PAUL PRESTON is ~~~~~~~~~~~~~ essor of Contemporary Spanish F~~~~~~~~~~~~~ le Cañada Blanch Centre for Contemporary Spanish Studies at the LSE. He was born in Liverpool in 1946 and educated there and at Oxford University. Between 1975 and 1991 he was a lecturer at the University of Reading then successively Lecturer in, Reader in and Professor of History at Queen Mary College, University of London. He has frequently acted as a commentator on Spanish affairs on radio and television in Britain and in Spain, and contributed articles on music, history and politics to leading newspapers and magazines in both countries. Among his many works, which have been translated into French, German, Italian Portuguese, Dutch, Catalan and Spanish, are *The Triumph of Democracy in Spain* (1986), *The Politics of Revenge: Fascism and the Military in Twentieth-Century Spain* (1990), *Franco: A Biography* (1993), *A Concise History of the Spanish Civil War* (1996), *Comrades* (1999), *Doves of War: Four Women of Spain* (2002) and *Juan Carlos* (2004). He is a Fellow of the British Academy, was decorated by Spanish King Juan Carlos a Comendador de la Orden de Mérito Civil and in 2000 was awarded a CBE.

Praise for *A Concise History of the Spanish Civil War*:

'[Preston's] economical style, together with a telling choices of quotes and mordant use of irony, serve his purpose admirably ... it is founded upon a vast knowledge and will not easily be refuted.'   *History Today*

International praise for *(A Concise History of)* The Spanish Civil War:

'A very fine and concise account of heroism and horror, of passions given full rein – and the vividness and scholarship make it all the harder to reconcile what was then with what is now.'
The Tablet

'Concisely written, it covers the complexities of the war with an assuring thoroughness.'
Sunday Boston Herald

'Mr Preston has provided as fair a history of the war as I have read, giving the many parties their just deserts. It is a good book for the ordinary reader interested in learning about what many have called a prelude to World War II.'
New York Times Book Review

'Not just a detailed description of events but a real interpretation of the causes and course of the war. By allowing the actors of the great Spanish drama to speak, he captures the dynamics of the civil war.'
La Stampa

'Paul Preston's book throws new, definitive light on the conflict of 1936.'
L'Unità

'An important and valuable contribution to the estimation of the anti-fascist war in Spain. It should be read by all who wish to deepen their understanding of the period.'
The Morning Star

Praise for *Franco*:

Yorkshire Post Book of the Year 1994
Runner-Up for the NCR Award 1994

'Brilliantly clear-minded and detailed ... the definitive

biography of Franco; there is nothing to match it in Spanish. It is a triumph of clarity, judicious analysis and detailed research.'   COLM TÓIBÍN, *Sunday Times*

'Magisterial . . . as engagingly readable as a good novel.'
PAUL HEYWOOD, *Observer*

'No previous study has told us so much about the formation of Franco's character. It grips the reader even in familiar passages of Franco's life. Its poised judgements and masterful scholarship make it certain to endure and difficult to refute.'
FELIPE FERNANDEZ-ARMESTO, *European*

Praise for *Comrades*:

'*Comrades* presents us with fascinating portraits, case studies that illustrate variously nobility, arrogance, self-delusion and evil. It remains difficult to comprehend the passions that lead to civil war; but this book helps us to understand.'
MICHAEL PORTILLO, *Sunday Telegraph*

Praise for *Doves of War*:

'A magnificent achievement. Preston combines the skills of the professional historian with a profound understanding of women. Eminently readable, this is narrative history at its best.'   *Literary Review*

'Written with a shrewd eye and a sure touch, the book is full of wonderful stories and acute observations. Above all, these are compellingly human dramas in which moral issues, right and wrong, Fascism and Communism, melt away.'
Sunday Telegraph

'Newcomers to the Spanish conflict could hardly find a better place to start.'   *Sunday Times*

'Passionate and deeply moving. . . when Preston writes about these women, you feel as if you are in their company.'
Scotland on Sunday

Praise for *Juan Carlos*:

'This is that rare thing – a work of academic history that is also an absorbing narrative. And its great merit is to remind us that at the centre of all the dynastic wrangling, political conspiracy and media speculation stands a man who has often felt very alone.'   *The Economist*

'An excellent biography . . . It reads like a spy thriller . . . There is no doubt that Preston is an ardent fan of Juan Carlos, and his compelling style carries the reader with him . . . Preston's great skill is to re-create real suspense over the 35 years that elapsed between Juan Carlo's arrival in Spain as a boy and the irreversible entrenchment of democracy in the 1980s.'   *Sunday Times*

'As with most of Preston's work, his eye for the winning detail makes his subjects quite human and enlivens the world of political manoeuvring into something other than dry history.'   *Washington Post*

PAUL PRESTON

The Spanish Civil War

REACTION, REVOLUTION AND REVENGE

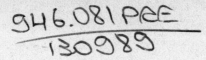

HARPER PERENNIAL
London, New York, Toronto and Sydney

Harper Perennial
An imprint of HarperCollins*Publishers*
77–85 Fulham Palace Road,
Hammersmith, London w6 8jb

www.harpercollins.co.uk

Published by Harper Perennial in 2006
9

This book is a revised and updated version of
A Concise History of the Spanish Civil War,
first published by Fontana Press in 1986, revised and updated from
The Spanish Civil War 1936–1939,
first published by Weidenfeld & Nicolson in 1986.

Map © Hardlines Ltd

A catalogue record for this book
is available from the British Library

ISBN-13 978-0-00-723207-9
ISBN-10 0-00-723207-1

Set in Janson by Rowland Phototypesetting Ltd,
Bury St Edmunds, Suffolk

Printed and bound in Great Britain by Clays Ltd, St Ives plc

This book is dedicated to the memory of
David Marshall and to the other men and women
of the International Brigades who fought and died
fighting fascism in Spain.

Contents

Acknowledgements

The author and publishers are grateful to the following archives, institutions and private collectors for their assistance in the location of the photographs used in this book: the Cañada Blanch Centre for Contemporary Spanish Studies, London School of Economics & Political Science, Dr Sheelagh Ellwood, Manuel González García, *Historia 16* (Madrid), the Instituto de España, the International Brigade Association, the Ministerio de Información, the Partido Comunista de España, Ramón Serrano Suñer.

List of Plates

The division of Spain into Republican and Nationalist zones, as of 22 July 1936

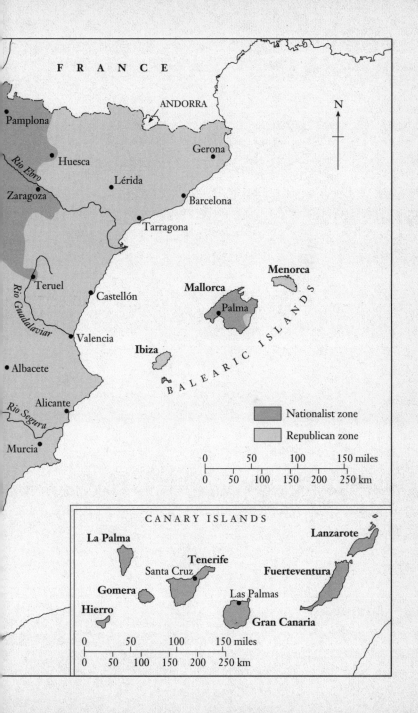

F R A N C E

ANDORRA

Pamplona

Rio Ebro

Huesca

Gerona

Lérida

Zaragoza

Barcelona

Tarragona

Rio Guadalaviar

Teruel

Castellón

Mallorca

Menorca

Palma

Valencia

Ibiza

B A L E A R I C   I S L A N D S

Albacete

Alicante

Rio Segura

Murcia

Nationalist zone

Republican zone

| 0 | 50 | 100 | 150 miles |
| 0 | 50 | 100 | 150 | 200 | 250 km |

N

CANARY ISLANDS

La Palma

Lanzarote

Tenerife

Santa Cruz

Fuerteventura

Gomera

Las Palmas

Hierro

Gran Canaria

| 0 | 50 | 100 | 150 miles |
| 0 | 50 | 100 | 150 | 200 | 250 km |

Preface

I wrote the first version of this book twenty years ago. My intention then was to provide the new reader with a manageable guide to the bibliographical labyrinth constituted by the fact that the Spanish Civil War has continued to be fought on paper. Even then there had been several thousand books on the Spanish Civil War and many of them were extremely long. Because the flow did not stop, I rewrote the book in 1996 in order to take account of what had been published in the ten years following its first appearance. At that point, I could not have imagined how much more was still to come. Accordingly, this much expanded version is an attempt to come to terms with the very considerable body of scholarship which has been published in Spanish, Catalan, English and other European languages since 1996. It also draws on my own ongoing research on Franco, the Francoist repression and Mussolini's role in the Spanish Civil War.

Inevitably, the new book is much longer – the text is 50 per cent longer than in 1996. Like the two earlier versions, it is interpretative rather than descriptive although even more ample use has been made of contemporary quotation to give a flavour of the period. It is not a book which sets out to find a perfect balance between both sides. I lived for several years under Franco's dictatorship. It was impossible not to be aware of the repression of workers and students, the censorship and the prisons. As late as 1975 political prisoners were still being executed. Despite what Franco supporters claim, I do not believe that Spain derived any benefit from the military rising of 1936 and the Nationalist victory of 1939. Many years devoted to the study of Spain of before, during and after the

1930s have convinced me that, while many mistakes were made, the Spanish Republic was an attempt to provide a better way of life for the humbler members of a repressive society. Against such temerity, the revenge taken by Franco and his followers was brutal and pitiless. Accordingly, there is little sympathy here for the Spanish right, but I hope there is some understanding.

My early interest in Spain was stimulated by the postgraduate seminar run at the University of Reading by Hugh Thomas and by Joaquín Romero Maura in Oxford. Over many years, I learned an enormous amount during my friendship with Herbert Southworth who was always prodigal with his hospitality and his knowledge. When I wrote the 1996 version, I was aware of how much I had derived from conversations over many years with Raymond Carr, Norman Cooper, Denis Smyth, Angel Viñas, Julián Casanova, Jerónimo Gonzalo and Martin Blinkhorn. Throughout the 1990s, the historiography of the Spanish Civil War was profoundly changed by the research of Ángela Cenarro, Helen Graham, Gerald Howson, Enrique Moradiellos, Alberto Reig Tapia and Ismael Saz. I continue to gain greatly from reading their work and many hours of conversation with them.

My friends Paul Heywood and Sheelagh Ellwood gave me marvellous support during the writing of the first edition. Their role in the second version was assumed by Helen Graham. For this third attempt, my ongoing discussions with Helen Graham have been supplemented by constant interchanges of ideas and information with Hilari Raguer and Francisco Espinosa Maestre. I would also like to thank Francisco Moreno Gómez, Isabelo Herreros and Luis Miguel Sánchez Tostado for help with particular issues.

My wife Gabrielle is, as ever, my shrewdest critic. With such a team of friends to help, it seems astonishing that any book could still have shortcomings. Unfortunately it does and they are mine.

INTRODUCTION

The Civil War Seventy Years On

On 19 October 2005 the ninety-year-old Santiago Carrillo was awarded an honorary doctorate by the Universidad Autónoma de Madrid. Carrillo was Secretary General of the Partido Comunista de España (PCE) for three decades from 1956 to 1985. He was a crucial, if not uncontroversial, figure in the resistance against Franco's dictatorship. The granting of the degree (*título de doctor*) was largely in recognition of his role in the struggle for democracy and his 'extraordinary merits, and particularly his contribution to the policy of national reconciliation, and his decisive contribution the process of democratic transition in Spain'. Carrillo had come to be widely revered for his moderate and moderating role at a crucial stage in the transition from dictatorship to democracy. However, during the Civil War, at the age of twenty-one, he had been security chief in the Madrid defence junta when large numbers of rightist prisoners were murdered at Paracuellos. Accordingly, the degree ceremony was disrupted by militants chanting '¡Paracuellos Carrillo asesino!' ('Paracuellos – Carrillo murderer'). It was not the first time that Carrillo had been the target of violent ultra right-wing attacks. Ever since his return to Spain in 1976, he had been the object of abuse for his alleged role in the killings at Paracuellos. On 16 April 2005, at the launch of a book called *The Two Spains*, by the historian Santos Juliá, where Carrillo was scheduled to speak, the event was interrupted when the bookshop was ransacked by extreme rightists. Barely a week later, a wall adjacent to his apartment block was scrawled with the words 'this is how the war began and we won', 'Carrillo, murderer, we know where you live' and 'where is the Spanish gold?'.

These incidents are symptomatic of the way in which the Spanish Civil War retains a burning relevance in contemporary Spain. In geographical and human scale, never mind technological horrors, the Spanish Civil War has been dwarfed by later conflicts. Nonetheless, it has generated more than twenty thousand books, a literary epitaph which puts it on a par with the Second World War. In part, that reflects the extent to which, even after 1939, the war continued to be fought between Franco's victorious Nationalists and the defeated and exiled Republicans. Even more, certainly as far as foreigners were concerned, the survival of interest in the Spanish tragedy was closely connected with the sheer longevity of its victor. General Franco's uninterrupted enjoyment of a dictatorial power seized with the aid of Hitler and Mussolini was an infuriating affront to opponents of fascism the world over. Moreover, the destruction of democracy in Spain was not allowed to become just another fading remnant of the humiliations of the period of appeasement. Far from trying to heal the wounds of civil strife, Franco worked harder than anyone to keep the war a live and burning issue both inside and outside Spain.

Reminders of Francoism's victory over international communism were frequently used to curry favour with the outside world. This was most dramatically the case immediately after the Second World War when frantic efforts were made to dissociate Franco from his erstwhile Axis allies. This was done by stressing his enmity to communism and playing down his equally vehement opposition to liberal democracy and socialism. Throughout the Cold War, the irrefutable anti-communism of the Nationalist side in the Civil War was used to build a picture of Franco as the bulwark of the Western system, the 'Sentinel of the West' in the phrase coined by his propagandists. Within Spain itself, memories of the war and of the bloody repression which followed it were carefully nur-tured in order to maintain what has been called 'the pact of blood'. The dictator was supported by an uneasy coalition of the highly privileged, landowners, industrialists and bankers; of what might be called the 'service classes' of Francoism, those members of the middle and working classes who, for whatever reasons – opportunism, conviction or wartime geographical loyalty – threw in their lot with the regime; and finally of those ordinary Spanish Catholics who supported the Nationalists as the defenders of religion and law and order. Reminders of the war were useful to rally the wavering loyalty of any or all of these groups.

The privileged usually remained aloof from the dictatorship and disdainful of its propaganda. However, those who were implicated in the regime's networks of corruption and re-pression, the beneficiaries of the killings and the pillage, were especially susceptible to hints that only Franco stood between them and the revenge of their victims. In any case, for many who worked for the dictator, as policemen, Civil Guards, as humble *serenos* (night-watchmen) or *porteros* (doormen), in the giant bureaucracy of Franco's single party, the *Movimiento*, in its trade union organization, or in its huge press network, the Civil War was a crucial part of their curriculum vitae and of their value system. They were to make up what in the 1970s came to be known as the *bunker*, the die-hard Francoists who were prepared to fight for the values of the Civil War from the rubble of the Chancellery. A similar, and more dangerous, commitment came from the praetorian defenders of the legacy of what Spanish rightists refer to broadly as *el 18 de julio* (from the date of the military rising of 1936). Army officers had been educated since 1939 in academies where they were taught that the military existed to defend Spain from communism, anarch-ism, socialism, parliamentary democracy and regionalists who wanted to destroy Spain's unity. Accordingly, after Franco's death the *bunker* and its military supporters were to attempt once more to destroy democracy in Spain in the name of the Nationalist victory in the Civil War.

For these ultra-rightists, Nationalist propaganda efforts to maintain the hatreds of the Civil War were perhaps gratuitous. However, the regime clearly thought it essential for the less partisan Spaniards who rendered Franco a passive support ranging from the grudging to the enthusiastic. Catholics and members of the middle classes who had been appalled by the view of Republican disorder and anti-clericalism generated by the rightist press were induced to turn a blind eye to the more distasteful aspects of a bloody dictatorship by constant and exaggerated reminders of the war. Within months of the end of hostilities, a massive 'History of the Crusade' was being published in weekly parts, glorifying the heroism of the victors and portraying the vanquished as the dupes of Moscow, as either squalidly self-interested or the blood-crazed perpetrators of sadistic atrocities. Until well into the 1960s, a stream of publications, many aimed at children, presented the war as a religious crusade against Communist barbarism.

Beyond the hermetically sealed frontiers of Franco's Spain, the defeated Republicans and their foreign sympathizers rejected the Francoist interpretation that the Civil War had been a battle of the forces of order and true religion against a Jewish–Bolshevik–Masonic conspiracy. Instead, they maintained consistently that the war was the struggle of an oppressed people seeking a decent way of life against the opposition of Spain's backward landed and industrial oligarchies and their Nazi and Fascist allies. Unfortunately, bitterly divided over the reasons for their defeat, they could not present as monolithically coherent a view of the war as did their Francoist opponents. In a way which weakened their collective voice, but immeasurably enriched the literature of the Spanish Civil War, they were sidetracked into vociferous debate about whether they might have beaten the Nationalists if only they had unleashed the popular revolutionary war advocated by anarchists and

Trotskyists as opposed to mounting the conventional war effort favoured by the Republicans, the Socialists and the increasingly powerful Communists.

Thereafter, the debate over 'war or revolution' engaged Republican sympathizers unable to come to terms with the leftist defeat. During the Cold War, it was used successfully to disseminate the idea that it was the Stalinist suffocation of the revolution in Spain which led to Franco's victory. Several works on the Spanish Civil War were sponsored by the CIA-funded Congress for Cultural Freedom to propagate this idea. The success of an unholy alliance of anarchists, Trotskyists and Cold Warriors has obscured the fact that Hitler, Mussolini, Franco and Chamberlain were responsible for the Nationalist victory, not Stalin. Nevertheless, new generations have continued to discover the Spanish Civil War, sometimes scouring for parallels, in the light of national liberation struggles in Vietnam, Cuba, Chile and Nicaragua, sometimes just seeking in the Spanish experience the idealism and sacrifice so singularly absent from modern politics.

The relevance of the Civil War to Franco's supporters and to left-wingers throughout the world does not fully explain the much wider fascination which the Spanish conflict still exercises today. In the aftermath of the Second World War, Korea and Vietnam, it can only seem like small beer. As Raymond Carr has pointed out, compared to Hiroshima or Dresden the bombing of Guernica seems 'a minor act of vandalism'. Yet it has provoked more savage polemic than virtually any incident in the Second World War. That is not, as some would have it, because of the power of Picasso's painting but because Guernica was the *first* total destruction of an undefended civilian target by aerial bombardment. Accordingly, the Spanish Civil War is burned into the European consciousness not simply as a rehearsal for the bigger world war to come, but because it presaged the opening of the floodgates to a new and horrific form of modern warfare that was universally dreaded.

It was because they shared the collective fear of what defeat for the Spanish Republic might mean that men and women, workers and intellectuals, went to join the International Brigades. The left saw clearly in 1936 what for another three years even the democratic right chose to ignore – that Spain was the last bulwark against the horrors of Hitlerism. In a Europe still unaware of the crimes of Stalin, the Communist-organized brigades seemed to be fighting for much that was worth saving in terms of democratic rights and trade union freedoms. The volunteers believed that by fighting fascism in Spain they were also fighting it in their own countries. Hindsight about the sordid power struggles in the Republican zone between the Communists on the one hand and the Socialists, the anarchists and the quasi-Trotskyist Partida Obrero de Unificación Marxista (POUM) on the other cannot diminish the idealism of the individuals concerned. There remains something intensely tragic about Italian and German refugees from Mussolini and Hitler finally being able to take up arms against their persecutors only to be defeated again.

To dwell on the impact of the horrors of the Spanish war and on the importance of the defence against fascism is to miss one of the most positive factors of the Republican experience – the attempt to drag Spain into the twentieth century. In the drab Europe of the Depression years, what was happening in Republican Spain seemed to be an exciting experiment. Orwell's celebrated comment acknowledged this: 'I recognized it immediately as a state of affairs worth fighting for.' The cultural and educational achievements of the Spanish Republic were only the best-known aspects of a social revolution that had an impact on the contemporary world which Cuba and Chile never quite attained in the 1960s. Spain was not only nearby, but its social experiments were taking place in a context of widespread disillusion with the failures of capitalism. By 1945, the fight against the Axis had become linked with the preservation of the old world. During the Spanish Civil War, however, the struggle against fascism was still seen as merely the first step to building a new egalitarian world out of the Depression. In the event, the exigencies of the war effort and internecine conflict stood in the way of the full flowering of the industrial and agrarian collectives of the Republican zone. Nevertheless, there was, and is, something inspiring about the way in which the Spanish working class faced the dual tasks of war against the old order and of construction of the new. The anarchist leader Buenaventura Durruti best expressed this spirit when he told a reporter, 'We are not afraid of ruins, we are going to inherit the earth. The bourgeoisie may blast and ruin their world before they leave the stage of history. But we carry a new world in our hearts.'

All of this is perhaps to suggest that interest in the Spanish Civil War is made up of nostalgia on the part of contemporaries of right and left and political romanticism on the part of the young. After all, there is a strong case to be made for presenting the Spanish Civil War as 'the last great cause'. It was not for nothing that the Civil War inspired the greatest writers of its day in a manner not repeated in any subsequent war. However, nostalgia and romanticism aside, it is impossible to exaggerate the sheer historical importance of the Spanish war. Beyond its climactic impact on Spain itself, the war was very much the nodal point of the 1930s. Baldwin and Blum, Hitler and Mussolini, Stalin and Trotsky all had substantial parts in the Spanish drama. The Rome–Berlin Axis was clinched in Spain at the same time as the inadequacies of appeasement were ruthlessly exposed. It was above all a Spanish war – or rather a series of Spanish wars – yet it was also the great international battleground of fascism and communism. And while Colonel von Richthofen practised in the Basque Country the *Blitzkrieg* techniques he was later to perfect in Poland, agents of the NKVD endeavoured to re-enact the Moscow trials on the leaders of the POUM because it was made up of dissident anti-Stalinist Marxists and one of its founders, along with Joaquín Maurín, was Andreu Nin, who had once been Trotsky's secretary in Moscow. The Russians were thwarted by the Spanish Republicans' insistence on proper judicial procedure.

Nor is the Spanish conflict without its contemporary relevance. The war arose in part out of the violent opposition of the privileged and their foreign allies to the reformist attempts of liberal Republican–Socialist governments to ameliorate the daily living conditions of the most wretched members of society. The parallels with Chile in the 1970s or Nicaragua in the 1980s hardly need emphasizing. Equally, the ease with which the Spanish Republic was destabilized by skilfully provoked disorder had sombre echoes in Italy, and even Spain, in the 1980s. Fortunately, Spanish democracy survived in 1981 the attempts to overthrow it by military men nostalgic for a Francoist Spain of victors and vanquished. The Spanish Civil War was also fought because of the determination of the extreme right in general and the army in particular to crush Basque, Catalan and Galician nationalisms. Spain did not witness 'ethnic cleansing' of the kind seen in the civil war in the former Yugoslovia. Nevertheless, Franco made a systematic attempt during and after the war to eradicate all vestiges of local nationalisms, political and linguistic. Although ultimately in vain, the cultural genocide thus pursued by Castilian centralist nationalism has provoked comparisons between the Spanish and Bosnian crises.

In Spain itself, the fiftieth anniversary of the war in 1986 was marked by a silence that was almost deafening. There was a television series and some discreet academic conferences, one of which, held under the title 'Valencia: Capital of the Republic', had its publicity poster, designed by the poet and artist Rafael Alberti on the basis of the Republican flag, unofficially, but effectively, banned. There was no official commemoration of the war. That was an act of political prudence on the part of a Socialist government fully aware of the sensibilities of a military caste brought up in the anti-democratic hatreds of Francoism. More positively it was a contribution to what has been called the 'pact of oblivion' (*pacto del olvido*), the tacit, collective agreement of the great majority of the Spanish people to renounce any settling of accounts after the death of Franco. A rejection of the violence of the Civil War and the regime which came out of it overcame any thoughts of revenge.

In fact, in 1986, the fiftieth anniversary of the outbreak of a war which would see Spain suffer nearly forty years of international ostracism, the country was formally admitted into the European Community. Ten years later, the withering away of Francoism and continued consolidation of democracy were demonstrated when the Spanish government, with all-party support, granted citizenship to the surviving members of the International Brigades who fought against fascism during the Civil War. It was a welcome but belated gesture of gratitude and reconciliation which serves as a reminder of a violent and bloody Spain which has perhaps gone for ever.

It might therefore be expected that, by 2006, passionate interest in the Spanish Civil War would at last be fading. This has not happened. Indeed, the very opposite is the case. It is only in recent years that for many families a major area of unfinished business, the location, proper burial and mourning of the dead, has begun in earnest. It is a process that, for half of Spain, was completed more than sixty years ago. That it has been denied the other half of the country until so recently is one of the main reasons for the continuing ability of the Spanish Civil War to provoke passion.

On 26 April 1942 Franco's government set in train a massive investigation called the 'Causa General'. Its immediate objective was to gather evidence of Republican wrongdoing. The 'material' gathered ranged from documents to unsubstantiated hearsay. It was an invitation to all those with genuine grievances – the relatives of those murdered or those who had been imprisoned or had had property confiscated or stolen in the Republican zone – to vent their desire for revenge. It also permitted anyone with a personal score to settle or who coveted someone's property or wife to smear their enemies. Although the procedures were lax in the extreme, the declarations made, substantiated or otherwise, were used to intensify the general-ized image of Republican depravity. It was a part of a general pattern that had been seen since July 1936 in every part of the Nationalist zone as it fell to rebel forces. Once the Nationalists were in control, those rightists killed by the left were identified and buried with honour and dignity in ceremonies that were often followed by acts of extreme violence against the local left. In the case of extremely famous victims of the war, such as the Falangist leader José Antonio Primo de Rivera or the original leader of the military coup, General José Sanjurjo, their bodies were exhumed and then reinterred in elaborate ceremonies.

The consequence of these various procedures was that the large majority of the victims of crimes in the Republican zone were identified and counted. Their families could mourn them and very often their names were engraved in places of post-humous honour, inscribed in the crypts of cathedrals or on the external walls of churches, with crosses or plaques placed where they died or even, in some cases, with streets named after them. The structures of law and order disappeared in Republican Spain as a result of the military coup and it took several months for them to be re-established. Accordingly, the atrocities in the Republican zone were often the work of criminal elements or out-of-control extremists, although also, less frequently, of deliberate policy by leftist groups determined to eliminate their political enemies. This great variety of crimes was portrayed for nearly forty years by the propaganda machine of the victorious regime, written largely by policemen, priests and soldiers, as if it were the official policy of the Republic. The purpose of such writing was to justify the military coup of 1936, the slaughter it provoked and the subsequent dictatorship. Through the press and radio of the *Movimiento*, the education system and the pulpits of Spain's churches, a single, monolithic interpretation of the Spanish Civil War was propagated. Until 1975, official propaganda carefully nurtured memories of the war and the bloody repression not only to humiliate the defeated, but also to help the victors recall what they owed Franco. For those who were complicit in the regime's networks of corruption and repression, it served to remind them that they needed Franco and the regime as a bulwark against the return of their victims who, they imagined, would want to wreak bloody revenge.

For those on the left there had been no equivalent process of closure. There were thousands of the 'disappeared' (*desaparecidos*), their bodies not located, their manner of death not confirmed. Unlike the families of the Nationalist victims of Republican violence, the relatives of the Republican victims of the Nationalist repression could not mourn openly, let alone bury their dead. Even after the death of Franco, the problem of confronting the memory of the Civil War remained immensely difficult because the hatreds of the war had continued to fester for thirty-seven years after its formal conclusion. The dictatorship had imposed a single vision of the past but there were many other memories, hidden and repressed. Many thousands of families wanted to know what had happened to their loved ones and if, as they feared, they had been murdered, where their bodies lay. In the first months of the transition to democracy, fear of a new civil war wrestled with the desire to know about the Republican past. In the event, the drive to guarantee the re-establishment and, later, the consolidation of democracy weighed more both with politicians and with the bulk of ordinary people. The formal renunciation of revenge which was an essential precondition for change was enshrined in a political amnesty not just for those who had opposed the dictatorship but also for those guilty of crimes against humanity committed in the service of the dictatorship. The amnesty text of 14 October 1977 was supported by the majority within the political spectrum. The ghosts of the Civil War and of Francoist repression weighed on Spain, but to prevent the reopening of old wounds successive governments, both conservative and Socialist, were extremely cautious when it came to funding commemorations, excavations and research connected to the war.

The determination of the great majority of the Spanish people to secure a bloodless transition to democracy and to avoid a repetition of the violence of another civil war not only overcame any desire for revenge but also saw the sacrifice of the desire for knowledge. Thus, the 'pact of oblivion' saw a curtain of silence drawn over the past in the interests of a still-fragile democracy. Accordingly, there were not only very few official initiatives aimed at commemorating the past but also a certain reticence within the education system about teaching the history of the Civil War and its aftermath. Nevertheless, at a local level many historians continued to pursue research into the Francoist repression, and, for many victims, appearance in the lists compiled in their books was their only gravestone or memorial. Despite its crucial value in political terms and its importance as a measure of the great political maturity of the Spanish people, the *pacto del olvido* did not apply to historians. In fact, from the first, in La Rioja, in Catalonia and in Aragón, there had been considerable research into the most disagreeable aspects of the Civil War, despite the *pacto*. Elsewhere, the uneasy truce with the past was soon broken, with the appearance of several important works on the repression in Andalusia, Extremadura, Galicia and other regions that had found themselves within the Nationalist zone during all or part of the war. In the last ten years, what began as a trickle has become a torrent of books which, although written from many widely differing perspectives, has produced a generally critical vision of the insurrectionary officers of 1936.

In addition to the flood of historical works, over the last five years there has emerged a popular movement in favour of the detailed reconstruction of the war and Franco's dictatorship at a local level. The creation of a series of organizations and associations dedicated to what has come to be called 'the recovery of historical memory'. Several factors lie behind this development. On the one hand, there is a sense that democracy is now sufficiently consolidated to be able to withstand a serious debate about the Civil War and its consequences. Underlying this is also a terrible urgency driven by an awareness of the dwindling numbers of surviving witnesses. Without engaging in the thorny issue surrounding the fact that there are many different historical memories of the same events, it remains true that the concept of recovering memory has had a profound impact on a people whose collective memory was kept behind bars for so many decades. A process has begun involving the excavation of common graves (*fosas*), the recording of the testimonies of survivors and the proliferation of innumerable television documentaries about what happened. In consequence, today, seventy years after its outbreak, the Spanish Civil War and its aftermath are again generating passionate and, at times, bitter argument.

The breaking of the taboo associated with the *pacto del olvido* has had a dramatic and unexpected impact. The creation of associations dedicated to the recovery of historical memory and the efforts to locate the mortal remains of the disappeared have helped close the emotional wounds of many families. Newspapers regularly print accounts of exhumations. Barely a week passes without the publication of a detailed account of the repression in some town or province and the number of known victims is rising. Indeed, after years of such figures being reduced, they are now rising towards the levels once suggested by horrified eyewitnesses during and immediately after the war itself. In some places, 'memory routes' have been created along which it is possible to see places where atrocities or acts of resistance took place, all of which has created enormous discomfort, not just among the perpetrators or their relatives. The outrage caused has extended even beyond those nostalgic for the dictatorship. It has also caused distress to extended sections of society which, over time, derived benefit from the regime. It is to this audience that a series of immensely successful historical polemics have been directed.

While there is at work a veritable army of serious researchers, there has emerged a small group of authors and broadcasters who barrack from the sidelines. Their cry is that the sufferings of Republican victims were notably less than has been claimed and that any such sufferings were, in any case, their own fault. Accordingly, the Spanish Civil War is being fought all over again on paper. These self-styled 'revisionists' allege that the historiographical advances of the last thirty years, in all their infinite variety, are the result of a sinister conspiracy in which almost the entire historical profession and many amateur historians are involved. A wide range of historians from conservatives and clerics to liberals and leftists, as well as regional nationalists, are accused of linking arms to impose a monolithic and politically motivated interpretation of the history of the Spanish Civil War and the regime that followed it. There is little in terms of research that is new about the revisionist works. They resuscitate the basic theses of Francoist propaganda, of writers like Tomás Borrás, or the secret policemen Eduardo Comín Colomer and Mauricio Karl. In some cases, they have even recycled the titles of famous Francoist texts. The only thing that is new is the addition, in both books and inflammatory *tertulias*, or radio debates, of the techniques of reality television in insulting the authors of the new historiography rather than debating with them.

The consequence has been to introduce a level of abrasive tension to daily political discourse in Spain. The bulk of the historiography of the Civil War is comprised of more or less seriously researched history, which, unusually for such research, is feeding a popular demand. In contrast, the works of the revisionists have exactly the contemporary political purpose which they denounce in others. Their criticism of the Republic is implicitly a criticism of those of its values which have survived the dictatorship or been reborn in contemporary Spanish democracy. This is particularly the case with regard to the federal elements of Spain's current structure, revisionist ire having been provoked by the fact that the present left-wing coalition government in Catalonia is actively sponsoring research into the repression. Even before this, the right had been outraged by the successful Catalan campaign for the return of tonnes of documents plundered by the Francoists in 1939. This documentation, housed in Salamanca, was originally seized to be scoured for names of leftists and liberals. Organized by archivists provided by the Gestapo, it was used, with similarly sequestered documentation from other conquered areas, to build up a file card index which became the infrastructural tool of the repression. In the view of the fiercely anti-Catalanist revisionists the Republic was, and by extension the present Socialist government is, 'Balkanizing' Spain. The revisionists have also derived some succour from the re-emergence in the United States of a fiercely Cold War vision of the Spanish Civil War which portrays the vanquished as the puppets of Moscow. This view, and the response it has provoked from historians within Spain and Great Britain, has also contributed to the ongoing renovation of the historiography of the Civil War.

It is possible that the revisionists are inadvertently helping to consolidate democracy in that the Civil War will not cease to be a ghost at the feast of democracy until the resentments and hatreds associated with it are vented. They have underlined the urgency of the task at hand: not to stir up the ashes, which is what they accuse historians of the repression of doing, but to investigate, demonstrate and remember what the Civil War really was – not a war of good and evil according to the prejudices of whoever happens to be writing, but a traumatic experience of mass suffering, in which there were few winners and many losers. As one of the most dedicated and thoughtful historians of the repression, Francisco Espinosa Maestre, put it recently, 'oblivion is not the same as reconciliation and memory is not the same as revenge'.

ONE

A Divided Society: Spain Before 1931

The origins of the Spanish Civil War lie far back in the country's history. The notion that political problems could more naturally be solved by violence than by debate was firmly entrenched in a country in which for a thousand years civil war has been if not exactly the norm then certainly no rarity. The war of 1936–9 was the fourth such conflict since the 1830s. The religious 'crusade' propaganda of the Nationalists joyfully linked it with the Christian *Reconquista* of Spain from the Moors. On both sides, heroism and nobility vied with primitive cruelty and brutality in a way that would not have been out of place in a medieval epic. Yet, in the last resort, the Spanish Civil War is a war firmly rooted in the modern period. The interference of Hitler, Mussolini and Stalin ensured that the Spanish Civil War would be a defining moment in twentieth-century history. Yet, leaving that international dimension aside, the myriad Spanish conflicts which erupted in 1936, regionalists against centralists, anti-clericals against Catholics, landless labourers against *latifundistas*, workers against industrialist, have in common the struggles of a society in the throes of modernization.

To understand Spain's progress to the bloodshed of 1936 it is necessary to make a fundamental distinction between the war's long-term structural origins and its immediate political causes. In the hundred years before 1931, it was possible to discern the gradual and immensely complex division of the country into two broadly antagonistic social blocks. However, when the Second Republic was established on 14 April 1931 amidst scenes of popular rejoicing, few Spaniards outside the lunatic fringes of the extreme left and right, the conspiratorial monarchists and the anarchists, believed that the country's problems could be solved only by resorting to violence. Five years and three months later, large sections of the population believed that war was inevitable. Moreover, a substantial proportion of them felt that war would be a good thing. Accordingly, it is necessary to establish exactly what happened between 14 April 1931 and 18 July 1936 to bring about that change. Nevertheless, the political hatreds which polarized the Second Republic in those five and a quarter years were a reflection of the deep-rooted conflicts within Spanish society.

The Civil War was the culmination of a series of uneven struggles between the forces of reform and reaction which had dominated Spanish history since 1808. There is a curious pattern in Spain's modern history, arising from a frequent *desfase*, or lack of synchronization, between the social reality and the political power structure ruling over it. Lengthy periods during which reactionary elements have attempted to use political and military power to hold back social progress have inevitably been followed by outbursts of revolutionary fervour. In the 1850s, the 1870s, between 1917 and 1923, and above all during the Second Republic, efforts were made to bring Spanish politics into line with the country's social reality. This inevitably involved attempts to introduce fundamental reform, especially on the land, and to carry out redistributions of wealth. Such efforts in turn provoked reactionary efforts to stop the clock and reimpose the traditional balance of social and economic power. Thus were progressive movements crushed by General O'Donnell in 1856, by General Pavia in 1874 and by General Primo de Rivera in 1923.

Accordingly, the Civil War of 1936–9 represented the

ultimate expression of the attempts by reactionary elements in Spanish politics to crush any reform which might threaten their privileged position. The recurring dominance of reactionary elements was a consequence of the continued power of the old landed oligarchy and the parallel weakness of the progressive bourgeoisie. A concomitant of the tortuously slow and uneven development of industrial capitalism in Spain was the existence of a numerically small and politically insignificant commercial and manufacturing class. Spain did not experience a classic bourgeois revolution in which the structures of the *ancien régime* were broken. The power of the monarchy, the landed nobility and the Church remained more or less intact well into the twentieth century. Unlike Britain and France, nineteenth-century Spain did not see the establishment of a democratic polity with the flexibility to absorb new forces and to adjust to major social change. That is not to say that Spain remained a feudal society but rather that the legal basis for capitalism was established without there being a political revolution. Accordingly, with the obvious difference that her industrial capitalism was extremely feeble, Spain followed the pattern established by Prussia.

Indeed, even until the 1950s, capitalism in Spain was predominantly agrarian. Spanish agriculture is immensely variegated in terms of climate, crops and land-holding systems. There have long existed areas of commercially successful small and medium farming operations, especially in the lush, wet hills and valleys of those northern regions which also experienced industrialization, Asturias, Catalonia and the Basque Country. However, throughout the nineteenth century and for the first half of the twentieth, the dominant sectors in terms of political influence were, broadly speaking, the large landowners. In the main, the *latifundios*, the great estates, are concentrated in the arid central and southern regions of New Castile, Extremadura and Andalusia, although there are also substantial *latifundios* to be found scattered in Old Castile and particularly in Salamanca.

The political monopoly of the landed oligarchy was periodically challenged by the emasculated industrial and mercantile classes with virtually no success. Until well after the civil war, the urban *haute bourgeoisie* was obliged to play the role of junior partner in a working coalition with the great *latifundistas*. Despite sporadic industrialization and a steady growth in the national importance of the political representatives of the northern industrialists, power remained squarely in the hands of the landowners.

There was never any strong possibility in Spain that industrialization and political modernization would coincide. In the first half of the nineteenth century, the progressive impulses, both political and economic, of the Spanish bourgeoisie were irrevocably diverted. The removal of feudal restrictions on land transactions combined with royal financial problems in the 1830s and the 1850s to liberate huge tracts of aristocratic, ecclesiastical and common lands. This not only diminished any impetus towards industrialization but, by helping to expand the great estates, also created intense social hatreds in the south. The newly released land was bought up by the more efficient among existing landlords and by members of the commercial and mercantile bourgeoisie attracted by its cheapness and social prestige. The *latifundio* system was consolidated and the new landlords were keen for a return on their investment. Unwilling to engage in expensive projects of irrigation, they preferred instead to build their profits on the exploitation of the great armies of landless day labourers, the *braceros* and *jornaleros*. The departure of the more easy-going clerics and nobles of an earlier age together with the enclosing of common lands removed most of the social palliatives which had hitherto kept the poverty-stricken south from upheaval. Paternalism was replaced by repression as the Civil Guard was created to form a rural armed police with the principal function of guarding the big estates from the labourers who worked on them. Thus, the strengthening of the landed oligarchy exacerbated an explosive social situation which could only foster the reactionary tendencies of the owners. At the same time, the syphoning into the land of the capital owned by the merchants of the great sea ports and Madrid bankers correspondingly weakened their interest in modernization.

Continued investment in land and widespread inter-marriage between the urban bourgeoisie and the landed oligarchy debilitated those forces committed to reform. The feebleness of the Spanish bourgeoisie as a potentially revolutionary class was underlined in the period from 1868 to 1874, which culminated in the chaos of the First Republic. With population growth in the middle of the century increasing pressure on the land, unskilled labourers had flocked to the towns and swelled the mob of unemployed who were highly sensitive to increases in bread prices. Hardly less wretched was the position of the urban lower middle class of teachers, officials and shopkeepers. Conditions were perhaps worst in the Catalan textile industry which produced all the horrors of nascent capitalism – long hours, child labour, overcrowding and low wages. When the American Civil War cut off supplies of cotton in the 1860s, the consequent rise in unemployment combined with a depression in railway construction to drive the urban working class to desperation. In 1868, this popular discontent combined with a movement of middle-class and military resentment of the clerical and ultra-conservative leanings of the monarchy. A number of *pronunciamientos* by liberal army officers together with urban riots led to the overthrow of Queen Isabel II in September 1868. The two movements were ultimately contradictory. The liberals were terrified to find that their constitutionalist rebellion had awakened a revolutionary movement of the masses. To make matters worse, a rebellion began in Spain's richest surviving colony, Cuba. The chosen replacement monarch, Amadeo of Savoy, abdicated in despair in 1873. In the ensuing vacuum, the First Republic was established after a number of working-class risings, an intolerable threat to the established order which was crushed by the army in December 1874.

In many respects, 1873–4 was to Spain what 1848–9 had been elsewhere in Europe. Having plucked up the courage to challenge the old order, the bourgeoisie was frightened out of its reforming ambitions by the spectre of proletarian disorder. When the army restored the monarchy in the person of Alfonso XII, reform was abandoned in return for social peace. The subsequent relation of forces between the landed oligarchy, the urban bourgeoisie and the remainder of the population was perfectly represented by the political system of the 1876 monarchical restoration. Two political parties, the Conservative and the Liberal, represented the interests of two sections of the landed oligarchy, respectively the wine and olive growers of the south and the wheat growers of the centre. The differences between them were minimal. They were both monarchist and were divided not on social issues but over free trade and, to a much lesser extent, over religion. The northern industrial bourgeoisie was barely represented within the system but was, for the moment, content to devote its activities to economic expansion in an atmosphere of stability. Until, in the twentieth century, they could organize their own parties, the Catalan textile manufacturers were inclined to support the Liberals because of their shared interest in restrictive tariffs, while the Basques, exporters of iron ore, tended to support the Conservative free traders.

It was virtually impossible for any political aspirations to find legal expression outside the two great oligarchical parties. Liberal and Conservative governments followed one another with soporific regularity. When results were not falsified in the Ministry of the Interior, they were fixed at the local level. The system of electoral falsification rested on the social power of local town bosses, or *caciques* (a South American Indian word meaning 'chief'). In the northern smallholding areas, the *cacique* was usually a moneylender, one of the bigger landlords, a lawyer or even a priest, who held mortgages on the small farms. In the areas of the great *latifundio* estates, New Castile, Extremadura or Andalusia, the *cacique* was the landowner or his agent, the man who decided who worked and therefore who did not starve. *Caciquismo* ensured that the narrow interests represented by the system were never seriously threatened.

On occasion, overzealous local officials would produce majorities by more than 100 per cent of the electorate. It was not unknown for results to be published before the elections took place. As the century wore on, casual falsification became somewhat more difficult and, if the requisite number of peasant votes could not be mustered, the *caciques* were said sometimes to register as voters the dead in the local cemetery. In consequence, politics became an exclusive minuet danced out by a small, privileged minority. The nature of politics in the period of *caciquismo* is illustrated by the celebrated story of the *cacique* of Motril in the province of Granada. When the coach with the election results arrived from the provincial capital, they were brought to him in the local *casino* (club). Leafing through them, he pronounced to the expectant hangers-on the following words: 'We the Liberals were convinced that we would win these elections. However, the will of God has decreed otherwise.' A lengthy pause. 'It appears that we the Conservatives have won the elections.' Excluded from organized politics, the hungry masses could choose only between apathy and violence. The inevitable outbreaks of protest by the unrepresented majority were dealt with by the forces of order, the Civil Guard and, at moments of greater tension, the army.

Challenges to the system did arise, however, and they were linked to the painfully slow but inexorable progress of industrialization and to the brutal social injustices intrinsic to the *latifundio* economy. The 1890s were a period of economic depression which exacerbated the grievances of the lower classes, especially in the countryside. Land hunger was creating an increasingly desperate desire for change, the more so as the southern labourers came under the influence of anarchism. Giuseppe Fannelli, an Italian disciple of the Russian anarchist Mikhail Bakunin, was sent to Spain by the First International in November 1868. His inspirational oratory soon secured him his own evangelists who took anarchism to one village after another. The message that land, justice and equality should be seized by direct action struck a chord among the starving day labourers, or *braceros*, and gave a new sense of hope and purpose to hitherto sporadic rural uprisings. Fannelli's eager converts took part in outbreaks of occasional violence, crop-burnings and strikes. However, poorly organized, easily defeated revolutionary outbursts began to alternate with periods of apathy.

It was but a short step from direct action to individual terrorism. The belief that any action was licit against the tyranny of the state saw increasing levels of social violence. In January 1892, an army of *braceros*, armed only with scythes and sticks but driven by hunger, invaded and briefly held the town of Jerez before being driven out by the police and the Civil Guard. As anarchism took root in the small workshops of the highly fragmented Catalan textile industry, there was a wave of bomb outrages that provoked savage reprisals from the forces of order. In August 1897 mass arrests and the use of torture provoked the assassination of the Spanish Prime Minister Cirilo Cánovas by a young Italian anarchist. A mass campaign against the torturing of anarchist prisoners in Barcelona's Montjuich prison, the Spanish Bastille, saw the rise to fame of the buccaneering demagogue Alejandro Lerroux.

The system was rocked in 1898 by defeat at the hands of the USA and the loss of the remnants of empire, including Cuba. This was to have a catastrophic effect on the Spanish economy especially in Catalonia for whose products Cuba had been a protected market. Barcelona was the scene of sporadic strikes and acts of terrorism by both anarchists and government *agents provocateurs*. Moreover, by the turn of the century, a modern capitalist economy was developing around the textile

and chemical industries of Catalonia, the iron and steel foun-
dries of the Basque Country and the mines of Asturias,
although the Spanish economy remained essentially agrarian.
Asturian coal was of lower quality and more expensive than
British coal. Neither Catalan textiles nor Basque metallurgy
could compete with British or German products in the international market, and their growth was stifled by the poverty of
the Spanish domestic market. Nonetheless, even the limited
growth of these industries in the north saw the emergence of
a militant industrial proletariat. Industrial development also
witnessed the beginnings of nationalist movements in Catalonia and the Basque Country born of resentment that Basques
and Catalans paid a very high proportion of Spain's tax revenue
but had little or no say in a government dominated by the
agrarian oligarchy. In 1901 the Catalanist party known as the
Lliga Regionalista won its first electoral victory.

In the two decades before the First World War the working-
class aristocracy of printers and craftsmen from the building
and metal trades in Madrid, the steel and shipyard workers in
Bilbao and the coal miners of Asturias began to swell the ranks
of the Partido Socialista Obrero Español (PSOE), the Socialist
Party founded in 1879, and its trade union organization, the
Unión General de Trabajadores (UGT). However, any possibility of overall unity within the organized workers' movement
was eliminated when the Socialists made the decision, in 1899,
to move the headquarters of the UGT from the industrial
capital, Barcelona, to the administrative capital, Madrid. To a
large extent this cut off the Socialist option for many Catalan
workers. Moreover, the PSOE was hobbled by its reliance
on a rigid and simplistic French Marxism, mediated through
the dead hand of the party's rigid leader, Pablo Iglesias. The
party was isolationist, committed to the view that the workers'
party should struggle for workers' interests, convinced of the
inevitability of revolution, without, of course, preparing for it.

The traditional dominance of the political establishment by

representatives of the landed oligarchy was thus gradually being undermined by industrial modernization but it would not be surrendered easily. In addition to the differing challenges represented by powerful industrialists and the organized working-class movement, a more cerebral opposition to the system came from a small but influential group of middle-class Republicans. As well as distinguished intellectuals like the philosopher Miguel de Unamuno and the novelist Vicente Blasco Ibáñez, increasingly there were dynamic new political groupings. In Asturias, the moderate liberal Melquiades Álvarez worked for a democratization of the monarchical system, in 1912 creating the Reformist Party. Álvarez's project for modernization attracted many young intellectuals who would later find prominence in the Second Republic, most notably the intensely scholarly man of letters Manuel Azaña, who would come to represent modernity and the European Spain of the distant future.

The rise of republicanism persuaded some elements within the PSOE, notably the young Asturian journalist Indalecio Prieto, of the need for the establishment of liberal democracy and they therefore fought for an electoral alliance with middle-class Republicans. Prieto had seen in Bilbao that, alone, the Socialists could do little, while, with the Republicans, they could secure election success. His advocacy of a Republican–Socialist electoral combination in 1909 opened up the long-term prospect of building socialism from parliament but also brought him into conflict with other leaders such as the UGT vice-president Francisco Largo Caballero, who advocated a strategy of confrontational strike action. Republican–Socialist collaboration would be the basis of eventual PSOE success. Indeed, Pablo Iglesias himself was elected to parliament in 1910. However, Prieto had earned the lifelong hostility of Largo Caballero, whose rancour would bedevil his existence and, eventually, have devastating consequences for Spain.

Another Republican movement that seemed to be threatening the system was the brainchild of the outrageous rogue Alejandro Lerroux. Born in Córdoba, Lerroux started his adult life as an army deserter after squandering his military academy fees in a casino. As a journalist he leapt to fame in 1893 by dint of an inadvertent victory in a duel with a newspaper editor. His exposés of the Montjuich tortures gained him a popular following. His skills as a demagogue gave him the leadership of a mass Republican movement in the slums of Barcelona and his ability as an organizer built a formidable electoral machine. It was revealed that he was receiving money from the central government, common practice in a period when politicians paid for the inclusion or suppression of news in newspapers. This gave rise to the widespread belief that his rabble-rousing in Barcelona was a Madrid-inspired operation to divide the anarcho-syndicalist masses and undermine the rise of Catalan nationalism. Probably no government slush fund could have achieved what he did. To become 'Emperor of the Paralelo', the Barcelona district where misery, criminality and prostitution held sway, required more genuine appeal than anything that could be conjured up in Madrid offices. This was achieved largely by the near pornographic techniques of anti-clerical demagogy in which he enjoined his followers, the 'young barbarians', to murder priests, sack and burn churches and 'liberate' nuns. Lerroux tapped into the profound anti-clericalism of immigrant workers. For them, the Church was the defender of the brutally unjust rural social order from which they had fled.

The first decade of the twentieth century therefore tasted an explosive cocktail of intransigence, on the part of landowners and industrialists, and subversion from a disparate array of Socialists, anarchists, Radicals, moderate Republicans and regional nationalists. It was a period in which rapid but sporadic industrialization and partial labour organization coincided with major post-imperial trauma. A resentful army disappointed in Cuba turned inwards, determined not to lose further battles, and became obsessed with the defence of national unity and the existing social order. Accordingly, the officer corps was increasingly hostile both to the left and to the regional Nationalists who were perceived as 'separatists'. Right-wing, centralist and constantly needled by the Catalan anti-militarist press, in November 1905 the army shook off its immediate post-war shame with an assault by three hundred officers on the premises of the satirical journal *¡Cu-cut!* and the Catalanist newspaper *La Veu de Catalunya*, during which forty-six people were seriously injured. To appease the army, the government introduced the Law of Jurisdictions which deemed that any criticism of the army, the monarchy or Spain itself would result in the perpetrators being tried by the military justice system. It was a dangerous step in the process whereby the officer corps came to consider itself the ultimate arbiter in politics. Moreover, the Spanish army was not prepared merely to be the defender of a constitutional regime whose decadence it despised. It hoped to find a solution in a new imperial endeavour in Morocco, made possible by British desires for a Spanish buffer against French expansionism on the southern shores of the Strait of Gibraltar. However, woefully unprepared, the new adventure stimulated massive popular hostility against conscription, thereby intensifying the hatred of the military for the left. At the same time, after 1905 Lerroux began to lose support precisely because of the fierce sincerity with which he revealed his pro-militaristic and centralist abhorrence of Catalanism.

The volatility of the situation was revealed by the events known as the *Semana Trágica* which took place in Barcelona in July 1909. The colonial disaster of 1898 *had* fed widespread working-class pacifism and ensured that, unlike France or Britain, Germany or Italy, Spain could not use imperialist adventures to divert attention from domestic social conflict. Spain's Moroccan entanglement was popularly regarded as the narrow personal undertaking of the King and the owners of the iron mines. In 1909, the government of the conservative

Antonio Maura, under pressure from both army officers close to Alfonso XIII and investors in the mines, sent an expeditionary force to expand Spain's Moroccan territory to encompass some important mineral deposits. Large numbers of reservists, mainly married men with children, were called up and embarked from Barcelona. Untrained and ill-equipped, the Spanish army was in the throes of being defeated by the Rif tribesmen at the battle of Barranco del Lobo. There were anti-war demonstrations in Madrid, Barcelona and cities with railway stations from which conscripts were departing for the war. A general strike broke out in Barcelona on 26 July. The Captain-General of the region decided to treat it as insurrection and declared martial law. Barricades were set up and anti-conscription protests escalated into anti-clerical disturbances and church burnings. The movement was put down with the use of artillery. Numerous prisoners were taken and 1725 people were subsequently tried, of whom five were sentenced to death. In military eyes the repression was necessary because the disturbances had connotations of anti-militarism, anti-clericalism and Catalan separatism. In this sense, during the *Semana Trágica* the hostility between the military and the labour movement prefigured the violent hostilities of the civil war.

The *Semana Trágica* certainly took Spain a step further towards the conflicts of the 1930s in terms of developments within the anarchist movement. Lerroux's pro-militaristic stance had exposed the fraudulence of his radicalism and saw the bulk of his 'young barbarians' drift towards anarchism. In the autumn of 1910, a variety of anarchist groups united to form an anarcho-syndicalist trade union known as the Confederación Nacional del Trabajo (CNT). The new organization rejected both individual violence and parliamentary politics, opting instead for revolutionary syndicalism. This involved a central contradiction which would hinder the organization throughout its existence. On the one hand, it would act as a conventional trade union defending the interests of its members within the existing order while at the same time advocating direct action to overthrow that system. The involvement of its members in violent acts of industrial sabotage and strikes meant the new organization was soon declared illegal.

Surprisingly, however, when the next explosion came it was precipitated not by the rural anarchists or the urban working class but by the industrial bourgeoisie. Nevertheless, once the crisis started, proletarian ambitions came into play in such a way as to ensure that the basic polarization of Spanish political life became starker than ever. The geometric symmetry of the Restoration system – with political power concentrated in the hands of those who also enjoyed the monopoly of economic power – already under pressure, was shattered by the outbreak of the First World War. Not only were political passions aroused by a bitter debate about whether Spain should intervene and on which side, accentuating growing divisions within the Liberal and Conservative parties, but massive social upheaval followed in the wake of the war. The fact that Spain was a non-belligerent put her in the economically privileged position of being able to supply both the Entente and the Central Powers with agricultural and industrial products. Coal mine owners from Asturias, Basque steel barons and ship-builders, Catalan textile magnates all experienced a wild boom which constituted the first dramatic takeoff for Spanish industry. The balance of power within the economic elite shifted somewhat. Agrarian interests remained pre-eminent but industrialists were no longer prepared to tolerate their subordinate political position. Their dissatisfaction came to a head in June 1916 when the Liberal Minister of Finance, Santiago Alba, attempted to impose a tax on the notorious war profits of northern industry without a corresponding measure to deal with those made by the agrarians. Although the move was blocked, it so underlined the arrogance of the landed elite that it precipitated a bid by the industrial bourgeoisie to carry through political modernization.

The discontent of the Basque and Catalan industrialists had already seen them mount challenges to the Spanish establishment by sponsoring their respective regionalist movements – the Partido Nacionalista Vasco (PNV) and the Lliga Regionalista. The leader of the Lliga, the shrewd Catalan financier Francesc Cambó, emerged as spokesman for the industrialists and bankers. He believed that drastic action was necessary if a major revolutionary cataclysm was to be avoided. Now the reforming zeal of industrialists enriched by the war coincided with a desperate need for change from a proletariat impoverished by it. Boom industries had attracted rural labour to towns where the worst conditions of early capitalism prevailed. This was especially true of Asturias and the Basque Country. At the same time, massive exports created shortages, rocketing inflation and plummeting living standards. After a number of dramatic bread riots, the Socialist UGT and the anarcho-syndicalist CNT were drawn together in the hope that a joint general strike might bring about free elections and then reform. While industrialists and workers pushed for change, middle-ranking army officers were protesting at low wages, antiquated promotion structures and political corruption. A bizarre and short-lived alliance was forged in part because of a misunderstanding about the political stance of the army.

Military discontent was related to a division within the army of those who had volunteered to fight in Africa – *Africanistas* – and those who had remained on the peninsula – *peninsulares*. For those who had fought in Africa the risks were enormous but the prizes, in terms of adventure and rapid promotion, high. The rigours and horrors of the Moroccan tribal wars brutalized the beleaguered *Africanistas*, who began to see themselves as a heroic band of warriors who, in their commitment to defending the Moroccan colony, were alone concerned with the fate of the *patria*. Long before the establishment of the Second Republic, this had developed into contempt for professional politicians, for the pacifist left-wing masses and, to a certain extent, for the *peninsulares*. The mainland represented a more comfortable but boring existence with promotion only by strict seniority. When salaries started to be hit, like those of civilians, by wartime inflation, there was resentment among the *peninsulares* against the *Africanistas* who had gained more rapid promotion. The *peninsulares* created the Juntas Militares de Defensa, rather like trade unions, to protect the seniority system and to seek better pay.

The Juntas' complaints were couched in the language of reform which had become fashionable after Spain's loss of empire in 1898. The intellectual movement known as 'Regenerationism' associated the defeat of 1898 with political corruption. Ultimately, 'Regenerationism' was open to exploitation by either the right or the left since among its advocates there were those who sought to sweep away the degenerate *caciquista* system by democratic reform and those who planned simply to crush it by the authoritarian solution of 'an iron surgeon'. However, in 1917 the officers who mouthed empty 'Regenerationist' clichés were acclaimed as the figureheads of a great national reform movement. For a brief moment, workers, capitalists and the military were united in the name of cleansing Spanish politics of the corruption of *caciquismo*. Had the movement been successful in establishing a political system capable of permitting social adjustment, the Civil War would not have been necessary. As things turned out, the great crisis of 1917 merely consolidated the power of the entrenched landed oligarchy.

Despite a rhetorical coincidence of their calls for reform, the ultimate interests of workers, industrialists and officers were contradictory and the system survived by skilfully exploiting these differences. The Prime Minister, the astute Conservative Eduardo Dato, conceded the officers' economic demands and promoted the ringleaders of the Juntas. He then provoked a strike of Socialist railway workers, forcing the UGT to act before the CNT was ready. Now at peace with the system, army officers – both *peninsulares* and *Africanistas* – were happy to defend it in August 1917 by crushing the striking Socialists, which they did with considerable bloodshed. Alarmed by the prospect of militant workers in the streets, the industrialists dropped their own demands for political reform and, lured by promises of economic modernization, joined in a national coalition government in 1918 with both Liberals and Conservatives. Once again the industrial bourgeoisie had abandoned its political aspirations and allied with the landed oligarchy out of a fear of the lower classes. Short-lived though it was to be, the coalition symbolized the slightly improved position of industrialists in a reactionary alliance still dominated by the landed interest.

By 1917, Spain was divided more starkly even than before into two mutually hostile social groups, with landowners and industrialists on one side and workers and landless labourers on the other. Only one numerous social group was not definitively aligned within this broad cleavage – the smallholding peasantry. Significantly, in the years before and during the First World War, efforts were made to mobilize Catholic farmers in defence of big landholding interests. With anarchism and Socialism making headway among the urban workers, the more far-sighted landowners were anxious to stop the spread of the poison to the countryside. Counter-revolutionary syndicates were financed by landlords from 1906 but the process was systematized after 1912 by a group of dynamic social Catholics led by Ángel Herrera, the *éminence grise* of political Catholicism in Spain before 1936. Through his organization of determined social Christian activists, the Asociación Católica Nacional de Propagandistas, Herrera helped set up a series of provincial Catholic Agrarian Federations which tried to prevent impoverished farmers turning to the left by offering them credit facilities, agronomic expertise, warehousing and machinery in return for their adoption of virulent anti-socialism. Many of those recruited were to play an important role when the landed oligarchy was forced to seek more modern forms of defence in the 1930s first by voting for the legalist parties of the right during the Second Republic and later by fighting for Franco.

In the aftermath of the crisis of 1917, however, the existing order survived in part because of the organizational naïvety of the left and even more because of its own ready recourse to armed repression. The foundation of the Communist International (Comintern) in March 1919 imbued the Spanish ruling classes with the same fear of bolshevism that afflicted all European countries. The defeat of the urban Socialists in 1917 had not marked the end of the assault on the system. Between 1918 and 1921, three years known as the *trienio bolchevique*, the anarchist day-labourers of the south took part in a series of risings. Eventually put down by a combination of the Civil Guard and the army, the strikes and land seizures of these years intensified the social resentments of the rural south. At the same time, urban anarchists were also coming into conflict with the system. Northern industrialists, having failed to invest their war profits in modern plant and rationalization, were badly hit by the post-war resurgence of foreign competition. The Catalans in particular tried to ride the recession with wage cuts and lay-offs. They countered the consequent strikes with lockouts and hired gunmen. The anarchists retaliated in kind and, from 1919 to 1921, the streets of Barcelona witnessed a terrorist spiral of provocations and reprisals. A split in the PSOE over whether or not to join the Comintern led to a factional split with the more radical elements forming the Communist Party in November 1921. The Communists' influence was immediately felt in a series of strikes in the Asturian coal mines and the Basque iron and steel industry. It was obvious that Restoration politics were no longer an adequate mechanism for defending the economic interests of the ruling classes. Moreover, the credibility of the system was rocked by the overwhelming defeat of the Spanish forces by Moroccan tribesmen at Annual in June 1921.

On 23 September 1923 a *coup d'état* was carried out by General Miguel Primo de Rivera. Ostensibly, Primo came to power to put an end to disorder and to prevent the King being embarrassed by the publication of an awkward report on the responsibility for Annual. However, as Captain-General of Barcelona and intimate of the Catalan textile barons, Primo was fully aware of the anarchist threat to them. Moreover, coming from a large landowning family in the south, he also had experience of the peasant risings of 1918–21. He was thus the ideal praetorian defender of the coalition of industrialists and landowners which had been consolidated during the great crisis of 1917. Initially, his dictatorship had two great advantages – a general revulsion against the chaos of the previous six years and an upturn in the European economy. He outlawed the anarchist movement and made a deal with the UGT whereby it was given a monopoly of trade union affairs. A massive public works' programme, which involved a significant modernizing of Spanish capitalism and the building of a communications infrastructure that would bear fruit only thirty years later, gave the impression that liberty was being traded in for prosperity.

The Primo de Rivera dictatorship was to be regarded in later years as a golden age by the Spanish middle classes and became a central myth of the reactionary right. Paradoxically, however, its short-term effect was to discredit the very idea of authoritarianism in Spain. This fleeting phenomenon was born partly of Primo's failure to use the economic breathing space to construct a lasting political replacement for the decrepit constitutional monarchy, but more immediately it sprang from his alienation of the powerful interests which had originally supported him. A genial eccentric with a Falstaffian approach to political life, he governed by a form of personal improvization which ensured that he bore the blame for his regime's failures. Although by 1930 there was hardly a section of Spanish society that he had not offended, his most crucial errors led to the estrangement of industrialists, landowners and the army. Attempts to standardize promotion machinery outraged army officers. The Catalan bourgeoisie was antagonized by an offensive against regionalist aspirations. Northern industrialists were even more enraged by the collapse of the peseta in 1928, which they attributed to his inflationary public spending. Perhaps most importantly, the support of Primo's fellow landowners was lost when efforts were made to introduce arbitration committees for wages and working conditions into rural areas. At the end of January 1930, Primo resigned.

There was no question of a return to the pre-1923 political system. Apart from the fact that it had fallen into disrepute by the time Primo seized power, significant changes had taken place in the attitudes of its personnel. Among the senior politicians, death, old age and, above all, resentment of the King's cavalier abandonment of the constitution in 1923 had taken their toll. Of the younger men, some had opted for the Republican movement, partly out of pique, partly out of a conviction that the political future lay in that direction. Others, especially those Conservatives who had followed the authoritarian implications of 'Regenerationism' to the logical extreme, had thrown themselves wholeheartedly into the service of the dictator. For them, there could be no going back. Their experiences under Primo had left them entrenched in the view that the only feasible solution to the problems faced by the right was a military monarchy. They would form the general staff of the extreme right in the Second Republic and were to provide much of the ideological content of the Franco regime.

In desperation, therefore, Alfonso XIII turned to another general, Dámaso Berenguer. His mild dictatorship floundered in search of a formula for a return to constitutional monarchy but was undermined by Republican plots, working-class agitation and military sedition. When he held municipal elections on 12 April 1931, Socialists and liberal middle-class Republicans swept the board in the main towns while monarchists won only in the rural areas where the social domination of the local bosses, the *caciques*, remained intact. Faced by the questionable loyalty of both army and Civil Guard, the King took the advice of his counsellors to depart gracefully before he was thrown out by force. The attitude of the military reflected the hope of a significant section of the upper classes that, by sacrificing the King, it would be possible to contain the desires for change of both the progressive bourgeoisie and the left. That was to be an impossible ambition without some concessions in the area of land reform.

The conflicts of the *trienio bolchevique* had been silenced by repression in 1919–20 and by the Primo de Rivera dictatorship, but they continued to smoulder. The violence of those years had ended the uneasy *modus vivendi* of the agrarian south. The repression had intensified the hatred of the *braceros* for the big landowners and their estate managers. By the same token, the landlords were outraged by insubordinate behaviour of the day-labourers whom they considered almost sub-human. Accordingly, the elements of paternalism which had previously mitigated the daily brutality of the *braceros'* lives came to an abrupt end. The gathering of windfall crops or the watering of beasts, even the collection of firewood were deemed to be 'collective kleptomania' and were prevented by the vigilance of armed guards. In consequence, the new Republic was to inherit a situation of sporadic social war in the south which was dramatically to diminish its possibilities of establishing a regime of co-existence. Nevertheless, with goodwill on both sides, everything, even peace, was possible in 1931. Within weeks of the Republic being established, however, it was clear that among the erstwhile supporters of Alfonso XIII and within the anarchist movement there was anything but goodwill to Spain's new democracy.

TWO

The Leftist Challenge, 1931–1933

The coming of the Second Republic signified a threat to the most privileged members of society and raised inordinate hopes among the most humble. Ultimately, the new regime was to fail because it neither carried through its threatened reforms nor fulfilled the utopian expectations of its most fervent supporters. The success of the right in blocking change would so exasperate the rural and urban working classes as to undermine their faith in parliamentary democracy. Once that happened, and once the left had turned to revolutionary solutions, the rightist determination to destabilize the Republic would be enormously facilitated. Yet given the failures of both the monarchy and the dictatorship, the majority of Spaniards had been prepared in 1931 to give the Republic a chance. However, behind the superficial goodwill, there was potentially savage conflict over the scale of the social and economic reform it should pursue, or, to use the jargon of the day, over what the 'content' of the Republic should be. In this sense, the seeds of war were buried near the surface of a Republic which was the source of hope to the left and of fear to the right.

Before 1931, social, economic and political power in Spain had all been in the hands of the same groups, the components of the reactionary coalition of landowners, industrialists and bankers. The challenge to that monopoly mounted by the disunited forces of the left between 1917 and 1923 had exposed the deficiencies of the Restoration monarchy. The defence of establishment interests was then entrusted to the military dictatorship of General Primo de Rivera. Because of its failure, the idea of an authoritarian solution to the problems facing the beleaguered oligarchy was briefly discredited. Moreover, the coming of the Republic found the right temporarily bereft of political organization. Accordingly, the upper classes and large sectors of the middle classes acquiesced in the departure of Alfonso XIII because they had little alternative. They did so in the hope that, by sacrificing a King and tolerating a President, they might protect themselves from greater unpleasantness in the way of social and economic reform.

However, the establishment of the Republic meant that for the first time political power had passed from the oligarchy to the moderate left. This consisted of representatives of the most reformist section of the organized working class, the Socialists, and a mixed bag of petty bourgeois Republicans, some of whom were idealists and many of whom were cynics. Therein lay a major weakness of the new government. Beyond the immediate desire to rid Spain of the monarchy, each of its components had a different agenda. The broad Republican–Socialist coalition ranged from conservative elements who wanted to go no further than the removal of Alfonso XIII, via a centre of the often venal Radicals of Alejandro Lerroux whose principal ambition was to derive profit from access to the levers of power, to the leftist Republicans and the Socialists who had ambitious, but different, reforming objectives. Together, they saw themselves using state power to create a new Spain. However, to do so required a vast programme of reform which would involve destroying the reactionary influence of the Church and the army, more equitable industrial relations, breaking the near feudal powers of the *latifundio* estate-owners and meeting the autonomy demands of Basque and Catalan regionalists.

Given that both economic power – ownership of the banks and industry, of the land and dominance of the landless labourers who worked it – and social power – control of the press and the radio, what passed for the mass media, and of the largely private

education system – remained unchanged, this disparate programme constituted a dauntingly tall order. Broadly speaking,
the masters of social and economic power were united with the
Church and the army in being determined to prevent any
attacks on property, religion or national unity. They were quick
to find a variety of ways in which to defend their interests.
Ultimately, then, the Spanish Civil War was to grow out of
the efforts of the progressive leaders of the Republic to carry
out reform against the wishes of the most powerful sections of
society.

When the King fled, power was assumed by the Provisional
Government whose composition had been agreed in August
1930 when Republican and Socialist opponents of the King had
met and forged the Pact of San Sebastián. The Prime Minister
was Niceto Alcalá Zamora, a landowner from Córdoba and
an ex-minister of the King. The Minister of the Interior was
Miguel Maura, the son of the celebrated Conservative politician Antonio Maura. The Minister of the Economy was the
liberal Catalan Lluis Nicolau D'Olwer. Both Alcalá Zamora
and Maura were Catholic conservatives and served as a guarantee to the upper classes that the Republic would remain within
the bounds of reason. The Radical Alejandro Lerroux was Minister of Foreign Affairs and the deputy leader of his party, the
altogether more upright and honest Diego Martínez Barrio,
was Minister of Communications. The remainder of the cabinet was made up of four left Republicans and three reformist
Socialists, unanimous in their desire to build a Republic for all
Spaniards. Inevitably, therefore, the coming of the parliamentary regime constituted far less of a change than was either
hoped by the rejoicing crowds in the streets or feared by the
upper classes.

Socialist ambitions were restrained. The PSOE leadership
hoped that the political power that had fallen into their hands
would permit the improvement of the living conditions of the
southern *braceros*, the Asturian miners and other sections of the

industrial working class. They realized that the overthrow of capitalism was a distant dream. What the most progressive members of the new Republican–Socialist coalition failed to perceive at first was the stark truth that the great *latifundistas* and the mine-owners would regard any attempt at reform as an aggressive challenge to the existing balance of social and economic power. However, in the days before they realized that they were trapped between the impatient mass demand for significant reform and the dogged hostility to change of the rich, the Socialists approached the Republic in a spirit of self-sacrifice and optimism. In Madrid on 14 April, members of the Socialist Youth Movement prevented assaults on buildings associated with the right, especially the royal palace. The Socialist ministers acquiesced in Maura's refusal to abolish the Civil Guard, a hated symbol of authority to workers and peasants. Also, in a gesture to the wealthy classes, the Socialist Minister of Finance, Indalecio Prieto, announced that he would meet all the financial obligations of the Dictatorship.

However, the potential state of war between the proponents of reform and the defenders of the existing order was not to be ignored. Rightist hostility to the Republic was quickly revealed. Prieto announced at the first meeting of ministers that the financial position of the regime was being endangered by a large-scale withdrawal of wealth from the country. Even before the Republic had been established, followers of General Primo de Rivera had been trying to build barricades against liberalism and republicanism. They started to collect money from aristocrats, landowners, bankers and industrialists to publicize authoritarian ideas, to finance conspiratorial activities and to buy arms. They realized that the Republic's commitment to improving the living conditions of the poorest members of society inevitably threatened them with a major redistribution of wealth. At a time of world depression, wage increases and the cost of better working conditions could not simply be absorbed by higher profits. Indeed, in a contracting economy they seemed like revolutionary challenges to the established economic order.

From the end of April to the beginning of July, the Socialist Ministers of Labour, Francisco Largo Caballero, and of Justice, Fernando de los Ríos, issued a series of decrees which aimed to deal with the appalling situation in rural Spain, shattered by a drought during the 1930–31 season and thronged by returning emigrants. De los Ríos rectified the imbalance in rural leases which favoured the landlords. Eviction was made almost impossible and rent rises blocked while prices were falling. Largo Caballero's measures were much more dramatic. The so-called 'decree of municipal boundaries' prevented the hiring of outside labour while any local workers in a given municipality remained unemployed. It struck at the landowners' most potent weapon, the power to break strikes and keep down wages by the import of cheap blackleg labour. In early May, Largo Caballero did something that Primo de Rivera had tried and failed to do – he introduced arbitration committees (known as *jurados mixtos*) for rural wages and working conditions which had previously been subject only to the whim of the owners. One of the rights now to be protected was the newly introduced eight-hour day. Given that, previously, the *braceros* had been expected to work from sun up to sun down, this meant that owners would either have to pay overtime or employ more men to do the same work. Finally, in order to prevent the owners sabotaging these measures by lockouts, a decree of obligatory cultivation prevented them taking their land out of operation. None of these decrees was applied ruthlessly and nothing was done about the owners who refused to pay hours worked over eight hours. However, together with the preparations being set in train for a sweeping law of agrarian reform, they alarmed the landowners who began to complain loudly of agriculture being ruined.

The response of the right was complex. At a local level, landlords simply ignored the new legislation, letting loose their armed retainers on the trade union officials who complained. The implementation in the countryside of the reforming decrees would depend on the efficacy and commitment of the civil governor of each province. In general terms, however, the Republican government faced enormous difficulty in finding competent and experienced personnel for its ministries. The problem was most acute at a local level. Miguel Maura wrote later of his despair at finding suitable governors for forty-nine provinces. The men recommended to him by his fellow ministers were often comically inadequate – one he rejected was a shoeshine boy who had lent money to Marcelino Domingo in harder times. In his memoirs, he wrote 'Governors! After thirty years, just thinking about them still gives me goose flesh.' Many governors were thus not up to the job of standing up to the landowners who openly flouted legislation. In their weakness, they often ended up as more loyal to local elites than to central government.

In terms of national politics, the powerful press networks of the right began to present the Republic as responsible for all the centuries-old problems of the Spanish economy and as the fount of mob violence. More specifically, there were two broad responses, known at the time as 'accidentalist' and 'catastrophist'. The 'accidentalists' took the view that forms of government, Republican or monarchical, were 'accidental' as opposed to fundamental. What really mattered was the social content of a regime. Thus, inspired by Ángel Herrera, the leader of the Asociación Católica Nacional de Propagandistas (the ACNP), the 'accidentalists' adopted a legalist tactic. The ACNP was an elite Jesuit-influenced organization of about five hundred prominent and talented Catholic rightists with influence in the press, the judiciary and the professions – a predecessor of Opus Dei. Herrera, who would end life as a Cardinal, was the editor of the most modern right-wing daily in Spain, *El Debate*. From within the ACNP a clever and dynamic leader, the lawyer José María Gil Robles, created an organization called Acción

Popular by welding together a general staff from the ACNP and the Catholic smallholding masses from the old Catholic Agrarian Federations. Its few elected deputies used every possible device to block reform in the parliament, or Cortes. Massive and extraordinarily skilful efforts of propaganda were made to persuade the smallholding farmers of northern and central Spain that the agrarian reforms of the Republic damaged their interests every bit as much as those of the big landowners. The Republic was presented to the conservative Catholic smallholders as a godless, rabble-rousing instrument of Soviet communism poised to steal their lands and dragoon their wives and daughters into an orgy of obligatory free love. With their votes thereby assured, by 1933 the legalist right was to wrest political power back from the left.

At the same time, the various 'catastrophist' groups were fundamentally opposed to the Republic and believed that it should be overthrown by some great catastrophic explosion or uprising. It was their view which was to prevail in 1936, although it should not be forgotten that the contribution of the 'accidentalists' in stirring up anti-republicanism among the smallholding peasantry was crucial for Franco's war effort. There were three principal 'catastrophist' organizations. The oldest was the Traditionalist Communion of the Carlists, anti-modern advocates of a theocracy to be ruled on earth by warrior priests. Antiquated though its ideas were, it was well supplied with supporters among the farmers of Navarre and had a fanatical militia called the *Requeté* which, between 1934 and 1936, was to receive training in Mussolini's Italy. The best financed and ultimately the most influential of the 'catastrophists' were the one-time supporters of Alfonso XIII and General Primo de Rivera. These Alfonsine monarchists, with their journal *Acción Española* and their political party Renovación Española, were the general staff and the paymasters of the extreme right. Both the rising of 1936 and the structure and ideology of the Francoist state owed an enormous amount to the Alfonsines. Finally, there were a number of unashamed Fascist groups, which finally coalesced between 1933 and 1934 under the leadership of the Dictator's son, José Antonio Primo de Rivera, as Falange Española. Also subsidized by Mussolini, the rank-and-file Falangists supplied the cannon fodder of the 'catastrophist' option, attacking the left and provoking the street fights which permitted other groups to denounce the 'disorder' of the Republic.

Among the Republic's enemies two of the most powerful were the Church and the army. Both were to be easily drawn into the anti-Republican right, in part because of errors made by the Republic's politicians but also because of the actions of the Church's own hardliner fundamentalists, or *integristas*. They were committed to the necessity of a 'Confessional State' that forcibly, by civil war if necessary, imposed the profession and practice of the Catholic religion and prohibited all others. Among this group were to be found the Cardinal Primate of All Spain, the Archbishop of Toledo, Pedro Segura, and the Bishop of Tarazona in the province of Zaragoza, Isidro Gomá. They formed a semi-clandestine group within the Church, whose members communicated with one another in code, a fact revealed when left-wingers found the secret archives of Isidro Gomá in the Archbishop's palace at Toledo in July 1936. On 24 April, a mere ten days after the proclamation of the Republic, Spain's bishops received a letter from the Apostolic Nuncio informing them that 'It is the wish of the Holy See that Your Eminence recommend to the priests, religious and faithful of your diocese to respect the constituted powers and obey them in the interests of public order and the common good.'

In response, on 1 May, Bishop Gomá wrote an intransigent pastoral letter which passed virtually unnoticed in comparison with the scandal provoked by that of the ambitious and irascible Archbishop Segura. Segura spent much of his life attempting to prohibit any modern dancing in which the couples touched and his pugnacity in matters theological led the monarchist intellectual José María Pemán to compare him to 'a bullfighter in doctrinal and pastoral issues'. Now, Segura's letter, addressed to all the bishops and the faithful of Spain, called for the mass mobilization of all in a crusade of prayers to unite 'seriously and effectively to ensure the election to the Constituent Cortes candidates who offer guarantees that they will defend the rights of the Church and the social order'. In irresponsibly provocative language, in a context of popular enthusiasm for the Republic, he went on to praise the monarchy and its links to the Church.

An outraged government immediately insisted on Segura's immediate removal by the Vatican. Before a response was received, Segura, believing himself to be in danger of reprisals, requested a passport and went to Rome. However, on 11 June he slipped back into Spain and began to organize clandestine meetings of priests. Accordingly, the deeply Catholic Minister of the Interior, Miguel Maura, without consulting the rest of the cabinet, took the decision to expel him from Spain. Newspaper photographs of the Cardinal Primate of Spain being escorted by police and Civil Guards from a monastery in Guadalajara was immediately produced as evidence of Republican persecution of the Church. The see of Toledo would remain vacant until 12 April 1933 when Segura was replaced by an equally vehement enemy of the Republic, Isidro Gomá.

Meanwhile, in the spring of 1931, the episode over Segura's pastoral had done nothing to soften the Republican view that the Church was the bulwark of black reaction. Thus, on May 11, when a rash of church burning spread through Madrid, Málaga, Seville, Cádiz and Alicante, the cabinet refused to call out the Civil Guard. Manuel Azaña, the immensely talented left Republican Minister of War, proclaimed that 'all the convents in Madrid are not worth the life of one Republican', a statement which was exploited by the rightist press to persuade its middle-class readership that Azaña somehow approved of the actual burnings. Certainly, the government demonstrated a notable lack of energy in dealing with the fires, which does not mean that it was to blame for them. The indifference of the watching crowds reflected just how strongly ordinary people identified the Church, the monarchy and right-wing politics. The Republican press claimed that the fires were the work of *agents provocateurs* drawn from the scab union, the *Sindicatos Libres*, in an effort to discredit the new regime. Indeed, it was even claimed that the young monarchists of the Círculo Monárquico Independiente (CMI) had distributed leaflets inciting the masses to attack religious buildings. On May 22, full religious liberty was declared. The monarchist daily *ABC* and the Catholic *El Debate* howled abuse and were briefly closed down by the government.

Several issues were to cause friction between the Republic and the armed forces but none more than the new regime's readiness to concede regional autonomy. On 14 April, Colonel Macià, the leader of the Catalan Esquerra Republicana de Catalunya (Republican Left of Catalonia), declared an independent Catalan republic. A deputation from Madrid persuaded him to await government action by promising a rapid statute of autonomy. Inevitably, this aroused the suspicions of the army which had shed so much blood in the fight against Catalan separatism. To make matters worse, the Minister of War, Azaña, began in May to prepare reforms to cut down the inflated officer corps and to make the army more efficient. It was thereby hoped to reduce the political ambitions of the armed forces. It was a necessary reform and, in many respects, a generous one, since the eight thousand surplus officers were retired on full pay. However, military sensibilities were inflamed by the insensitivity with which various aspects of the reforms were implemented. Azaña's decree of 3 June 1931 insisting on the so-called *revisión de ascensos* (review of promotions) reopened some of the promotions on merit given during the Moroccan wars. Many distinguished right-wing generals including Francisco Franco faced the prospect of being reduced to the rank of colonel. The commission carrying out the revision took more than eighteen months to report, causing unnecessary anxiety for the nearly one thousand officers affected, of whom only half had their cases examined. On 30 June 1931, Azaña closed the General Military Academy in Zaragoza for budgetary reasons and because he believed it to be a hotbed of reactionary militarism. This guaranteed Azaña the eternal enmity of its Director, General Franco.

Since Azaña's reforms involved the abolition of the army's jurisdictions over civilians thought to have insulted it, many officers regarded them as a savage attack. Those who were retired, having refused to take the oath of loyalty to the Republic, were left with the leisure to plot against the regime. This was encouraged by the conservative newspapers read by most army officers, *ABC*, *La Época* and *La Correspondencia Militar*, which presented the Republic as responsible for the economic depression, for the breakdown of law and order, and for disrespect for the army and anti-clericalism. In particular, a campaign was mounted alleging that Azaña's intention was to '*triturar el Ejército*' (crush the army). Azaña never made any such remark, although it has become a commonplace that he did. In fact, far from depriving the army of funds and equipment, Azaña, who had made a lifetime study of civil–military relations, merely ensured that the military budget would be used more efficaciously. If anything, Azaña tended to be punctilious in his treatment of a shambolic and inefficient force which compared poorly with the armies of countries like Portugal or Romania. Ironically, the military readiness of the Spanish army in 1936 owed as much to the efforts of Azaña as to those of his successor, the rightist José María Gil Robles. Azaña was converted by the rightist propaganda machine into the bogey of the military because he wanted to provide Spain with a non-political army. For the right, the army existed above all to defend their social and economic interests. Azaña was therefore presented as a corrupt monster, determined to destroy the army, as he was allegedly determined to destroy the Church, because it was part of the Jewish–Bolshevik–Masonic conspiracy to do so. Curiously, he had a much higher regard for military procedures than his predecessor, General Primo de Rivera. A general who presumed to 'interpret the widespread feeling of the nation' to Azaña was told forthrightly, 'Your job is merely to interpret regulations.' That was not how Spanish generals expected to be treated by civilians.

From the very first days of the Republic right-wing extremists disseminated the idea that an alliance of Jews, Freemasons and the working-class Internationals was conspiring to destroy Christian Europe, with Spain as a principal target. Anti-semitism, even in a country whose Jews had been expelled four and a half centuries earlier, was a potent weapon. Already in June 1931 the Carlist newspaper *El Siglo Futuro* had denounced Niceto Alcalá Zamora, Miguel Maura and his Minister of Justice, Fernando de los Ríos, as Jews. The Catholic press in general made frequent reference to the Jewish–Masonic–Bolshevik conspiracy. The Editorial Católica, which owned a chain of newspapers including *El Debate*, would soon be publishing the deeply anti-semitic and anti-masonic magazines *Gracia y Justicia* and *Los Hijos del Pueblo*. Even the more moderate Catholic daily, *El Debate*, referred to De los Ríos as 'the rabbi'. The attribution of the Republic's reforming ambitions to a sinister foreign Jewish–Masonic–Bolshevik plot made it that much easier to advocate violence against it. As this propaganda intensified over the next five years, the conviction grew on the extreme right that the Spanish supporters of this filthy foreign conspiracy had to be exterminated.

Such propaganda was soon widespread. However, the first major political contest of the Republic had taken place before the right was properly organized. The June 1931 elections were won by the Socialists in coalition with the left Republicans. Republicanism tended to be a movement of intellectuals and the petty bourgeoisie, more an amorphous improvised grouping than a united left-wing force. The only centre grouping, the Radicals, had, on the other hand, started out as a genuine mass movement in Barcelona in the early years of the century. Led by the fiery orator and corrupt machine politician Alejandro Lerroux, the Radicals were to become progressively more conservative and anti-Socialist as the Republic developed. They did immense damage to the Republic by their readiness to opt for the winning side at any given time. The polarization brought about by the pendulum effect of a big left-wing victory in the 1931 elections followed by an equally dramatic rightist triumph in 1933 was greatly intensified by the fact that the Radicals had changed sides.

The centrifugal dynamic of Republican politics was in itself the inadvertent consequence of a set of electoral regulations which were drawn up in such a way as to avoid the political fragmentation that destroyed the Weimar Republic. To ensure strong government majorities, in any given province, 80 per cent of the seats were given to the party or list with most votes over 40 per cent of those cast. The other 20 per cent block of seats went to the list that was second past the post. Accordingly, small fluctuations in the number of votes cast could lead to massive swings in the number of parliamentary seats actually won. The pressure to form coalitions was obvious. The elections of 28 June 1931 for the Constituent Cortes therefore registered a heavy victory for the broad coalition of Socialists, the left Republicans and the Radicals, with a total of 250 seats. The PSOE had gained 116 seats. In the flush of victory, little thought seems to have been given by the Socialist leadership to the long-term implications of the fact that Lerroux's Radicals, with a campaign that was unashamedly conservative, not to say right wing, had gained ninety-four seats and become the second largest party in the Constituent Cortes. The somewhat heterogeneous right gained only eighty seats. By 1933, however, the success of rightist tactics in blocking reform and the consequent disappointment of the left-wing rank and file had provoked a significant realignment of forces. By then, the anarchists who had voted for the leftist parties in 1931 were committed to abstention. The Socialists had so lost faith in the possibilities of bourgeois democracy that they refused to make a coalition with the left Republicans. The apparatus of the state would thus be allowed to slip out of the grasp of the left in the November 1933 elections.

That change was a reflection of the enormity of the task that faced the 1931 parliament, known as the Constituent Cortes because its primary task was to give Spain a new Constitution. For the Republic to survive it had to increase wages and cut unemployment. Unfortunately, the regime was born at the height of the world depression. With agricultural prices falling, landowners had let land fall out of cultivation. The landless labourers, who lived near starvation at the best of times, were thus in a state of revolutionary tension. Industrial and building workers were similarly hit. To make matters worse, the wealthy classes were hoarding or exporting their capital. This posed a terrible dilemma for the Republican government. If the demands of the lower classes for expropriation of the great estates and takeovers of the factories were met, the army would probably intervene to destroy the Republic. If revolutionary disturbances were put down in order to appease the upper classes, the government would find the working class arrayed against it. In trying to tread the middle course, the Republican–Socialist coalition ended up enraging both sides.

This was demonstrated within a week of the Cortes' first session. A general strike called by the anarchists led to thousands of CNT telephone workers leaving work. The strike achieved its most notable successes in Seville and Barcelona and was an intense embarrassment to the government which was anxious to prove its ability to maintain order. The Ministry of Labour declared the strike illegal, and the Civil Guard was called in. In Seville the CNT attempted to convert the strike into an insurrection. Miguel Maura, Minister of the Interior, decided on drastic action: martial law was declared and the army sent in to crush the strike. Maura authorized the shelling of an anarchist meeting place, the Casa Cornelio. Local rightist volunteers were permitted to form a 'Guardia Cívica' and killed several leftists, including four anarchists shot in cold blood in the Parque de María Luisa. The revolutionary nature of the strike frightened the upper classes, while the violence with which it was put down – thirty killed and two hundred wounded – confirmed the anarchists in their hostility to the Republic.

The CNT was increasingly falling under the domination of the Federación Anarquista Ibérica (FAI), the secret organization founded in 1927 to maintain the ideological purity of the movement. In the summer of 1931 there was a split between the orthodox unionists of the CNT and FAI members who advocated continuous revolutionary violence. The FAI won the internal struggle and the more reformist elements of the CNT were effectively expelled. The bulk of the anarcho-syndicalist movement was left in the hands of those who felt that the Republic was no better than either the monarchy or the dictatorship of Primo de Rivera. Thereafter, and until the CNT was uneasily reunited in 1936, the anarchists embarked on a policy of 'revolutionary gymnastics' – anti-Republican insurrectionary strikes which invariably failed because of lack of coordination and fierce repression, but enabled the rightist press to identify the Republic with violence and upheaval.

In the autumn of 1931, however, before the waves of anarchist agitation were fully under way, the Cortes was occupied with the elaboration of the new Constitution. After an earlier draft by the conservative politician Angel Ossorio y Gallardo had been rejected, a new constitutional committee, under the Socialist law professor Luis Jiménez de Asúa, met on 28 July. It had barely three weeks to draw up its draft. In consequence, some of its unsubtle wording was to give rise to three months of acrimonious debate. Presenting the project on 27 August, Jiménez de Asúa described it as a democratic, liberal document with great social content. An important Socialist victory was chalked up by Luis Araquistain, later to be one of Largo Caballero's radical advisers, when he prevailed on the chamber to accept Article 1, which read 'Spain is a republic of workers of all classes'. Article 44 stated that all the wealth of the country must be subordinate to the economic interests of the nation and that all property could be expropriated, with compensation, for reasons of social utility. Indeed, the Constitution finally approved on 9 December 1931 was as democratic, laic, reforming and liberal on matters of regional autonomy as the Republicans and Socialists could have wished. It appalled the most powerful interests in Spain, landowners, industrialists, churchmen and army officers.

The opposition of the conservative classes to the Constitution crystallized around Articles 44 and 26. The latter concerned the cutting off of state financial support for the clergy and religious orders; the dissolution of orders, such as the Jesuits, that swore foreign oaths of allegiance; and the limitation of the Church's right to wealth. The Republican–Socialist coalition's attitude to the Church was based on the belief that, if a new Spain was to be built, the stranglehold of the Church on many aspects of society must be broken. That was a reasonable perception, but it failed to take into account the sensibilities of Spain's millions of Catholics. Religion was not attacked as such, but the Constitution was to put an end to the government's endorsement of the Church's privileged position. To the right, the religious settlement of the Constitution was a vicious onslaught on traditional values. The debate on Article 26, the crucial religious clause, coming in the wake of the bitterness provoked by Azaña's military reforms, intensified the polarization which was to end in civil war.

Substantial popular support for right-wing hostility to the Republic was secured during the so-called revisionist campaign against the Constitution. The opposition to the Constitution's religious clauses was equalled in bitterness by that to the clauses concerning regional autonomy for Catalonia and agrarian reform. The legalization of divorce and the dissolution of religious orders contained in Article 26 infuriated the Catholic establishment and the right-wing press, which attributed the measures to evil Jewish–Masonic machinations. During a debate late into the night of 13 October 1931, Gil Robles turned to the Republican–Socialist majority in the Cortes and declared: 'Today, in opposition to the Constitution, Catholic Spain takes its stand. You will bear responsibility for the spiritual war that is going to be unleashed in Spain.' Five days later, on 18 October 1931, in the Plaza de Toros at Ledesma (Salamanca), Gil Robles called for a crusade against the Republic, claiming that 'while anarchic forces, gun in hand, spread panic in government circles, the government tramples on defenceless beings like poor nuns'.

Indeed, the passing of the Constitution marked a major change in the nature of the Republic. By identifying the Republic with the Jacobinism of the Cortes majority, the ruling coalition alienated many members of the Catholic middle classes. The perceived ferocity of the Constitution's anticlericalism provoked the right into organizing its forces at the same time as the union made at San Sebastián in 1930 began to break up. During the debate of 13 October, later described by Alcalá Zamora as the saddest night of his life, the defence of the religious clauses of the Constitution fell to Manuel Azaña. In the course of his intervention, he made the remark that 'Spain has ceased to be Catholic', which was taken by the right as proof that the Republic was determined to destroy the Church. He was merely commenting on a reality already accepted by the more liberal elements of the Church hierarchy that, sociologically, Catholicism no longer enjoyed the pre-eminence that it had once had. Nevertheless, in October both Alcalá Zamora and Miguel Maura resigned and Azaña, who had risen to prominence during the debate, became Prime Minister. This upset Lerroux, who had been grooming himself for the job, and was excluded because of widespread fear in political circles that he would be unable to keep his hands out of the till. He went into opposition with his Radicals. Thus Azaña was forced to rely more heavily upon the Socialists. This in turn made it more difficult for him to avoid provoking the enmity of the Right.

In fact, Azaña was caught between two fires – that of the left, which wanted reform, and that of the right, which rejected it. This was made apparent when he came to deal with the agrarian problem. Agrarian violence was a constant feature of the Republic. Based on the crippling poverty of rural labourers, it was kept at boiling point by the CNT. The anarchists, together with the Socialist Landworkers' Federation (FNTT: Federación Nacional de Trabajadores de la Tierra, founded in April 1930), were calling for expropriation of estates and the creation of collectives. The Republicans, as middle-class intellectuals, respected property and were not prepared to do this. Largo Caballero, as Minister of Labour, had improved the situation somewhat with the four decrees that he had introduced in the spring. However, the limits of such piecemeal reform were starkly exposed in December 1931 when the Badajoz section of the FNTT called a general strike. It was in the main a peaceful strike, in accordance with the instructions of its organizers. In one isolated village called Castilblanco, however, there was bloodshed. When the strike was called, the FNTT members in Castilblanco had already endured a winter without work. On 31 December, while they were holding a peaceful and disciplined demonstration, the Civil Guard started to break up the crowd. After a scuffle, a Civil Guard opened fire, killing one man and wounding two others. The hungry villagers, in a frenzy of fear, anger and panic, fell upon the four guards and beat them to death with stones and knives.

General José Sanjurjo, the Director General of the Civil Guard, told journalists that one of the PSOE's parliamentary deputies for Badajoz, the fiery Jewish feminist Margarita

Nelken, was responsible for the entire incident. He went on to compare the workers of Castilblanco to the Moorish tribesmen whom he had fought in Morocco, commenting, 'In a corner of the province of Badajoz, Rif tribesmen have a headquarters'. He also declared – mendaciously – that after the colonial disaster of Annual in 1921, 'even in Monte Arruit, when the Melilla command collapsed, the corpses of Christians were not mutilated with such savagery'. Sanjurjo's words seemed to justify the subsequent revenge taken by the Civil Guard. More importantly, his identification of the Spanish rural proletariat and with the rebels of the Rif indicated how little the army felt that its job was to protect the Spanish people from an external enemy. The Spanish proletariat was clearly 'the enemy'. In that sense, the mentality of the *Africanista* high command reflected one of the major consequences of the colonial disaster of 1898. This was simply that the right coped with the loss of a 'real' overseas empire by internalizing the empire; that is to say, by regarding metropolitan Spain as the empire and the proletariat as the subject colonial race.

Almost before the cabinet had time to come to terms with Castilblanco, Sanjurjo's men had wreaked a bloody revenge which killed eighteen people. Three days after Castilblanco the Civil Guard killed two workers and wounded three more in Zalamea de la Serena (Badajoz). Two days later, a striker was shot dead and another wounded in Calzada de Calatrava and one striker was shot in Puertollano (both villages in Ciudad Real), while two strikers were killed and eleven wounded in Épila (Zaragoza), and two strikers killed and ten wounded in Jeresa (Valencia). On 5 January the most shocking of these actions occurred when twenty-eight Civil Guards opened fire on a peaceful demonstration at Arnedo, a small town in the northern Castilian province of Logroño. Several workers had been sacked from the local shoe factory at the end of 1931 for belonging to the UGT. At a public protest, the Civil Guard opened fire, killing a worker and four women bystanders, one of them a twenty-six-year-old pregnant mother whose two-year-old son also died. A further fifty townspeople were wounded, including many women and children, some of them babes in arms. Over the next few days, five more people died of their wounds and many had to have limbs amputated, among them a five-year-old boy and a widow with six children.

Then, in early 1932, an anarchist strike was put down with considerable severity, especially in Alto Llobregat in Catalonia. Arrests and deportations followed. Anarchist and Socialist workers were simply being exasperated at the same time as the right was being left with its belief that the Republic meant only chaos and violence. Nevertheless, the need for reform was self-evident, particularly in the rural south where, despite promises of agrarian reform, conditions remained brutal. All over the south, many owners had declared war on the Republican–Socialist coalition by refusing to plant crops.

The response of the big landowners to reform measures had been rapid, both nationally and locally. Their press networks spouted prophecies of the doom that would ensue from government reforms while in reality they themselves simply went on as if the decrees had never been passed. What the vituperative outbursts of the landowners' organizations failed to stress was the extent to which Socialist measures remained little more than hopes on paper. There was virtually no machinery with which to enforce the new decrees in the isolated villages of the south. The social power consequent on being the exclusive providers of work remained with the owners. The Civil Guard was skilfully cultivated by, and remained loyal to, the rural upper classes. Socialist deputies from the south regularly complained in the Cortes about the inability of provincial civil governors to apply government legislation and to oblige the Civil Guard to side with the *braceros* rather than with landowners.

Throughout 1932, the FNTT worked hard to contain the growing desperation of its southern rank and file. With agrarian reform in the air, the landowners did not feel disposed to invest in their land. The law of obligatory cultivation was effectively ignored and labour was not hired to do the tasks essential for the spring planting. *Braceros* were refused work because they belonged to the landworkers' union. Nonetheless, the FNTT continued to adhere to a moderate line, and appealed to grass-roots militants to refrain from extremism and not to expect too much from the forthcoming agrarian reform. Unfortunately, the statute did little largely because its cautious provisions had been drawn up for Marcelino Domingo, the new Minister of Agriculture, by conservative agronomists and property lawyers. After painfully slow progress through the Cortes between July and September, it provided for the setting up of an Institute of Agrarian Reform to supervise the break-up of estates over 56 acres (22.5 hectares). Therefore it did absolutely nothing for the smallholders of the north. Moreover, the devices used by landowners to avoid declaring their holdings, together with the fact that the reform law's provisions were riddled with loopholes and exceptions, ensured that it did little for the labourers of the south either. Largo Caballero described it as 'an aspirin to cure an appendicitis'. And, if it did nothing to abate the revolutionary fervour of the countryside, it did even less to allay the hostility of right-wing landowners towards the Republic.

Another source of fierce opposition to the Republic was the statute of Catalan autonomy. Providing for Catalan control of local administration with a local parliament, the Generalitat, the statute was regarded by the army and the conservative classes as an attack on national unity. In the Cortes, a determined Azaña battled it out with right-wing deputies. In fact, the statute of Catalan autonomy, drawn up by a coalition headed by Francesc Macià, the intransigent Catalan nationalist, was far from the maximalism that had been expected by the Madrid politicians. Nevertheless, they were loath to allow the Generalitat, and particularly Macià, any real autonomy. They regarded his party, the Esquerra, as a short-lived, opportunistic coalition, dependent for its viability on the votes of the CNT rank and file. This did not prevent the right from presenting Azaña's cabinet as hell bent on destroying centuries of Spanish unity.

However, religion remained the most potent weapon in the right-wing armoury and, to a certain extent, it was put there by Republican and Socialist imprudence. Indeed, justification for blanket hostility to the Republic could easily be found in various manifestations of anti-clericalism. Given the Church's historic association with, and legitimization of, the most reactionary elements in Spanish society, it was not difficult to understand the extent of popular anti-clericalism. However, considerable distress was caused to ordinary Catholics by many measures which did not attack the institutional Church so much as the shared rituals that were so important in much of provincial life. Municipal authorities were forbidden to make financial contributions to the Church or its festivals. In many towns and villages the banning of religious processions was gratuitously provocative. When processions did take place, they often clashed with new laic festivals. In Seville, fear of attack led to more than forty of the traditional fraternities (*cofradías*) withdrawing from the Holy Week procession in the city. Many, but not all, of the members of the *cofradías* were militants of Acción Popular and of the Carlist Comunión Tradicionalista. Their gesture led to the popularization of the phrase 'Sevilla la mártir', despite the fact that every effort was made by Republican authorities to see that the processions went ahead. The issue was manipulated politically to foment hostility to the Republic by creating the impression of religious persecution.

In January 1932, Church cemeteries passed under the jurisdiction of municipalities. There were cases of left-wing mayors (*alcaldes*) imposing a tax on Catholic burials or funeral processions being prohibited altogether. The state recognized only civil marriage, so those who had a Church wedding were required to visit a registry office. The removal of crucifixes from schools and of religious statues from public hospitals, along with the prohibition on the ringing of bells, caused ordinary Catholics to see the Republic as their enemy. There were many cases of left-wing *alcaldes* placing a local tax on the ringing of bells, to make the Church contribute to social welfare. Religious friction at both local and national level created an ambience that rightist politicians found easy to exploit. The attribution of the Republic's reforming ambitions to a sinister foreign Jewish–Masonic–Bolshevik plot went hand in hand with claims that it must be destroyed and its supporters exterminated.

Indeed, the right soon demonstrated that it would not scruple to use violence to change the course of the Republic. Army officers enraged by the military reforms and autonomy statute were joined by monarchist plotters in persuading General José Sanjurjo that the country was on the verge of anarchy and ready to rise at his bidding. General Sanjurjo's attempted coup took place on 10 August 1932. Badly planned, it was easily defeated both in Seville, by a general strike of CNT, UGT and Communist workers, and in Madrid, where the government, warned in advance, quickly rounded up the conspirators. In a sense, this attack on the Republic by one of the heroes of the old regime, a monarchist general, benefited the government by generating a wave of pro-Republic fervour. The ease with which the *Sanjurjada*, as the fiasco was known, was snuffed out enabled the government to generate enough parliamentary enthusiasm to get the agrarian reform bill and the Catalan statute of autonomy through the Cortes that September. Nevertheless, among those who supported the coup were the same rightists who had taken part in the shootings in the Parque de María Luisa in Seville in 1931. They would soon be at liberty and with plenty of time to repeat their exploits in 1936.

The government's prestige was at its height yet the situation was much less favourable than it appeared. The *Sanjurjada* showed the hostility with which the army and the extreme right regarded the Republic. Moreover, while the government coalition was crumbling, the right was organizing its forces. This process was aided by the insurrectionism of the CNT. The rightist press did not make subtle distinctions between the CNT, the UGT and the FNTT. Although the CNT regarded the Republic as being 'as repugnant as the monarchy', its strikes and uprisings were blamed on the Republican–Socialist coalition which was working hard to control them. However, while the extreme right in the *pueblos* (villages) was content to engage in blanket condemnation of disorder, the more far-sighted members of the rural bourgeoisie, who had found a home in the Radical Party, were able to use the CNT's hostility towards the Socialists in order to drive wedges between the different working-class organizations. The most dramatic example of this process took place as a result of a nationwide revolutionary strike called by the CNT for 8 January 1933 and of its bloody repercussions in the village of Casas Viejas in the province of Cádiz. In the lockout conditions of 1932, four out of five workers in Casas Viejas were unemployed for most of the year, dependent on charity, occasional road-mending jobs and scouring the countryside for food in the shape of wild asparagus and rabbits. Their desperation, inflamed by an increase in bread prices, ensured a ready response on 11 January to the earlier CNT call for revolution. Their hesitant declaration of libertarian communism led to savage repression in which twenty-four people died.

The rightist press moved swiftly from issuing congratulations to the forces of order to a realization that the situation could be exploited. The subsequent smear campaign, in which the right-wing papers howled that the Republic was as barbaric, unjust and corrupt as all the previous regimes, ate into the morale of the Republican–Socialist coalition. The work of the government was virtually paralysed. Although the Socialists stood loyally by Azaña, who bore the brunt of rightist abuse for Casas Viejas, the incident heralded the death of the coalition, symbolizing as it did the government's failure to resolve the agrarian problem. Henceforth, at a local level, the FNTT was to become more belligerent and its attitude filtered through into the Socialist Party in the form of a rejection of collaboration with the Republicans. The anarchists, meanwhile, stepped up the tempo of their revolutionary activities. The Radicals under Lerroux, ever-anxious for power, drew increasingly to the right and began a policy of obstruction in the Cortes.

The latent violence at local level was transmitted to national politics, where there developed increasing hostility between the PSOE and the newly created rightist group, the Confederación Española de Derechas Autónomas (CEDA). The new party, which had grown out of Acción Popular and at least forty other rightist groups, was the creation of José María Gil Robles. In his closing speech at the founding congress in Madrid, in February 1933, he told his audience:

> When the social order is threatened, Catholics should unite to defend it and safeguard the principles of Christian civilization ... We will go united into the struggle, no matter what it costs ... We are faced with a social revolution. In the political panorama of Europe I can see only the formation of Marxist and anti-Marxist groups. This is what is happening in Germany and in Spain also. This is the great battle which we must fight this year.

Later on the same day, at another meeting in Madrid, he said that he could not see anything wrong with thinking of fascism to cure the evils of Spain. The Socialists were convinced that the CEDA was likely to fulfil a Fascist role in Spain, a charge only casually denied by the Catholic party, if at all. A majority in the PSOE led by Largo Caballero came to feel that if bourgeois democracy was incapable of preventing the rise of fascism, it was up to the working class to seek different political forms with which to defend itself.

In the meanwhile, throughout 1933, the CEDA was spreading discontent with the Republic in agrarian circles. Gil Robles specialized in double-edged pronouncements, and fuelled the Socialists' sensitivity to the danger of fascism. Weimar was persistently cited as an example by the right and as a warning by the left. Parallels between the German and Spanish Republics were not difficult to find. The Catholic press applauded the Nazi destruction of the German Socialist and Communist movements. Nazism was much admired on the Spanish right because of its emphasis on authority, the fatherland and hierarchy – all three central preoccupations of CEDA propaganda. More worrying still was that, in justification of the legalistic tactic in Spain, *El Debate* pointed out that Hitler had attained power legally. The paper frequently commented on Spain's need for an organization similar to those which had destroyed the left in Germany and Italy, and hinted that Acción Popular/ CEDA could fulfil that role.

It was in such an atmosphere that elections were called for November. In contrast to 1931, this time the left went to the polls in disarray. The right, on the other hand, was able to mount a united and generally bellicose campaign. Gil Robles had just returned from the Nuremberg rally and appeared to be strongly influenced by what he had seen. Indeed, the CEDA election campaign showed that Gil Robles had learned his lessons well. Determined on victory at any price, the CEDA election committee decided for a single anti-Marxist counter-revolutionary front. Thus, the CEDA had no qualms about going into the elections in coalition with 'catastrophist' groups such as Renovación Española and the Carlists or, in other areas, with the cynical and corrupt Radicals.

A vast amount of money was spent on the right's election campaign. The CEDA's election fund was enormous, based on generous donations from the well-to-do like Juan March, the millionaire enemy of the Republic. The climax of the CEDA's campaign came in a speech given in Madrid by Gil Robles. His tone could only make the left wonder what a CEDA victory might mean for them:

> We must reconquer Spain . . . We must give Spain a true unity, a new spirit, a totalitarian polity . . . It is necessary now to defeat socialism inexorably. We must found a new state, purge the fatherland of judaising freemasons . . . We must proceed to a new state and this imposes duties and sacrifices. What does it matter if we have to shed blood! . . . We need full power and that is what we demand . . . To realize this ideal we are not going to waste time with archaic forms. Democracy is not an end but a means to the conquest of the new state. When the time comes, either parliament submits or we will eliminate it.

The Socialists, who had decided to contest the elections on their own, could not match the massive propaganda campaign mounted by the right. Gil Robles dominated the campaign of the rightist coalition, as Largo Caballero did that of the Socialists, mirroring the radical extremism of his opponent. Declaring that only the dictatorship of the proletariat could carry out the necessary economic disarmament of the bourgeoisie, he delighted his supporters but antagonized the right and helped justify its already aggressive stance.

The arguments of the moderate Indalecio Prieto that the PSOE must maintain its electoral alliance with the left Republicans were dismissed by the more radical elements of the party led by Largo Caballero. Their imposition of the decision to go it alone was an irresponsible one. They were simultaneously blaming the left Republicans for all the deficiencies of the Republic and confidently assuming that all the votes cast in 1931 for the victorious Republican–Socialist coalition would stay with the PSOE. In fact, that coalition had ranged from the middle classes to the anarchists. The Radicals were now on the right and, in the wake of Casas Viejas, the hostility of the anarchists to the Republic ensured that they would abstain. The Socialists were committing a fatal tactical error. Given the existing electoral law which favoured coalitions, together with the CEDA's readiness to make alliances, it took twice as many Socialist votes to elect a deputy as rightist ones. The election results brought bitter disappointment to the Socialists, who won only fifty-eight seats. After local deals between the CEDA and the Radicals designed to take advantage of the electoral law, the two parties finished with 115 and 104 deputies respectively. The right had regained control of the apparatus of the state. It was determined to use it to dismantle the reforms of the previous two years. However, expectations had been raised during that time which could only ensure burning popular fury when the right put back the clock to the days before 1931.

THREE

Confrontation and Conspiracy,
1934–1936

In the following two years, which came to be known as the *bienio negro* (black two years), Spanish politics were to be bitterly polarized. The November 1933 elections had given power to a right wing determined to avenge the injuries and indignities which it felt it had suffered during the period of the Constituent Cortes. This made conflict inevitable, since, if the workers and peasants had been driven to desperation by the inadequacy of the reforms of 1931–2, then a government set on destroying these reforms could only force them into violence. At the end of 1933, 12 per cent of Spain's workforce was unemployed and in the south the figures were nearer 20 per cent. Employers and landowners celebrated the victory by cutting wages, sacking workers, evicting tenants and raising rents. Even before a new government had taken office, labour legislation was being blatantly ignored.

The Socialists' outrage knew no bounds. Their own tactical error in not allying with the Republicans had made a crucial contribution to their electoral defeat. However, the PSOE was convinced that the elections had been fraudulent. In the south, they had good reason to believe that they had been swindled out of seats by the *caciques'* power over the starving *braceros*. In rural areas of high unemployment, it had been easy to secure votes by the promise of jobs or the threat of dismissal. Armed thugs employed by the *caciques* prevented Socialist campaigners speaking at some meetings and were a louring presence next to the glass voting urns on election day. In Spain as a whole, the PSOE's one and a half million votes had won it 58 seats in the Cortes, while the Radicals' eight hundred thousand votes had been rewarded with 104 seats. According to calculations made by the PSOE, the united parties of the right had together got 3,345,504 votes and 212 seats at 15,780 votes per seat, while the disunited left had received 3,375,432 votes and only ninety-nine seats at 34,095 votes per seat. In some areas of the south – Badajoz, Córdoba and Málaga, for example – the margin of right-wing victory was small enough for electoral malpractice to have made all the difference. Rank-and-file bitterness at the cynical union of Radicals with the CEDA and at losing the elections unfairly quickly gave way to dismay at the untrammelled offensive of the employers. Popular outrage was all the greater because of the restraint and self-sacrifice that had characterized Socialist policy between 1931 and 1933. Now, in response to the consequent wave of militancy, the Socialist leadership began to adopt a tactic of revolutionary rhetoric. Their vain hope was that they could both scare the right into limiting its belligerency and persuade the President of the Republic, Niceto Alcalá Zamora, to call new elections.

Although he was not prepared to go that far, Alcalá Zamora did not invite Gil Robles to form a government despite the fact that the CEDA was the biggest party in the Cortes, albeit one without an overall majority. The President suspected the Catholic leader of nurturing more or less Fascist ambitions to establish an authoritarian, corporative state. Thus, Alejandro Lerroux, as leader of the second largest party, became Prime Minister. Dependent on CEDA votes, the Radicals were to be the CEDA's puppets. In return for harsh social policies in the interests of the CEDA's wealthy backers, the Radicals were to be allowed to enjoy the spoils of office. The Socialists were appalled. Largo Caballero was convinced that in the Radical

Party there were those who, 'if they have not been in jail, deserve to have been'. Once in government, they set up an office to organize the sale of state favours, monopolies, government procurement orders, licences and so on. The PSOE view was that the Radicals were hardly the appropriate defenders of the basic principles of the Republic against rightist assaults.

The first violent working-class protest, however, came from the anarchists. With irresponsible naïvety, an uprising was called for 8 December 1933. However, the government had been forewarned of the anarcho-syndicalists' plans and quickly declared a state of emergency. Leaders of the CNT and the FAI were arrested, press censorship was imposed and syndicates were closed down. In traditionally anarchist areas, Aragón, the Rioja, Catalonia, the Levante, parts of Andalusia and Galicia, there were sporadic strikes, some trains were blown up and Civil Guard posts were assaulted. The movement was quickly over in Barcelona, Madrid and Valencia. In the Aragónese capital Zaragoza, however, the rising did get off the ground. Workers raised barricades, attacked public buildings and engaged in street fighting. The response of the government was to send in the army, which took four days with the aid of tanks to crush the insurrection.

Violent incidents involving the CNT diverted attention from the growing problem of malnutrition in the southern provinces. This was a consequence not only of the determination of landowners to slash wages and refuse work to union members but also of significant rises in the price of basic necessities. The Radical government had removed controls on the price of bread and it had risen by 25 to 70 per cent. Demonstrations by starving women, children and the aged calling for bread became a frequent sight. The spread of hunger in the south was also mirrored in the intensification of militancy within the principal landworkers' union, the FNTT. Its president, the moderate Lucio Martínez Gil, was replaced by one of the more radical young followers of Largo Caballero, Ricardo

Zabalza Elorga. At the end of 1933, then, the Socialist leaders were faced with a rising tide of mass militancy, which was a consequence both of the employers' offensive and their own feeling of bitterness at the perceived unfairness of electoral defeat. Largo Caballero reacted by intensifying his revolutionary threats although his noisy rhetoric was not matched by any serious revolutionary intentions. His was verbal revolutionism both to satisfy rank-and-file aspirations and to pressure Alcalá Zamora to call new elections. It was a dangerous game, since, if the President did not succumb to such pressure, the Socialists would be left with the choice of stepping up their threats or losing credibility with their own militants. The resulting situation could benefit only the CEDA.

With a pliant Radical government in power, the success of Acción Popular's 'accidentalist' tactics could hardly have been more apparent. 'Catastrophism' was for the moment eclipsed. Nevertheless, the extreme right remained unconvinced by Gil Robles' democratic tactic and so continued to prepare for violence. Carlists were collecting arms and drilling in the north and the spring of 1934 saw Fal Conde, the movement's secretary, recruiting volunteers in Andalusia. In March, representatives of both the Carlists and the Alfonsine monarchist party, Renovación Española, led by Antonio Goicoechea, went to see Mussolini who promised money and arms for a rising. Both groups were convinced that even a strong rightist government did not constitute an adequate long-term guarantee for their interests, because it would be subject to the whims of the electorate in a still democratic Republic. In May 1934, the monarchists' most dynamic and charismatic leader, José Calvo Sotelo, returned after three years exile to take over the leadership from Antonio Goicoechea. Henceforth, the monarchist press, in addition to abusing Gil Robles' weakness, began increasingly to talk of the conquest of the state as the only sure road to the creation of a new authoritarian, corporative regime.

Even Gil Robles was having trouble controlling his forces.

His youth movement, the Juventud de Acción Popular (JAP), was seduced by the German and Italian examples. Great Fascist-style rallies were held at which Gil Robles was hailed with the cry '*¡Jefe! ¡Jefe! ¡Jefe!*' (the Spanish equivalent of *Duce*) in the hope that he might start a 'March on Madrid' to seize power. Monarchist hopes, however, centred increasingly on the openly Fascist group of José Antonio Primo de Rivera, Falange Española, as a potential source of shock troops against the left. The Falange had been founded in October 1933 with monarchist subsidies. As a landowner, an aristocrat and well-known socialite, José Antonio Primo de Rivera served as a guarantee to the upper classes that Spanish fascism would not get out of their control in the way of its German and Italian equivalents. Falange Española merged in 1934 with the pro-Nazi Juntas de Ofensiva Nacional-Sindicalista of the pro-German Ramiro Ledesma Ramos, becoming Falange Española de las JONS. Perpetually short of funds, the party remained during the Republican period essentially a small student group preaching a utopian form of violent nationalist revolution. The Falangist leader's cult of violence facilitated the destabilization of the politics of the Second Republic. His blue-shirted militias, with their Roman salutes and their ritual chants of *¡ARRIBA ESPAÑA!* and *¡ESPAÑA! ¡UNA! ¡ESPAÑA! ¡LIBRE! ¡ESPAÑA! ¡GRANDE!*, aped Nazi and Fascist models. From 1933 to 1936, FE de las JONS functioned as the cannon fodder of the *haute bourgeoisie*, provoking street brawls and helping to generate the lawlessness which, exaggerated by the right-wing press, was used to justify the military rising. Its importance lay in the role played by its political vandalism in screwing up the tension which would eventually erupt into the Civil War.

The left was very aware of such developments and was determined to avoid the fate of the German and Austrian left. As 1934 progressed there were growing numbers of street battles between left and right. Events within the orthodox political arena did little to cool tempers. Lerroux resigned in April after Alcalá Zamora had hesitated about signing an amnesty bill which reinstated the officers involved in the Sanjurjo rising of 1932. Socialists and Republicans alike felt that the government was signalling to the army that it could make a coup whenever it disliked the political situation. The left was already suspicious of the government's reliance on CEDA votes, since Gil Robles continued to refuse to swear his loyalty to the Republic. Moreover, since he made it quite clear that when he gained power he would change the Constitution, the left was coming to believe that strong action was necessary to prevent him doing so. In fact, even if Gil Robles was not quite as extreme as the left believed him to be, he managed to convey the impression that the Radical government, backed with CEDA votes, was intent on dismantling the progressive, reforming Republic that had been created in 1931.

In this context, it was difficult for the Socialist leadership to hold back its followers. Largo Caballero tended to give way to the revolutionary impatience of the masses, although his rhetoric, which they cheered to the echo, was unspecific and consisted largely of Marxist platitudes. No concrete relation to the contemporary political scene was ever made in Largo Caballero's speeches of early 1934 and no timetable for the future revolution was ever given. However, rank-and-file pressure for the radicalization of the Socialist movement, particularly from its youth movement, the Federación de Juventudes Socialistas (FJS), and its Madrid organization, the Agrupación Socialista Madrileña, developed throughout 1934. This led to important divisions within the PSOE. The right-wing of the party, led by the professor of logic Julián Besteiro, tried several tactics to slow down the process of bolshevization which was taking place within the party. This merely earned Besteiro the vehement hostility of the radical youth. The centre, led by the ever-pragmatic Indalecio Prieto, reluctantly went along with the revolutionary tactic out of party loyalty. The young followers of Largo Caballero came to dominate the party and the UGT, with the organizations of the Socialist movement falling into their hands in quick succession.

Thus, political tension grew throughout 1934. In March, the anarchists held a four-week strike in Zaragoza to protest against the maltreatment of prisoners taken after the December rising. Then the CEDA made a sinister gesture in the form of a large rally of its youth movement, the JAP. The choice of Philip II's monastery of El Escorial as venue was an unmistakably anti-Republican gesture. In driving sleet, a crowd of twenty thousand met in a gathering which closely resembled a Nazi rally. They swore loyalty to Gil Robles, 'our supreme chief', and chanted '*¡Jefe! ¡Jefe! ¡Jefe!*'. The JAP's nineteen-point programme was recited, with emphasis on point two, 'our leaders never make mistakes', a direct borrowing from the Italian Fascists. One CEDA deputy declared that 'Spain has to be defended against Jews, heretics, freemasons, liberals and Marxists'. Another, the deputy for Zaragoza, Ramón Serrano Suñer, brother-in-law of General Franco and later architect of the post-Civil War National-Syndicalist state, denounced 'degenerate democracy'. The high point of the rally was a speech by Gil Robles. His aggressive harangue was greeted by delirious applause and prolonged chanting of '*¡Jefe!*'. 'We are an army of citizens ready to give our lives for God and for Spain,' he cried. 'Power will soon be ours . . . No one can stop us imposing our ideas on the government of Spain'.

The young revolutionaries of the FJS were convinced that Gil Robles was aiming to take over the government in order to bring the Republic to an end. Various Radical ministries were incapable of allaying the suspicion that they were merely Gil Robles' Trojan Horse. By repeatedly threatening to withdraw his support, Gil Robles provoked a series of cabinet crises by complaining that the cabinet was too liberal. As a result, the Radical government was adopting an ever-more conservative veneer. On each occasion, Lerroux, who was desperate to stay in power, would force the more liberal elements of his party out of the cabinet. Accompanied by like-minded friends, they then quit the party, leaving the rump ever more dependent on CEDA whims. After the first of the reshuffles, in March 1934, Gil Robles found a Radical minister who enjoyed his unalloyed trust. This was Rafael Salazar Alonso, the Minister of the Interior and a representative of the aggressive landowners of Badajoz. One of his first acts as minister was to call in the Inspector General of the Civil Guard, Brigadier General Cecilio Bedia de la Cavallería, and make it clear that his forces should not be inhibited in their repression of social conflicts. Although Lerroux resisted the temptation to declare all strikes unlawful, he delighted the right by announcing that strikes with political implications would be ruthlessly suppressed. For both the CEDA and Salazar Alonso, all strikes were deemed to be political. He provoked a number of strikes throughout the spring and summer of 1934 which enabled him to pick off the most powerful unions one by one, beginning with the printers in March. The Radical–CEDA determination to undermine the Republic's most loyal support became clear when the government clashed successively with the Catalans and the Basques.

The sympathy shown by the Constituent Cortes to autonomist aspirations was now dropped in favour of right-wing centralist bias. This was particularly the case with regard to Catalonia. Unlike the rest of Spain, Catalonia was governed by a truly Republican party, the Esquerra, under Lluis Companys. In April, Companys passed an agrarian reform, the *Ley de contratos de cultivo*, an enlightened measure to protect tenants from eviction by landowners and the right to buy land which they had worked for eighteen years. The law was opposed by the landowners and the Catalan conservative party, the Lliga, protested to the Madrid government with the backing of the CEDA. The right of the central government to intervene in Catalonia over this issue was not clear. Under pressure from the CEDA, the Radical cabinet handed the question to the Tribunal of Constitutional Guarantees, whose membership was predominantly right wing. On 8 June, by a small majority, the Tribunal found against the Generalitat. Nevertheless, Companys went ahead and ratified the law. Meanwhile, the government began to infringe the Basques' tax privileges and, in an attempt to silence protest, forbade their municipal elections. Such high-handed centralism could only confirm the left's fears of the Republic's rapid drift to the right.

Trouble increased during the summer. Rural labourers were suffering immense hardship through increased aggression from employers, which had been greatly facilitated by the repeal in May of the law of municipal boundaries. Coming just before the harvest, this permitted landlords to import cheap Portuguese and Galician migrant workers to undercut local wages. The defences of the rural proletariat were falling rapidly before the right-wing onslaught. The last vestige of protection that left-wing landless labourers had for their jobs and their wages was that provided by the Socialist majorities on many town and village councils. Socialist mayors were the only hope that rural workers had of the local landowners being obliged to observe social legislation or of municipal funds being used for public works that would provide some employment. The Radicals had been systematically removing them, Salazar Alonso using flimsy pretexts such as 'administrative irregularities'. He ordered provincial civil governors to remove *alcaldes* who 'did not inspire confidence in matters of public order' – which usually meant Socialists.

After much agonized debate within the FNTT, Ricardo Zabalza began to advocate a general strike in order to put a stop to the patronal offensive. Older heads within the UGT were opposed to what they saw as a rash initiative which might squander worker militancy and thus undermine the possibility of a future defence against attempts to establish a reactionary corporative state. The harvest was ready at different times in each area, so the selection of a single date for the strike would lead to problems of coordination. Moreover, a general strike, as opposed to one limited to large estates, would cause hardship to leaseholders and sharecroppers who needed to hire one or two workers. There was also the danger that the provocative actions of the owners and the Civil Guard could push the peasants into violent confrontations which they could only lose. Nevertheless, under extreme pressure from a hungry rank and file pushed beyond endurance by the constant provocation of *caciques* and Civil Guard, the FNTT called for a series of strikes, to be carried through in strict accordance with the law.

While the strike action could hardly be considered revolutionary, Salazar Alonso was not prepared to lose this chance to strike a blow at the largest section of the UGT. His measures were swift and ruthless. Within weeks of taking over the Ministry of the Interior, in meetings with the head of the Civil Guard General Bedia de la Cavallería and the Director General de Seguridad José Valdivia, he had already made specific plans for the repression of such a strike. Accordingly, just as Zabalza's hopes of compromise negotiations between the FNTT and the Ministers of Agriculture and Labour were about to be fulfilled, Salazar Alonso issued a decree criminalizing the actions of the FNTT by declaring the harvest a national public service and the strike a 'revolutionary conflict'. Liberal and left-wing individuals in the country districts were arrested wholesale, including four Socialist deputies. This was a flagrant violation of Articles 55 and 56 of the Constitution. Several thousand peasants were loaded at gunpoint onto lorries and deported hundreds of miles from their homes and then left without food or money to make their own way back. Workers' centres were closed down and many town councils were removed, to be replaced by government nominees. Although most of the labourers arrested were soon released, emergency courts sentenced prominent workers' leaders to four or more years in prison. The workers' societies in each village, the *Casas del*

Pueblo, were closed and the FNTT was effectively crippled until 1936. In an uneven battle, the FNTT had suffered a terrible defeat. Salazar Alonso had effectively put the clock back in the Spanish countryside to the 1920s.

The politics of reprisal were beginning to generate an atmosphere, if not of imminent civil war, certainly of great belligerence. The left saw fascism in every action of the right; the right smelt revolution in every left-wing move. Violent speeches were made in the Cortes and, at one point, guns flourished. In the streets shots were exchanged between Socialist and Falangist youths. Juan Antonio Ansaldo, a well-known monarchist playboy and aviator, had joined the Falange in the spring to organize terrorist squads. A plan to blow up the Madrid *Casa del Pueblo* was thwarted when the police discovered a large cache of arms and explosives. The actions of the Falangist hit squads provoked reprisals by the would-be revolutionaries of the Federación de Juventudes Socialistas. The government's attacks on regional autonomy and the increasingly threatening attitude of the CEDA were driving the Socialists to play with the idea of a revolutionary rising to forestall the destruction of the Republic.

The JAP held another rally, on 9 September, this time at Covadonga in Asturias, the starting point for the reconquest of Spain from the Moors. This was clearly a symbol of warlike aggression which foreshadowed the Francoist use after 1936 of the violent crusade imagery of the *Reconquista*. Gil Robles spoke in violent terms of the need to annihilate the 'separatist rebellion' of the Catalans and the Basque Nationalists. Revelling in the adulation of the assembled ranks of the JAP, the supreme *Jefe* worked himself up to a frenzy of patriotic rhetoric calling for nationalism to be exalted 'with ecstasy, with paroxysms, with anything; I prefer a nation of lunatics to a nation of wretches'. Behind his apparently spontaneous passion was a cold-blooded determination to provoke the left. Gil Robles knew full well that the left considered him a Fascist. He was also aware that it intended to prevent the CEDA coming to power, although he was confident that the left was not in a position to succeed in a revolutionary attempt.

The preparations for revolution of the young Socialists had consisted largely of Sunday picnics in Madrid's Casa del Campo during which military manoeuvres, without weapons, were amateurishly practised. Salazar Alonso had had no difficulty in tracking down the few revolvers and rifles that had been acquired by means of expensive encounters with unscrupulous arms dealers. Thanks to informers in the PSOE or to the arms dealers themselves, when the police subsequently raided the houses of militants and on *Casas del Pueblo* they seemed to know exactly where guns were concealed behind partitions or under floorboards. The most notorious arms purchase was carried out by Prieto, when arms – initially ordered by exiled enemies of the Portuguese dictatorship who could not pay for them – were shipped to Asturias on the steamer *Turquesa*. In a bizarre incident, the shipment fell largely into the hands of the police although Prieto escaped. Only in Asturias was the local working class even minimally armed, as a result of pilfering from local small-arms factories and dynamite available in the mines.

On 26 September the CEDA opened the crisis by announcing that it could no longer support a minority government. Lerroux's new cabinet, announced late at night on 3 October, included three CEDA ministers. To the left, it seemed as if this was the first step towards the imposition of fascism in Spain. The reaction of the Republican forces was abrupt. Azaña and other leading Republicans denounced the move and even the conservative Miguel Maura broke off relations with the President. The Socialists were paralysed with doubt. They had hoped that threats of revolution would suffice to make Alcalá Zamora call new elections. Now, the UGT gave the government twenty-four hours' notice of a pacific general strike. The Socialists hoped that the President would change his mind but they merely succeeded in giving the police time to arrest working-class leaders. In most parts of Spain, the strike was a failure largely because of the prompt action of the government in declaring martial law and bringing in the army to run essential services.

In Barcelona, events were more dramatic. In an attempt to outflank extreme Catalan nationalists, and seriously alarmed by developments in Madrid, Companys proclaimed an independent state of Catalonia 'within the Federal Republic of Spain'. It was a protest against what was perceived as the Fascist betrayal of the Republic. The CNT stood aside since it regarded the Esquerra as a purely bourgeois affair. In fact, the rebellion of the Generalitat was doomed when Companys refused requests to arm the workers. Bloodshed was avoided by his moderation, which was matched by that of General Domingo Batet, the officer in command of the Catalan military region (or Fourth Organic Division, as it was called). General Batet employed common sense and restraint in restoring the authority of the central government. He ordered his men to be 'deaf, dumb and blind' before any provocations. In so preventing a potential blood bath, he incurred the wrath of General Francisco Franco, who was directing the repression from Madrid. Franco had sent warships to bombard the city and troops of the Foreign Legion. Batet ignored Franco's recommendation to use the Foreign Legion to impose savage punishment on the Catalans and thus kept casualties to a minimum. In avoiding the exemplary violence that Franco regarded as essential, however, Batet was paving the way to his own execution by the Francoists during the Spanish Civil War.

The only place where the protests of the left in October 1934 were not easily brushed aside was in Asturias. There, spontaneous rank-and-file militancy impelled the local PSOE leaders to go along with a revolutionary movement organized jointly by the UGT, the CNT and, belatedly, the Communists, united in the *Alianza Obrera* (Workers' Alliance). The local Socialist leaders of the mineworkers knew that the strike was

1. *Above*: Civilians killed on 19 July 1936 combating the uprising in Barcelona.

2. *Right and below*: Nationalist propaganda linked Franco's cause both to Spain's imperial past and to contemporary Fascism and Nazism.

VIVA ESPAÑA

VIVA ITALIA — VIVA ALEMANIA — VIVA PORTUGAL

¡¡FRANCO!!

ESPAÑA FUE ES Y SERÁ INMORTAL

3. Official poster celebrating Franco's victory. In the bottom left-hand corner is the last of his daily war reports which reads 'Today, with the Red Army captive and disarmed, our victorious troops have achieved their final military objectives. The war is over.'

4. In Spanish cities, the establishment of the Second Republic on 14 April 1931 was greeted by popular rejoicing, typified by this celebration in the Plaza de Cibeles in Madrid.

5. The euphoria of the Republic's early days dissipated with the church burnings of May 1931 in Madrid and the south.

6. José María Gil Robles, leader of the Catholic authoritarian party, the CEDA, addresses a meeting during the campaign for the 1933 elections. The introduction of female suffrage was to benefit the right.

7. *Above left*: José Antonio Primo de Rivera, founder of Falange Española, idealized as *Jefe Nacional*.

8. *Above right*: The official portrait of Manuel Anzaña, the brilliant intellectual who was successively Minister of War, Prime Minister and President of the Republic.

9. *Below*: Monarchists give the fascist salute at the funeral of their assassinated leader, José Calvo Sotelo.

10. The De Havilland D. H. 89 Dragon Rapide hired by Luis Bolín in Croydon to take Franco to Morocco to lead the Spanish colonial Army in Africa in the uprising.

11. Franco in Tetuán shortly after his arrival from the Canary Islands.

12.*Above left*: Diego Martínez Barrio, briefly Prime Minister on 19 July 1936, tried in vain to negotiate a compromise peace with General Mola.

13. *Above*: General Gonzalo Quiepo de Llano seized Seville for the rebels and then ran Andalucia as an autonomous fief. He was famous for his obscene radio broadcasts aimed at terrorizing the Republican population with accounts of the bloodthirsty exploits of his troops.

14. *Left*: British International Brigaders return to the front after convalescence.

15. Republican militiamen settle in the main square of Toledo for a long seige of the Alcázar.

16. Generals of the Nationalist *Junta de Defensa* arrive on 21 September 1936 at an airfield near Salamanca for the meeting at which Franco was chosen as commander-in-chief. In the centre, the tall Alfredo Kindelán, the bearded Miguel Cabanellas, Franco, to his left Queipo de Llano and Mola.

17. *Left*: Franco harangues the survivors of the siege of Alcázar de Toledo on 29 September 1936.

18. *Below*: General José Moscardó, commander of the Alcázar of Toledo, revisits the ruins. The boy in his arms is Restituto Valero, born during the siege. In 1975, then a captain, Valero was expelled from the Army for participation in the Unión Militar Democrática.

19. The 'Cockney Express', a van sent from London with food for besieged Madrid.

20. A Republican column in the Sierra de Guadarama.

21. Spanish Republican militia of the Socialist Unión General de Trabajadores

22. The encircling Francoist forces subject Madrid to massive bombardment.

23. The citizens of Madrid shelter from bombardments in the underground (Metro).

24. Letter from General 'Mancini (the pseudonym used by Roatta) congratulating Italian troops for their capture of Malaga in February 1937.

COMANDO PRIMA BRIGATA VOLONTARI

(Dio lo vuole!)

ORDINE DEL GIORNO N.° 3

del 10 Febbraio 1937 XV

Il Generale di Divisione Comm. Mancini comandante in capo delle forze volontarie ha inviato alle truppe dipendenti della 1.ª Brigata che hanno conquistato Malaga il seguente proclama in data 9 Febbraio:

"Da oggi la 1.ª Brigata Volontari assume la denominazione di:

f.ª DIVISIONI VOLONTARI

"LEGIONARI DELLA 1.ª DIVISIONE VOLONTARI!

Avete scritto a Malaga una gloriosa pagina!
In tre giorni di lotte e di marce avete liberato una provincia dalla barbarie rossa; le avete ridato la pace, la libertà, la vita!
Così procede il Fascismo; e Voi, sua avanguardia armata in lotta per un ideale, ne avete interpretato lo spirito, ne avete manifestato il dinamismo.
A Voi, Ufficiali e Volontari, al Vostro Comandante Generale Arnaldi, che vi ha condotto alla conquista di Malaga, il mio ringraziamento, che esprime ed interpreta il pensiero di CHI da lontano vi segue!"

UFFICIALI E VOLONTARI DELLA 1.ª DIVISIONE: A NOI! "il generale di divisione capo missione fto MANCINI.

Malaga 10 Febbraio 1937 XV

IL GENERALE COMANDANTE

Giangualtiero Arnaldi

25. Basque refugee children stuff mattresses with straw at a camp near Southampton.

26. Italian volunteers of the Garibaldi Battalion of the International Brigades fought Mussolini's Corpo di Truppe Volontarie at Guadalajara.

doomed without support from the rest of Spain but they opted to stay with their men. The Minister of War, the Radical Diego Hidalgo, had given Franco informal control of operations. He made him his 'adviser' and used him as an unofficial Chief of the General Staff, by dint of marginalizing his own staff and dutifully signing the orders drawn up by Franco. The Minister's decision was entirely comprehensible. Franco had detailed knowledge of Asturias, its geography, communications and military organization. He had been stationed there, had taken part in the suppression of the general strike of 1917 and had been a regular visitor since his marriage to an Asturian woman, Carmen Polo. What delighted the Spanish right was that Franco responded to the rebellious miners in Asturias as if he were dealing with the recalcitrant tribes of Morocco.

To this end, Franco brought in the hardened mercenaries of Spain's colonial Army of Africa. Uninhibited by the humanitarian considerations which made other more liberal officers hesitate to use the full weight of the armed forces against civilians, Franco regarded the problem before him with the same icy ruthlessness that had underpinned his successes in the colonial wars. The miners organized a revolutionary commune with transport, communications, hospital facilities and food distribution, but had few weapons. Armed largely with dynamite, they were reduced to submission by both heavy artillery attacks and bombing raids. The Spanish Foreign Legion committed atrocities, many women and children were killed and, when the principal Asturian cities, Gijón and Oviedo, fell, the army carried out summary executions of leftists. Franco commented casually to a journalist, 'The war in Morocco, with the Regulares and the Legion, had a certain romantic air, an air of reconquest. But this war is a frontier war and its fronts are socialism, communism and whatever attacks civilization in order to replace it with barbarism.'

The Asturian rising demonstrated to the left that it could carry out change only by legal means. It also demonstrated to the right that its best chance of preventing change lay with the instruments of violence provided by the armed forces. In that sense, it marked the end for the Republic. To Gerald Brenan, the great British writer on Spain who lived in Málaga at the time, it was 'the first battle of the Civil War'. The conflict did not end with the defeat of the miners. As their leader, Belarmino Tomás, put it, 'our surrender today is simply a halt on the road, where we make good our mistakes, preparing for the next battle'. There could be no going back. The October revolution had terrified the middle and upper classes; and in their terror they took a revenge which determined the left that they must reunite in order to win power electorally. The Socialist movement was, in fact, badly scarred by the events of October 1934. The repression unleashed in the aftermath of the October rising was truly brutal. In Asturias, prisoners were tortured. Thousands of workers were imprisoned. Virtually the entire UGT executive was in jail. The Socialist press was silenced.

Nothing was done in the next fifteen months to reconcile the hostilities aroused by the revolution and its repression. Despite the CEDA's much-vaunted aim of beating the revolution by a programme of social reform, proposals for moderate land reform and for tax reforms were defeated by right-wing intransigence. Indeed, Manuel Giménez Fernández, the CEDA Minister of Agriculture, encountered embittered opposition within his own party to his mildly reformist plans. He was denounced as the 'white Bolshevik'. There was room only for the punishment of the October rebels. Gil Robles demanded the 'inflexible application of the law'. Companys was sentenced to thirty years imprisonment. The thousands of political prisoners remained in jail. A vicious campaign was waged against Azaña in an unsuccessful attempt to prove him guilty of preparing the Catalan revolution. The Catalan autonomy statute was suspended.

Then, when the CEDA failed to secure the death penalty for two Asturian Socialist leaders, its three ministers resigned.

Gil Robles thus resumed his tactic of provoking cabinet crises in order to weaken the Radicals. He hoped to move crab-like towards taking power himself. He was rewarded in early May when Lerroux's new government contained five *Cedistas*, including Gil Robles himself as Minister of War. It was a period of open reaction. Landlords halved wages and order was forcibly restored in the countryside. Gil Robles purged the army of loyal Republican officers and appointed known opponents of the regime to high positions – Francisco Franco became Chief of the General Staff, Manuel Goded Inspector General and Joaquin Fanjul Under-Secretary for War. In a number of ways – regimental reorganization, motorization, equipment procurement – Gil Robles continued the reforms of Azaña and effectively prepared the army for its role in the Civil War.

In response to rightist intransigence, the left was also growing in strength, unity and belligerence. In jail, political prisoners were soaking up revolutionary literature. Outside, the economic misery of large numbers of peasants and workers, the savage persecution of the October rebels and the attacks on Manuel Azaña combined to produce an atmosphere of solidarity among all sections of the left. After his release from jail, Azaña, and Indalecio Prieto, who was in exile in Belgium, began a campaign to ensure that the disunity behind the 1933 electoral defeat would not be repeated. Azaña worked hard to reunite the various tiny Republican parties, while Prieto concentrated on countering the revolutionary extremism of the Socialist left under Largo Caballero. A series of gigantic mass meetings in Bilbao, Valencia and Madrid were addressed by Azaña in the second half of 1935. The enthusiasm for left-wing unity shown by the hundreds of thousands who came from all over Spain to attend these *discursos en campo abierto* (open-air speeches) helped convince Largo Caballero to abandon his opposition to what eventually became the Popular Front. At the same time, the Communists, prompted by Moscow's desire for alliance with the democracies, frightened of being excluded, also used their influence with Largo Caballero in favour of the Popular Front. They knew that, in order to give it the more proletarian flavour that he wanted, Largo Caballero would insist on their presence. In this way, the Communists found a place in an electoral front which, contrary to rightist propaganda, was not, in Spain, a Comintern creation but the revival of the 1931 Republican–Socialist coalition. The left and centre left closed ranks on the basis of a programme of amnesty for prisoners, of basic social and educational reform and trade union freedom.

When a combination of Gil Robles' tactic of erosion of successive cabinets and the revelation of two massive scandals involving followers of Lerroux led to the collapse of the Radicals, the CEDA leader assumed that he would be asked to form a government. Alcalá Zamora, however, had no faith in the CEDA leader's democratic convictions. After all, only some weeks before Gil Robles' youthful followers of the JAP had starkly revealed the aims of the legalist tactic in terms which called to mind the attitude of Joseph Goebbels to the 1933 elections in Germany: 'with the weapons of suffrage and democracy, Spain must prepare itself to bury once and for all the rotting corpse of liberalism. The JAP does not believe in parliamentarianism, nor in democracy.' It is indicative of Alcalá Zamora's suspicion of Gil Robles that, throughout the subsequent political crisis, he had the Ministry of War surrounded by Civil Guards and the principal garrisons and airports placed under special vigilance. Gil Robles was outraged and, in desperation, he investigated the possibilities of staging a *coup d'état*. The generals whom he approached, Fanjul, Goded, Varela and Franco, felt that, in the light of the strength of working-class resistance during the Asturian events, the army was not yet ready for a coup.

Elections were announced for February. Unsurprisingly, the election campaign was fought in a frenetic atmosphere. Already, in late October, Gil Robles had requested a complete range of Nazi anti-Marxist propaganda pamphlets and posters, to be used as a model for CEDA publicity material. In practical terms, the right enjoyed an enormous advantage over the left. Rightist electoral finance dramatically exceeded the exiguous funds of the left. Ten thousand posters and fifty million leaflets were printed for the CEDA. They presented the elections in terms of a life-or-death struggle between good and evil, survival and destruction. The Popular Front based its campaign on the threat of fascism, the dangers facing the Republic and the need for an amnesty for the prisoners of October. The elections held on 16 February resulted in a narrow victory for the Popular Front in terms of votes, but a massive triumph in terms of power in the Cortes.

The left had won despite the expenditure of vast sums of money – in terms of the amounts spent on propaganda, a vote for the right cost more than five times one for the left. Moreover, all the traditional devices of electoral chicanery had been used on behalf of the right. Because the election results represented an unequivocal statement of the popular will, they were taken by many on the right as proving the futility of legalism and 'accidentalism'. The savagery of rightist behaviour during the last two years ensured that the left's tactical error of 1933 was unlikely to be repeated. The hour of the 'catastrophists' had struck. The CEDA's youth sections and many of the movement's wealthy backers were immediately convinced of the necessity of securing by violence what was unobtainable by persuasion. The elections marked the culmination of the CEDA attempt to use democracy against itself. This meant that henceforth the right would be more concerned with destroying the Republic than with taking it over. Military plotting began in earnest.

There was an almost instant return to the rural lockout of 1933 and a new aggression from industrialists. The rural and industrial working classes were equally militant, determined to secure some redress for the anti-union repression of the *bienio negro* from November 1933 to November 1935. Helpless in the midst of the conflict stood the government, weak and paralysed. Indeed, the central factor in the spring of 1936 was the fatal weakness of the Popular Front cabinet. The weakness was born not just of right-wing hostility but even more of the fact that it was in no meaningful sense representative of the electoral coalition which had voted it into power. In turn, that was the consequence of the ambiguity of PSOE attitudes to the Republic in the wake of the disappointments of 1931–3 and the suffering of the *bienio negro*. While Prieto was convinced that the situation demanded Socialist collaboration in government, Largo Caballero, fearful of a rank-and-file drift to the anarcho-syndicalist CNT, insisted that the liberal Republicans govern alone. He fondly believed that the Republicans should carry out the Popular Front electoral programme until they reached their bourgeois limitations. Then, in his fanciful scenario, they would be obliged to make way for an all-Socialist government. He used his immense influence to prevent the participation in the government of the more realistic Prieto. In consequence, only Republicans sat in the cabinet.

Largo Caballero's revolutionism was never more than verbal but his rhetoric was enough to intensify the fears of a middle class already terrified by rightist propaganda and increasing levels of disorder on the streets. In the south, demonstrations in favour of amnesty for the prisoners of 1934 frequently turned into acts of vandalism against churches and the property of the rich. The task of pacification and reconciliation facing Azaña was enormous given the simmering hatred left by the previous two years. On 9 March, Falangist gunmen in Granada attacked a group of workers and their families, wounding many women and children. On the following day, during a strike called in protest, the local headquarters of the Falange and Acción Popular, the offices of the right-wing newspaper *Ideal* and two churches were set on fire. On 12 March, Falangist gunmen tried to assassinate Luis Jiménez Asúa, the architect of the

Constitution. On 16 March, Largo Caballero's house was fired on by another rightist terror squad. Azaña's cabinet was barely equal to the problems it faced. The likeable Minister of the Interior, Amós Salvador, lacked the will to control the spiral of provocation and reprisal. As long as Azaña remained Prime Minister, the government's authority could just be maintained.

Unfortunately, in April and May there was to occur a series of events which gave credence to the view that the most malignant of fates presided over Spain's destiny. In order to put together an even stronger team, Azaña and Prieto plotted to remove the more conservative Alcalá Zamora from the presidency. Alcalá Zamora was constantly meddling in the work of the government and had little liking for Azaña. He had virtually no support since the left could not forgive him for permitting the entry of the CEDA into the government in October 1934 and the right could not forgive him for failing to invite Gil Robles to be Prime Minister at the end of 1935. In the Cortes on 7 April, Azaña and Prieto combined to have him impeached on the grounds that he had exceeded his constitutional powers in dissolving the Cortes. The removal of Alcalá Zamora seemed to open up the prospect of overcoming the difficulties caused by Largo Caballero's hostility to Socialist participation in government. Prieto and Azaña had the skill and the popularity to stabilize the tense situation of the spring of 1936. With one as Prime Minister and the other as President, it might have been possible to maintain reform on a scale to diminish left-wing militancy while dealing determinedly with right-wing conspiracy and terrorism.

In the hope of putting a strong team at the head of the Republican state, neither man considered the consequences of neither of them being able to lead the cabinet. The first part of the plan worked but not the second. Azaña was elevated to the presidency on 10 May and immediately asked Prieto to form a government. He had detailed plans for social reforms and for a crackdown on the extreme right. However, he needed the backing of Largo Caballero, who controlled large sections of the Socialist movement – he was president of the UGT, of the largest section of the party, the Agrupación Socialista Madrileña, and also of the parliamentary party which he ruled with a rod of iron. Prieto faced his fellow parliamentary deputies twice, on 11 and 12 May. He knew when he had backed Azaña for the presidency that Largo Caballero and his followers would refuse to support a government under his premiership. He could have formed a government with the backing of the Republicans and about a third of the Socialist deputies. However, when faced with the prospect of splitting the party to which he had devoted his life, he could not do so. It was, at best, a mixture of weakness and decency; at worst, of defeatism and irresponsibility. Azaña had been removed from the cabinet and would now be replaced by a feeble substitute, his friend Santiago Casares Quiroga. Largo Caballero remained naïvely confident that, if what he saw as the inevitable transfer of power from an exclusively Republican to an exclusively Socialist cabinet provoked a Fascist or military uprising, it would be defeated by the revolutionary action of the masses.

The consequences could not have been worse. A shrewd and strong Prime Minister was lost. To make matters worse, on assuming the presidency, Azaña increasingly withdrew from everyday politics. He took enormous delight in his ceremonial functions, in the restoration of monuments and palaces and in being a patron of the arts. His replacement as Prime Minister, Casares Quiroga, suffering from tuberculosis, was hardly the man to provide the determined leadership necessary in the circumstances.

Immediately the election results were known, exuberant workers had set about reaping revenge for the starvation and wage cuts of the *bienio negro* and for the brutal repression which had followed the Asturian rising. In any case, natural disaster intensified the social misery of the south. After drought in 1935, 1936 began with heavy rainstorms which decimated olive, wheat and barley production. Unemployment was rocketing and the election results had raised the hopes of the *braceros* to fever pitch. Throughout March, the Socialist land-workers' union, the FNTT, encouraged its members to take at its word the new government's proclaimed commitment to rapid reform. In Salamanca and Toledo, Córdoba and Jaén, there were invasions of estates by peasants who stole olives or cut down trees. The most substantial land seizures took place in Badajoz. On 29 May, in Yeste in the province of Albacete, seventeen peasants were killed, and many others wounded, by the Civil Guard. They had attempted to chop wood on land that had once belonged to the village and been taken from it by legal subterfuge in the nineteenth century. In general, what most alarmed the landlords was the assertiveness of labourers whom they expected to be servile but now found to be deter-mined not to be cheated out of reform as they had between 1931 and 1933. Many landowners withdrew to Seville or Madrid, or even to Biarritz or Paris, where they enthusiastically joined, financed or merely awaited news of ultra-rightist plots against the Republic.

Many sectors of right-wing society were anxious to role back the reforms associated with the Spanish Republic. This was most starkly clear in the rural areas where the Republic had raised hopes that challenged the existing social balance. It was also true in terms of the Republic's concessions to regional nationalisms, which unleashed military centralism, and of Republican efforts to break the educational and religious mo-nopolies held by the Catholic Church. One change initiated by the Republic which was less dramatic in its immediate impact yet ignited deep-seated hostility was the movement towards the emancipation of women. The Republic gave much to women but Franco's victory in the Spanish Civil War would take away even more.

In the five and a quarter years before the right-wing backlash culminated in the military coup of 18 July 1936, cultural and

educational reform had transformed the lives of many Spaniards, particularly women. Before 1931, the Spanish legal
system had been astonishingly retrograde – women were not
permitted to sign contracts, to administer businesses or estates
or to marry without risk of losing their jobs. The Republican
Constitution of December 1931 gave them the same legal
rights as men, permitting them to vote and to stand for parliament and legalizing divorce. Pressure for the female vote had
come not from any mass women's movement but from a tiny
elite of educated women and some progressive male politicians,
most notably in the Socialist Party. Accordingly, much of this
legislation was excoriated as 'godless' by a majority of Catholic
women influenced by their priests. At the same time, the right
was far more successful than the left in mobilizing newly eman-
cipated female voters to its cause. In any case, in the period
from 1931 to 1936, women of both the left and the right were
mobilized politically and socially as never before. They were
involved in electoral campaigns, trade union committees, protest demonstrations and in the educational system, both
through the massive expansion of primary schooling and the
opening up of the universities.

Nevertheless, public life remained a predominantly male
precinct. The woman rash enough to put her head over the
parapet and intrude upon the patriarchal territory of politics
faced accusations of being brazen and – as happened to both
Margarita Nelken and Dolores Ibárruri – from there it was but
a short step to being regarded as a whore. Such misogyny was
less prevalent in the more cosmopolitan atmosphere of the
left in Madrid and Barcelona, although even there it was not
uncommon. On the right, female independence was heavily
frowned upon. The further one travelled from the metropolis,
the more acute the problem became.

There were very few female parliamentary deputies even of
the left and centre left. Indeed, of the 1004 parliamentary
deputies of the three Republican Cortes of 1931, 1933 and

1936, only ten were women. One, Dolores Ibárruri, was a Communist, five – Margarita Nelken, María Lejárraga, Matilde de la Torre, Julia Álvarez Resano and Veneranda García Blanco y Manzano – were Socialists. Two – Victoria Kent and Clara Campoamor – were left-of-centre Republicans. Only two women gained a parliamentary seat on the right, Ángeles Gil Albarellos and Francisca Bohigas Gavilanes, both of the Catholic CEDA. It is noteworthy that three of the ten – Dolores Ibárruri, Matilde de la Torre and Veneranda García Blanco y Manzano – represented the mining districts of Asturias. Once war broke out, the political role of women would expand massively, as, inevitably, would the corresponding and violent determination of right-wing men to put back the clock.

It was not only in rural areas that the middle and upper classes feared that a rising tide of 'red' violence was about to inundate society. The CEDA's failure to secure electoral success meant the end of moderation. The right turned from Gil Robles to the more belligerent José Calvo Sotelo, the monarchist leader. The *Jefe* of the CEDA, however, convinced that the legal road to corporativism was blocked, did everything possible to help those who were committed to violence. As he later boasted, he had already made an incalculable contribution to the creation of mass right-wing militancy. His efforts to block and later to dismantle reform had done much to undermine Socialist faith in the possibilities of bourgeois democracy. Now he handed over the CEDA's electoral funds to the head of the military conspiracy, General Emilio Mola. Gil Robles' day had passed and nothing more starkly demonstrated the change in atmosphere than the startling rise of the Falange. Cashing in on middle-class disillusionment with the CEDA's legalism, the Falange expanded rapidly. Moreover, attracted by its code of violence, the bulk of the JAP went over en masse.

The Falangist terror squads continued to work hard to create an atmosphere of disorder which would justify the imposition of an authoritarian regime. They helped to ensure the escalation of a spiral of mindless violence which rendered rational discussion impossible. At no time during the Second Republic was there a greater need for strong and decisive government. The young activists of right and left were clashing on the streets. Military plotters were working to overthrow the regime. Prieto realized, as did few others, that attempts at revolutionary social change would only enrage the middle classes and drive them to fascism and armed counter-revolution. Instead, Prieto was convinced that the answer was to restore order and accelerate reform. He had plans to remove unreliable military commanders, reduce the power of the Civil Guard and disarm the Fascist terror squads. He was also anxious to promote massive public works, irrigation and housing schemes and speed up agrarian reform. It was a project which, pursued with energy and will, might have prevented civil war. Largo Caballero, however, had ensured that Prieto's vision would not be realized.

Indeed, while Prieto counselled caution, Largo Caballero did exactly the reverse. Intoxicated by Communist flattery – *Pravda* had called him 'the Spanish Lenin' – he toured Spain, prophesying the inevitable triumph of the coming revolution to crowds of cheering workers. His dearest ambition was to bring the whole of the workers' movement under Socialist control. Given his presidencies of the UGT, of the Madrid section of the PSOE and of the parliamentary party, he was in an excellent position from which to pursue this policy. Largo, however, then made a naïve error. Convinced that he was taking a step towards realizing his dream of uniting the working class under PSOE hegemony, he acquiesced in the fusion of the Socialist and Communist youth movements. The Communists happily agreed that the newly united youth movement should carry a name which gave the impression of a Socialist takeover – Juventudes Socialistas Unificadas. In fact, the new movement quickly fell totally under the dominance of the more dynamic Communists. It meant the eventual loss of forty thousand young Socialists of the Federación de Juventudes Socialistas to the PCE. Santiago Carrillo, the FJS leader, had long since drawn close to Moscow. Since he had already started attending meetings of the Central Committee of the Communist Party, it is difficult to believe that he had not already passed from the PSOE to the PCE.

In fact, though, it is debatable whether Largo Caballero was ever genuine in his revolutionary pronouncements. Always a pragmatist concerned to further the interests of his UGT members, Largo Caballero tended to 'lead from behind', going along with the rank and file less out of conviction than out of a determination not to be out of step. For all the rhetoric, the only real weapon at the left's disposal in early 1936, the revolutionary general strike, was never used. Indeed, when serious proposals for revolution were made in April by Joaquín Maurín, one of the leaders of the quasi-Trotskyist POUM, he was scorned as a dangerous utopian by Largo Caballero's supporters. The divisions between Largo and Prieto ultimately weakened the Republic. The left-wing of the party made regular statements – about the death agony of capitalism and the inevitable triumph of socialism – which Prieto, with some justification, regarded as insanely provocative. In fact, party discipline was maintained in such a way as to contribute to the stability of the Republican government. However, the May Day marches, the clenched fist salutes, the revolutionary rhetoric and violent attacks on Prieto frightened elements of the middle classes into taking action to avoid their apparently impending doom.

In fact, the Socialists were caught on the horns of a genuine dilemma. Prieto believed that strong reforming government was the only answer to the right's threats to the Republic. However, there was nothing about right-wing attitudes at the time to suggest that military conspiracy would have been voluntarily abandoned for anything less than social policies like those pursued under the Radical–CEDA coalition of 1934–5.

Largo Caballero was convinced, after the experience of the Constituent Cortes, that a Republican–Socialist coalition such as Prieto advocated would be incapable of carrying out adequate measures. This division of opinion, exacerbated by personal animosity between Largo Caballero and Prieto, effectively paralysed the political initiative of the Socialist movement. That the strongest party of the Popular Front was not therefore able to participate actively in using the apparatus of the state to defend the Republic was all the more tragic in the light of the inefficacy of Casares Quiroga. The new Prime Minister was no match for the problems he was called upon to solve. Under constant attack in the Cortes from an angry right wing, harassed by the destruction of public order by the Falange and the anarchists, and undermined by the lack of Socialist support, Casares nonetheless seemed to have little appreciation of the gravity of the situation. He shrugged off Prieto's warnings about military plotters with the offensive comment 'I will not tolerate your menopausic outbursts'.

The government could not therefore prevent politics degenerating into open conflict. While bombs were being planted and public officials murdered, there could be no compromise. In the Cortes, the violence of speeches by José Calvo Sotelo or by the fiery Communist Dolores Ibárruri (known as 'Pasionaria') underlined the impossibility of any accord. The move to extremism was revealed in the fact that the Falange was breaking up CEDA meetings, the Socialist Youth attacking the followers of Prieto. While Largo Caballero made empty prophesies of revolution, Calvo Sotelo talked in chillingly convincing terms of violent counter-revolution. The purpose of his speeches was to prevent any possible reconciliation between moderates on both sides. Since parliamentary debates received full uncensored press coverage, he dwelt on disorder, often generated by Falangists subsidized by his party, in order to persuade the middle classes of the need for military insurrection. Throughout the spring of 1936, Calvo Sotelo provided the army with a theory of political action and the right-wing masses with an urgent sense of the need to confront the twin threats of 'communism' and 'separatism', both of which were presented as consubstantial with the Republic. His speeches provoked scuffles in the Cortes. On one occasion, a Socialist deputy offered to fight him in the street and called him a 'pimp'. On another, after declaring himself a Fascist, he made an unmistakable overture to the army when he said that 'the soldier who, faced with his destiny, is not prepared to rise for Spain and against anarchy, is out of his mind'.

In fact, several generals had already decided that power should be taken away from a government which was both helpless to stop what they saw as the break-up of Spain at the hands of regional separatists and responsible for policies that were undermining the structure of society. In consequence, they concluded that the time had come for a Primo de Rivera-style 'iron surgeon'. Many of the high command in 1936, faced by the chaos of the Popular Front, a chaos orchestrated by their rightist allies, had no qualms about intervening in politics. Senior officers who could remember the Cuban disaster – men of Primo de Rivera's generation like Generals José Sanjurjo and Gonzalo Quiepo de Llano – had long since developed a haughty contempt for what they saw as the ineptitude of the professional politicians. The younger generals had little sense of loyalty to a regime which they believed to be impermanent. At all levels, there was a belief that the army had the right to intervene in politics to defend both the social order and the territorial integrity of Spain.

The military uprising which took place on 17–18 July 1936 was more carefully planned than any previous coup. The lesson of the *Sanjurjada* of 10 August 1932 – that casual *pronunciamientos* would no longer work against a proletariat ready to use the weapon of the general strike – had been well learned. General Emilio Mola, the 'Director' of the plot, realized that there would have to be a coordinated seizure of power in garrisons of all of Spain's fifty provinces and a swift annihilation of the organized working class. In the first of his secret instructions to fellow conspirators, issued in April 1936, he recognized the importance of terror. He declared, 'It has to be borne in mind that the action has to be violent in the extreme to reduce as soon as possible the enemy which is strong and well-organized. Of course, all leaders of political parties, societies and trade unions which are not linked to the movement will be imprisoned and exemplary punishment carried out on them in order to strangle any rebellion or strikes.'

The preparation of the rising, or *alzamiento*, was made more difficult by the efforts of the Republican government to neutralize suspect generals. On 21 February, at the suggestion of the new Minister of War, General Carlos Masquelet, Franco was sacked as Chief of Staff and sent to the Canary Islands as military commander; Goded was removed as Inspector General and transferred to the Balearic Islands to be military commander there; and Mola was posted from command of the Army of Africa to be military governor of the Navarrese capital, Pamplona. This last transfer was short-sighted, to say the least. Pamplona was the centre of Carlist monarchism, and of its militia force, the *requetés*. Consequently, Mola found himself in an excellent place from which to organize plans for the mainland insurrection, although his relations with the Carlists were not without friction. The obvious figurehead was the veteran of African wars and earlier coups, Sanjurjo. Indeed, Sanjurjo played an important role in cementing the agreement between Mola and the Carlist leader, Manuel Fal Conde. José Antonio Primo de Rivera, imprisoned by the government in mid-March in an attempt to control the Falange, was more cautious, but agreed to support the uprising lest his movement be left behind. However, the crucial impetus for the conspiracy came from junior officers sympathetic to authoritarian ideas.

Certain factors made the conspirators' task much easier than it might otherwise have been. The government continued to ignore the repeated warnings that it received of the plot. The Director General of Security pointed the finger at Mola but no serious action was taken. Both Azaña and Casares Quiroga were singularly unaware of the danger. Shortly after Casares was appointed Prime Minister, his military aide, the air force major Ignacio Hidalgo de Cisneros, informed him of the activities of a group of anti-Republican pilots who were storing weapons and bombs. Hidalgo de Cisneros then accompanied Casares Quiroga to Azaña's country retreat to report on this. Azaña cut him off, saying brusquely that it was dangerous to make such accusations. On their way back to Madrid, Casares said, 'After what you've just seen, you'll understand how difficult it is for me to take action against suspects.'

On 12 June, Casares met Colonel Juan Yagüe, whom he had summoned to Madrid because of deafening (and accurate) rumours that he was the effective leader of the military conspiracy in Morocco. Hidalgo de Cisneros had urged the Minister to seize the opportunity to keep Yagüe in Madrid and replace him with a trustworthy officer. Casares Quiroga offered Yagüe a transfer, either to a desirable post on the Spanish mainland or to a plum position as a military attaché abroad. Yagüe replied that he would rather burn his uniform than not be able to serve with the Legion. After a long meeting, Casares emerged, saying to Hidalgo, 'Yagüe is a gentleman, a perfect officer, and I am sure that he would never betray the Republic. He has given me his word of honour and his promise as an officer that he will always loyally serve the Republic and men like Yagüe stand by their commitments.' By weakly permitting Yagüe to return to Morocco, Casares committed a major political blunder which allowed the conspiracy to flourish among the colonial garrisons.

Three days later, Casares compounded his error. On 15 June, at the Monastery of Irache, near Estella in Navarre, Mola held a secret meeting with the commanders of the garrisons of Pamplona, Logroño, Vitoria and San Sebastián. The

Mayor of Estella, on hearing of this conspiratorial gathering, informed the Civil Governor of Navarre who posted units of Civil Guards around the monastery. When he telephoned Casares Quiroga for further instructions, the Prime Minister indignantly ordered him to remove them, saying, 'General Mola is a loyal Republican who deserves therefore the respect of the authorities.'

Just over a week went by before yet another mistake was made. A curious warning came from the pen of General Franco. He wrote to Casares Quiroga on 23 June 1936 a letter of labyrinthine ambiguity, both suggesting that the army would be loyal if treated properly and insinuating that it was hostile to the Republic. The clear implication was that, if only Casares would put Franco in charge, the plots could be dismantled. At that stage, Franco was some way back in the seniority stakes by the side of the principal conspirators. In later years, his apologists were to spill many gallons of ink trying to explain away this letter, presenting it as either a skilful effort to put Casares off the scent or a last magnanimous, peacemaking gesture. In the event, Casares took no more notice of Franco than he had of Prieto. In fact, the letter had offered Casares the opportunity to neutralize Franco either by buying him off or having him arrested. It was typical of the Prime Minister's insouciance that he did neither.

General Franco's letter was a prime example of his *retranca*, the hesitant peasant cunning associated with the natives of Galicia. His determination to be on the winning side without taking any substantial risks hardly marked him as a likely charismatic leader. Nonetheless, for several reasons, Mola and the other conspirators were loath to proceed without him. He had enormous influence in the officer corps, having been for a time Director of the Military Academy in Zaragoza as well as Chief of the General Staff under Gil Robles. In particular, he was greatly respected in the Spanish Moroccan Army, the country's toughest military force, in which he had made his own meteoric career. The *Africanista* officers respected him for his icy ruthlessness; the Moorish troops because his numerous escapes from death convinced them that he possessed the mystical power of *baraka*, or invulnerability. The coup could not possibly have a chance of succeeding without the Moroccan Army and Franco was the obvious man to lead it. Moreover, his part in suppressing the working-class rebellions in Asturias in 1917 and 1934 had made him something of a hero among the more hysterical sections of the middle and upper classes. Yet, as the letter to Casares Quiroga indicated, in the early summer of 1936 Francisco Franco was a less determined plotter than might have been expected. He preferred to wait in the wings, improving his golf in the Canary Islands and making abortive efforts to learn English. His coy hesitation saw his exasperated comrades bestow upon him the ironic nickname 'Miss Canary Islands 1936'. Sanjurjo was heard to say that the rising would go ahead 'with or without Franquito'.

When Franco finally decided to join in, he was given a vitally important but second-ranking role. The future Head of State after the triumphant coup was to be Sanjurjo. As technical mastermind of the plot, Mola was then expected to have a decisive role in the politics of the victorious regime. Then came a number of generals, each of whom was assigned a region, among them Franco with Morocco. Several of them were equally as prominent to Franco, especially Joaquin Fanjul, who was in charge of the rising in Madrid, and Manuel Goded, who was given Barcelona. Moreover, even if Franco had been *primus inter pares*, even if Sanjurjo and Mola had not outranked him in the conspiratorial hierarchy, his future in the post-coup polity could only lie in the shadow of the two charismatic politicians of the extreme right, José Calvo Sotelo and José Antonio Primo de Rivera. That situation was to change with astonishing rapidity and, in the eyes of some observers, with sinister symmetry.

The arrangements for Franco's part in the coup had been

made even before his participation was finally confirmed. On 5 July, the Marqués de Luca de Tena, owner of the monarchist daily *ABC*, instructed his London correspondent, the unpleasant Luis Bolín, to charter an aircraft to take Franco from the Canaries to Morocco where he was to take command of the Army of Africa. Bolín hired a De Havilland Dragon Rapide in Croydon and arranged for a group of what appeared to be holidaying passengers to mask the aeroplane's real purpose. Douglas Jerrold, an English right-wing Catholic, was involved in the arrangements. In his autobiography, Jerrold wrote of his role in helping 'to save a nation's soul':

> We lunched at Simpson's and de la Cierva completed the party.
> 'I want a man and three platinum blondes to fly to Africa tomorrow.'
> 'Must there really be *three*?' I asked, and at that Bolín turned triumphantly to De la Cierva. 'I told you he would manage it.'
> I rang Hugh Pollard. 'Can you fly to Africa tomorrow with two girls?' I asked, and heard the expected reply.
> 'Depends upon the girls.'

Leaving Croydon on 11 July, the plane arrived in Casablanca, via Bordeaux, the following day. Three days later, it arrived at the airport of Gando near Las Palmas on the island of Gran Canaria.

In the meanwhile, however, dramatic events had been taking place on the Spanish mainland. On the afternoon of 12 July, Falangist gunmen had shot and killed a leftist officer of the Republican Assault Guards, Lieutenant José del Castillo. Castillo was number two on a blacklist of pro-Republican officers allegedly drawn up by the ultra-rightist Unión Militar Española, an association of conspiratorial officers linked to Renovación Española. The first man on the blacklist, Captain

Carlos Faraudo, had already been murdered. Enraged comrades of the murdered Castillo responded with massive and irresponsible reprisals. In the early hours of the following day they set out to avenge his death by murdering a prominent right-wing politician. Failing to find Gil Robles, who was holidaying in Biarritz, they kidnapped and shot Calvo Sotelo. On the evening of the 13th, Indalecio Prieto led a delegation of Socialists and Communists to demand that Casares distribute arms to the workers before the military rose. The Prime Minister refused, but he could hardly ignore the fact that there was now virtually open war.

The political scandal which followed the discovery of Calvo Sotelo's body was enormous and played neatly into the hands of the military plotters. The murder provided graphic justification for their contention that Spain needed military intervention to save her from anarchy. It clinched the commitment of many ditherers, including Franco, and obscured how long the coup of 17–18 July had been in the making. It also deprived the conspirators of an important leader. As a powerful figure and a cosmopolitan rightist of wide experience, Calvo Sotelo would have been a senior civilian leader after the coup. Unlike the various ciphers that were to be used by Franco, he would have imposed his personality on the post-war state. Now, however, he was dead, and even if no one could have judged it in such terms at the time his death removed an important political rival to Franco.

In the short term, Calvo Sotelo's assassination gave a new urgency to plans for the uprising. Franco had acute immediate problems which took precedence over any long-term ambitions. As military commander of the Canary Islands, his headquarters were in Santa Cruz de Tenerife. The Dragon Rapide from Croydon had landed on Gran Canaria perhaps because it was nearer to mainland Africa, perhaps because of the low cloud afflicting Tenerife, perhaps because it was feared that Franco was being watched. In order to travel from Santa Cruz to Gran Canaria, Franco needed the authorization of the Ministry of War. Apparently his request for an inspection tour of Gran Canaria was turned down. The rising was scheduled to start on 17 July, so Franco would have to leave for Morocco on that day at the latest. In the event he did so, yet none of his biographers seem to regard it as odd that the Dragon Rapide should have been directed to Gran Canaria with confidence in Franco's ability to get there too. That he got there at all was the result of either an amazing coincidence or foul play.

On the morning of 16 July, General Amado Balmes, military commander in Gran Canaria and an excellent marksman, was shot in the stomach and died of his wounds while trying out various pistols on a shooting range. Francoist historiography has played down the incident as a tragic, but fortunately timed, accident. To counter suggestions that Balmes was removed by members of the military conspiracy, Franco's official biographer claimed that Balmes was himself an important figure in the plot. Strangely, however, Balmes never featured in the subsequent pantheon of heroes of the 'crusade'. Other sources suggest that Balmes was a loyal officer who had withstood intense pressure to join the rising. If that was true, he had, like many other Republican officers, put his life in danger. It is virtually impossible now to say if his death was accidental, suicide or murder, but what is certain is that he died at precisely the right time for Franco. The need to preside over the funeral gave Franco the perfect excuse to travel to Las Palmas on 17 July. Coordinated risings were planned to take place all over Spain the following morning. However, indications that the conspirators in Morocco were about to be arrested led to the action being brought forward there to the early evening of 17 July. The garrisons rose in Melilla, Tetuan and Ceuta in Morocco. In the early morning of 18 July, Franco and General Luis Orgaz took over Las Palmas.

When news reached Madrid of the rising in Morocco, Azaña asked Casares what Franco was doing, to which he replied complacently, 'He's in storage in the Canary Islands.' Casares telephoned his friend, the distinguished physiologist Professor Juan Negrín, and told him, 'this coup is guaranteed to fail. The Government is master of the situation. It will all be over soon.' The Spanish Civil War had begun and Casares's complacency already left the government at a major disadvantage.

FOUR

'The Map of Spain Bleeds': From Coup d'État to Civil War

The plotters had not foreseen that their rising would turn into a long civil war. Their plans had been for a rapid *alzamiento*, or rising, to be followed by a military directory like that established in 1923, and they had not counted on the strength of working-class resistance. It was only in some areas, however, that there was certainty of success. In fact, the triumph or defeat of the military coup followed the electoral geography of the country. In Pamplona, the Carlist population turned the coup into a popular festival, thronging the streets and shouting *¡Viva Cristo Rey!* (Long live Christ the King). The conservative ecclesiastical towns of León and Old Castile – Burgos, Salamanca, Zamora, Segovia and Avila – fell almost without struggle although it took Generals Saliquet and Ponte nearly twenty-four hours to crush the Socialist railway workers of Valladolid. According to the *Diario de Burgos* of 20 July, 'the Assault and Civil guards joined in the Movement from the first moment'. In the Canary Islands, the local press displayed a misplaced optimism typical of the rebel zone in the early days of the war. It was announced in the *Gaceta de Tenerife* on 21 July that José Antonio Primo de Rivera (actually now in a Republican jail in Alicante) was marching on Madrid with a column of Falangists, that Azaña had been arrested in Santander and that Mola had seized the Ministry of the Interior in Madrid. The rebels adopted the title of '*Nacionales*', rather stronger in its connotations of 'the only true Spaniards' than the usual English rendition of 'Nationalists'.

In the Catholic heartlands, where the rising had enjoyed instant success, blood soon started to flow with the blanket repression of Republicans of all kinds. It was not just the region's relatively few anarchists, Communists and Trotskyists who were rounded up and shot but also moderate Socialists and centre-left Republicans. General Mola's conviction that terror behind the lines would play a crucial role was harshly revealed when he called a meeting of all of the *alcaldes* of the province of Pamplona and told them: 'It is necessary to spread terror. We have to create the impression of mastery eliminating without scruples or hesitation all those who do not think as we do. There can be no cowardice. If we vacillate one moment and fail to proceed with the greatest determination, we will not win. Anyone who helps or hides a Communist or a supporter of the Popular Front will be shot.'

Those who claimed to be rising in defence of law and order and of eternal Catholic values inaugurated a savage purge of leftists and Freemasons which was to leave a smouldering legacy of hatred in the area for more than forty years. The killings did not just take place in areas of resistance. It is noteworthy that, in places where the military coup was immediately successful, the number of killings was in the thousands. In the three overseas bases of the Canary Islands, Ceuta and Melilla, 2768 people were killed; in Galicia, 3000, in Zamora, 3000, in Valladolid, 3430, and in Navarra, 2789.

Outside the areas which in a sense had been secured for the right twenty years before by the success of the Catholic Agrarian Federations and during the Republic by the propaganda efforts of Acción Popular, Nationalist victories were gained against hostile populations by various combinations of surprise, trickery and the swift crushing of working-class resistance. Thus, in Oviedo, Colonel Antonio Aranda, pretending to be loyal to the Republic, convinced local miners' leaders that they could safely dispatch their men to help relieve Madrid. Once their trains had left, Aranda declared for the rebellion. Determined officers in Galicia took Vigo and La Coruña after heavy fighting with the unarmed population. Remarkable successes were achieved in Andalusia, but the way that they were won suggested that a long and bloody struggle lay ahead. Of all the various conflicts which had contributed to the outbreak of the Spanish Civil War, none had been fiercer than the agrarian war in the south. In consequence, once the outbreak of hostilities removed all restraints, latent social hatreds ensured that in the villages and towns of Andalusia and Extremadura horrific cruelties would be unleashed.

In the rural districts, the local *braceros*, fervent supporters of the Republic, were usually able to overpower small Civil Guard garrisons. In some towns, cruel reprisals were then taken against those landowners not rich enough to have removed themselves to the safety of Seville or the South of France, and also against the priests who had legitimized the tyranny of the *caciques* and *latifundistas*. Equally, in many other southern towns, the rightists known to support the uprising were merely detained for their own safety. Then, within days of the *alzamiento*, the local branches of the Socialist FNTT and of the CNT went about collectivizing the big estates. The stores of the great *cacique* families were broken open and their flour, hams and olive oil distributed by the revolutionary committees. Special pastures given over to the breeding of fighting bulls, a caprice of the owners which had contributed to local misery, were ploughed over. In the months before new crops would be available, plans were made by the local revolutionary committees to slaughter the bulls for food. Strictly rationed, it was hoped that they would keep everyone fed until the harvest. For most of them, used to a meagre diet of bread and *gazpacho*, a soup made of tomatoes, onions, peppers and garlic, augmented by the occasional rabbit, it was the first time they had ever tasted beef, if not meat. However, retribution in the villages would not be long behind once the major Andalusian cities had fallen to the rebels. Even in those towns where there had been no right-wing victims, reprisals were savage. The excuse given was that the left had simply not had time to carry out the evil plans they were assumed to have harboured – '*les faltaban tiempo*'.

A general strike in Cádiz seemed to have won the town for the workers but after a fierce encounter the rebel garrison gained control with the help of rich Falangists led by José de Mora Figueroa, the Marqués de Tamarón. After the capture of the city, Mora Figueroa took his men to Jerez de la Frontera where he organized a column which set about conquering the remaining towns of the province. Córdoba, Huelva, Seville and Granada all fell after savage elimination of working-class opposition. Seville, the Andalusian capital and the most revolutionary southern city, fell to the eccentric General Gonzalo Queipo de Llano in remarkable fashion – albeit not nearly so remarkable as he was later to claim. Queipo de Llano was related by marriage to Alcalá Zamora and had been a fervent supporter of the Republic in 1931. Having been involved in the abortive military rising of December 1930 in which Republicans, Socialists and left-wing army officers had hoped to overthrow Alfonso XIII, he was not entirely trusted by the rebels. However, on 17 July he arrived in Seville in his capacity as general in command of the *Carabineros* (frontier guards) ostensibly to inspect customs posts in the port.

Within a year of the events, he claimed that he had captured the city with spontaneous bravery and the help of only 130 soldiers and fifteen civilians. In a radio broadcast on 1 February 1938, he exaggerated even more wildly, declaring that he had taken the city with fourteen or fifteen men. He claimed that, gun in hand, he had announced to the commander of the Second Military Division, Major General José Fernández Villa-Abrille, 'I have come to tell you that the time has come to decide whether you support your comrades in arms or the government that is leading Spain to ruin.' Allegedly, he then browbeat the rest of the initially loyal local garrison into joining the rising. In fact, the coup had been meticulously planned by a major of the general staff stationed in Seville, José Cuesta Monereo, and carried out by a force of four thousand men. General Villa-Abrille and his staff were aware of what was being prepared, yet did nothing to prevent it. The great majority of the Seville garrison were involved, including units of artillery, cavalry, communications and transport.

This large force seized the nerve centres of the city, taking the telephone building, the town hall and the headquarters of the Civil Governor by artillery bombardment, establishing control of the main access routes into the centre and then applying indiscriminate terror. By the second day, they were assisted by the first troops of the Spanish Foreign Legion to arrive from Africa. With fifty Carlist *requetés*, fifty Falangists and another fifty Civil Guards, they immediately began the bloody suppression of the working-class districts of Triana, La Macarena, San Julián and San Marcos. Despite first being bombarded with artillery, the resistance was dogged until the rebels, using women and children as human shields, were able to enter and begin the repression in earnest. Moorish mercenaries, the *Regulares*, were given a free hand to loot and to butcher men, women and children. On 25 July, Queipo signed a declaration that all the leaders of any labour union on strike would 'immediately be shot' as well as 'an equal number of carefully chosen rank-and-file members'.

Events in Granada were equally bloody and typical of the rebels' determination to win by the application of terror. The brutality and ruthlessness of Queipo de Llano in particular were illustrated by the fate of the military commander of Granada, General Miguel Campins. Loyal to the Republic, he had refused to obey Queipo's command that he declare martial law. However, Campins did send a telegram putting himself under the orders of his friend, General Franco, with whom he had served as deputy director of the General Military Academy in Zaragoza. Placed under arrest by junior officers who had joined the conspiracy, he was tried in Seville for 'rebellion' on 14 August and shot two days later. Franco allegedly sent letters asking that mercy be shown to Campins but Queipo, who loathed the future Caudillo, tore them up.

In the meanwhile, in Granada, the working-class district of the Albaicín was shelled and bombed. When control of the city centre was assured, the military authorities allowed the Falangist 'Black Squad' to sow panic among the population by taking leftists from their homes at night and shooting them in the cemetery. In the course of the war, about five thousand civilians were shot in Granada. The caretaker of the cemetery went mad and was committed to an asylum. One of the most celebrated victims of rightist terror, not just in Granada but in all Spain, was the poet Federico García Lorca. Years later, the Francoists were to claim that Lorca had died because of an apolitical private feud related to his homosexuality. In fact, Lorca was anything but apolitical. In ultra-reactionary Granada, his sexuality had given him a sense of apartness which had grown into a sympathy for those on the margins of respectable society. In 1934, he had declared, 'I will always be on the side of those who have nothing.' His itinerant theatre *La Barraca* was inspired by a sense of social missionary zeal. Lorca regularly signed anti-Fascist manifestos and was connected with organizations such as International Red Aid.

In Granada itself he was closely linked with the moderate left. His views were well known and it would not have escaped the notice of the town's oligarchs that he considered the Catholic conquest of Moorish Granada in 1492 to have been a disaster. Flouting a central tenet of Spanish right-wing thinking, Lorca believed that the conquest had destroyed a unique civilization and created 'a wasteland populated by the worst bourgeoisie in Spain today'. When rightists hunting for 'reds' began to look for him, he took refuge in the home of his friend the

Falangist poet Luis Rosales. It was there that he was arrested by the sinister Ramón Ruiz Alonso, a prominent member of the local CEDA who had hitched his cart to the Falange. Having been denounced as a Russian spy by Ruiz Alonso, Federico García Lorca was shot at dawn on 19 August 1936. The cowardly murder of a great poet was, however, like that of the loyal General Campins, merely a drop in an ocean of political slaughter.

In the provinces of Seville and Córdoba, many landowners supported the rising and joined mixed columns made up of soldiers, Civil Guards, Carlist *requetés* and Falangists. Some financed the columns or supplied them with horses and men. They played a prominent role in choosing the victims to be executed in the conquered villages. After the suppression of the working-class districts of Seville, a Carlist column organized by a retired major, Luis Redondo García, carried out operations against towns in the south-east of the province. Other columns were organized by wealthy volunteers with access to vehicles and weapons. A typical example was that led by Ramón de Carranza, the man imposed by Queipo de Llano as *Alcalde* of Seville. It was no coincidence that in many localities of the province conquered by his column there were substantial landholdings of the families of Carranza and other wealthy members of the column. After the capture of each town, Carranza established new right-wing town councils (*ayuntamientos*) and transported large numbers of prisoners to Seville for execution.

On 27 July, Carranza's column reached one such town, Rociana in Huelva, where the left had taken over in response to news of the military coup. There had been no right-wing casualties, but the premises of the landowners' association (Asociación Patronal) and two clubs had been destroyed, twenty-five sheep had been stolen and the parish church and rectory had been burned, although the parish priest, Father Martínez Laorden, had been saved by local Socialists and given refuge in the house of the mayor. On 28 July, after Carranza's arrival, the parish priest made a speech from the balcony of the town hall: 'You all no doubt believe that, because I am a priest, I have come with words of forgiveness and repentance. Not at all. War against all of them until the last trace has been eliminated.' A large number of men and women were arrested. The women had their heads shaved and one was dragged around the town by a donkey before being murdered. Over the next three months, sixty people were shot. In January 1937, Father Martínez Laorden made an official complaint that the repression had been altogether too lenient.

The scale of terror and repression in those areas which had been easily won by the rebels made it clear that their objective was not simply to take over the state but to exterminate an entire liberal and reforming culture. The rebels were waging war on the urban and rural workers who had benefited from the reforms of the Republic, on the officials, the mayors and parliamentary deputies who were regarded as the instruments of reform and on the teachers and intellectuals seen as responsible for spreading the poison of new ideas. The extent to which this was a war of old against new was summed up by General Mola's apocalyptic, and somewhat premature, declaration in Burgos: 'The government which was the wretched bastard of liberal and Socialist concubinage is dead, killed by our valiant army. Spain, the true Spain, has laid the dragon low, and now it lies, writhing on its belly and biting the dust. I am now going to take up my position at the head of the troops and it will not be long before two banners – the sacred emblem of the Cross and our own glorious flag – are waving together in Madrid.'

Nevertheless, the scale of working-class resistance in many areas where the rising triumphed suggested that if the government had taken the decisive action of issuing guns to the workers the rebellion might have been crushed at birth. Understandably, however, the moderate liberal cabinet of Santiago

Casares Quiroga had refused to do so. In part this was because
the Prime Minister still seemed not to believe that the situation
was serious. It also derived from a reluctance to hand over
power to working-class organizations which would be unlikely
to hand it back once the military rising had been crushed.
Then valuable time was lost in a search for a compromise
solution. Left-wing demonstrations calling for arms were
ignored – guaranteeing the success of the rising in many places.

Throughout 18 July there seemed no end to the stream
of bad news reaching Prime Minister Casares Quiroga. At
6.00 p.m. he had been appalled by a suggestion from Largo
Caballero that there was no option but to arm the workers.
Three hours later, he had resigned. Tortured by remorse for
neglecting to heed warnings of the military conspiracy, he
blamed himself for the triumphs of the rebels. In an effort
to expiate his guilt by exposing himself to danger, he joined
a workers' militia unit. In blue overalls, he fought against
Mola's advancing forces at the Sierra de Guadarrama and then
remained in the besieged capital until the end of 1938.

Following Casares Quiroga's resignation, President Azaña
called on the moderate centre Republican Diego Martínez
Barrio to form a broad coalition government to negotiate with
the rebels. At 11.00 p.m., Largo Caballero opposed Martínez
Barrio's suggestion, brought by Prieto, for Socialist participation in the new cabinet because the proposed coalition was
intended to include groupings to the right of the Popular
Front. Feeling that the absence of the PSOE might facilitate
talks with the military rebels, Martínez Barrio finally formed a
government of Republicans in the early hours of the morning of
19 July. He began immediately to telephone military garrisons
and, despite individual assurances of personal loyalty to him, he
soon realized how little room for manoeuvre he had. In Burgos,
the loyal General Domingo Batet was virtually a prisoner. In
Zaragoza, General Miguel Cabanellas made it clear that he
could – and would – do nothing to stop the rebels taking over.

Martínez Barrio spoke twice to General Mola. So resounding had been the victory of the rebels in Pamplona that he was
in no mood for compromise. The new Prime Minister assured
him that his government would pursue a more right-wing
policy and re-impose law and order. Mola rejected an offer of
the post of Minister of War in the new cabinet. The Minister of
War, General José Miaja, also tried unsuccessfully to negotiate
Mola's surrender. Rumours of the conciliation attempts led to
popular protest demonstrations in the streets of Madrid. By
midday on 19 July, Martínez Barrio had been forced to resign.
A conservative cabinet had been tried in the hope of compromise with the rebels. The only remaining option was to fight
and that meant arming the workers. Already unhappy about
the working-class radicalism manifested during the spring of
1936, few Republicans were prepared to contemplate such an
option.

The quest for compromise was abandoned but it was not
easy to find a Prime Minister prepared to grasp the nettle.
Martínez Barrio was replaced finally by José Giral, a left
Republican follower of Azaña. His cabinet was little distin-
guishable from that of Casares Quiroga. With an eye on international opinion, there was no attempt to include members of
the working-class parties – although Prieto was to be the real
power behind the throne, working tirelessly as Giral's principal
adviser. Giral quickly took the dramatic step of authorizing the
distribution of arms to the workers. It was to be crucial in the
defeat of the rebellion in many places, although an equally
decisive role was played by the forces of order, the Assault
Guards and the Civil Guards. Where these forces remained
loyal – and they usually did so in cities of substantial proletarian
strength – the rebels were generally defeated.

On the same afternoon of 19 July, General Joaquín Fanjul,
aided by some Falangists, tried to start the rising in Madrid
from the Montaña barracks. His troops were immediately surrounded by a vast crowd of workers reinforced by loyal Assault

Guards. After white flags were flown, the Madrileños advanced on the barracks to accept its surrender, only to be fired on. Infuriated, they murdered several of the officers when the barracks was captured at noon on 20 July. In the euphoria of the moment, it was seen as the equivalent of the storming of the Bastille during the French Revolution. Among the crowd was Valentín González, a road mender from Extremadura, who was shortly to acquire fame as 'El Campesino', the peasant soldier. He was just one of the volunteers in those first days who would later emerge as a significant military leader. They ranged from cosmopolitan figures like the playboy intellectual Gustavo Durán to the uneducated quarryman Enrique Líster. Gustavo Durán, a pianist and composer and a close friend of Lorca, joined a militia group of Socialist railway workers. He discovered remarkable military talents and rose to important positions of command. Enrique Líster had worked in Cuba and on the tunnelling for the Moscow Metro, before returning to Spain as a Communist Party agitator. During the Civil War, he would show himself to be a resourceful battlefield commander, his determination and ruthlessness getting the best out of poorly trained and badly equipped troops.

Many volunteers joined up as the left-wing parties of Madrid formed militias and columns and set off to repel General Mola's troops at the Somosierra pass north of the capital. In the fierce fighting there, 'El Campesino' emerged as a potential military leader. Enrique Líster was instrumental in the militarization of the militias through his role in creating the crack *Quinto Regimiento*, which became the nucleus of the Popular Army. Other spontaneous left-wing militiamen from the capital headed south to reverse the success of the rising in Toledo. With loyal regular troops, they captured the town but the rebels retreated into the Alcázar, the impregnable fortress which dominates both Toledo and the river Tagus which curls around it. Command was taken by the fifty-eight-year-old Colonel José Moscardó, the Director of the Escuela de Gimnástica (Gymnastics School) of the Infantry Academy.

In Barcelona, Companys refused to issue arms but depots were seized by the CNT. In the early hours of 19 July, rebel troops began to march on the city centre. They were met by anarchists and the local Civil Guard which, decisively, had stayed loyal. The CNT stormed the Atarazanas barracks, where the rebels had set up headquarters. When General Goded arrived by seaplane from the Balearic Islands to join them, the situation was already lost for the rising. Captured, he was forced to broadcast an appeal to his followers to lay down their arms. This was a vital victory for the government, for it ensured that all of Catalonia would remain loyal.

The capture of Fanjul in Madrid and Goded in Barcelona constituted not entirely unforeseeable blows for the Nationalists. Both generals had realized that they faced immensely difficult tasks. However, as Mola and other successful conspirators awaited the arrival of General Sanjurjo from his Portuguese exile to lead a triumphal march on Madrid, they received some entirely unexpected bad news: Sanjurjo had been killed in bizarre circumstances. On 19 July, Juan Antonio Ansaldo, a famous air ace and monarchist playboy who had once organized Falangist terror squads, had arrived in Estoril at the summerhouse where General Sanjurjo was staying. Ansaldo had been sent by Mola to collect Sanjurjo and bring him to the rebel zone. The aircraft that Ansaldo used – a tiny De Havilland Puss Moth two-seater – was a less than appropriate choice for the mission. Moreover, the far more suitable Dragon Rapide which had taken Franco from the Canary Islands to Morocco had arrived in Lisbon at the same time. It could easily, and more comfortably, have taken Sanjurjo to Burgos. However, on his arrival in Estoril, in front of a group of the general's hangers-on, Ansaldo had greeted him dramatically as the Spanish Chief of State. Overcome with emotion at this theatrical display of public respect, Sanjurjo agreed to travel with him.

To add to the problems posed by the minuscule scale of

Ansaldo's aeroplane, the Portuguese authorities now intervened. Although Sanjurjo was legally in the country as a tourist,
the Portuguese government did not want trouble with Madrid.
Accordingly, Ansaldo was obliged to clear customs and depart
alone from the airport of Santa Cruz. He was then to return
towards Estoril and collect Sanjurjo at a disused racetrack
called La Marinha at Boca do Inferno (the mouth of hell) near
Cascaes. In addition to his own rather portly self, Sanjurjo had,
according to Ansaldo, a large suitcase containing full-dress
uniforms and medals for his expected triumphal entry into
Madrid. Because of the wind, Ansaldo chose, rather recklessly,
to take off in the direction of some trees. The overweight
aircraft had insufficient lift to prevent the propeller, or possibly
the fixed undercarriage, clipping the tree tops. It crashed and
burst into flames. Sanjurjo died although his pilot escaped
virtually unhurt. Contrary to Ansaldo's version, it was later
claimed, somewhat implausibly, in Portugal that the crash was
the result of an anarchist bomb.

Whatever the cause it was to have a profound impact on the
course of the war and on the career of General Franco. It was
later asserted that Sanjurjo would have pushed for an early
negotiated settlement before the battle fronts hardened,
although this seems unlikely given Mola's rejection of Martínez
Barrio's peace overtures and was not something which would
have found a sympathetic response among the revolutionary
masses of the Republican zone. More concretely, however,
with Fanjul and Goded eliminated (they were executed in
August) the demise of Sanjurjo meant that only General Mola,
in his capacity as 'Director' of the rising, was even remotely in
a position to challenge Franco for the leadership of the rebels.
However, Franco was his senior officer – a major general while
Mola was only a brigadier general. Queipo de Llano was a
major general of greater seniority than Franco but his Republican connections ensured that most rebel officers found him
unacceptable as leader. In any case, the decisive factor in the

power stakes was Franco's control of the 47,000 well-armed and well-trained men of the Moroccan Army. The battle-hardened colonial army, consisting of the professionals of the Spanish Foreign Legion and Arab mercenaries of the *Regulares Indígenas* (native regulars), was to be the cornerstone of Nationalist success. Apart from Mola, the only other potential challenger to Franco's growing pre-eminence was the Falangist leader José Antonio Primo de Rivera, but he was in a Republican prison in Alicante.

In these early days of the war, the quietly ambitious Franco made winning the war his main priority. Nevertheless, neither he nor his subordinates lost any opportunity, in conversations with journalists and diplomats, of referring to 'his troops on the mainland'. Within a week of the uprising, in Foreign Ministries around Europe, the rebels were being referred to as the 'Francoists'. Nevertheless, the death of Sanjurjo served as a reminder that the *alzamiento* was far from the instant success that the conspirators had hoped for. The rebels controlled about a third of Spain in a huge block including Galicia, León, Old Castile, Aragón and part of Extremadura, together with isolated enclaves like Oviedo, Seville and Córdoba. They had the great wheat-growing areas, but the main centres of both heavy and light industry in Spain remained in Republican hands. The revolt had collapsed in Madrid, Barcelona, Valencia, Málaga and Bilbao. The insurgents therefore had quickly to evolve a plan of attack to conquer the rest of Spain. Since Madrid was seen as the hub of Republican resistance, their strategy was to take the form of drives on the Spanish capital by Mola's northern army and Franco's African forces. The rebels, however, confronted unexpected problems. The columns sent by Mola had not anticipated being halted at the Sierra north of Madrid by the untrained workers' militias from the capital. The northern army was also impeded by lack of arms and ammunition. Franco's army was paralysed by the problem of transport across the Strait of Gibraltar. Sea passage was impossible since the

Strait was controlled by Republican warships whose crews had mutinied against their rebel officers. In the face of these difficulties, the rebels turned to fellow rightists abroad for help.

On 19 July, Luis Bolín had set off for Rome to ask Mussolini for transport planes. While Bolín was still travelling, Franco had managed to convince both the Italian Consul in Tangier, Pier Filippo De Rossi del Lion Nero, and the military attaché, Major Giuseppe Luccardi, that he was a winner. Over the next week, they sent a stream of telegrams to Rome which together conveyed Franco's skilful appeal to Mussolini. On one of the first such requests for twelve bombers or civilian transport aircraft, Mussolini simply scribbled at the bottom of the telegram 'NO'. On a second desperate telegram from Franco, the Duce wrote only 'FILE'. Bolín arrived in Rome on 21 July and, the following day, armed with a letter of introduction from the exiled Spanish King, Alfonso XIII, he saw the recently appointed Italian Foreign Minister, Mussolini's son-in-law Count Galeazzo Ciano. Despite Ciano's initial sympathy, Bolín did not receive the assistance he had hoped for. At this stage, Mussolini was concerned by reports that the French were about to help their sister Popular Front in Spain. The Duce's principal foreign policy objective was to bring down the Anglo–French hegemony in the Mediterranean but he was too cautious to want to risk war with either prematurely.

However, Mussolini's interest in the Spanish situation and in the role of General Franco was being maintained by telegrams from Tangier. The pleas from Franco offered certain success, a flattering promise to emulate Italian fascism in Spain, future subservience and all at a bargain price. The Duce still hesitated. A prestigious delegation sent by General Mola saw Ciano on 25 July. It consisted of prominent monarchists including Antonio Goicoechea, the head of Renovación Española, who had visited Rome in March 1934. Recent research has shown that this delegation did not play the decisive role often attributed to it. In fact, Mussolini began gradually to incline towards support for Franco between 25 and 27 July as a result of several factors. He was much impressed by reports from Paris which showed that the French were pulling back from offering aid to the Republic. For a variety of reasons, he came to the conclusion that the British Establishment supported the Spanish military rebels. He and Ciano were convinced, for instance, that Portuguese support for the rebels would not have been possible without the tacit permission of the British. The clinching factor in favour of Franco was news which reached Rome on 27 July that the Kremlin was deeply embarrassed by events in Spain and had no intention of helping the Spanish Republic.

Accordingly, arrangements were made during the night of 27 July and the early morning of 28 July for help to be sent to Franco. A squadron of twelve Savoia-Marchetti S.81 bombers was assembled in Sardinia prior to flying to Spanish Morocco on the following day. Two merchant ships were also loaded, one with twelve FIAT C.R.32 fighters, accompanied by pilots and mechanics, and the other with ammunition and fuel for the aircraft. In the course of the war, 377 FIAT C.R.32s sent to Spain would carry out the bulk of rebel fighter operations. The squadron of Savoia-Marchetti S.81s, led by Lieutenant Ruggiero Bonomi, was briefly and symbolically escorted by General Guseppe Valle, chief of staff of the Italian Regia Aeronautica and effective Minister of Aviation. General Valle had instructed the crews that, once in Morocco, they should enlist in the Foreign Legion as a cover. However, strong headwinds saw them run low on fuel and three of the twelve came down, one in the sea and two in French Morocco, one of which made a forced landing and the other crashed. Although Ciano was to deny categorically any official Italian involvement, the crashes alerted the world to the fact that Mussolini was helping Franco.

Franco secured Italian aid by dint of his personal efforts to convince the Italian officials in Tangier of his prospects for success. He pursued a parallel process with Adolf Langenheim and Johannes Bernhardt, two German businessmen who were the local representatives in Spanish Morocco of the overseas section of the Nazi Party, the Ausland-Organization. In consequence, on 22 July he was able to send a further request for aid to Hitler via Bernhardt, through a complex chain involving a large cast of Ausland-Organization, Nazi Party and SS personages who greased the wheels to the Führer. Bernhardt made contact with Ernst Wilhelm Bohle of the Ausland-Organization, Bohle with Friedhelm Burbach, the head of the AO for Spain, Burbach with his old school chum Alfred Hess, Hess with his brother Rudolf, Hitler's lieutenant, and finally Rudolf Hess with the Führer himself, who was staying at Villa Wahnfried, the Wagner residence, while attending the annual Wagnerian festival in Bayreuth.

The Führer received Franco's emissaries on his return from a performance of *Siegfried*, conducted by Wilhelm Furt-wängler. They brought a terse letter from General Franco requesting rifles, anti-aircraft guns and fighters and transport planes. Hitler's initial reaction to the letter was one of doubt: noting the insurgents' lack of financial resources, he commented, 'That's no way to start a war.' However, after an interminable harangue about the Bolshevik threat, he decided to launch what he called *Unternehmen Feuerzauber* (Operation Magic Fire), apparently still under the influence of the opera that he had just attended – particularly, the 'Magic Fire' music which accompanies Siegfried's heroic passage through the flames to liberate Brünnhilde. Goering, after initially expressing doubts about the risks, became an enthusiastic supporter of the idea. There was no continuity between Hitler's spontaneous decision and long-standing contacts between the Nazi Ausland-Organization and Spanish rightists. These contacts were exposed when the Barcelona offices of the Ausland-Organization were ransacked by anarchists. The documents seized were published in 1937 as *The Nazi Conspiracy in Spain*. However, Operation Magic Fire was the real start of German intervention in the Spanish conflict.

Mussolini and Hitler thus turned a *coup d'état* going wrong into a bloody and prolonged civil war. Twenty Junkers Ju 52 transport aircraft joined the Italian bombers and so permitted Franco to launch the first significant military airlift in history. Throughout the war, another one hundred Junkers Ju 52s would arrive from Germany and play the principal role in rebel bombing operations. On 5 August, Franco gave further proof of his will to win when, against the advice of his closest collaborators, he decided to punch a hole in the Republican blockade with a small convoy of fishing boats carrying troops. The crossing of the Strait by the so-called 'convoy de la victoria' was covered by the recently arrived Savoia-Marchetti. He was banking on the inexperience of the Republican crews limiting their capacity to manoeuvre large warships. His success struck a significant psychological blow since the news that the ferocious Army of Africa was starting to land on the mainland spread fear throughout the Republican zone. In the first week of August, an air ferry of troops from Morocco to Seville began and within ten days 15,000 troops were transported across. By 6 August, there were troop ships crossing the Strait under Italian air cover. The Germans also sent some Heinkel fighters and volunteer pilots from the Luftwaffe. Within a week, the rebels were receiving regular supplies of ammunition and armaments from both Hitler and Mussolini.

The arrival of foreign aid now enabled the Nationalist rebels to undertake two campaigns which considerably improved their situation. General Mola began an attack on the Basque province of Guipúzcoa with the intention of capturing Irún and San Sebastián and cutting off the province from France. Irún was attacked daily by Italian bombers. Its poorly armed and untrained militia defenders fought bravely but were overwhelmed on 3 September. In the midst of the fighting, arms supplies to the defenders from France had been stopped. Claude Bowers, historian and American Ambassador to Spain, wrote, 'When the defenders of Irún fled across the border to

Hendaye, because of the exhaustion of ammunition, they found six freight cars loaded with ammunition from Catalonia sent across the southern border of France. This munition had been stopped by "Non-intervention" at the critical hour.' The defence of the entire north was thus placed in jeopardy.

Meanwhile, Franco's Army of Africa advanced northwards to Madrid, commanded in the field by Colonel Juan Yagüe, the hardened veteran of the Moroccan wars and the most influential military supporter of the Falange. Heading out of Seville, the African army took village after village leaving a horrific trail of slaughter in its wake. In one town after another, the occupying troops raped working-class women and looted their houses. Moorish soldiers and Legionaries selling radios, clocks, watches, jewellery and even items of furniture became a common sight along the way. On August 10, Yagüe's forces reached Mérida, an old Roman town near Cáceres, which had fallen at the beginning of the rising. Thus, the two halves of Nationalist Spain were joined. Yagüe's troops then turned back to capture Badajoz, the capital of Extremadura, near the Portuguese border. The decision to do so was Franco's and it delayed the advance of his African columns. Even though still in the hands of the Republic, Badajoz could not threaten Yagüe's troops from the rear and could have been picked off at the rebels' leisure. Franco was being cautious, consolidating the unification of the two segments of the rebel zone. After heavy artillery and bombing, the walls were breached and a savage repression began during which nearly two thousand people, including many innocent civilians, were shot. The streets ran with blood and the piles of corpses provided a sight of what the Portuguese journalist Mario Neves called 'desolation and dread'. Yagüe's men were sending a message to the citizens of Madrid as to what they could expect if they did not surrender before the arrival of the African columns.

The *Legionarios* and *Regulares*, and the Falangists who had accompanied them, unleashed yet another orgy of looting in shops and houses, most of which belonged to the very rightists who were being 'liberated'. Yet again, anything portable – jewellery and watches, radios and typewriters, clothing and bales of cloth – was carried off through streets strewn with corpses and drenched with blood. Jay Allen, an American journalist writing for the *Chicago Tribune*, arrived shortly afterwards. He saw Falangist patrols stop workmen in the streets and check if they had fought to defend the city by ripping open their shirts in order to see if their shoulders bore the telltale bruises of recoiling rifles. Those whose did were carted off to the bullring where Allen saw files of men, arms raised in the air, being brought in: 'At four o'clock in the morning they are turned out into the ring through the gate by which the initial parade of the bullfight enters. There machine guns await them. After the first night the blood was supposed to be palm deep on the far side of the lane. I don't doubt it. Eighteen hundred men – there were women, too – were mowed down there in some twelve hours. There is more blood than you would think in 1800 bodies.'

Although the massacre was also witnessed by French and Portuguese journalists, it was fiercely denied by the Nationalist press service. Speakers in the United States were paid to denigrate Jay Allen. Colonel Yagüe, however, laughed at such denials. He told another American journalist accompanying the Nationalist army, John T. Whitaker of the *New York Herald Tribune*, 'Of course we shot them. What do you expect? Was I supposed to take 4000 reds with me as my column advanced, racing against time? Was I supposed to turn them loose in my rear and let them make Badajoz red again?' Bodies were left for days in the streets to terrorize the population.

As African columns advanced, by September 1936, in southern Spain, there were more and more refugees in flight. As towns and villages along the road from Seville to Mérida were taken by the African columns, many workers and their families had already fled westwards. At the same time, some had fled northwards from the repression in Cádiz and Huelva. Others went southwards from Badajoz and Mérida after the capture of both cities. The result was a large number of desperate refugees in the western part of Badajoz, cut off to their east by the Seville–Mérida road and to the north by the Mérida–Badajoz road, to the south by the advancing columns and to their west by the Portuguese frontier. By mid-September, about eight thousand men, women, children and old people had collected in open country near the town of Valencia del Ventoso, where the local population did its best to feed them at rapidly organized soup kitchens.

On 18 September, faced with the prospect of being driven into Nationalist hands, the trade union and political leaders among them organized the refugees into columns to undertake a desperate forced march towards Republican lines. It was decided to divide this wretched human mass into two groups. The first contingent consisted of approximately two thousand people, the second of six thousand. The first had a dozen men armed with rifles and about one hundred with shotguns, the second about twice as many. These exiguous forces had to protect two lengthy columns of horses, mules and other domestic animals and carts containing whatever possessions the refugees had managed to grab from their homes before taking flight. Alongside walked young children, women – with babes in arms, others pregnant – and many old people.

Moving at different speeds, the groups spread out. Most successfully crossed the road from Seville to Mérida and some made it to Castuera in the Republican zone. However, the bulk of the refugees moved slowly, throwing up dust clouds which made it easy for rebel reconnaissance aircraft to pinpoint their position. The headquarters in Seville of General Gonzalo Queipo de Llano, the rebel commander in the south, were fully informed of the movements, the civilian composition of the columns and their sparse armament. Nevertheless, preparations were made to attack them as if they were well-equipped military units. They walked into an elaborate ambush. Machine guns were placed on the hills overlooking their route and, when the refugees were within range the rebels opened fire. Large numbers of refugees were killed during the fighting; more than two thousand were taken prisoner and transported to Llerena. Many hundreds scattered into the surrounding countryside. Families were separated, some never to meet again. Some wandered in the unfamiliar territory for weeks, only to be killed or captured by search parties of Civil Guard and mounted Falangists. A few made it through to the Republican zone. In Llerena, where the prisoners were held, a massacre took place, with prisoners machine-gunned in the bullring.

The terror which surrounded the advance of the Moors and the Legionnaires was one of the Nationalists' greatest weapons in the drive on Madrid. It explains why Franco's troops were initially so much more successful than those of Mola. The scratch Republican militia would fight desperately as long as they enjoyed the cover of buildings or trees, but even the rumoured threat of being outflanked by the Moors would send them fleeing, abandoning their weapons as they ran. An advance was now begun up the valley of the Tagus towards Toledo and Madrid. The last town of importance in their way, Talavera de la Reina, fell on 2 September. John Whitaker, recalled later, 'I never passed a night in Talavera without being awakened at dawn by the volleys of the firing squads. There seemed no end to the killing. They were shooting as many at the end of the second month as in my first days there. They averaged perhaps thirty a day. They were simple peasants and workers. It was sufficient to have carried a trade-union card, to have been a free-mason, to have voted for the Republic.'

It was not just the Army of Africa which executed the conquered population. On the island of Mallorca, where the rising had been initially successful, a Republican invasion took place in mid-August. However, with Italian help, the rebels had recaptured the island at the beginning of September. For the next four months, a terrible repression was carried out under the supervision of the head of the small Italian invasion force, the deranged Fascist Arconovaldo Bonacorsi, known as 'Conte Rossi'. Georges Bernanos, the French Catholic novelist, was horrified by what took place in Mallorca. He saw truckloads of men being carried to their deaths:

> The lorries were grey with road-dust, the men too were grey, sitting four by four, grey caps slung crosswise, hands spread over their tent-cloth trousers, patiently. They were kidnapping them every day from lost villages, at the time when they came in from the fields. They set off for their last journey, shirts still clinging to their shoulders with perspiration, arms still full of the day's toil, leaving the soup untouched on the table, and a woman, breathless, a minute too late, at the garden wall, with a little bundle of belongings hastily twisted into a bright new napkin.

On 21 September, Yagüe's army captured the town of Santa Olalla on the road to Madrid. John Whitaker was appalled by the mass execution of six hundred captured militiamen which took place in the main street of Santa Olalla: 'They were unloaded and herded together. They had the listless, exhausted, beaten look of troops who can no longer stand out against the pounding of German bombs.' As they clustered together, Moorish troops set up two machine guns and, firing short lazy bursts, mowed down the prisoners.

Of course, the atrocities were not confined to the rebel zone. At the beginning of the war, particularly, there were waves of assassinations of priests and suspected Fascist sympathizers. Militia units set themselves up to purge their towns of known rightists and especially churchmen. Churches and religious monuments were destroyed. More than six thousand priests and religious were estimated to have been murdered.

Falangists and members of yellow unions were favourite targets of the spontaneous *checas*, or pseudo-secret police units, set up by various left-wing groups, particularly the anarchists. In part, this was the consequence of the fact that the military coup had provoked a collapse of the structures of law and order that, in turn permitted an outburst of revolutionary optimism in the midst of which the prisons in the Republican zone had been emptied of common criminals. Some of the groups that carried out the grisly work of repression, such as the self-styled Brigadas de Investigación Criminal, under the leadership of the sinister Agapito García Atadell, were driven by greed and bloodlust rather than any political motivation.

The Republican repression also reflected the fact that the military coup itself provoked fear and suspicion of right-wingers known, or thought, to sympathize with the objectives of the rebels. On 23 August 1936, rumours of an escape bid by prisoners led to the murder of seventy prisoners in Madrid's Cárcel Modelo, including Azaña's friend Melquíadez Álvarez, as well as several ultra right-wingers. It was, in part, a reprisal for the news of the massacre of Badajoz that had been carried to the capital by terrified refugees from Extremadura. After the slaughter in the Cárcel Modelo, Giral wept. President Azaña was devastated, saying to his brother-in-law, Cipiriano Rivas Cherif, 'the bloodshed disgusts me. I can't go on. It will drown us all.'

If there was a difference in the killings in the two zones it lay in the fact that the Republican atrocities tended to be the work of uncontrollable elements at a time when the forces of order had rebelled, while those committed by the Nationalists were officially condoned by those who claimed to be fighting in the name of Christian civilization. Nationalist propaganda naturally tried to present the killings in the Republican zone as part of official government policy. This, it was claimed, was bolshevism in action. Indeed, there were many on the Republican side who were intensely aware of the damage being done to their cause by indiscriminate killing. The attacks on priests and the wanton destruction of churches were of considerable service to the rebels. Eventually, the popular perception of this unwitting cooperation with the Nationalist cause led to extensive measures being taken to put an end to the Republican repression. On 24 August 1936, the day after the killings in the Cárcel Modelo, *tribunales populares* (people's courts) were set up in an effort to plug the gap left by the collapse of the justice system and to stop the uncontrolled killings.

The rebels consolidated their position considerably throughout August and September. The African veteran and Carlist sympathizer Colonel (soon to be General) José Enrique Varela was connecting up Seville, Córdoba, Granada and Cádiz. For the Republicans, there were no such spectacular advances. In Oviedo, the outraged miners had returned and were besieging Colonel Aranda, who had taken their city by trickery. The rebel garrison of Toledo was still under siege in the fortress of the Alcázar. On 23 July, anarchist militia columns had set out from Barcelona in an attempt to recapture Zaragoza. Like Seville, the Aragónese capital was a CNT stronghold and had also fallen quickly to the rebels. It thus became a futile point of honour for the CNT to take Zaragoza. Its militia set off in a frenzy of enthusiasm, got within striking distance and then halted. In a small-scale parody of the Nationalist siege of Madrid, they were to remain bogged down for eighteen months. Only twelve miles away from their lines, they could see Zaragoza at night, 'a thin string of lights like the lighted portholes of a ship', wrote Orwell. Thus, for the Republic, the war was turning into an unending cycle of losses or, at best, stalemates. Moreover, Republican attempts to gain foreign aid had been less successful than those of the rebels.

On 19 July, Giral had sent a telegram appealing for assistance to Léon Blum, Prime Minister in the French Popular Front government. It read, 'SURPRISED BY

DANGEROUS MILITARY COUP STOP BEG YOU TO HELP US IMMEDIATELY WITH ARMS AND AEROPLANES STOP FRATERNALLY YOURS GIRAL.' A Nationalist victory would mean a third Fascist state on France's borders. This, in turn, would seriously damage France's international position because it would mean the loss of Spain as a land bridge for the incorporation into national defence of French colonial forces – 30 per cent of her total military capacity. Blum, encouraged by his Air Minister, Pierre Cot, decided initially in favour of sending help. Moreover, as leader of a sister regime himself, he was moved by Giral's appeal. However, his shaky coalition cabinet was split over the issue, with the Defence Minister Yvon Delbos especially hostile to the Spanish Popular Front. Pro-rebel staff in the Spanish Republican Embassy in Paris leaked news of Giral's request and Blum's response. This was seized upon by the rightist press, which was already raging about the threat to French investments from Spanish revolutionaries. Blum was now accused of risking war with Germany and Italy. As Blum wavered, he was made aware during a visit to London on 23 and 24 July that the British were against his sending aid. In the lobby of Claridges Hotel, Sir Anthony Eden warned him, 'Be prudent.' Ostensibly British caution arose from fears that French assistance to the Republic might provoke a widening of hostilities but it also reflected the fact that British commercial interests in Spain inclined the Baldwin government towards the Nationalists.

As the French rightist press went on the rampage, the Radical ministers in the Popular Front coalition declared that they would back Blum only if he got assurances of British approval. Faced by the storm in the press and fearful of losing British support, by 25 July Blum had drawn back from his earlier commitment to aid and proposed instead that the principal European powers agree not to intervene in Spain. In the light of French hesitation, José Giral wrote to the Soviet Ambassador in France appealing to him 'to notify your government about the desire and necessity, which our government is experiencing, for supplies of arms and ammunition of all categories, and in very great quantities, from your country'. It would be some weeks before the Russians would react favourably. On 6 August, however, the Spanish Republic did receive some aircraft from France, but not as many as were needed. Blum hoped vainly that by preventing the international participation which would favour the rebels he could give the Spanish Popular Front government a reasonable chance to suppress the military rising. Since Non-intervention was to be an empty farce, cynically exploited by Germany and Italy, and later by the Soviet Union, the Spanish Republic was in fact doomed.

In the heat of the Spanish summer of 1936, however, that was far from clear. Franco was occupied by the need to take a major decision concerning the route to be taken by the Army of Africa. By 21 September, his columns had reached Maqueda, an important crossroads where the road from the south divided to go north to Madrid or east to Toledo. The columns could either press on towards Madrid, or else turn to Toledo, to relieve the Nationalist garrison there, besieged by Republican militiamen. The one thousand Civil Guards and Falangists who had retreated into the Alcázar in the early days of the rising had taken with them as hostages approximately two hundred women and children, the families of known leftists. The militia had wasted vast amounts of time, energy and ammunition in trying to capture this strategically unimportant fortress. The resistance of the besieged garrison had thus become the great symbol of Nationalist heroism. Naturally, the existence, and later disappearance, of the hostages was entirely forgotten. A story about the siege propagated by both Spanish and English supporters of the Nationalist cause remained current throughout the Civil War and for many years after. It was claimed that, on 23 July, the Republican militia commander in charge of the siege had telephoned Colonel Moscardó, the garrison's senior officer, and told him that if he did not surrender, his son would be executed.

Moscardó reputedly told his son to commend his soul to God and to die bravely. Allegedly, he then heard over the telephone the shot which ended his son's life. The story is almost certainly apocryphal for a variety of reasons, not least because of its suspicious resemblance to the legend of Guzmán el Bueno who bravely sacrificed the life of his son during the thirteenth-century siege of Tarifa by the Moors. It fitted all too conveniently into the Nationalist effort to link the Civil War against other Spaniards with the *Reconquista* of Spain from the infidel. Moscardó's son was in fact shot on 23 August but not because of the threat supposedly made against his father. He was executed, along with other prisoners, as a reprisal for a Nationalist air raid on Toledo. It is odd that, if the telephone link with the Alcázar was functioning on 23 July, further contact was never attempted. Such details hardly mattered. The Alcázar and heroic anecdotes linked to it were of immense propaganda value to the Nationalists.

On 9 September, an officer was sent to Toledo with a sheet containing three conditions for the garrison's surrender: that Moscardó guarantee the lives of all those in the fortress; that all women, children and youths under the age of sixteen be released immediately; and that all others would be given a fair trial to ascertain their responsibilities. A major of the Republican General Staff, Vicente Rojo, volunteered in the hope of saving the hostages. He felt that he might succeed because he had spent a decade as a lecturer in tactics at the Infantry Academy in Toledo and many of those within the Alcázar were friends and ex-colleagues. He entered the fortress under a white flag of truce, was blindfolded and taken to see Colonel Moscardó who glanced at the list of conditions and, without hesitation, rejected them. This is what Rojo had predicted would happen, 'because, if I were in there, I wouldn't surrender'. While he was inside, Rojo received requests for help from some of the besieged officers. His friend Captain Luis Alamán gave him the details of where his wife and two daughters were hiding in Madrid and asked Rojo to help them. Moscardó asked him to get a priest to come to hear confessions and say mass. On his return to Madrid, Rojo made the arrangements for a priest to go into the Alcázar on the next day. He also found the family of Captain Alamán and gave them refuge in his own house situated, ironically, in Guzmán el Bueno 50.

The job of finding a priest fell to the artist Luis Quintanilla. After receiving a refusal from a canon of the Cathedral of Toledo, he found a priest in Madrid who was ready to undertake the mission. On entering the fortress, Father Enrique Vázquez Camarasa was blindfolded and taken, in total silence, before the gaunt figure of Moscardó. When Father Vázquez Camarasa enquired delicately about the situation of the many women and children, Moscardó replied brusquely that it was none of his business and that he could hear confessions, say mass and give communion but nothing more. He was then taken to a pestilent cellar where he said mass before a large number of emaciated women and crying children. Deeply shocked by this hellish agglomeration of living corpses, he tried to talk to the officers of the need to have pity on them. Moscardó never forgave him. After the fortress was finally relieved, following another seventeen days of privation, a press campaign was unleashed in the Nationalist zone against Vázquez Camarasa, who was denounced as 'the red priest'. At the end of the Civil War, he was obliged to go into exile, dying in Buenos Aires in 1946.

The decision about whether or not to relieve the Alcázar was closely related to the power struggle which had begun to unfold in the Nationalist camp. An obvious advantage enjoyed by the Nationalists over the Republic was their unity, symbolized by the establishment on 24 July of the Burgos Junta under the nominal presidency of General Miguel Cabanellas. However, despite the existence of the Burgos Junta, Nationalist

Spain was effectively divided into three power blocks. In the power stakes, one of them, the almost medieval fief of General Queipo de Llano in Seville, did not count. The others were dominated by General Mola in Burgos and by General Franco, moving onto Madrid with his Army of Africa. Although younger at only forty-three, Franco was the senior officer, a major general, while the forty-nine-year-old Mola was only a brigadier general. In addition, Franco's early hesitations had been more than redeemed by the spectacular way in which his troops had swept northwards. Furthermore, through General Alfredo Kindelán and Colonel Juan Yagüe, Franco had let both monarchists and Falangists think that he would further their aims. Kindelán organized a meeting of the ranking Nationalist generals on 21 September at an airfield near Salamanca. All the leading generals, except Cabanellas, agreed that a commander in chief should be nominated to replace Sanjurjo. There were not only sound military reasons for this but it would also facilitate ongoing negotiations for aid from Hitler and Mussolini.

At the Salamanca meeting, Franco was chosen as single commander. Later on the same day he decided to divert his advance against Madrid in order to relieve the Alcázar. By diverting his troops to Toledo, he lost an unrepeatable chance to sweep onto the Spanish capital before its defences were ready. Malicious tongues spread the rumour that he was trying to influence the power struggle with an emotional victory and a great journalistic coup. The delay certainly gave Madrid breathing space in which to organize its defences. It was, militarily speaking, an unnecessary gesture since an uninterrupted push on the capital would in itself have been likely to provoke the abandonment of the siege of the Alcázar. Whatever Franco's motives, his decision did him little harm. By 26 September, Nationalist forces were outside Toledo. The Jesuit chronicler Father Alberto Risco described the passage of the Moroccan *Regulares* of El Mizzian through the outlying districts: 'with the breath of God's vengeance on the blades of their machetes, they pursue, they destroy, they kill ... and intoxicated with blood, the column moves on'.

On the following day, the African columns entered the city and were able to liberate their besieged comrades. A bloodbath ensued. While it took place, the press was prevented from entering the city. What they saw, when they were allowed in on 29 September, shocked them deeply. John Whitaker reported, 'The men who commanded them never denied that the Moors killed the wounded in the Republican hospital housed in the hospice of San Juan Bautista on the outskirts of Toledo. They boasted of how grenades were thrown in among two hundred screaming and helpless men.' Whitaker was referring to the Tavera Hospital, housed in the hospice of San Juan Bautista on the outskirts of Toledo. Webb Miller of the United Press also reported on what happened there, claiming that one hundred men were shot where they lay. At the maternity hospital, more than twenty pregnant women were forced from their beds, loaded onto a truck and taken to the municipal cemetery where they were shot. The hostages had already been shot. Webb Miller reported seeing the beheaded corpses of *milicianos* in the streets. Father Risco describes men and women committing suicide to avoid capture by the African columns. Those who were taken in the house-to-house searches, he commented, 'had to die'. They were rounded up and taken to the various town squares where they were shot in groups of twenty or thirty. The nearly eight hundred people shot were buried in a mass common grave in the infamous lot 42 of the municipal cemetery.

Whatever the military efficacy of his action, the political benefits to Franco were enormous. In the middle ages, Toledo had been the first major Muslim city to be reconquered by Christian forces. Now, Franco was symbolically associating himself with the great warriors of the *Reconquista* and the Republican defenders with the infidel. The liberation was restaged on the following day for newsreel cameras. Cinema audiences throughout the world saw Franco touring the rubble of the Alcázar with a gaunt and bearded Moscardó. Franco thereby came to symbolize the Nationalist war effort. Both inside and outside Spain, he was emerging as the leader on whom rightist hopes were focused. With a little chicanery by General Kindelán and Franco's brother, Nicolás, the diminutive Galician general was able to press his advantage to become not only single commander but also Chief of State. He was soon being hailed as Caudillo (the nearest Spanish equivalent to Führer) by ecstatic Nationalist crowds.

In contrast to the joy in Nationalist ranks, the situation for the Republic looked bleak. San Sebastián had surrendered on 13 September because the Basques did not want to risk the destruction of their elegant city. Colonel Varela continued his march into Andalusia, advancing eastwards from Seville. It was an offensive of little military importance but one which clearly underlined the socio-economic motives of the Nationalist war effort. The Nationalist army was accompanied by the sons of *latifundistas* who had formed volunteer cavalry units. Throughout August, defended only by peasants armed with pitchforks, shotguns and old blunderbusses, village after village fell. Swarms of terrified refugees clutching their few possessions fled before the looting Moorish mercenaries and Carlist *requetés*. Cruel acts of revenge against the *braceros* who had collectivized the land were then often supervised by the very landowners who had fled in the spring. In the small town of Lora del Río in the province of Seville, where the only victim of the left had been the particularly despotic *cacique*, the Nationalists shot three hundred citizens as a reprisal. In nearby Palma del Río in the neighbouring province of Córdoba, Civil Guards and Falangists smashed down doors and drove out those villagers who had not managed to flee. Under the supervision of the local *cacique*, they were lined up and he marched along the lines picking out those who were to be shot in atonement for the killing of his bulls. More than two hundred were herded into the estate yard and machine-gunned down. Elsewhere, the prisoners underwent a rudimentary trial and were shot for crimes such as failing to go to mass, reading Rousseau and Kant, criticizing Hitler and Mussolini or admiring Roosevelt.

On 16 September, Varela's troops captured Ronda in the province of Málaga. Mola's forces were heading towards Madrid once again, and on 7 October the Army of Africa resumed its northward march. Supplies of arms had been collected and they were augmented by the arrival of Italian artillery and armoured cars. Already the Nationalists occupied most towns within fifteen miles of Madrid, so the capital was inundated with refugees and had major problems of food and water distribution. Now the militia columns were also falling back on Madrid in total disarray. Franco had announced to newspaper correspondents that he would take the capital on 20 October. Nationalist radio stations broadcast the news that Mola was preparing to enter Madrid's Puerta del Sol on a white horse. He even offered to meet the *Daily Express* correspondent there for coffee and wags set up a table to await him. Telegrams addressed to Franco congratulating him on his victory were piling up at the Telefónica building. There seemed little hope for Madrid. Then, on 15 October, the first arms began to arrive from the Soviet Union. The Kremlin's initial reluctance to help the Republic had given way to a determination that Germany and Italy should not be allowed to use Spain to alter the European balance of power. There would now be no easy victory for the Nationalists.

FIVE

'Behind the Gentleman's Agreement': The Great Powers Betray Spain

To a large extent the reaction of foreign powers dictated both the course and the outcome of the Civil War. That was hardly surprising since the Spanish conflict was only the latest and fiercest battle in a European civil war which had been raging intermittently for the previous twenty years. The Russian Revolution of October 1917 had provided a dream and an aspiration for the left throughout Europe. Ever since, the right in Europe had been trying both internationally and domestically to build barriers against both real and perceived revolutionary threats. The savage repression of revolution in Germany and Hungary after the First World War, the destruction of the left in Italy by Mussolini, the establishment of dictatorships in Spain and Portugal and even the defeat of the General Strike in Great Britain had been part of this process. The crushing of the German left in 1933 and of the Austrian in 1934 were its continuation. On a wider canvas, fear and suspicion of the Soviet Union had been a major determinant of the international diplomacy of the Western powers throughout the 1920s and even more so in the 1930s. The early tolerance shown to both Hitler and Mussolini in the international arena was a tacit sign of approval of their policies towards the left in general and towards communism in particular. Gradually, it became apparent that the corollary of the rearrangement of the domestic power balance in Italy and Germany in favour of capitalism was to be an effort to alter the balance of foreign competition by policies of imperialist aggression. Yet even then, the residual sympathy for fascism of the policy-makers of the Great Powers ensured that their first response would be simply to try to divert such ambitions in an anti-Communist, and therefore eastwards, direction.

Throughout the Republican period, the Spanish right and the left had both been intensely aware of their part in that wider European process. Gil Robles attended the Nuremberg rally and based much CEDA propaganda on techniques learned while on a study tour of Nazi Germany. Both Renovación Española and Carlists had close relations with the Italian Fascists. The Falange was actually subsidized by the Italian government. 'Accidentalists' and 'catastrophists' never tired of expressing admiration of and a determination to emulate both Hitler and Mussolini. The left was equally sensitive to European parallels, its daily press full of horror stories of fascism. German, Italian and Austrian exiles wrote dire warnings in Spanish leftist periodicals of the need to fight fascism. Accordingly, when the war broke out in Spain, both sides were aware of taking part in a conflict with wide international ramifications. Without German and Italian aircraft, the rebel generals would not have been able to transport their best troops for use on the Spanish mainland. Similarly, Soviet arms played a crucial part in the defence of Madrid. Indeed, in the last resort, the availability of international credit and arms supplies were of sufficiently crucial importance to make it seem that the outcome of the war was determined in the chancelleries of Europe rather than on the battlefields of Spain.

Nonetheless, the official international line on the Spanish crisis was one of Non-intervention. This institutionalized hypocrisy originated in a suggestion by the French. At first in favour of aiding the Republic, the French premier Léon Blum had been virtually told by the British that if, as a result of their assistance to Spain, war resulted (presumably with Germany or Italy) then Britain would not help her. It was hoped that if Non-intervention could be imposed, the Spanish war would peter out for lack of arms and ammunition. None of the great powers had a policy ready when the Spanish crisis broke on them in the summer of 1936. Each responded to Non-intervention in the way that best agreed with the policy it was already following: the Fascist powers with instinctive aggression, the democracies with caution. This was particularly the case with Britain. By tradition and as a reaction against the horrors of the First World War, the British were determined to avoid a general war. The Spanish Republicans, however, found it hard to believe that this could outweigh an awareness of the need to avoid strengthening the position of Nazi Germany. After the Civil War had come to an end, the Republican Minister of Foreign Affairs in both the Largo Caballero and Negrín cabinets, the Socialist Julio Alvarez del Vayo, wrote, 'Not a day passed until almost the end, when we did not have fresh reasons to hope that the Western democracies would come to their senses and restore us our rights to buy from them. And always our hopes proved illusory.' The British, however, saw the Spanish conflict in the context of a wider foreign policy which involved issues far more complex than the Republic's rights to buy arms. Like the French, the British government was committed at all costs to diminishing the risks of a European conflagration. In addition, an implicit goal of British appeasement was to persuade the Germans that they should look to the East if they wished to expand. Hence the willing sacrifice of Austria and Czechoslovakia; hence the attempts by Chamberlain to extricate Britain from her agreement to go to Poland's aid in the event of attack. This was the logical concomitant of British policy since 1935, during which period a blind eye had been turned to Germany's open rearmament and to the Italian invasion of Abyssinia, a member state of the League of Nations.

Public opinion in Britain was overwhelmingly on the side

of the Spanish Republic. Even as late as January 1939, when defeat was certain, 70 per cent of those polled considered the Republic to be the legitimate government. However, among the small proportion of those who supported Franco, never more than 14 per cent, and often lower, were those who would make the crucial decisions. Where the Spanish war was concerned, Conservative decision-makers tended to let their class prejudices prevail over the strategic interests of Great Britain. The journalist Henry Buckley was told by a British diplomat, 'the essential thing to remember in the case of Spain is that it is a civil conflict and that it is very necessary that we stand by our class'. This was obvious from the first. On 28 July 1936, Count Galeazzo Ciano made it clear to Edward Ingram, the British chargé d'affaires in Rome, that he believed Portugal's full and open support for the Spanish military rebels would simply not be possible without British encouragement. Ingram replied that 'the Foreign Office had understood the Italian initiative in its precise significance'.

That British support for the rebels was widely taken for granted on the European right was revealed on the very next day when Franco himself, in an interview published in the Toulouse daily *La Dépêche*, declared, 'The question is not just a national but an international one. Certainly, Great Britain, Germany and Italy should view our plans with sympathy.' Franco would never admit in public that 'perfidious Albion' made an enormous contribution to his eventual success. However, as early as 10 August the hastily created Ministry of State in Burgos reported to the Junta de Defensa Nacional, 'Overall, the English favour us, as can be appreciated by the forthright, open and admirable assistance given us by Portugal, a country tied to the British to such an extent that it must be admitted that Oliveira Salazar has the fullest approval of the British Government in aiding us on the scale that he does.' In early August, Juan de la Cierva, the Spanish inventor of the autogyro and the man who had helped arrange Franco's flight from the Canary Islands to Morocco, had already told the Italian chargé in London, Leonardo Vitetti, that he had bought all the aircraft available on the free market in Britain and was about to send them to Mola. De la Cierva said that 'the British authorities had given him every facility even though they knew only too well that the aircraft were destined for the Spanish rebels'.

The British were inclined by their considerable commercial interests in Spain, with substantial investments in mines, sherry, textiles, olive oil and cork, to be anything but sympathetic to the Republic. The business community inevitably tended towards the Nationalist side since it was believed that the anarchists and other Spanish revolutionaries were liable to seize and collectivize British holdings.

Equally, members of the British government and the diplomatic corps, for reasons of class and education, sympathized with the anti-revolutionary aims of the Nationalists as they did with those of Hitler and Mussolini. It was commonplace for Spanish aristocrats and the scions of the main sherry exporting families to be educated at English Catholic public schools such as Beaumont, Downside, Ampleforth and Stonyhurst. They spoke the same language as the upper-class Englishmen with whom they pleaded Franco's cause. There was thus a nexus of upper-class contacts and friendship which intensified the underlying hostility of British Conservatives to the Spanish Republic. Added to the determination to avoid war, these factors made the adoption of a policy of Non-intervention a logical step. Above all, it would serve to neutralize and localize the Spanish war. But it had a further advantage for the British Conservatives. Non-intervention treated both sides in the Civil War as equally reprehensible, although one was the legal government and the other a group of rebellious generals. Both sides were denied aid, although the Republic had a right under international law to buy arms and supplies. By denying the Republic this right, Non-intervention absolved the British from any fear that they might be helping the forces of revolution.

This fear was stoked by the spine-chilling reports of Norman King, the British Consul in Barcelona, which were printed and distributed to cabinet members in London. King, who believed Spaniards to be 'a bloodthirsty race', announced on 29 July that, if the military rebellion were defeated, 'Spain will be plunged into the chaos of some form of bolshevism and acts of savage brutality can be expected'. Sir Henry Chilton, the British Ambassador in Spain in 1936, was openly and unremittingly hostile to the government to which he was accredited. The American Ambassador, Claude Bowers, wrote that Chilton 'was violently against the loyalists from the first day, and he habitually called them "reds"'. From his splendid French residence in St Jean de Luz, where he remained until his retirement in late 1937, Chilton maintained cordial relations with the military rebels on the other side of the border. Day-to-day contact with the Republican government was left in the hands of a chargé d'affaires, George Ogilvie Forbes, first in Madrid and later in Valencia.

At the end of November 1937, the British government appointed an official representative to Nationalist Spain in the person of Sir Robert Hodgson. Married to a ferociously anti-Communist White Russian, he had been British representative to Admiral Kolchak's 'All Russian Government' in Omsk during the Russian Civil War, and thereby developed a loathing of the Communists. As far as Hodgson and his wife were concerned, the Spanish Civil War was an opportunity to reverse the victory of the Bolsheviks. He made no secret of his sympathy for the Nationalist view that the Republicans were 'Communist-controlled hordes, inspired by the Comintern and supported by the human scum, largely alien, from which the Republican forces are recruited'. His despatches from Burgos referred in lyrical terms to the Nationalists. After his first interview with Franco, for instance, he reported to the Foreign Office on the Caudillo's 'very attractive personality' and the 'marked kindliness of expression' emanating from his eyes. In his memoirs, Hodgson referred proudly to 'the cause', by which he meant the Nationalist war effort.

It is not the case, though, that in Britain either the Conservative or the Labour Party was undivided on the issue of Spain. Atrocity stories about sex-crazed, looting Spanish anarchists were spread by British Catholic supporters of the Nationalists. Through the Right Book Club and the conservative press, they had considerable impact on the middle classes. Even without their efforts, the majority of Conservatives accepted Chamberlain's policy of appeasement at virtually any price. Nevertheless, he was opposed by a significant minority. Anthony Eden, for instance, came increasingly to distrust Italian motives. Churchill believed that Britain should remain neutral. However, he gradually altered his stance as he brooded on the scale of German and Italian intervention.

Writing on the Spanish crisis in the *Evening Standard* on 10 August 1936, Churchill commented:

> It is of the utmost consequence that France and Britain should act together in observing the strictest neutrality themselves and endeavouring to induce it in others. Even if Russian money is thrown in on the one side, or Italian and German encouragement is given to the other, the safety of France and England requires absolute neutrality and non-intervention by them. French partisanship for the Spanish Communists, or British partisanship for the Spanish rebels, might injure profoundly the bonds which unite the British Empire and the French Republic. This Spanish welter is not the business of either of us. Neither of these Spanish factions expresses our conception of civilization.

However, in the course of 1938, representations from the Republican Ambassador, Pablo de Azcárate, and from the pro-Republican Conservative Duchess of Atholl, eventually provoked him into a rethink.

On 16 April 1938, Chamberlain signed the Anglo–Italian Pact. Azcárate protested that the deal permitted the Italians to keep troops in Spain, despite the Non-Intervention Agreement. Churchill wrote to Eden: 'A complete triumph for Mussolini, who gains our cordial acceptance for his fortification of the Mediterranean against us, for his conquest of Abyssinia, and for his violence in Spain.' Fearing that Francoist Spain might become an Axis satellite, Churchill now held an amicable conversation with Azcárate, expressing sympathy for the Republic, after dinner at the Soviet Embassy. Churchill told a Buenos Aires newspaper: 'Franco has all the right on his side, because he loves his country. Also Franco is defending Europe against the Communist danger – if you wish to put it in those terms. But I – I am English, and I prefer the triumph of the wrong cause. I prefer that the other side wins because Franco would be an upset to British interests.' Churchill had effectively concluded that Britain would be risking its Great Power status in the Mediterranean if it helped create a Fascist Spain.

In the Labour Party division rested on less imperialistic considerations. Sympathy for Spanish democracy was balanced by much hostility, particularly amongst trade unionists, to the Communists, who had only recently been instructed by the Comintern to abandon their denunciation of reformist social democratic parties as 'social fascists'. The fiercely anti-Communist leader of the powerful Transport and General Workers' Union, Ernest Bevin, argued that in any case Britain was not in a position to help Spain. On the other hand, leaders like Aneurin Bevan and Stafford Cripps expressed public support for the Republic although in general they remained opposed to rearmament. Clement Attlee, leader of the Parliamentary Labour Party, publicly pledged 'all practicable support to our Spanish comrades' four days after the military rebellion. The contradictions in Labour's position were exploited by

Bevin and led to their defeat when they attempted at the 1936 Party Conference in Edinburgh to commit the party to supporting the Republic. Yet at that Conference delegates claiming to represent the opinion of ordinary party members managed to express support for the Republic: 'Our hearts and sympathies are with them in their struggle.'

At an individual level, rank-and-file members of the Labour Party worked hard to help Spain in many ways, including donations of money and service in the International Brigades. Official Labour Party policy was opposed to members joining the International Brigades and, until 1937, supported the National government in adhering to the Non-Intervention Agreement. Nevertheless, Labour Party members, including Jack Jones, a Labour councillor in Liverpool, actively participated in the recruitment of volunteers for the International Brigades. Several Labour councillors would fight in Spain. Once there, Jack Jones, who would later himself be leader of the Transport and General Workers' Union, became political commissar of the Major Attlee Company, one of the very few non-Communist commissars. Eventually, in October 1937, the party formally rejected Non-intervention and, in December 1937, Attlee visited Spain to demonstrate his personal admiration for the Brigades.

Non-intervention was equally convenient for the French. Although Léon Blum was anxious to help the Spanish Republic, even he could see positive benefits in the policy of Non-intervention. Certainly he had to contend with intense pressure against aid for Spain, both from Britain and from within his own country. Amongst those opposed to any French involvement in the Spanish conflict were the French President, Radical Party ministers in Blum's Popular Front cabinet and the combined forces of the French right. The British attitude was also crucial. Since 1918, the French had been haunted by the memory of their casualties in the First World War and hence obsessed with an unending quest for security. When the

Nazi–Polish non-aggression pact broke the French network of alliances in Eastern Europe, France was forced to rely almost totally on British support. Dread of losing this support was enough to incline France towards Non-intervention once the official British position became clear. The Italians had reliable reports that British support for French proposals for Non-intervention was based entirely on the belief that it was a useful device for preventing French help to the Spanish Republic. It is unlikely that Blum was unaware of this. In any case, Blum's domestic problems precluded international tight-rope walking. Large sections of French society sympathized with the Spanish Nationalists at the same time as they bitterly resented Blum's Popular Front government. Caught between this right-wing opposition and a rash of left-wing strikes and riots, the French government understandably took the line of least resistance in foreign affairs. Fears of provoking civil war in France played a not inconsiderable role in Blum's decision to adopt Non-intervention. Had he intervened on the side of the Spanish Popular Front, he believed that there would have been a Fascist rising in France with the consequence that 'Spain could not have been saved, but France would have gone Fascist'.

The United States was too wrapped up in its New Deal isolationism to be overly preoccupied by what was happening in Spain. American strategic interests in Spain were insignificant. However, US investments in Spain amounted to eighty million dollars in 1936. That part of politically influential opinion which followed events in Europe was bitterly divided over Spain. Liberal, Protestant and left-wing groups favoured the Republic. The right, business and the bulk of the Catholic Church supported the rebels. The Hearst press chain was unequivocally behind Franco. A typical headline carried by its paper the *Journal* on 3 August 1936 declared, 'Red Madrid Ruled By Trotsky'. President Roosevelt bowed to the power of the rightist-Catholic lobby and on 7 August his acting

Secretary of State, William Phillips, announced that the United States would 'scrupulously refrain from any interference whatsoever in the unfortunate Spanish situation'. Seven days later, speaking at Chautauqua in New York State, the President himself presented the formula of a 'moral embargo' on arms sales to Spain as a way of maintaining international peace.

Without taking specific legislative action, the US government was effectively extending the 1935 Neutrality Act. The liberal weekly *The Nation* protested that this meant taking sides against the Republic. The embargo certainly hurt Franco far less than it did the Republic. The pro-Nazi President of the Texaco oil company, Thorkild Rieber, for instance, risked six million dollars by supplying the Nationalists with a substantial proportion of their oil needs on credit. He was penalized by a small fine. The Glenn A. Martin Aircraft Corporation of Baltimore and Robert Cuse, a businessman specializing in aircraft parts, however, were refused export licences for the shipment of long-standing orders to the Spanish Republic. Protestants were appalled at the Spanish Nationalists' hostility to democracy and freedom of worship. They filled the press with letters expressing disquiet at the use of religious arguments to justify atrocities. Claude Bowers bombarded the President with detailed letters urging him to help the Republic. Roosevelt replied nonchalantly, 'Do write me some more marvellous letters like that last one.' In 1939, when Bowers returned to Washington, Roosevelt told him, 'We have made a mistake; you have been right all along.' The distinguished American diplomat Sumner Welles, Under-Secretary of State from 1937 to 1943, wrote later that, 'of all our blind isolationist policies, the most disastrous was our attitude on the Spanish Civil War'.

The Soviet Union's attitude was complex and rather more subtle. Although diplomatic relations with Spain had been established on 27–28 July 1933, the centre-right governments in power from late 1933 to early 1936 had not wished to implement the agreement. Accordingly, Moscow was unable to name a diplomatic representative until 29 August 1936, more than six weeks after the military uprising. The USSR was extremely slow to come to the aid of the Spanish Republic and, even when it did, the guiding principle behind its policy could hardly have been further removed from the goal of spreading revolution. In May 1934, the Comintern had given the signal for a radical change in Communist Party tactics. No longer were social democratic parties in Europe to be excoriated as 'social fascist'. Instead, in order to facilitate the forging of alliances between the Soviet Union and the Western bourgeois states, Communist parties were to propose joint action with Socialist parties. This represented a fundamental shift in Comintern tactics, bringing to an end ten years of isolationist and sectarian rigidity. The reasons for the shift lay in Stalin's altered assessment of the foreign policy interests of the Soviet Union. The rise of fascism in Italy and even more so of Nazism in Germany had convinced the Soviet leader of the need to seek alliances with the democratic capitalist states, France and Britain. Thus, *L'Humanité*, the French Communist newspaper, called for a united front with the French Socialists. The corollary of this was a diplomatic effort to revive the traditional anti-German defensive alliance between Russia and France. On 2 May 1935, a Franco–Soviet Pact of Mutual Assistance was signed in Paris.

Shortly after the signing of this pact, the Seventh Congress of the Comintern opened in Moscow, and the policy of the 'People's Front' was officially adopted. The main concern of the Comintern Congress was to formulate a strategy to safeguard the Soviet Union from external attack. The central slogan chosen for the Communist parties was 'The fight for peace and for the defence of the USSR'. The Italian Communist leader Palmiro Togliatti, who was to be a Comintern representative in Spain during the Civil War, spelt things out clearly during the Congress when he stated, 'For us it is absolutely indisputable that there is complete identity of aim between the peace policy of the Soviet Union and the policy of the working class and the Communist parties of the capitalist countries. There is not, and cannot be, any doubt in our ranks on this score. We not only defend the Soviet Union in general. We defend concretely its whole policy and each of its acts.'

Comintern policy, like that of the Russian Foreign Ministry, was a response to Hitler's well-advertised designs on Soviet territory. Defence of Russian territory would take precedence over the encouragement of revolution. When intervention took place in Spain, it was to be made starkly clear that the agents of the Comintern were not the general staff of world revolution but the frontier guards of the Soviet Union.

Stalin was concerned above all with collective security, co-operation with Britain and France against the German threat. Conscious of the Soviet Union's unpreparedness for war, not least because of his own purges of the officer corps of the Red Army, he had been virtually silent on the new Nazi regime. Indeed, he had gone to great lengths to ensure that Russia would remain for as long as possible on the same terms with the Third Reich as with Weimar Germany. The Spanish conflict thus came as a profound embarrassment to Stalin. There was animated debate in the Comintern about how to react. Enthusiastic revolutionaries were all for aiding the Spanish Republic, but Stalin crucially sided with the more thoughtful moderates. Accordingly, it was decided to do nothing beyond platonic declarations of support for the Spanish Republic. By 29 July, when Dolores Ibárruri, the Spanish Communist parliamentary deputy, appealed to the countries of the world to save Spanish democracy, there had been no overt reaction from the Soviet Union. Stalin's dilemma was obvious. On the one hand he could not stand back and let the Spanish Republic go under, for another Fascist state on the borders of France would so strengthen the French right and weaken the left as to increase the probability of the Franco–Soviet Pact being abrogated.

Even if that did not happen, the pact would be devalued by the reduction in French military power as a consequence of the loss of the Spanish route for the colonial army back to metropolitan France. On the other hand, victory for the Spanish left could lead to an all-out social revolution in the Iberian peninsula, which would alienate the conservative Western powers being courted by the Soviet Union. Stalin dreaded the prospect of the democracies being driven to line up with the Fascist dictators against Soviet Spain and Soviet Russia.

Stalin started his gradual and hesitant move away from his original decision to do nothing in Spain as a result of the news that two of the Italian bombers en route to Spanish Morocco had crash-landed in French North Africa. The initial Soviet reaction to this evidence of Fascist intervention in Spain was cautious. On 3 August, a crowd of 150,000 people gathered in Red Square in Moscow to express solidarity with the Spanish Republic. Collections for Spain were held in Soviet factories and Russian workers allegedly voted unanimously to donate 0.5 per cent of their salaries to help the Republic. On 18 September, the first shipment of food thus purchased left Russia for Spain. These were clear indications of official policy. Although Stalin was never especially sensitive to the views of the workers of other countries, he was aware that it would be immensely damaging in propaganda terms if the Soviet Union, the 'First Workers' State', failed to come to the aid of a beleaguered Popular Front government. Indeed, on the evening of 3 August, a senior Soviet official had told the American chargé d'affaires in Moscow that, despite doubts over the wisdom of being seen to help the Spanish Republic, the Kremlin had decided that 'if the Soviet Union is to continue to maintain hegemony over the international revolutionary movement, it must not hesitate in periods of crisis to assume the leadership of that movement'. More importantly, Stalin was aware that untrammelled success for the Nationalists in Spain would, in turn, strengthen the international positions of Hitler and Mussolini to the detriment of those of France and, by extension, of Stalin.

Stalin's policy towards the Spanish conflict was therefore conditioned by the need to resolve an appalling dilemma. He had to attain a balance whereby Soviet aid to Spain would prevent a major alteration to the international balance of power in favour of Germany yet at the same time not provoke the conservative reflexes of Stanley Baldwin or the French right. Essentially, he needed to prevent the Republic being defeated, but he also wished to avoid an outright victory for the Spanish revolutionary left. Thus, his reaction to the proposal of Non-intervention was one of unalloyed relief and, on 22 August, the Soviet Union signed the agreement. It seemed to free him from the decision of whether to abandon the Spanish left or risk an international war for which the Soviet Union was not ready. In the same spirit, in response to wildly optimistic reports from Madrid, the Comintern had already instructed the Spanish Communist Party to support the Republican government and to do nothing to take advantage of the revolutionary possibilities of the breakdown of order. Then, on 28 August, the Soviet Union officially declared that it would not export arms to the Spanish Republic.

At the beginning of the war, Russia had no Ambassador in Spain. It was not until the end of August that a mission was sent, including a veteran diplomat, Marcel Rosenberg, as Ambassador, and a military mission led by General Ian Pavlovich Berzin. The *Realpolitik* that informed the Soviet caution was explained with startling clarity in the British Communist newspaper the *Daily Worker* on 9 September:

Had the Soviet Union not agreed to the French proposal for neutrality, it would have very seriously embarrassed the [French] Government, and considerably assisted fascists in France and England, as well as the governments of Germany and Italy, in their campaign against the Spanish people . . . If the Soviet Government took any step which added further fuel to the present inflammable situation in Europe, it would be welcomed by the Fascists of all countries and would split the democratic forces, thus directly preparing the way for so-called 'preventive warfare' against Bolshevism as represented by the USSR.

However, already in August a trickle of Soviet military personnel, including air force pilots, had journeyed to Spain. Then, as September progressed, Stalin became increasingly alarmed by unmistakable evidence that the Non-Intervention Agreement was doing nothing to prevent German, Italian and Portuguese aid to Franco. The consequence was, as Comintern reports to Moscow were now making clear, the probable defeat of the Spanish Republic and, with it, a significant change in the European balance of power to the detriment of the Soviet Union. There were Russian warnings aplenty to Great Britain, France and the other members of the Non-intervention Committee that Moscow might be obliged to breach the agreement if violations by Germany and Italy were ignored. Arms supplies to Spain began only once it became unavoidably clear that Germany and Italy were merely using Non-intervention as a convenient front for their aid to the Nationalists. By 14 September, Stalin appointed a committee to investigate the feasibility of sending full-scale military assistance to Spain, including aircraft and tanks. Its conclusions were approved by the Politburo on 29 September. The first Soviet ship containing heavy weaponry, the *Komsomol*, left Odessa on 7 October and docked in Cartagena on 15 October. Subsequent shipments throughout October and November would give the Republic short-lived air superiority during the battle for Madrid.

Stalin had decided to supply enough arms to keep the Republic alive, while instructing his agents in Spain to make every effort to ensure that the revolutionary aspects of the struggle were silenced. Accordingly, aid for Spain came with a hidden condition attached which was effectively that the Spanish proletariat should go no further than was acceptable to French and British policy-makers. Stalin helped the Spanish Republic not in order to hasten its victory but rather to prolong its existence sufficiently to keep Hitler bogged down in an expensive venture. The most that Stalin wished for the Republic was that there might be a compromise solution acceptable to the Western democracies. He was less concerned about the fate of the Spanish people than that his cooperation with the democracies in the fight against Fascist aggression should be sealed by an ostentatious Soviet readiness to keep social revolution in check. Thus, through an irony of history, the revolutionary elements in the Republican zone – the anarchists and the quasi-Trotskyists of the POUM – would face the most determined opposition not from the Fascist forces of Franco, but from the Moscow-dominated Communists.

Thanks to the research of the Spanish historian Ángel Viñas, there exists little doubt with regard to the reasons behind Nazi involvement in the Spanish Civil War. German support to the rebel generals came about as a result of a deliberate decision by Hitler, who saw aid to Franco as serving essential foreign policy interests of the Third Reich. This remained the case throughout the duration of the war. The Führer saw in the Spanish conflict an opportunity to push appeasement to its limits and thereby undermine Anglo–French hegemony of international relations. Hitler was well aware of British fears of the Communist threat and quite consciously played on these. In the words of the then French Ambassador in Berlin, André François-Poncet:

> Rarely have I seen so strong an effort made by the National Socialist Government to influence Great Britain. It believes that the events in Spain will impress English conservatives and, by opening their eyes to the reality of the Bolshevik peril and the dangers of an over

close friendship with an already contaminated France, will detach them from our country. It is lavishing attentions upon Sir Robert Vansittart who is in Berlin on a visit. Its hope that circumstances are working for an Anglo–German rapprochement keeps on growing.

Hitler himself talked to Count Ciano about what he referred to as 'the tactical field' of anti-Bolshevism, by which he meant that Axis intervention in Spain should be presented to the democracies as disinterested anti-Communism. Nonetheless, Hitler also had a genuine and extreme ideological antipathy towards Bolshevism and the Soviet Union. This was reflected in the attempts by the Nazis to argue that the anarchy and disorder associated with the Spanish conflict had in fact been planned by the Kremlin, despite the obvious fact that the Soviet Union had been taken by surprise by the events in Spain.

However, like that of the Soviet Union, the German response to the Spanish Civil War was determined by its broad strategic assessment of the international situation. Hitler was as fearful of the idea of a Communist Spain as Stalin was of the idea of a Fascist Spain. The reason for this was that, for both Germany and the Soviet Union, the position of France in the mid-1930s was crucial, and the French situation was seen as intimately related to events in Spain. As the British Ambassador in Moscow, Viscount Chilston, commented, 'any danger to France is a danger to the Soviet Union'. In Hitler's calculation, a victory for the Popular Front forces in Spain would go some way towards creating a leftist bloc in Europe, which would stand in the way of the Third Reich's plans for imperialist expansion into Central and Eastern Europe. The quest for *Lebensraum* was dependent on a prior defeat of France and that defeat would be endangered if the Spanish Popular Front were not first eliminated.

Suggestions that Hitler's intervention in Spain was motivated by the possibilities of economic advantage have been overplayed. Although Spain's mineral resources were tempting to a Germany bent on rearmament, this was not the main initial attraction for Hitler. Spanish iron ore had constituted only 6.6 per cent of German consumption in 1935. Spanish pyrites made up 46 per cent of total German pyrites imports. However, in neither case was there any threat to supplies through normal channels. Indeed, even at the time of the Third Reich's great foreign exchange crisis in early 1936, imports of Spanish ores were unaffected given Germany's extremely favourable balance of trade with Spain. Rather, the German position was in some ways the mirror image of that of the Soviet Union. Hitler wished to avoid the creation of a 'Soviet Spain', but nor was he yet ready to provoke a European conflict through excessive involvement in Spanish affairs. Just as Stalin wanted a Republican victory without any revolutionary overtones, so Hitler supported a victory for the rebel forces, but did not want to alarm or antagonize the Western powers.

Instead, he used the Spanish conflict as a form of preparation for the struggle in Europe which would inevitably break out in due course. This much was admitted by Hermann Goering, Commissioner for Air during the Third Reich, at the Nuremberg trials:

> When the civil war broke out in Spain, Franco sent a call for help to Germany and asked for support, particularly in the air. One should not forget that Franco with his troops was stationed in Africa and that he could not get the troops across, as the fleet was in the hands of the Communists ... The decisive factor was, first of all, to get his troops over to Spain. The Führer thought the matter over. I urged him to give support under all circumstances, firstly, in order to prevent the further spread of communism in that theatre and, secondly, to test my young Luftwaffe at this opportunity in this or that technical respect. With the permission of the Führer, I sent

a large part of my transport fleet and a number of experi-
mental fighter units, bombers, and anti-aircraft guns; and
in that way I had an opportunity to ascertain, under
combat conditions, whether the material was equal to the
task. In order that the personnel, too, might gather a
certain amount of experience, I saw to it that there was a
continuous flow, that is, that new people were constantly
being sent and others recalled.

Goering had clearly forgotten that nine years before he had
been initially less enthusiastic to help Franco than Hitler.
Nonetheless, once the decision was taken, his commitment
to using Spain as a testing ground was unquestionable. The
volunteer members of the crack Condor Legion, private soldiers as well as officers, were paid executive salaries to fight in
Spain. Hitler was also soon to be attracted by the opportunities
offered by aid to Franco in terms of securing Germany's long-
term needs in strategic raw materials.

Italy was the one European power whose policy most lacked
consistency and rationality. Her geographical position and lack
of strategic raw materials dictated that she follow a modest and
realistic policy of alignment with England, the dominant naval
power in the Mediterranean. Mussolini's policy, however, was
always dominated by the restless desire to redress the perceived
injustices of the Versailles peace settlement. By striking out at
random, whether in Corfu or Abyssinia, Mussolini hoped 'to
make Italy great, respected and feared'. A desire for a dynamic
restructuring of the world order in favour of fascism led
eventually to alignment with Nazi Germany and the Rome–
Berlin Axis. Mussolini took immensely seriously his position
as the founder of fascism. The caution that he had displayed
in the first ten days of the Spanish Civil War was short-lived.
Given that the Spanish war was widely seen as the beginning
of a world counter-offensive against fascism, he was unable
to resist the urge to intervene. The defeat of the Spanish

Nationalists would be a defeat for what he saw as a sister movement and the Duce could not contemplate that, not least because of the deferential way in which Franco had placed himself under his protection. In any case, Mussolini was always looking for an arena in which to flex the muscles of his armed forces. To a certain extent, Spain was seen by the Italians, as by the Germans, as a possible testing ground for men and equipment. More crucially, however, Mussolini believed that immersion in blood and violence was the only way to forge the spirit of the new Fascist man.

From the mid-1920s, the Duce had declared that Italian men would be educated in brutal virility and pitiless xeno-phobia. At the same time, Italian women would be urged to produce more male children to be the warriors who would make up the armies of the future. The goal was a nation of sixty million Italians who 'will make the weight of their numbers and their strength felt in the history of the world'. What this meant, he declared early on, was to put an end to 'the blackmail of grain and coal' and 'to collaborate in demolishing the British empire'. In 1925, he had confided to the diplomat Salvatore Contarini that 'Gibraltar, Malta, Suez and Cyprus represent a chain that permits England to encircle, to imprison Italy in the Mediterranean'. Over the next few years, the need to smash the bars of the prison was to become one of Mussolini's most constant (albeit private) refrains. Nevertheless, the Duce was torn between a desire to destroy the British and curry favour with them.

Accordingly, as Mussolini hesitated over whether to respond favourably to Franco's request for aid, he was greatly comforted by the fact that all the feedback from London reinforced his assumption that the British would do nothing to stand in his way. He was seemingly being offered the best of both worlds – the British would stand aside while, in Spain, he undermined their Mediterranean hegemony. Even as the first Italian aircraft were on their way to Morocco, the Italian chargé in London,

Vitetti, reported on the widespread sympathy to be found within the highest reaches of the Conservative Party for the Spanish rebels and for Italian fascism. Vitetti's conclusions derived from conversations with Conservative MPs, including Captain David Margesson, the Conservative leader of the House, with senior Tories at the Carlton Club and with representatives of the Rothemere press. Tory Members of Parliament told him of their conviction that the events in Spain were the direct consequence of 'subversive Soviet propaganda' and of their anxiety to see the Spanish left crushed. The right-wing Leo Amery, who had been First Lord of the Admiralty in the early 1920s, had told him that the Spanish war raised 'the problem of the defence of Europe against the threat of bolshevism'. In January 1937, Mussolini would tell Goering in the Palazzo Venezia that 'the English Conservatives have a great fear of Bolshevism, and this fear could very well be exploited politically'.

Economic factors were of even less importance in Mussolini's decision to help the Spanish rebels than they had been in Hitler's. The position of France was the key factor. Indeed, motivated by a determination to undermine French power, he had been infuriated by the early news that Blum planned to aid the Spanish Republic. However, it was an impotent rage since he did not want to risk outright confrontation with the French. However, once he knew, on 25 July, of the disarray in Paris which meant that the French would not be helping the Spanish Republic, he changed his mind. He saw the possibility of killing off for the foreseeable future the prospect that the Popular Front governments of Spain and France would be drawn together to the detriment of Italian ambitions in the Mediterranean. By helping Franco, he was not only pandering to his own egoistical view of himself as the senior figure in world fascism, but he knew, once French hesitations and pusillanimity had become obvious, that he had the opportunity to alter the European, and particularly Mediterranean, balance of power in Italy's favour. A Nationalist victory might lead to the expulsion of the British from Gibraltar. It would probably give Italy access to bases in the Balearic Islands. In either eventuality, it was an excellent opportunity to weaken Britain's communications with Suez. And it seemed as if all this could be secured at the bargain price of a few transport aircraft. In fact, the limited risk of 28 July would, in less than six months, have escalated to all-out, if undeclared, war against the Spanish Republic. By August 1936, Franco's requests for equipment would become more daring. Soon there would be an Italian expeditionary force in Mallorca under Arconovaldo Bonacorsi. As Franco encountered ever-greater difficulties in his march on Madrid, he would turn to Italy as a matter of course. And the more Mussolini said 'yes', the more difficult it became to say 'no' since, for all that the democracies turned a blind eye, the world knew that the cause of Franco was the cause of the Duce. Franco could not be allowed to lose.

The extent to which Italian intervention in Spain suited Hitler's foreign policy interests and damaged those of the democracies was shrewdly perceived by Ulrich von Hassell, the German Ambassador in Rome. In a report sent to Berlin on 18 December 1936, he wrote enthusiastically:

> Germany has in my opinion every reason for being gratified if Italy continues to interest herself deeply in the Spanish affair. The role played by the Spanish conflict as regards Italy's relations with France and England could be similar to that of the Abyssinian conflict, bringing out clearly the actual, opposing interests of the powers and thus preventing Italy from being drawn into the net of the Western powers and used for their machinations. The struggle for dominant political influence in Spain lays bare the natural opposition between Italy and France; at the same time the position of Italy as a power in the Western Mediterranean comes into competition with

that of Britain. All the more clearly will Italy recognize
the advisability of confronting the Western powers
shoulder to shoulder with Germany.

For Mussolini, then, Spain provided a splendid opportunity to
try to impress the Germans of Italy's claims to be an indispensable ally. Unfortunately, the desire to show off Italy's 'iron
military strength' would end in the humiliation of the battle of
Guadalajara, about which Lloyd George wrote a mocking
article under the heading 'The Italian Skedaddle'. In consequence, hurt vanity led to Mussolini trying to prove his mettle
to Hitler by unswerving commitment to the Rome–Berlin Axis.
Italy was therefore pushed ever closer to Germany and ultimately into the Second World War on Hitler's side.

It was the French, conscious of their pivotal role, who proposed an agreement of Non-intervention in the Spanish conflict. In August 1936, twenty-seven European nations formally
adhered to such an agreement. In the event, it was to mean
little: intervention continued as if the agreement had never
existed. Thus, the Non-intervention Committee, set up on
9 September 1936, and based in London, was little more than
a sham. However, it was a sham which worked in the interest
of the rebel forces in Spain, and which hindered the efforts of
the legitimate Republican government to stage an effective
defence against the insurgents. The Soviet Union, which believed neither in the legality nor the efficacy of the Non-
Intervention Agreement, initially decided to adhere to its terms
out of a desire to keep its relations with the West cordial. The
Germans and Italians, however, openly flouted the Agreement.
They found it so convenient a cloak for their activities on
behalf of the Spanish Nationalists that they were to be found
cynically defending its existence against the criticisms of the
Russians.

Scrupulous observation of the Non-Intervention Agreement
would have suited Stalin's plans. It was Italo–German arms

shipments to the Nationalists which obliged him to provide support for the Republic, which he did cautiously while continuing to proclaim Soviet neutrality. Had it been possible to stop German and Italian aid to the rebels, then Stalin would gladly have stopped Soviet shipments to the Republic. As it was, the Non-Intervention Committee achieved virtually nothing. Under the chairmanship of the Conservative Lord Plymouth, the Committee consistently revealed a bias against the Soviet Union whilst always being extremely polite to the Fascist powers. The Soviet Ambassador to London, Ivan Maisky, commented of Lord Plymouth: 'In this large, imposing and well-groomed body dwelt a small, slow-moving and timid mind. Nature and education had made Plymouth a practically ideal personification of English political mediocrity, nourished by the traditions of the past and by well-worn sentiments. As Chairman of the Committee, Plymouth presented an entirely helpless and often comic figure.'

Plymouth's daily bewilderment and his readiness to meet urgent problems by adjourning the Committee enabled both the Italians and Germans to continue openly to assist Franco's forces. The flamboyant Italian representative, Dino Grandi, and the German Ambassador in London, the bumbling ex-champagne salesman Joachim von Ribbentrop, put on virtuoso displays of mendacity. They combined to render Non-intervention a tragic mockery of the position of the Spanish Republic. Under Plymouth's chairmanship, the Committee moved with agonizing slowness, stopping for long-drawn-out discussions of such topics as whether gas masks constituted armaments but always ready to ignore hard evidence of the Agreement being breached.

In the words of Pandit Nehru, Non-intervention was 'the supreme farce of our time'. It left the Republic at a clear disadvantage in comparison to the rebels and thereby confirmed the anti-revolutionary trend of international diplomacy since 1917. On a visit to Gibraltar, the English poet Stephen

Spender was appalled to find that the Governor's house was full of rich Spanish refugees who recounted stories of atrocity and that the local English gentry were outraged because the Spanish Civil War had brought the Gibraltar Royal Calpe Hunt to a stop. The Republican fleet was refused refuelling facilities at Gibraltar, where the Governor was principally preoccupied with the re-establishment of regular hunting. Nothing sustained Nehru's view more than the fact that naval supervision of the east coast of Spain from Almeria to Alicante should be confided to the Germans, and from there to the French border placed in the hands of the Italians. This permitted both to intercept Russian supplies while ensuring free rein for their own attacks on the Levante coast. On 29 May 1937, the pocket battleship *Deutschland* was attacked by Republican bombers and twenty-three German sailors were killed. Their bodies were taken to Gibraltar where they were buried with full military honours. In reprisal, the Germans mounted a large-scale artillery bombardment of Almería causing notable loss of life among the undefended civilian population.

The Spanish democratic regime was to be as much a victim of the pusillanimity of the Western powers as were Austria and Czechoslovakia. However, it would be wrong to see the international diplomacy of the Spanish Civil War as merely a microcosm of Western appeasement, Fascist aggression and Soviet duplicity. When also seen in the context of the post-1917 series of defeats suffered by the European left, the abandonment of Spain to fascism assumes an iron logic. What is remarkable is that the political representatives of the Spanish Republic were so shocked by the nonchalance of the Western powers. In a perceptive, and sorrowful, entry in his diary on 31 May 1937, Manuel Azaña wrote:

> Our greatest enemy until now has been the British government. All the schemes devised for non-intervention and their consequences have damaged the government and

favoured the rebels. Their hypocrisy has become so obvious that it seemed infantile cynicism. It is a great thing to say that this is done to preserve peace in Europe. But to think that Germany or Italy would declare war on Britain or France if the Spanish Government bought arms in these two countries is sheer stupidity. The best way to avoid a general war is not to permit Germany and Italy to do what they like in Spain. How can the triumph of the rebels, the protégées of Germany and Italy, be in the interests of the British?

Azaña and the other leaders of the Republic had witnessed fascism in action and could not believe that British and French statesmen could be so blind to its threat. Eventually, even the conservative leaders of the democracies would perceive the danger. In 1936, however, their attitude to fascism, and therefore to the Spanish conflict, was compounded of an understandable desire to avoid war and a quiet glee that they might be able to do so by turning Hitler and Mussolini against the European left. They thereby passed a death sentence on the Spanish Republic and dramatically weakened the Western powers.

This had been implicitly recognized in a prophetic article by Churchill published in the *Daily Telegraph* on 30 December 1938. He wrote:

It must be admitted that if at this moment the Spanish Government were victorious they would be so anxious to live on friendly terms with Great Britain, they would find so much sympathy among the British people for them, that we should probably be able to dissuade them from the vengeance which would have attended their earlier triumph in the struggle. On the other hand, if Franco won, his Nazi backers would drive him to the same kind of brutal suppressions as are practised in the Totalitarian

States. The victory of the Spanish Republic would, therefore, not only be a strategic security for British Imperial communications through the Mediterranean, but gentler and reconciling forces would play a larger part.

Elsewhere in the article, he wrote 'Nothing has strengthened the Prime Minister's hold upon well-to-do society more remarkably than the belief that he is friendly to General Franco and the Nationalist cause in Spain. But these sentiments on either side may be pushed beyond the bounds of British interest. It would seem that today the British Empire would run far less risk from the victory of the Spanish Government than from that of General Franco.'

SIX

'Madrid is the Heart':
The Central Epic

The inexorable advances of the Nationalists in the first months of the war exposed the inadequacies of the Giral government. Like Casares Quiroga, Giral had been in the absurd position of presiding over a cabinet representing only a small section of the Popular Front coalition which had won the February 1936 elections. Largo Caballero, who must bear the ultimate responsibility for the crucial absence of the PSOE from the cabinet, remained committed to the idea of an exclusively workers' government. However, with Franco's African columns moving towards Talavera de la Reina, the last major town before Madrid, and Mola on the verge of taking Irún, Largo Caballero had eventually been brought round to acknowledge the need for a change. With some hesitation, at the prompting of his adviser, Luis Araquistain, he finally accepted the view of his arch-rival Indalecio Prieto that, given the international situation, the survival of the Republic required a cabinet backed by both the working-class parties and the bourgeois Republicans. On 4 September 1936, a true Popular Front government was formed with Largo Caballero as both Prime Minister and Minister of War. It contained Communists as well as Socialists and Republicans. Two months later, on 4 November, with the Nationalists already at the gates of Madrid, four representatives of the anarcho-syndicalist CNT also joined the cabinet. It was an indication of the gravity of the situation that the CNT should thus abandon its most sacred principles in order to help defend the beleaguered democratic regime.

Already in mid-October the artillery fire of the approaching Army of Africa had been heard in Madrid. The armies of Franco and Mola were aiming to meet in the capital. The rebels had amassed considerable supplies of arms, and these were supplemented by Italian weaponry. By 1 November, 25,000 Nationalist troops under General José Varela had reached the western and southern suburbs of Madrid. Their aim was to cut through the Casa del Campo, the old royal hunting ground, and the University City. They were considerably strengthened by the arrival in mid-November of the newly created German Condor Legion under General Hugo Sperrle. This was a force of specialized units, equipped with the latest developments in German bomber and fighter aircraft and motorized weapons which were to be tested out in Spain. Indeed, so sure was the Republican government that Madrid would fall that it left for Valencia on 6 November, and placed the protection of the city in the hands of General Miaja, who was left to improvise the creation of the Junta de Defensa (Defence Council).

The decision to move the Republican government to Valencia was divisive and controversial. The four newly incorporated anarchist ministers, Juan García Oliver (Justice), Juan López (Commerce), Federica Montseny (Health) and Juan Peiró (Industry), were reluctant to abandon Madrid. According to Indalecio Prieto, the anarchists 'considered themselves victims of a deception, thinking that they had been made ministers only in order to implicate them in such a serious measure, and they resisted giving their approval'. The decision to leave Madrid, though, was not a last-minute act of desperation. The transfer of government headquarters had been discussed previously. Moreover, not all members of the government saw the abandonment of Madrid as an admission that the city was bound to fall to the rebels. The Communist Party representatives in Largo Caballero's cabinet, Jesús Hernández (Education) and Vicente Uribe (Agriculture), had argued in October that the defence of Madrid and the evacuation of the government were not incompatible objectives. The four anarchists, however, regarded leaving the capital as cowardice and proposed to remain in Madrid while the other members of the cabinet left. This was firmly rejected by Prieto who was quick to perceive the political advantage that their bravery would confer upon the CNT.

Prieto, who had joined the cabinet as Navy and Air Force Minister, was, however, distressed by the manner in which the government proposed to leave. Although with characteristic pessimism, Prieto, like Largo Caballero, was convinced that Madrid would swiftly fall to the insurgents, he believed the government should announce in advance its plans to leave the capital. He later claimed that some weeks before he had proposed that the government should leave, but do so with adequate publicity. Prieto was anxious that the transfer should not take place suddenly and unexpectedly at the last moment and thereby give the impression of a desperate flight. He considered it advisable that the people of Madrid should be psychologically prepared so that they would find the measure as militarily justifiable and not the act of cowardly fugitives. As so often, Largo Caballero ignored the advice of Prieto.

The cabinet debate on the Prime Minister's evacuation proposal was extremely tense. After asking permission to discuss the matter privately, the four CNT ministers withdrew and only after considerable delay did they return to say that they agreed. Largo Caballero announced that the new seat of government would be Valencia and not Barcelona, which had originally been the expected choice because the President of the Republic, Manuel Azaña, had already moved there. Prieto announced that he had made two passenger aircraft available to ferry the cabinet members to Valencia but none took him up on his offer. Largo Caballero left by the main Madrid–Valencia

road that passed through the town of Tarancón which was
occupied by anarchist militiamen under a certain Colonel
Rosal. Rosal impeded the passage of ministers and civil ser-
vants. Julio Alvarez del Vayo, the left Socialist Foreign Minister, was jostled and insulted. Juan Peiró and Juan López,
respectively the CNT Ministers of Industry and of Commerce,
were turned back to Madrid and forced to travel to Valencia
by plane with Prieto.

According to Prieto, Largo had decided unilaterally that
the government should go to Valencia. In his own memoirs,
however, Largo states that it had been a unanimous cabinet
decision to go to Valencia, and that Azaña had changed his
mind and gone to Barcelona on 19 October without consulting
anyone. Whatever the truth of the matter, there can be little
doubt that the manner in which the government left Madrid
created a very poor impression and allowed the Communist
Party to assume the lead in defending Madrid, and thereby to
enhance its own prestige. It was an important step along the
path to its ultimate takeover of the whole Republican war
effort. In the meantime, the main issue was the situation in
the Spanish capital, suddenly bereft of a government. The
atmosphere in the city on the evening of 6 November is well
conveyed by Mikhail Koltsov, the Soviet journalist, often
described as Stalin's personal emissary, who was portrayed by
Hemingway in *For Whom the Bell Tolls* as 'Karkov':

> I made my way to the war ministry, to the commissariat
> of war ... Hardly anyone was there ... I went to the
> offices of the Prime Minister. The building was locked.
> I went to the Ministry of Foreign Affairs. It was deserted
> ... In the foreign press censorship an official ... told me
> that the government, two hours earlier, had recognized
> that the situation of Madrid was hopeless .... and had
> already left. Largo Caballero had forbidden the publi-
> cation of any news about the evacuation 'in order to avoid

panic' . . . I went to the Ministry of the Interior . . . The
building was nearly empty . . . I went to the central committee of the Communist Party. A plenary meeting of
the Politburo was being held . . . They told me that this
very day Largo Caballero had suddenly decided to evacuate. His decision had been approved by the majority of
the cabinet . . . The Communist ministers wanted to
remain, but it was made clear to them that such a step
would discredit the government and that they were
obliged to leave like all the others . . . Not even the most
prominent leaders of the various organizations, nor the
departments and agencies of the state, had been informed
of the government's departure. Only at the last moment
had the Minister told the Chief of the Central General
Staff that the government was leaving . . . The Minister
of the Interior, Galarza, and his aide, the Director of
Security Muñoz, had left the capital before anyone else
. . . The staff of General Pozas, the commander of the
central front, had scurried off . . . Once again I went to
the War Ministry . . . I climbed the stairs to the lobby.
Not a soul! On the landing . . . two old employees are
seated, like wax figures, wearing livery and neatly shaven
. . . waiting to be called by the Minister at the sound of
his bell. It would be just the same if the Minister were
the previous one or a new one. Rows of offices! All
the doors are wide open . . . I enter the War Minister's
office . . . Not a soul! Further down, a row of offices –
the Central General Staff, with its sections; the General
Staff, with its sections; the General Staff of the Central
Front, with its sections; the quartermaster corps, with its
sections; the personnel department, with its sections.
All the doors are wide open. The ceiling lamps shine
brightly. On the desks there are abandoned maps, documents, communiques, pencils, pads filled with notes. Not
a soul!

There was deep confusion over how the defence of Madrid was to be organized when the government left. Moreover, there was a generalized sense of panic and disorder in the capital. The Socialist Arturo Barea, head of the Foreign Press and Censorship Bureau, described in his autobiography, *The Forging of a Rebel*, how he received the news of the government's departure:

> When Luis Rubio Hidalgo told me that the Government was leaving and that Madrid would fall the next day, I found nothing to say. What could I have said? I knew as well as anybody that the Fascists were standing in the suburbs. The streets were thronged with people who, in sheer desperation, went out to meet the enemy at the outskirts of their town. Fighting was going on in the Usera district and on the banks of the Manzanares. Our ears were forever catching the sound of bombs and mortar explosions, and sometimes we heard the cracking of rifle shots and the rattle of machine guns. But now the so-called War Government was about to leave, and the Head of its Foreign Press Department expected Franco's troops to enter ... I was stunned, while he spoke on urbanely.

The departing government had decided to entrust the defence of Madrid to General José Miaja. The hero of Madrid, as he was to become, had a chequered background. He had been Minister of War for several hours in the compromise cabinet formed by Martínez Barrio on the night of 18 July. Convinced that the rebels must win against the Republic, he had refused to continue in that post in the government of Giral, and was even accused of having been a member of the ultra-rightist Unión Militar Española. Transferred to command the 3rd Division in Valencia, he had then been beaten back in an attempt to take Córdoba and relieved of his command. He was thus under some suspicion when given the awesome task of organizing the defence of Madrid. Indeed, he was sure it was part of a deliberate attempt to sacrifice him in a futile gesture. According to Largo Caballero, Miaja's reaction on hearing the news of his unexpected, and probably unwanted, promotion was to turn pale, stammer and point out that, while he was at the orders of the Prime Minister, it should be remembered that his family was in prison in Nationalist-held Morocco and that he had business interests there.

On the same day, Largo, in his capacity as Minister of War, had drawn up with General José Asensio Torrado, his under-secretary, orders for the defence of Madrid. These were handed in sealed envelopes to Miaja, the newly appointed commander of the Madrid military district, and to General Sebastián Pozas, commander of the Army of the Centre, with further instructions that they were not to be opened until the following morning at six. Miaja and Pozas ignored orders and opened their envelopes on the evening of 6 November. It transpired that each had been given the other's orders, a mistake which remains a source of controversy. Miaja was instructed to set up a Junta de Defensa, made up of all parties to the Popular Front, and to defend Madrid 'at all costs'. Pozas received instructions on tactical movements and for the setting up of new headquarters. Nonetheless, according to Julián Zugazagoitia, editor of *El Socialista* and supporter of Prieto, no one in the government believed that Madrid could be defended, least of all Largo Caballero who was fully conversant with the prevailing state of military confusion and disintegration. The Prime Minister left Madrid as convinced as Prieto that it would fall to the enemy within a week.

However, the arrival of rebel forces had been delayed by Franco's decision to liberate the Alcázar of Toledo. This proved to be vital for the Republicans. The breathing space allowed the delivery of Soviet aid – which was paid for on 25 October by the sending of half of Spain's gold reserves to the Soviet Union, a move which also provided the Republic with considerable and desperately needed hard currency. The delay allowed Madrid to benefit from the arrival of the International Brigades. These were organized and recruited by the Comintern, which had quickly recognized the existence of a spontaneous urge to help Spain among workers throughout Europe and America. Volunteers from all over the world, anxious to fight fascism, were shipped to Spain via Paris where the organization was run by various agents including the future Marshal Tito. They began to arrive in October and were trained at Albacete under the direction of André Marty, the brutal French Communist. The first units reached Madrid on 8 November, and consisted of German and Italian anti-Fascists, plus some British, French and Polish left-wingers. Sprinkled among the Spanish defenders at the rate of one to four, the brigadiers both boosted their morale and trained them in the use of machine guns.

Known as the 'International Column' in the Republican press, the Eleventh International Brigade under the leadership of General Emilio Kléber, also known as Lazar Stern, was vital to the defence of Madrid. Kléber was an Austro-Hungarian who had been trained at the Frunze Academy in Moscow. Together with the Communist Party's Fifth Regiment, the most highly organized and disciplined force in the central zone, the Eleventh Brigade enabled Miaja to lead the entire population of Madrid in a desperate and remarkable defence. By early November, there was hand-to-hand fighting between militiamen and Moors in the university buildings. Yet the people fought on, under banners which proclaimed 'They Shall Not Pass' and 'Madrid Will Be The Tomb Of Fascism'. The fiery Communist orator Dolores Ibárruri rallied the defenders with ringing oratory: 'It is better to die on your feet than to live on your knees.' She harangued the women of Madrid: 'It is better to be the widow of a hero than the wife of a coward.' A women's brigade was in fact involved in the fighting. Working-class districts were shelled and bombed, although

Franco was careful to spare the plush Barrio de Salamanca, the residential districts where his fifth columnists lived. Those clandestine Franco supporters that were caught were slaughtered by the desperate militiamen.

Volunteers from all over the world flocked to fight for the Republic. Some were out of work, others were adventurers, but the majority had a clear idea of why they had come: to fight fascism. For the victims of the Fascist regimes of Mussolini and Hitler it was a chance to fight back against an enemy whose bestiality they knew only too well. Forced out of their own countries, they had nothing to lose but their exile and were fighting to go back to their homes. One of the battalions which saw its first action in Madrid, and which was to suffer enormous casualties, was the Thaelmann, consisting mainly of German, and some British, Communists. Esmond Romilly was a British member of the Thaelmann Battalion. He later wrote of his comrades-in-arms: 'For them, indeed, there could be no surrender, no return; they were fighting for their cause and they were fighting as well for a home to live in. I remembered what I had heard from them of the exile's life, scraping an existence in Antwerp or Toulouse, pursued by immigration laws, pursued relentlessly – even in England – by the Nazi Secret Police. And they had staked everything on this war.' Indeed, when the Republic finally fell in 1939, many German, as well as Italian, anti-Fascists were still fighting in Spain. They ended up in French camps, and many fell into the hands of the SS and died in the gas chambers.

For the British and American volunteers the need to fight in Spain was somewhat different. They made more of a conscious choice. The hazardous journey to Spain was undertaken out of the awful presentiment of what defeat for the Spanish Republic might mean for the rest of the world. One who made such a choice was Jason Gurney, a sculptor living in Chelsea, London, who went to fight and received a wound which would prevent his ever being able to sculpt again: 'The Spanish Civil War seemed to provide the chance for a single individual to take a positive and effective stand on an issue which appeared to be absolutely clear. Either you were opposed to the growth of Fascism and went out to fight against it, or you acquiesced in its crimes and were guilty of permitting its growth.' Gurney was typical of the volunteers who believed that, by combating fascism in Spain, they would be fighting against the threat of fascism in their own countries. They were offered nothing in the way of pay or even insurance. One man who asked the British recruiters about conditions of service was told, 'You're not the kind of bloke we want in Spain. So get out.' All they were offered – and all most of them wanted – was the chance to fight fascism.

In contrast, Franco always claimed that there were no foreigners among his troops. Despite being described as volunteers, all of the 20,000 Germans and many of the 80,000 Italians who fought with the rebels were properly trained, regular soldiers. They were paid in their home country and regularly rotated. Similarly, the Portuguese *viriatos* included a high proportion of regular soldiers on full pay whose service in Spain counted in their military record back home. Their numbers have been variously estimated from 4000 to 20,000, and were probably not more than 8000. However, there were also some genuine volunteers on the Francoist side, somewhere between 1000 and 1500. There were White Russians who had fought against the Bolsheviks in their own civil war and would go on to fight them again in Finland. The ferociously anti-semitic Romanian Iron Guard sent eight volunteers to help Franco in the 'battle with the red beast of the Apocalypse'. The Jean d'Arc battalion consisted of about 300 French from the Croix de Feu and other extreme rightist organizations. There was also a motley crew of Poles, Belgians and other extreme rightists, Catholics, Fascists and anti-semites from all over Europe. These included at least half a dozen Englishmen and an American. One of the Englishmen, Peter Kemp, became an officer first with the Carlists and then with the ferocious Spanish Foreign Legion.

However, the most well-known foreign volunteers for Franco were the seven hundred Blue Shirts of the Irish battalion under General Eoin O'Duffy. His Catholic volunteers were inflamed with a desire to fight in Spain by gory press reports of religious persecution in the Republican zone. For most of them this was no more or less than a religious crusade, as evidenced by the following extract from O'Duffy's *Crusade in Spain*, published in 1938:

> Before leaving, the volunteers were presented with Rosaries, Agnus Deis and other religious emblems, the gift of the Right Rev. Monsignor Byrne, Clonmel, Dean of Waterford. Seventeen counties were represented in this party, the largest contingent coming from Tipperary. Referring to their departure, the Right Rev. Monsignor Ryan, Dean of the Archdiocese of Cashel, preaching after Mass the following Sunday, said: 'They have gone to fight the battle of Christianity against Communism. There are hosts of difficulties facing the men whom General O'Duffy is leading, and only heroes can fight such a battle. Those at home can help the cause with their prayers. The Rosary is more powerful than weapons of war. In the presence of Our Lord Jesus Christ let us promise that we will offer one decade of the family Rosary daily for poor suffering Spain; for the Irish boys who have gone out to fight the desperate battle that is threatening desolation all over the world. Let us pray that the destruction of civilization may be averted, that Christ may live and reign, and that Communism and the power of Satan on earth may be brought to naught.'

O'Duffy himself had been Chief of the Irish Police until 1933. After being removed for political reasons, he became leader of the Army Comrades Association which he had quickly turned into the Fascist Blue Shirt movement. He hoped that success in Spain would further his own dictatorial ambitions in Ireland. In the event, O'Duffy's volunteers did not find the glory which might have facilitated a Fascist coup in Ireland. O'Duffy diminished the military efficacy of his brigade by giving the most responsible appointments to his own political supporters, regardless of their experience. Disaster followed and their first casualties were inadvertently at the hands of the Francoists. At the battle of the Jarama in February 1937, one of their companies was fired on by a Falangist unit which mistook them for International Brigaders and a minor skirmish ensued in which four Irishmen were killed. Their only actual battlefield experience at the Jarama was part of a diversionary attack launched half-heartedly to help the Italian advance on Guadalajara. The Irish suffered some casualties while contributing little to the rebel cause. In the summer of 1937, after a period of inaction during which O'Duffy drank heavily, they went home thoroughly disillusioned and with their leader's political reputation severely tarnished.

The recruitment of the Republican volunteers was largely organized by the Communist Party. This does not mean that they were all Communists, although a high proportion of them were. Hindsight about the awful crimes of Stalin or about the sordid power struggles within the Republican zone cannot diminish the idealism and heroism of those who sacrificed their comfort, their security and often their lives in the anti-Fascist struggle. Francoists and anti-Communist historians in the United States have presented the International Brigaders as the dupes of Moscow. This tendency reached its peak in a work in the 1980s which, somewhat bizarrely, drew much of its evidence from the records of the US Congress House Committee on Un-American Activities and of the hearings of the US Subversive Activities Control Board. The fact that the Brigades were largely Communist-organized should not be allowed to obscure the fact that the volunteers went to Spain to fight Hitlerism. They perceived, as democratic politicians evidently did not, what the poet Edgell Rickword vividly expressed in his satirical lines, 'In Hitler's frantic mental haze / Already Hull and Cardiff blaze, / And Paul's grey dome rocks to the blast / of air torpedoes screaming past'.

It was, nevertheless, left to the Communists to sneak the volunteers across the French border, either on foot or in buses. Some even crossed the Pyrenees wearing rope-soled sandals, or *alpargatas*. On the bus carrying Jason Gurney, one man began to scream 'I don't want to go'. To prevent him alerting the French authorities to their illegal crossing, Gurney hit him. He wrote later that the man 'cried a lot that night at Figueras but seemed quite content thereafter and never held it against me. But when I saw his body lying dead, two months later, on the Jarama fields, I felt like a murderer.' As the recruiters had warned, it was 'a bastard of a war'. When the volunteers arrived at Barcelona, they were greeted by bands and huge welcoming crowds. Most of them had no experience of warfare, and they had to be organized quickly into units and given a few hours rudimentary training. Often with inadequate equipment, they were then sent out to do battle with the Fascist forces. The first units reached Madrid on 8 November. Geoffrey Cox, the *News Chronicle* correspondent, was in the Spanish capital when they arrived:

> The few people who were about lined the roadway, shouting almost hysterically, '¡Salud! ¡Salud!', holding up their fists in salute, or clapping vigorously. An old woman with tears streaming down her face, returning from a long wait in a queue, held up a baby girl, who saluted with her tiny fist. The troops in reply held up their fists and copied the call of '¡Salud!' We did not know who they were. The crowd took them for Russians. The barman turned to me saying 'The Rusos have come. The

Rusos have come'. But when I heard a clipped Prussian voice shout an order in German, followed by other shouts in French and Italian, I knew they were not Russians. The International Column of Anti-Fascists had arrived in Madrid.

The boost to the morale of the *Madrileños* was incalculable.

Nevertheless, the role of the International Brigades in the defence of Madrid should not be exaggerated. They were one component of a heroic effort which involved the whole population. Women and children helped with food, communications and medical supplies. On 14 November, the column of the legendary anarchist fighter Buenaventura Durruti arrived. Durruti himself was to die within a week, killed in circumstances which remain a source of dispute. His death occurred near the University City but away from the thick of action and was almost certainly the result of a gun accidentally going off in his car. A story was issued that he had been shot by a Nationalist sniper. Many anarchists were unable to accept this and accused the Communists of having assassinated their heroic leader. The Communists countered with an assertion that Durruti had been killed by his own men resentful of his efforts to impose discipline. A gigantic funeral procession through Barcelona followed Durruti to his final resting place on 22 November. The hundreds of thousands of mourners who edged slowly through the streets constituted the last public demonstration of the CNT's mass strength. Thereafter, recriminations over Durruti's death provided a focus for bitter confrontation born of contradictory interpretations of how the struggle against the rebels should be carried out. The anarchists accused the Communists of imposing the authoritarian rigidity of Soviet communism over the spontaneity of the libertarian social revolution. The Communists responded with severe criticisms of the way anarchist inefficiency impeded the job of feeding the refugees crammed into the besieged city and mocked the performance of the Durruti column in defending the University City.

It is true that the Nationalists, in the form of Moorish troops, had been able to make significant advances and had crossed the Manzanares river. In the end, though, their surge forward was contained. In fact, Durruti's men had gone into action with some reluctance. The anarchist leader had insisted on his arrival in Madrid that his men needed to rest and reorganize. However, Durruti was subjected to enormous pressure by the recently formed Madrid Junta de Defensa, under Miaja, which had debated in its session of 14 November the placing of the anarchist column under its direct orders. This turned out to be unnecessary, for Durruti had agreed at the last moment to go to the Republican lines straightaway. His militiamen, however, were both ill-equipped and exhausted after two months of uninterrupted fighting on the Aragón front, and many of them fled in the face of Moorish attacks. The Moors almost reached the city centre, but they were driven back after a heroic struggle by the people of Madrid. By 23 November, the Nationalist attack was spent. For the moment the city was saved.

The great popular hero of the defence of Madrid was General Miaja. His success in holding off the rebel forces owed an enormous amount to the immediate offer of support to the Junta de Defensa by the Communist Party, its Fifth Regiment, and the Communist-dominated united Socialist youth movement, the Juventudes Socialistas Unificadas (JSU). Nonetheless, he was later to be vilified by the Communists after having been built up by them to the status of a living legend. This has been seen by some as part of a deliberate policy by the Communists in order to gain access to the leading positions in the Junta de Defensa. Having been abandoned by the Republican government and convinced that he had been chosen as a scapegoat, it was not surprising that Miaja looked to the

Communists. They in turn perceived that the battered spirits of the *Madrileños* needed a hero. Miaja was therefore put on a pedestal and became intoxicated by the praise lavished upon him. With a large escort of motorcyclists and guards in armoured cars, his arrival anywhere would be announced by a cacophony of sirens. He told Julián Zugazagoitia, 'When I am in my car women call out to me, "Miaja!" "Miaja!" And they scream to each other, "There goes Miaja! There goes Miaja!" ... and I greet them and they greet me. They are happy and so am I.' Throughout a lengthy visit to the various fronts around the capital, he repeated incessantly to Largo Caballero, '¡Soy la vedette de Madrid!' – 'I am the star of Madrid.'

To many, though, the rotund and scruffy Miaja was an unimpressive figure. Franco and Queipo de Llano, for instance, both thought that he was an incompetent coward. Herbert L. Matthews, the *New York Times* correspondent in Madrid, described Miaja as the very reverse of his image as the loyal, dogged, courageous defender of Madrid. Unlike the hero of the myth, he was weak, unintelligent, unprincipled. Prieto regarded him as venal and frivolous. Largo Caballero criticized bitterly the sumptuous banquets organized in Miaja's honour in the basement of the Ministerio de Hacienda (Finance Ministry) while the rest of the population went hungry. Azaña commented after a meeting with him, 'It is difficult to have an interesting conversation with this man. He is a loquacious gossip who flits like a bird from one subject to another, smiling and self-satisfied.'

The perceptive *Pravda* correspondent Mikhail Koltsov, meanwhile, maintained that the real director of operations in Madrid was the forty-two-year-old Vicente Rojo, who had taken the surrender conditions into the Alcázar of Toledo. Rojo, who had been promoted to lieutenant colonel on 10 October, was appointed Miaja's chief of staff by Largo Caballero just before the government left for Valencia. It was an inspired choice. Rojo had served in Africa but his real vocation had been as a student of military tactics. For ten years from 1922 to 1932, he had served as an instructor in the Academia de Infantería in Toledo. Appalled by the lack of decent textbooks, he wrote new ones and rewrote the syllabus. Thereafter, he had studied at the Escuela Superior de Guerra for entry into the Estado Mayor (General Staff) where he had been for just four months when the military coup took place. Rojo's speciality was topography and the use of maps and he was quick to bring his theoretical knowledge to bear. He was also a fervent believer in the importance of morale. With the spirits of the defenders at their lowest point after the departure of the government for Valencia, his skills as a motivator were to be as crucial as his technical abilities.

Mikhail Koltsov noted in his diary on 10 November:

> Miaja is very little involved in operational details; he even knows little about them. These are matters he leaves to his Chief of Staff and to the commanders of columns and sectors. Rojo wins the confidence of the men by his modesty, which conceals his great practical knowledge and unusual capacity for work. This is the fourth day that he has remained bent over the map of Madrid. In an endless chain, commanders and commissars come to see him, and to all of them, in a low, calm voice, patiently, as though in a railroad information office, sometimes repeating himself twenty times, he explains, teaches, indicates, annotates papers, and frequently draws sketches.

The average citizen of Madrid, however, knew little of the political difficulties within the Junta de Defensa. In fact, while Rojo concentrated on the technical military aspects of the capital's defence, Miaja devoted himself to touring the city, enjoying being seen and raising morale. Miaja's very approachability ensured his considerable success in this task.

The siege of the capital went on, with intermittent bombing and shelling, for nearly three years. Esmond Romilly was once caught in a Metro station during an air raid. His description gives an indication of the horrors undergone by the Madrid population four years before they would become commonplace for the citizens of London: 'We tried to get out on to the street, but a panic-stricken crowd made it impossible to move. The fear of suffocation was stronger than that of the bombs – women screamed and on the steps men were fighting to get into the shelter. As we heard the roar of the aero-engines overhead, I remembered the crowds gathered around the Metro station on our first day – bodies were still being excavated; two hundred people had been killed when an incendiary bomb burst over a "bomb-proof" shelter.'

Yet the horrors of the siege were not confined to the loyalist inhabitants of the city. Many Nationalist sympathizers lived through the siege in fear of their lives, hiding in the homes of friends and at foreign embassies, terrified of falling into the hands of the *checas*. Others were not so scared and emerged at night to act as snipers from rooftops and darkened windows. Substantial numbers of rightists had in fact been rounded up at the beginning of the war. Large numbers of them were to die in the course of the so-called *sacas*, or removals, of prisoners from Madrid's jails, the Cárcel Modelo, Porlier, Ventas and San Antón. Before the siege, the murders of imprisoned rightists had been the work of uncontrolled militia patrols and were often provoked by outrage at the numerous civilians killed in the constant Nationalist bombing attacks of the undefended city. After the fall of the town of Getafe immediately to the south of the capital on 4 November, popular panic and serious military trepidation had intensified. Reports reached Madrid of the slaughter of civilians in the streets as Franco's Moroccan troops moved through the southern suburb of Carabanchel. In the centre of Madrid, not just the thuds of artillery but also the crackle of rifle fire could be heard. Soon, a decision would be made to remove the prisoners on a large scale, with horrific consequences.

In part, the responsibility for what then happened belonged to General Mola. Already on 3 October, Dolores Ibárruri, 'Pasionaria', writing in the Communist daily *Mundo Obrero*, referred to an earlier broadcast in which Mola had stated that he had four columns poised to attack Madrid but that the attack would be initiated by a fifth column already inside the city. She called for the unhesitating elimination of this enemy within. The notion of a 'fifth column' emerged once more when, on 28 October, as the circle began to close around Madrid, Mola had transferred his headquarters from Burgos to Ávila for the final assault. There, he had confidently announced to journalists how Madrid would fall. According to one of the reporters present, the Australian Noel Monks of the *Daily Express*, he produced maps showing where the four attacking columns were positioned. When asked which of the four was likely to take the city, he said that it would be none of them but rather a fifth column, 'men now in hiding who will rise and support us the moment we march'. Thus, the phrase 'fifth column' became current and panic intensified in Madrid.

Like 'Pasionaria' before him, Enrique Líster, the commander of the Communist Fifth Regiment, reacted furiously to Mola's comments. He wrote later, 'The general's blustering boast gave us a timely warning and cost the fascists dear. The commanders of the forces attacking Madrid expected the "fifth column" to come out onto the streets, stab us in the back and create disorder among the population. It was essential to eliminate this danger and, even if it was not entirely crushed, the "fifth column" was hit sufficiently hard to leave it incapable of decisive action.' It was hardly surprising then that, besieged in the terror-stricken city, the population and the political leadership alike were concerned about the enemy within.

Apart from fifth columnists hiding in embassies, many of

whom were armed, the largest number – nearly eight thousand strong – were in Madrid's various prisons. As Líster's commentary makes clear, little or no distinction was made between the 'fifth column' and the rightist prisoners. With the rebels only two hundred yards from the largest of the prisons, the Cárcel Modelo, in the Argüelles district near the University City, it was feared that the hundreds of army officers among the prisoners could form the basis of new units for the Nationalist army which seemed on the point of taking the capital. From the late afternoon of 7 November, formal overall responsibility for the prisoners lay with the young Communist Secretary General of the JSU, Santiago Carrillo, who had just been made Councillor for Public Order in the Junta de Defensa. The fact that he held such an important position at the age of twenty-one indicated his special relations with the Russians. Among the Soviet personnel present at the time were General Ian Pavlovich Berzin, one-time head of Soviet Military Intelligence, and Mikhail Koltsov, whose official status as a journalist was belied by the enormous influence he wielded, which led to speculation that he was really Stalin's eyes and ears in Madrid. Koltsov was alarmed to hear reports that the prisoners were already crowing about their imminent liberation and their incorporation into the rebel forces. He, Berzin and other Russian advisers insisted that it would be suicidal not to evacuate dangerous prisoners. Indeed, Koltsov's own memoirs contain many references to one 'Miguel Martínez', a supposedly Latin American Comintern agent with sufficient influence to give advice at the highest level. It has been widely assumed that 'Miguel Martínez' was none other than Koltsov himself, not least because, at a meeting in Moscow, Stalin jokingly called him 'Don Miguel'. Nevertheless, there have recently been suggestions that 'Miguel Martínez' was another Soviet agent, a deep-penetration agent who had been in Spain for some time.

Whatever his own real identity, Koltsov's memoirs claim that 'Miguel Martínez' personally persuaded the Communists to evacuate the prisoners although it is much more likely that many people were involved in what was a complex process. It is certainly the case that on the morning of 7 November, some hours before the first official meeting of the Junta de Defensa, Koltsov/Miguel Martínez went to see Pedro Checa, of the Communist Party central committee, and urged him to proceed to the evacuation of the prisoners. It is also likely that, in the course of the day, as the Junta de Defensa was being put together, the issue of the danger posed by the prisoners was discussed by the Communist representatives and Miaja himself. The subject was certainly high on their agenda.

A document discovered in 2005 by the journalist Jorge M. Reverte indicates that, after the inaugural session of the Junta, which began at 6.00 p.m. on 7 November, a private meeting was held between representatives from the newly created Consejería de Orden Pública, Carrillo's office of public order, and the local Federation of the CNT. Since the Communists held sway within the city and there were many anarchist control points in the outskirts, such a meeting made sense. Unfortunately, the document does not give the names of the participants at this meeting, nor does it indicate the exact time it took place, although the implication is that it was on the night of 7 November. The document indicates that those present decided that the prisoners should be divided into three groups, into which it is to be presumed that they had already been classified. The fate of the first, consisting of 'fascists and dangerous elements', was to be 'Immediate execution', 'with responsibility to be hidden'. The second group, prisoners considered to be supporters of the military uprising but, because of age or profession, less dangerous, were to be evacuated to Chinchilla, near Albacete. The third, those least politically committed, were to be released. Although there remain several question marks in relation to this document, its clear implication is that the evacuation, arrangements for which were already being put into place by Pedro Checa in response to

Koltsov/Miguel Martínez, now had anarchist approval and collaboration.

In the event, the specific orders for the evacuation of prisoners were signed neither by Carrillo nor by any member of the Junta de Defensa, but by the second-in-command in the Dirección General de Seguridad, the policeman Vicente Girauta Linares. Equally, explicit orders for their execution have not been found. Nevertheless, about 1200 of them were loaded onto double-decker buses. Eighteen kilometres from Madrid, at the villages of Paracuellos del Jarama and Torrejón de Ardoz, they were made to get off and were shot. It was the greatest single atrocity in Republican territory during the war, its horror barely diminished by the particular conditions in the besieged capital. The Communists would subsequently claim that the buses had been waylaid at anarchist control posts on the outskirts of Madrid. Carrillo himself has consistently repeated that, in the chaos of the government's flight to Valencia, with insufficient soldiers to cover the entrances to the streets by which the rebels might enter the city, there was little planning and considerable improvisation.

It is certainly possible that those given the task of escorting the prisoners, imbued with the general hatred of the approaching rebels, would have needed no more than a hint that they should take the law into their own hands. Reports by the Norwegian and Argentinian chargés d'affaires alleged that among those escorting the prisoners was the notorious group of thugs led by Agapito García Atadell, a member of the JSU who had taken upon himself the task of rooting out Fifth Columnists. His gang, self-styled the Brigadas de Investigación Criminal, otherwise popularly known as the 'dawn patrol' (Esquadrilla del Amanecer), went far beyond this function, indiscriminately robbing and killing rightists in Madrid. In fact, García Atadell, fearing retribution for his crimes, had already fled the capital. However, if his group was entrusted with the job of evacuating the prisoners, then those in charge could have had few doubts about their likely fate. The fact that some of those evacuated safely got as far as Alcalá de Henares is consistent with the triage of prisoners referred to in the document found by Reverte although it might equally suggest that the escorts of each group made their own decisions.

As recently as November 2005, Carrillo refused to comment on the lately discovered document, simply repeating his contention that the killings were the work of uncontrolled elements:

> What there was in Madrid and outside the city was great hatred of the fascists; thousands of refugees from Extremadura and Toledo camping out as best they could in the outskirts and burning with desire for revenge. And there were also uncontrolled forces like the anarchist Del Rosal or Iron Columns which were hardly different from what nowadays are called warlords because of their total autonomy and lack of discipline in regard to official authorities. I can take no responsibility other than having been unable to prevent it.

This is ingenuous under any circumstances, but especially so in the light of the Reverte document. Moreover, Carrillo's claimed ignorance of what happened is at best amnesia since, according to the minutes of the meeting of the Junta de Defensa on 11 November 1936, he gave a detailed account of the measures that he had taken to organize the evacuations of prisoners from the Cárcel Modelo. At that meeting, he stated that the operation had had to be suspended because of protests emanating from the diplomatic corps.

In a later report to Stalin, the Bulgarian Stoyan Minev, alias Boris Stepanov, from April 1937 the Comintern's delegate in Spain, spoke proudly of the Communists taking the initiative in the task of cleansing Madrid of Fifth Columnists in the wake of Mola's statement. If prisoners and Fifth Columnists are taken to be one and the same, Stepanov's report coincides with the blunt statement of Enrique Líster. Subsequently, ignoring the context of a besieged city fearful of the enemy within, Nationalist propaganda built on the atrocity of Paracuellos to create a picture of *la barbarie roja* (red barbarism). The Francoists consistently claimed that 12,000 prisoners had been murdered. Despite the fact that Santiago Carrillo was only one of a number of people involved in the decision-making process, the Franco regime, and the Spanish right thereafter, never lost an opportunity to use Paracuellos to denigrate him during the thirty years that he was Secretary General of the Communist Party (1956–85) and after.

The prisoners of Paracuellos were not the only Nationalist victims of the panic provoked by the advance on Madrid. The most celebrated was José Antonio Primo de Rivera. Although the Falangist leader was in a Republican jail in Alicante, an escape bid or a prisoner exchange was not inconceivable. Several prominent Nationalists had crossed the lines in these ways, including important Falangists like Raimundo Fernández Cuesta, who was officially exchanged, and Ramón Serrano Suñer, who escaped. Obviously, given the pre-eminence of José Antonio Primo de Rivera, his release or escape would be far from easy. Yet there were attempts to liberate him. The first had been the work of isolated groups of Falangists in Alicante. Then, in early September, when the Germans had come to see the Falange as the Spanish component of a future world political order, more serious efforts were made, largely under the auspices of their Consul in Alicante, Joachim von Knobloch. A band of Falangists led by Agustín Aznar arrived on a German torpedo boat on 17 September. However, their plans for a *coup de main* were changed into an attempt to get Primo de Rivera out by bribery which failed when Aznar was caught and only narrowly escaped himself.

In October, von Knobloch and Aznar continued their efforts but came up against less than enthusiastic backing from Franco, newly elevated as Generalísimo of the Nationalist forces and

Head of the Nationalist State. The Caudillo, as he now styled himself, told the German authorities that he required that José Antonio be rescued without any money being handed over or at least haggled over to the last peseta. This considerably diminished the chances of success but the Germans in Alicante decided to go ahead. Franco then issued even more curious instructions regarding the fate of José Antonio once he had been liberated. Such an event was to be kept totally secret, the Falangist leader was to be kept apart from von Knobloch, who was the main link with the Falangist leadership, and he was to be interrogated only by someone sent by Franco. He was not to be landed in the Nationalist zone without the specific permission of Franco. The Caudillo made bizarre claims to the Germans to the effect that there existed doubts about the mental health of Primo de Rivera. Not surprisingly, the Germans decided to abort the operation.

The motivation behind Franco's crude and convoluted sabotage of a rescue attempt that had little chance of success was entirely understandable. The Caudillo needed the Falange both as a mechanism for the political mobilization of the civilian population and as a way of creating a spurious identification with ideals of his German allies. If the charismatic José Antonio Primo de Rivera were to have turned up at Salamanca, Franco could never have dominated and manipulated the Falange as he was later to do. After all, since before the war, José Antonio had been wary about too great a cooperation with the army for fear that the Falange would simply be used as cannon fodder and political trimming for the defence of the old order. In his last ever interview, with Jay Allen, published in the *Chicago Daily Tribune* on 9 October and in the *News Chronicle* two weeks later, the Falangist leader had expressed his dismay that the defence of traditional interests was taking precedence over his party's rhetorical ambitions for sweeping social change. Even taking into account the possibility that José Antonio was exaggerating his revolutionary aims to curry favour with his jailers, the implied clash with the political plans of Franco was clear.

On 6 October, Franco had been visited in Salamanca by Count du Moulin-Eckart, Counsellor at the German Legation in Portugal. The new Head of State informed his first diplomatic visitor that his main preoccupation was the 'unification of ideas' and the establishment of a 'common ideology' among the army, the Falange, the monarchists and the CEDA. Given the links of most of those groups with the old order, such unification could only be carried out at the cost of the political annihilation of the Falange, something hardly likely to be approved by its leader. Accordingly, the plans of von Knobloch and Aznar were not pressed forward with any urgency. A further possibility for Primo de Rivera's release arose from a suggestion by Ramon Cazañas, Falangist *Jefe* in Morocco. He proposed that an exchange be arranged for General Miaja's wife and daughters, who were imprisoned in Melilla. Franco apparently refused safe-conducts for the negotiators, although the family of General Miaja was later exchanged for the family of the Carlist Joaquín Bau. Similarly, the Caudillo refused permission for another Falangist, Maximiano García Venero, to drum up an international campaign to save José Antonio's life.

José Antonio Primo de Rivera was shot in Alicante prison on 20 November 1936. Eyewitness accounts testify that he died with great courage and dignity. The Caudillo rejoiced in private that a man whom he had always hated as an elegant playboy could not now be an inconvenient presence in Salamanca. He maliciously told Ramón Serrano Suñer, a close friend of José Antonio, that he had proof that the Falangist leader had died a coward. Nevertheless, he made full use of the propaganda opportunities provided by the execution. At first, he chose, at least publicly, to refuse to believe that José Antonio was dead. The Falangist leader was more use 'alive' – leaving the Falange leaderless while Franco made his own political arrangements. Franco's immediate private response to the news of the execution was enormously revealing of his peculiarly repressed way of thinking. 'Probably', he told Serrano Suñer, 'they've handed him over to the Russians and it is possible that they've castrated him.' Once the death was officially accepted, Franco used the cult of *el ausente* (the absent one) to take over the Falange. All its external symbols and paraphernalia were used to mask its real ideological disarmament. Even certain of Primo de Rivera's writings were suppressed and his designated successor, Manuel Hedilla, was imprisoned under sentence of death.

In Madrid, the rebel advance under Varela had finally been halted by 22 November when Franco was forced by the exhaustion of his troops to call off frontal assaults. It was the first major defeat suffered by Franco's forces. Had the Republic been in a position to counter-attack, the Nationalists might well have suffered a serious reverse. Varela and Yagüe told a German military adviser, in the presence of John Whitaker, 'We are finished. We cannot stand at any point if the Reds are capable of undertaking counter-attacks.' Franco's long-term optimism never flagged. He realized the significance of the fact that, four days earlier, both the Italians and Germans had announced their recognition of the Nationalist Junta at Burgos as Spain's legitimate government. The American Ambassador in Berlin, William E. Dodd, perceived, as did the Caudillo, that, 'having recognized Franco as conqueror when this has yet to be proved, Mussolini and Hitler must see to it that he is successful or be associated with a failure'. At the end of December 1936, Sir Robert Vansittart, Permanent Under-Secretary at the Foreign Office, would make a similar point in a secret report to the cabinet on 'The World Situation and British Rearmament': 'The two dictator States are creating a third; and, by recognizing General Franco's government before he is sure of winning, they have committed themselves irretrievably to making a success of his venture, thus limiting niceties as to means.'

In fact, there were other reasons for Franco's optimism. In October, the Asturian capital Oviedo had been 'liberated' from the miners who were beseiging it. *ABC* of Seville commented with joy on 18 October that the victorious Nationalist columns had entered the Asturian capital after a 'real butchery' of the miners. Further good news from the north came at the end of November with the defeat of a Basque offensive. Madrid, of course, remained the principal front. Both sides dug in and for a month things were relatively quiet. On 13 December, the Nationalists began an attempt to cut the Madrid–La Coruña road to the north-west. After crippling losses in fighting around the village of Boadilla del Monte, the attack was called off. On 5 January, the assault was renewed with increased ferocity. A slow tank advance was met by Republican forces. In four days, only ten kilometres of road had been taken and at enormous cost, each side having lost in the region of 15,000 men. Casualties among the International Brigades were particularly high.

Meanwhile, the farcical and somewhat dishonest attempts of the British and French to impose the policy of Non-intervention could do nothing to stop the flow of foreign Fascist assistance to Franco. In response, the legitimate Republican government, refused arms by the Western democracies, had been forced to turn to the Soviet Union. Largo Caballero had sent a letter to the Soviet ambassador on 17 October requesting that he ask his government if it would 'agree to the deposit of approximately 500 metric tons of gold, the exact weight to be determined at the time of delivery'. The role of the moderate Socialist Finance Minister, Dr Juan Negrín, was crucial in the transfer of the gold. In September, Negrín had taken the decision to transfer the gold reserves of the Bank of Spain to a more secure deposit in the caves used as ammunition dumps at the naval base of Cartagena. In October, along with Largo Caballero, he decided to send the gold to Moscow to be held there as credit for future arms purchases. Given the difficulties facing the Republic in purchasing arms legitimately within the democracies, this was an entirely sensible decision. Franco could rely on a regular stream of high technology assistance from Germany and Italy, complete with trained technicians, spare parts and the correct workshop manuals. The Republic, in contrast, had to send its ill-equipped and bookish emissaries to operate among the sharks of the open arms market and, in consequence, make do with overpriced and obsolete equipment from private arms dealers. Nevertheless, Negrín has been accused by right-wing historians of being no more than the stooge of the Russians.

Numerous accounts of the transactions between Madrid and Moscow imply that Spain was somehow cheated by the Soviet Union. However, the leading experts on the financing of the Civil War, Professor Ángel Viñas, and the English author Gerald Howson, are agreed that the accounting gap between the slightly more than four hundred tonnes of fine gold that was transferred to the Soviet Union and the cost of the equipment supplied was probably not significant. The equipment supplied, however, ranged dramatically from obsolete artillery and small arms to state-of-the-art aircraft, tanks and anti-tank guns. The gold also had to pay for the transport of equipment to Spain, a process during which some Soviet shipping was sunk, and also for the training of Spanish pilots. In any case, it is hard to see that Negrín had any real option but to buy arms from the Soviet Union with Spanish gold. Even Largo Caballero, who was later to turn against Negrín, asserted that the Finance Minister's request for authority to transfer the gold to an unnamed safe hiding place was entirely reasonable given the proximity of the rebel forces. If the gold had fallen into Nationalist hands, there would have been no more arms for the Republic and defeat would have been inevitable. According to Largo Caballero, once the gold had been transferred to Cartagena, fears of a Nationalist landing led Negrín to send it abroad. Since banking circles in England and France had already shown their hostility to the Republic by, in some cases,

freezing Spanish assets, virtually blocking credit and systematically hampering the Republic's financial transactions, there was
little alternative but Russia, where Republican funds were any-
way destined in order to pay for arms and food.

In contrast, the Nationalists, despite the fact that the
Spanish gold reserves remained in Republican hands, did not
encounter so much difficulty in financing their war effort. The
insurgents aimed from the outset to obtain as much aid in war
matériel as the Fascist powers were prepared to provide. While
the Italians were particularly generous, or irresponsible, the
Germans sought to derive some financial benefit from arms
supplies to the rebels. To this end, there was set up a firm
in Spain, the Compañía Hispano-Marroquí de Transportes
(HISMA), to handle transactions between Spain and Germany.
From September 1936, HISMA conducted German–Spanish
trade on the basis of bartering goods, thereby avoiding the use
of foreign currency, of which the Nationalists were very short.
In October 1936, a counterpart to HISMA, the Rohstoff-und-
Waren-Kompensation Handelsgesellschaft (ROWAK), was set
up in Berlin under the ultimate authority of Hermann Goering.
These two companies established for the Nazis a virtual monopoly of Nationalist commerce with the outside world. They
also played an important role in placing the Nationalist
economy on a war footing. In addition, the HISMA/ROWAK
system had far-reaching long-term effects on the Nationalist
economy. Spanish exports of most value to the German war
economy were diverted to the Third Reich, thereby reducing
the Nationalists' capacity to raise foreign currency elsewhere.

Some money was raised by a 'National Subscription'
whereby people in the Nationalist zone handed over their
jewellery, watches and gold coins. Sometimes money and
jewellery were given freely but there was also considerable
pressure. Not to give was to risk denunciation as 'disaffected'.
Substantial sums were also raised by the confiscation of the
property of those imprisoned or executed. A number of ex-

tremely rich businessmen – among them Juan March, Francesc Cambó and Ángel Pérez – put their fortunes at the disposal of the Nationalist cause. However, the basic mechanism relied upon by Franco was credit. Ángel Viñas has estimated that the Nationalists received approximately seven hundred million dollars' worth of resources and services on credit during the Civil War. Much aid, though, particularly from Italy, was given free of charge.

Between December 1936 and April 1937, the Italians sent nearly one hundred thousand troops to fight for Franco. They were given their first action in the south. To offset the stalemate in Madrid, the campaign to mop up the rest of Andalusia had been continued. It was a campaign almost as bloodthirsty as the march on Madrid had been. Under the extraordinary General Queipo de Llano, troops began to advance on Málaga from Marbella and Granada. Known as the 'Radio General', Queipo would broadcast nightly on the airwaves of Spain, telling tales full of sexual innuendo about 'the Jew Blum', Doña Manolita (Azaña), Miaja and Prieto, as well as relishing what his Moorish mercenaries would do to Republican women.

On 3 February 1937, motorized columns of Italians began to move on Málaga. After bombing raids by Italian aircraft and bombardment by Nationalist warships, the city collapsed easily. The speed and success of their tactics of *guerra celere* (the Italian version of *Blitzkrieg*) was to cause future difficulties for the Nationalists and their allies. The Republican defences were in some disarray from the outset, largely because there was little military discipline and organization, and because there was a shortage of arms. The Italian tanks, fast and light, succeeded in large part because, given the absence of Republican defences, they did not suffer any flank attacks to which they were particularly vulnerable. Accordingly, Franco and Mussolini drew conclusions about the invincibility of the Italian Missione Militare in Spagna under the command of General Mario Roatta. Franco was infuriated because Italian troops were first to enter Málaga and briefly ruled the city before Roatta sent him a telegram tactlessly worded as follows: 'Troops under my command have the honour to hand over the city of Málaga to Your Excellency.' Despite the ease of the victory, and the lack of resistance encountered, the Nationalists under Queipo showed no mercy. Within the city itself nearly four thousand Republicans were shot. Many rightists emerged claiming that they had escaped death at the hands of the 'reds' only because they had not had time to kill them. One of Queipo de Llano's officials commented sarcastically, 'In seven months, the Reds didn't have enough time. Seven days is more than enough for us. They really are suckers.'

After the battle, refugees escaping along the coast road were bombarded by the navy and air force. T. C. Worsley was an English volunteer ambulance driver on the road from Málaga to Almeria along which the refugees were fleeing. His description is harrowing:

> The refugees still filled the road and the further we got the worse was their condition. A few of them were wearing rubber shoes, but most feet were bound round with rags, many were bare, nearly all were bleeding. There were seventy miles of people desperate with hunger and exhaustion and still the streams showed no signs of diminishing. Then the faint hum of bombers. The sides of the road, the rocks and the shore were dotted with the refugees, pressed down on their faces burrowing into holes. Children lay flat, with one frightened eye turned upwards towards the sky, with their hands pressed tight over their ears or folded backwards to protect their vulnerable necks. Huddled groups crouched everywhere, mothers already on the brink of exhaustion, held down their children pushing them into every cranny and hollow, flattening themselves into the hard earth, while the planes droned nearer. They had been bombed before and

knew only too well what to do. We decided to fill the
lorry with kids. Instantly we were the centre of a mob of
raving shouting people, entreating and begging, at this
sudden miraculous apparition. The scene was fantastic,
of the shouting faces of the women holding up naked
babies above their heads, pleading, crying and sobbing
with gratitude or disappointment.

The crowds of refugees who blocked the road out of Málaga
had been in an inferno. They were shelled from the sea,
bombed from the air and then machine-gunned. The scale of
the repression inside the fallen city explained why they were
ready to run the gauntlet.

Encouraged by their success in the south, the rebels renewed
their efforts to take Madrid. While the Republicans were preparing a counter-attack, the Nationalist forces, under the direction of General Orgaz, launched a huge attack through the
Jarama valley on the Madrid–Valencia highway to the east of
the capital. This was defended fiercely by Republican troops
reinforced by the International Brigades. They were unprepared for the intensity of the Nationalist artillery fire or the
special ability of the Moorish mercenaries to move across
country without being seen. The outcome of the battle of the
Jarama valley was similar to that which took place for the La
Coruña road. The Nationalist front advanced a few miles, but
no strategic gain was made. The Republican forces had again
demonstrated that while they were heroically brave in defence,
they had little left for a counter-attack. Again the casualties
were enormous. The Republicans lost 25,000 including some
of the best British and American members of the Brigades, and
the Nationalists about 20,000. The Republican efforts had not
been helped by disputes between General Miaja and General
Pozas, head of the Army of the Centre. Since the Jarama valley
fell within Pozas' area of command, Miaja refused to send
troops until the government made him commander of the

entire zone. Nonetheless, it was the International Brigades which bore the brunt of the fighting. The British contingent was almost wiped out in one afternoon.

After these various stalemates, Franco came under pressure from the Germans and Italians to seek a rapid victory. In any case, he was desperate for some form of diversion which would allow some respite for troops exhausted by the bitter fighting in the Jarama. It was decided to make an attack on Guadalajara, forty miles north-east of Madrid. The Generalísimo perceived this as an ideal way to divert Republican troops away from the Jarama. The Italians, however, were aiming at a bold and decisive initiative in the wake of their triumph at Málaga. On 1 March, Franco agreed to an Italian proposal to close the circle around Madrid, with a joint attack south-west by the Italians from Sigüenza towards Guadalajara backed up by a north-eastern push by Nationalist troops from the Jarama towards Alcalá de Henares. On 8 March, the Italians under General Amerigo Coppi initially broke through the Republican defences. However, it became clear by the evening that Franco's promised attack from the Jarama had not materialized. This allowed the Republicans to draw reinforcements from the Jarama.

Moving rapidly towards Madrid, the Italians overextended their lines of communication. The Italians were caught in a heavy snowstorm. Coppi's columns were further disadvantaged by the weather. Equipped for African operations, they were unprepared for heavy snow and sleet. Operating from improvised fields, their aircraft were grounded in the mud and made easy targets for the Republican air force operating almost normally from permanent aerodromes. On 12 March, Republican troops, with the Garibaldi Battalion of the International Brigade and Soviet tanks, counter-attacked. Italian light tanks with fixed machine guns were vulnerable to the Republic's Russian T-26 with revolving turret-mounted cannon. With Roatta desperate for the promised southern arm of the pincer, Franco prevaricated, claiming unconvincingly that his generals were ignoring his orders.

Within five days, to the intense mortification of Mussolini, the Italian forces were routed. The Duce told the German Ambassador in Rome, Ulrich von Hassell, that no Italian would be permitted to return alive until victory over the Republic had erased the shame of Guadalajara. Franco's officers toasted 'Spanish heroism of whatever colour it might be'. The defeat at Guadalajara – the first for fascism – had many dimensions – the weather, the poor morale and inappropriate equipment of the Italians and the dogged courage of the Republicans. Nevertheless, if Franco's attack had taken place as promised, the outcome might have been very different. The Generalísimo's failure to commit his own troops and his apparent willingness to let the Italians be slaughtered in a bloodbath with the Republicans makes it difficult to avoid the conclusion that he was using Roatta's men as cannon fodder in his broad strategy of defeating the Republic by slow and gradual attrition. At best, he behaved as if the Italians were acting as a diversion for his beleaguered troops in the Jarama. Far from providing the support expected by the Italians for what they regarded as a major joint operation, he let the Italians bear the weight of the fighting while his own units regrouped.

Militarily, Guadalajara was only a minor defensive victory, but in terms of morale it was a huge Republican triumph. Much valuable equipment was captured and also documents which proved that the Italians were soldiers and not volunteers. However, the Non-Intervention Committee refused to accept this evidence because it was not presented by a country represented on the Committee. And to emphasize that the Republic could expect no help from the Committee, no protests were made when the Italian representative, Dino Grandi, echoed Mussolini's boast to von Hassell. On 23 March, Grandi announced that no Italian soldiers would be withdrawn until the Nationalist victory was secure.

Noel Monks sent a dispatch on the Fascist defeat to the *Daily Express* which was published with his by-line. He was summoned before Franco and threatened with execution. In the event, he was merely expelled from rebel Spain. Of his meeting with Franco, Monks wrote, 'He was paunchy even then, on this day in March 1937, when I stood before him. For the leader of a military revolt that had been going on now for nearly nine months, he was the most unmilitary figure I have ever seen. He seemed to be dominated by the massive desk he was sitting at. His face was flabby, and the eyes that glared into mine would have made good tors for a game of marbles, they seemed so hard.'

On 24 March 1937, Vicente Rojo was promoted to the rank of full colonel 'por méritos de guerra' (for achievements in battle). The Republicans were hanging on, but it was an increasingly desperate struggle merely to survive. What made their plight even more dire was the extent of the growing bitterness of the vicious political conflicts raging within the Republican camp as to how the struggle should be conducted. The intensity of these divisions would soon reach a point at which a civil war within the Civil War would break out.

SEVEN

Politics behind the Lines:
Reaction and Terror in the City of God

If Stalin was cautious in helping the Spanish Republic, Hitler and Mussolini were by comparison unstinting in their aid to Franco. Stalin's attitude was summed up in his admonition to the high-ranking Soviet advisers sent to Spain: 'Stay out of range of artillery fire.' However, just as important as the scale and enthusiasm of foreign assistance were to be the strings attached to it. Every bit as much as the Soviet Union, the Fascist powers sought the right to intervene in Spanish internal affairs as an additional levy on their aid. It was not just a question of German officers arrogantly demanding the best rooms in hotels, to be served first in restaurants or that other diners stand for the singing of the Nazi anthem, the 'Horst Wessel Song', nor of swaggering Italian officers making love to Spanish girls. Franco's pleas for help had been couched in terms that seemed to promise that, if victorious, his Spain would be a satellite of the Fascist powers. In the event, Franco would resist Mussolini's attempts to inject urgency and Italian direction into his lumbering military strategy but he would concede very considerable mineral resources and mining rights to the Germans.

Nevertheless, Axis help brought fewer complications than did Russian assistance to the Republic. The manner in which dependence on Soviet aid was manipulated to inflate the influence of the Spanish Communist Party exacerbated the Republic's greatest weakness, the interminable, and violent, polemics between its various factions as to how the war should be fought. The trappings and symbols of the Falange provided the necessary veneer of international Fascist solidarity. There were individual attempts to boost the Falange. Hitler's first envoy, General Wilhelm Faupel, meddled inconsequentially in support of the more pro-Nazi elements of the Falange. In March 1937, Mussolini sent Roberto Farinacci, the powerful Fascist boss of Cremona, to persuade Franco to introduce a Fascist-style 'Spanish National Party' to impose total control of political life. Both were politely ignored. Moreover, the German and Italian regular army officers in Spain tended to sympathize much more with the traditional values of their Spanish brothers-in-arms than with the anti-oligarchical rhetoric of Falangism. Thus, in the competition for power in the Nationalist zone, the Falange was not boosted by the Germans and Italians in the way that the Communist Party was elevated to a hegemonic position by the committed backing of the Russians. In consequence, the Nationalists enjoyed a dramatically higher level of unity behind their lines than did the Republicans.

This unity derived largely from the pre-eminence of the military. Virtually all other questions were relegated while the soldiers got on with the job of winning the war. Thus, despite the existence during the Second Republic of competing rightist political groups – the CEDA, Falangists, Carlists and Alfonsine monarchists – a moratorium was effectively placed on political activity once the war broke out. This was not especially difficult given the level of cooperation between them that had existed before 1936. Falangist terror squads had been financed by the monarchists of Renovación Española and their activities used by the CEDA to present the Republic as a regime of chaos and disorder. All owed a large part of their ideology to Carlism, the fountainhead of indigenous Spanish reactionary thought. The left regarded the tactical and rhetorical divisions of the various rightist groups as a smokescreen of trivia behind which they pursued their shared interests as specialist units in the same army. They shared a determination to establish an authoritarian corporative state, to smash the organizations of the working class and to dismantle the institutions of democracy. They addressed each others' meetings and wrote in each others' newspapers. They had been united in parliament and at election times. Now, during the Civil War, they accepted with alacrity that their future survival depended on the success of the military rising. Accordingly, while the Nationalist zone was not entirely free of rivalries, the generals faced relatively few problems in imposing unity within the rightist ranks.

For those who did not share the values and aspirations of the *Movimiento* but were unfortunate enough to find themselves in the Nationalist zone, unity was imposed by means of a vicious terror. Members of the Popular Front parties and the trade unions were shot in their thousands as the Nationalists conquered each new piece of territory. At first in Old Castile and Galicia, and then in newly conquered territories, a greatly expanded Falange, flooded with newcomers, became the blood-stained auxiliary repressive force which freed the military from the task of politically purging their civilian enemies of the left. In their religious fervour, the Carlist *requetés* were also often guilty of barbaric excesses. Details of appalling atrocities committed by Nationalist troops against women and men were published by the Madrid College of Lawyers. What made the horrors committed seem worse was that they were carried out under the benign gaze of the Church and perpetrated by the forces of law and order – the army, the Civil Guard and the police.

The Archbishop of Zaragoza, Rigoberto Doménech, declared on 11 August 1936, 'this violence is carried out not in the service of anarchy but legitimately for the benefit of order, the Fatherland and Religion'. Whereas bombing raids or news of atrocities elsewhere often provoked mob violence in the Republican zone, the violence in the Nationalist zone was rarely 'uncontrolled'. An illustrative example is what happened on 21 October 1936 near Monreal, a small town south-east of Pamplona. Three days earlier, in the town of Tafalla, after the funeral of a *requeté* lieutenant killed in battle, an enraged crowd went to the local prison determined to lynch the one hundred men and twelve women detained there. When the Civil Guard prevented a massacre, a delegation went to get written authorization from the military authorities. Three days later, in the early hours of the morning, sixty-five of the prisoners were taken to Monreal. They were shot by a group of *requetés* and the *coup de grâce* was administered by the deputy parish priest of Murchante, one of the many Navarrese priests who had left their congregations to go to war. The Bishop of Pamplona, Monsignor Marcelino Olaechea Loizaga, was sufficiently shocked by the regularity with which prisoners were murdered after the funerals of Carlist troops to deliver a strikingly unusual and exceptional sermon on 15 November. His text, which found no echo elsewhere in the Church, was 'no more blood in the name of revenge'.

Perhaps as many as 180,000 Freemasons, liberals and leftists lost their lives in the Francoist repression although there is still considerable controversy over exact figures. Francoists continue to produce spurious computations which diminish the number of leftist victims. However, in recent years there have been a number of detailed local studies which suggest that, if some of the older estimates are exaggerated, the real figures are still horrendous.

Three examples, Seville, Navarre and Córdoba, will suffice. Queipo de Llano's chief propaganda officer, Antonio Bahamonde, who, appalled by what he had witnessed in rebel-held territory, fled to the Republican zone, claimed that 150,000 had been executed in Andalusia and 20,000 in Seville alone before the end of 1938. Count Ciano complained in July 1939 that 80 people per day were still being shot in Seville although Bahamonde reckoned in 1938 that the figure then was between

20 and 25 per day. The most widely quoted Francoist authority on the repression, General Ramón Salas Larrazábal, in his nationwide survey of 1977 gave a figure of 2417 executions in the entire province of Seville during the war and after. Detailed ongoing research by local historians, using only verifiable data, has already reached the figure of 11,500 for Seville and for all of Andalusia of more than 55,000. In Navarre, a province in which the left was relatively weak, the Basque priest Fr Juan José Usabiaga Irazustabarrena ('Juan de Iturralde') was able to find in the course of the 1940s the names of 1950 people murdered by the right. In 1983, General Salas Larrazábal reached a figure of only 893 for Navarre. However, the research carried out in the 1980s and 1990s by the Navarrese collective Altaffaylla Kultur Taldea has found proof of 2789 deaths. In every province, the pattern of detailed, village by village, research is invariably pushing the numbers up towards the most horror-stricken contemporary estimates.

In 1946, an ex-CEDA notary estimated as 32,000 the number executed in the province of Córdoba since 1936. General Salas Larrazábal's 1977 figure for the Nationalist repression in the province over the same period was 3864. The exhaustive investigations of Francisco Moreno Gómez produced in 1985 definitive proof of the wartime executions of 7679 men and women throughout the province, with 2543 in the provincial capital alone. However, Dr Moreno Gómez estimated that these were certainly below the real figure not least because, since his research was completed, there had been a flood of people emboldened in the years of the democratic regime to register the wartime deaths of their relatives. His own research, and that of colleagues in Córdoba, continued. In 1987, he added figures of 1594 for the post-war repression in Córdoba. By 2001, he had found evidence of another 379 killed in the repression of the guerrilla resistance of the 1940s. As of 2005, Moreno Gómez's provisional figure stands at 9652 dead as a result of Nationalist repression, a figure to which should be added 756 who died of hunger and mistreatment in prison, and a further 223 Córdoban exiles from Francoism who died in German concentration camps. These figures are certainly still short of being definitive.

The journalist Noel Monks witnessed numerous atrocities and the problems of writing about them. In his memoirs, he commented:

In Talavera, because not much was going on at the front, one was fed on a steady diet of atrocity propaganda; the things the Reds did as they fell back into Madrid. And the strange thing was that the Spanish troops I met – Legionaires, Requetés and Falangists – bragged openly to me of what they'd done when they took over from the Reds. But they weren't atrocities. Oh no, señor. Not even the locking up of a captured militia girl in a room with twenty Moors. No, señor. That was fun. And I had pointed out to me the wife of a Falangist officer who used to follow the execution squads and deliver the *coup de grâce* with her husband's revolver as she shouted: 'Viva Franco.'

I began to get strange qualms about this great Catholic country fighting for the Faith. What was a crime, an atrocity, on one side was just clean fun and devotion to duty on the other. The humble, simple people I lived among for four months, dressed in perpetual mourning, seemed stunned by it all. Franco's censors knew the score though. You could put over all the 'Red' atrocities you wished, but try and write something the troops bragged to you they did, and not only would it be cut out of your dispatch but you would get a sharp reprimand from the chief censor. Of course both sides committed fiendish atrocities in Spain, as I was to discover. But somehow the ones committed in Franco's name had a certain dispensation about them, as far as the outside world was concerned, that was not accorded to the Government side.

Monks' perception was entirely correct. This was largely the result of the skill with which the Francoists issued publications like the *Preliminary Official Report on the Atrocities Committed in Southern Spain in July and August, 1936, By the Communist Forces of the Madrid Government*, which was a wildly exaggerated, and often fictitious, account of disorder in southern villages. Antonio Bahamonde described the process whereby 'atrocity' photographs were faked. Corpses of those shot were mutilated and burnt, eyes cut out, limbs amputated, stomachs cut open, then photographed as 'proof' of 'red outrages'. This, plus two subsequent 'reports' and the determined support of the conservative and Catholic press, ensured a sympathetic response to the Francoist claim that the rebels were carrying out a legitimate crusade against 'red' barbarity.

A clear symptom of this was the initial attitude of Winston Churchill to the situation in Spain. When the new Spanish Ambassador, Pablo de Azcárate, arrived in London in early September 1936, he was introduced by Lord David Cecil to Churchill. Despite the fact that Azcárate had been a highly respected functionary of the League of Nations, Churchill angrily rejected his outstretched hand, muttering, 'Blood, blood . . .' In an *Evening Standard* article on 2 October 1936, entitled 'Spain: Object Lesson For Radicals', Churchill claimed:

> The massacre of hostages falls to a definitely lower plane; and the systematic slaughter night after night of helpless and defenceless political opponents, dragged from their homes to execution for no other crime than that they belong to the classes opposed to Communism, and have enjoyed property and distinction under the Republican constitution, ranks with tortures and fiendish outrages in the lowest pit of human degradation. Although it seems to be the practice of the Nationalist forces to shoot a proportion of their prisoners taken in arms, they cannot

be accused of having fallen to the level of committing the atrocities which are the daily handiwork of the Communists, Anarchists, and the P.O.U.M., as the new and most extreme Trotskyist organization is called. It would be a mistake alike in truth and wisdom for British public opinion to rate both sides at the same level.

That terror was intended as a weapon to generate fear far and wide was made clear by the broadcasts of both General Mola in the north and, more systematically, by General Queipo de Llano in the south. His obscene descriptions of bloody atrocities were heard nightly from Seville and may have contributed to provoking his listeners to commit atrocities themselves. The savagery visited upon the towns conquered by Spanish colonial forces was simply a repetition of what they did when they attacked a Moroccan village. In a broadcast on 23 July, Queipo de Llano declared, 'We are determined to apply the law without flinching. Morón, Utrera, Puente Genil, Castro del Río, start digging graves. I authorize you to kill like a dog anyone who dares oppose you and I say that if you act in this way, you will be free of all blame.'

As news of the murders reached towns that were threatened by right-wing forces, reprisals were taken against the right-wing elements that were assumed to be planning to do the same. The uncontrolled Republican militias were not the same as the disciplined troops of the rebels, who were encouraged by their officers to carry out atrocities. Later in the same speech quoted above, Queipo de Llano said, 'Our brave Legionaries and Regulares have shown the red cowards what it means to be a man. And, incidentally, the wives of the reds too. These Communist and Anarchist women, after all, have made themselves fair game by their doctrine of free love. And now they have at least made the acquaintance of real men, and not milksops of militiamen. Kicking their legs about and struggling won't save them.'

The horrors of the military repression in Seville and the rest of western Andalusia in 1936 were gradually extended to the rest of Spain as Franco captured ever more territory. Considerable cruelty – rape, confiscation of goods, execution because of the politics of a son or husband – was carried out against women in the name of the Francoist concept of redemption. 'Red' women were depicted both as whores and 'not women'. These accusations, a reflection of the fear provoked in right-wing men by the liberation of women by the Republic, were specifically directed against politically active women like Dolores Ibárruri and Margarita Nelken and more generally against women on the left.

As the Francoist forces captured Republican territory – in Castile and Galicia in the first few days, in the southern provinces in the late summer of 1936, along the northern coast in 1937 and then all over Spain once the war ended on 1 April 1939 – the feminist revolution of the Second Republic was reversed with extreme savagery. In La Coruña, the civil governor Francisco Pérez Carballos was shot on 24 July 1936. His wife, Juana Capdevielle San Martín, was in an advanced state of pregnancy. She was arrested and imprisoned. When she heard the news of her husband's fate, she miscarried. She was released but some days later she was picked up by a Falangist paramilitary squad, raped and murdered. Republican women would be punished for their brief escape from gender stereotypes by humiliations both public and private. They were dragged through the streets after having their heads shaved, being tarred and feathered or forced to ingest castor oil so they would soil themselves in public. In Nationalist prisons, they were beaten and tortured. Sexual humiliation ranged from being paraded naked through the streets, via sexual harassment to rape.

The dour and humourless General Franco had learned to instil loyalty through fear during his time in Africa. His military style, appropriate to a minor colonial war, also reflected his experience in Morocco. He was cold, ruthless and secretive.

His taciturn *Gallego* caution tended to obscure his lack of clearly defined political views. No one, however, could doubt his sense of political purpose. This was made starkly clear by his conduct of the Nationalist war effort. Ponderous as a decision-maker, doubts have been cast on his military abilities. Certainly his leadership was dogged, uninspired and the despair of his German allies. Throughout the war he would sacrifice lives and waste time in unnecessary campaigns to gain militarily unimportant territory. However, his tortoise-like strategy of slowness facilitated the elimination of leftist and liberals which was to be one of his greatest sources of strength after 1939. His decision to liberate the Alcázar gave a breathing space to the Republicans and was indefensible in military terms, but it clinched his own grasp on power within the Nationalist Junta. In speeches and interviews, he made it clear that his strategy of attrition had a long-term political purpose. He did not speak of a Spanish equivalent to Hitler's thousand-year Reich but rather made it clear that he intended to eradicate socialism, communism, anarchism, liberal democracy and freemasonry from Spain for centuries to come.

After his appointment as 'Head of Government of the Spanish State', Franco set about limiting threats to his own long-term pre-eminence from the various rightist political groups. They were all broadly united behind the military in the desire to crush the left once and for all but still nurtured ambitions of putting their own special stamp on the authoritarian regime to which they all aspired. The monarchists wanted a restoration; the Carlists, a virtual theocracy under their own pretender; the Falange, a Spanish equivalent to the Third Reich. The CEDA had all but disappeared, its militants migrating to more extremist groups but its leader, Gil Robles, aspired to a significant role in the future. Since the generals had expected to take power swiftly, they had postponed resolving problems of political organization until after their expected victory. However, when it became apparent that a long struggle was necessary, it was recognized that some form of political structure would have to be produced to unite the Nationalist zone.

With cunning and determination, Franco had already headed off potential challenges to his own power. He had sabotaged the slim possibility of rescuing José Antonio Primo de Rivera. Gil Robles had virtually eliminated himself as a possible rival. At the beginning of the war, he had hedged his bets, resisting General Mola's call for prominent rightists to go to Burgos to give support to the rising. It was an error from which Franco ensured that he would never recover. He spent the first months of the war in Lisbon raising money, buying arms for the rebels and acting as unofficial intermediary between Franco and the Portuguese leader, Oliveira Salazar. However, in the autumn and winter of 1936, when he began to visit the rebel zone, he found a deeply hostile reception. In the febrile atmosphere of Salamanca, the *Jefe*'s legalist tactic during the Republic was reviled as having betrayed rightist interests by delaying the inevitable war against democracy and the left. There was sufficient competition for preferment for the consignment of Gil Robles to the dustbin of history to meet with general approval.

In general, the senior civilian monarchists were even less of a problem for Franco. Never having had any significant rank and file, they had no real power base and thus were happy to insinuate themselves as advisers to Mola and Franco. At the first glimmer of a threat to this agreeable situation, however, Franco acted swiftly. In mid-December 1936 he received a letter from Don Juan de Borbón, the son of Alfonso XIII and heir to the throne, requesting his permission to take part in the Nationalist war effort. As a one-time officer in the Royal Navy, Don Juan wanted to join the crew of the battle cruiser *Baleares* which was then nearing completion. The young prince promised to abstain from any political contacts, but Franco feared that he might become a figurehead for the Alfonsine monarchists, of whom there were many in the army. There was a danger that, with Don Juan in Spain, the Alfonsists would become a distinct group alongside the Falangists and the Carlists. The Caudillo's response was simple but cunning. He delayed some weeks before replying to Don Juan, then he gracefully refused the offer, on the grounds that he could not take responsibility for endangering the life of the heir to the throne. He thus consolidated his position among the monarchists while, at the same time, deriving considerable political capital within the Falange by letting it be thought that he had excluded Don Juan in order to facilitate the future Falangist revolution.

Despite the elimination of possible challenges from Don Juan, Gil Robles and José Antonio Primo de Rivera, there remained a larger problem. As the Army of Africa faced ever growing casualties, Franco had to rely increasingly on the recruitment of militia whose first loyalty was to a political group. Inevitably, that increased the political weight of the two parties which made the most substantial contribution, the Falange and the Carlist *Comunión Tradicionalista*. This did not in itself challenge Franco but, given the different long-term political ambitions of these groups, he perceived potential threats both to his single command of the armed forces and to his own political hegemony. Without José Antonio, the Falange was in some disarray. Accordingly, the Carlists represented, in the short term, a greater difficulty. Since late October, the President of their National War Junta, Manuel Fal Conde, had become vociferous in defence of Carlist autonomy. To this end, when the Francoist high command announced its decision to give regular army ranks to militia officers, and create short-term conversion courses to turn them into *alféreces provisionales* (provisional second lieutenants), the Carlists quickly set up an independent Real Academia Militar de Requetés. Since Franco's permission had not been sought, he seized the opportunity to clip Fal Conde's wings. After first neutralizing the easy-going head of the Traditionalist Communion, the Conde de Rosezno, he gave Fal Conde forty-eight hours either to leave Spain or face a court martial for mutiny. He then brought all the militia groups, whether of the CEDA, the Falange or the Carlists, under military command.

The decisive way in which Franco had removed his rivals was born of his belief that political power was merely an extension of the military command structure, *el mando*. The view that those who disobeyed were guilty of mutiny simplified many problems. However, the consolidation of the Generalísimo's undisputed authority was not the same as creating a permanent civilian infrastructure for his rule. Moreover, in early 1937, he was aware that both Queipo de Llano and Mola harboured long-term political ambitions. In the context of any future power struggle, control over the political groupings which increasingly supplied the bulk of the Nationalist troops, the Falange and the Carlists would be decisive. Franco was determined therefore to impose his command over subordinates and rivals alike. Moreover, his close relations with Hitler and Mussolini, and his desire for the Caudillo to be seen on a level with the Führer and the Duce, inclined him to copy their single-party systems.

The brains behind the creation of a formal state structure complete with a mass movement was to be Ramón Serrano Suñer, the Generalísimo's *cuñado* (brother-in-law). A prominent figure in the Juventud de Acción Popular, the CEDA's extremist youth movement, Serrano Suñer had been instrumental in bringing over much of its rank and file to the Falange in the spring of 1936. He had witnessed the murder of friends in jail in the Republican zone and only just escaped the *sacas*, in which his two brothers, José and Fernando, were murdered. In consequence, he was an emotional and totally committed opponent of democracy. After escaping from Madrid, he made his way to Salamanca in February 1936. There, living with his family in the attic of Franco's residence and headquarters, the Bishop's Palace, he had daily access to the Caudillo. Indeed, given that the cold and suspicious Franco had few confidants, it was assumed that his *cuñado* was the power behind the Generalísimo's throne. Malicious tongues quickly bestowed on Serrano Suñer the matching nickname the *cuñadísimo* (supreme brother-in-law).

In daily strolls around the episcopal gardens, Serrano Suñer explained to Franco that *un Estado campamental*, a battlefield state, which constantly had to pitch its tents anew, needed to be replaced by permanent political machinery. A brilliant lawyer, the handsome Serrano Suñer had both the intellect and the political credentials to be chief architect of the Francoist state. He was agreeable to Franco because of their family ties and because he had no power base of his own. He was also acceptable to many 'old-shirt' Falangists because he had been a lifelong personal friend of José Antonio Primo de Rivera. There were also other newly recruited pragmatists, less ideologically militant, who had been his followers in the Juventud de Acción Popular.

Together with Franco's brother, the amiable cynic Nicolás, Serrano Suñer devised a way to fill the political void on the Nationalist side. There was no question that the most feasible vehicles for the creation of a mass political movement were the Falange, whose membership had risen to nearly a million by early 1937, and the Carlist Traditional Communion. Since the autumn of 1936, Nicolás Franco had been toying unsuccessfully with the idea of uniting them. The notion now took off. The job was made easier by the fact that the Falange had been weakened by the arrest of many of its national and provincial leaders even before the war started. Decapitated by the execution of its founder, it was now in the throes of an increasingly bitter power struggle which was to be exploited with some finesse by Serrano Suñer, Nicolás Franco and other members of the political general staff operating from Franco's headquarters, the *Cuartel General*.

On one side of the Falange stood the radical followers of

José Antonio's designated successor, the provincial *Jefe* from Santander, Manuel Hedilla, an unsophisticated Fascist thug. Ranged against them was another group, known as the 'legitimists', of relatives and friends of José Antonio. This group was led by the aggressive head of the Falangist militias, Agustín Aznar, and his cousin, Sancho Dávila. They snobbishly regarded Hedilla as too proletarian. Franco and Serrano Suñer thought him too pro-Nazi and altogether too inclined to take seriously José Antonio's warnings about letting the Falange become a tame adjunct of the army. For their purposes, however, Hedilla had the advantage of guileless naïvety. Serrano Suñer and the *Cuartel General* let Hedilla think that, if he did not oppose the inevitable unification of the Falange and the Carlists, he would be left to run the new party. He was told that first he must suppress the 'legitimist' rebellion.

Armed Falangists from both groups thronged Salamanca. On 16 April, the 'legitimists' struck first, deposing Hedilla from the leadership. Believing that he had Franco's backing, Hedilla sent a group of his men to seize the party headquarters and arrest Aznar and his henchmen. In the early hours of the morning of 17 April there was a bloody brawl in which two Falangists were shot dead. Franco now acted: Aznar was arrested, accused of provoking disorder in the rearguard. No action was taken against Hedilla who could still, at this point, have played a subordinate role in Franco's orchestrated takeover of the Falange. On 18 April, a meeting of the Falange's national council, the Consejo Nacional, elected Hedilla supreme party chief, or *Jefe Nacional*. When he went to tell Franco, he found the Caudillo about to announce the fusion of the Falange and the Carlists. Ushered onto a balcony of the Bishop's Palace, Franco embraced him in front of a large crowd. In press and radio reports, it was made to appear that the recently elevated *Jefe Nacional* had handed over his powers to the Caudillo. A decree of unification, issued on 19 April, announced that the new party would be called Falange Española Tradicionalista y de las Juntas de Ofensiva Nacional Sindicalista. When the new party's leadership was announced four days later, Franco was *Jefe Nacional* and Hedilla merely a member of the Junta Política (executive committee). To accept was to condemn himself to impotence, so Hedilla, overestimating his own support among the 'old shirts', refused and instructed the provincial chiefs to obey only orders which came through him. On 25 April, Hedilla was placed under arrest along with several other Falangist dissidents. He was tried on 29 May, accused of planning to assassinate Franco. After intercession from Serrano Suñer, the sentence of death was commuted. Hedilla spent another four years in a Francoist jail.

Franco had had the decree of unification drawn up by Serrano Suñer (and the deranged Fascist writer Ernesto Giménez Caballero) without discussing the details with either Hedilla or the Carlist leadership. The bulk of the Carlists were furious but, in the interests of the war effort, they suppressed their outrage. The rank and file of the Nationalist zone welcomed the unification as a way of putting a stop to the friction between the various groups. However, since the new party was now the only political formation allowed in the Nationalist zone, the independence of the Spanish Fascist movement was at an end. Thereafter, the *Movimiento* (Movement), as the new single party was known, had little or no political autonomy. Forced to accept Franco as their new leader, the Falangists saw their ideological role usurped by the Church, their party turned into a machine for the distribution of patronage and their 'revolution' indefinitely postponed. In the event, Serrano Suñer had begun the process of making the Falange Francoist but he never managed to make a Falangist of Franco.

The unification enshrined Franco's determination to eliminate any political rivals. It was not a difficult task. Calvo Sotelo was dead. His deputy, the effete Antonio Goicoechea, dutifully accepted the decree of unification and dissolved Renovación Española. Gil Robles was a broken reed as far as the

Nationalists were concerned. Franco allegedly loathed him, resentful of the fact that, as Minister of War in 1935, Gil Robles had been his superior. His position was not enhanced by a fulsome acceptance of the unification any more than it had been by his instruction in February that the remnants of Acción Popular desist from political activity. Although little had been done to facilitate attempts to save José Antonio Primo de Rivera from execution, once he was dead Franco had no scruples about allowing his execution to be mythologized into martyrdom as a means of attracting supporters. A cult of his memory was generated in such a way as to legitimize Franco's leadership of the new party.

Franco's competitors within the army were also steadily eliminated. Sanjurjo had been killed at the outset, Goded and Fanjul executed by the Republicans in August 1936. This left just Mola as an even remotely realistic rival. If only in the suspicious mind of the Caudillo himself, Mola would always have been an implicit challenge. As it was, relations between the two men deteriorated after Franco's rise to power. Decisive and flexible in military matters, Mola was keen to terminate the war in the north. Franco's plodding style of military leadership drove him to distraction. Moreover, perhaps out of a desire to emphasize Mola's subordination, Franco constantly put obstacles in the way of the northern campaign. He interfered with Mola's air forces and often took troops away from the northern front to reinforce positions around Madrid. Just when some sort of clash seemed inevitable, Mola became the victim of a fatal air crash.

On 3 June 1937, Mola set out from Pamplona to Vitoria and thence to Valladolid to inspect the front. At Alcocero, in the province of Burgos, his plane crashed; everyone on board was killed. Franco received the news coldly. Wilhelm Faupel, the German Ambassador to the Nationalist government, wrote to the Wilhelmstrasse on 9 July that 'Franco undoubtedly feels relieved by the death of General Mola. He told me recently:

"Mola was a stubborn fellow, and when I gave him directives which differed from his own proposals he often asked me: 'Don't you trust my leadership any more?'".' Hitler is reported to have said that 'the real tragedy for Spain was the death of Mola; there was the real brain, the real leader . . . Franco came to the top like Pontius Pilate in the Creed.'

There have been many theories about what really happened. Rumours of conspiracy and sabotage abounded. The father of the dead pilot, Colonel Chamorro, thereafter kept two loaded pistols on a table in his home, awaiting the day when he would kill his son's murderers. As the official version claimed, the plane may simply have hit a hill known as the Monte de la Brújula in dense fog. Mola was flying in a British-built Airspeed A.S.6 Envoy which had been taken to the Nationalist zone by a defecting pilot. Its English markings, similar to planes used to fly supplies into the Republic from France, had not been entirely obliterated. Accordingly, it is also possible that the aircraft was mistakenly shot down by Nationalist fighters.

Franco now found himself without any serious competition. From the first floor of the Bishop's Palace in Salamanca he directed the Nationalist war effort. It was to be some time before Serrano Suñer's state-building exercise came to fruition in the creation of an organized bureaucracy. The improvisational nature of things was reflected in the rise to important positions of a number of bizarre characters. The much-mutilated General José Millán Astray, missing one arm and an eye, was appointed chief of the press and propaganda department. Famous as the frenzied founder of the Spanish Foreign Legion, he was hardly the best man to present the Nationalist cause to the outside world. On 12 October 1936 he had brought that cause into considerable international disrepute by his behaviour during the celebrations of the anniversary of Christopher Columbus's discovery of America. When a bystander shouted out the battle cry of the Legion, '*¡Viva la muerte!*' (Long live death), Millán Astray had responded with the triple Nationalist chant of '*¡España!*', and back came the three ritual replies of '*¡Una!*', '*¡Grande!*', '*¡Libre!*' (United! Great! Free!). When he was reproached by the Rector of the University of Salamanca, the philosopher Miguel de Unamuno, an apoplectic Millán Astray screamed, 'Catalonia and the Basque Country are two cancers in the body of the nation. Fascism, the cure for Spain, has come to exterminate them!'

In reply, Unamuno suggested that Millán Astray's bloodlust derived from a desire to see others as mutilated as himself. Again Millán Astray interrupted, shrieking, '*¡Mueran los intelectuales!*' (Death to intellectuals). When he had screamed himself hoarse in the midst of a deafening tumult, Unamuno rose again. In the tense silence, with violence floating in the air, Unamuno spoke calmly: 'This is the temple of intelligence and I am its high priest. I have always been, despite the words of the proverb, a prophet in my own country. You will win but you will not convince. You will win because you have more than enough brute force; but you will not convince because to convince means to persuade. And to persuade you need something which you lack: right and reason. It seems to me pointless to ask you to think about Spain.' He was threatened by Millán Astray's bodyguards and helped from the hall by Franco's wife, Carmen Polo. Unamuno was removed from his position in the university and held under virtual house arrest.

On 13 December 1936, Unamuno sent a letter to his friend Quintin de Torre about the Nationalist repression that he had witnessed in Salamanca, referring to 'the most bestial persecution and unjustified murders'. Regarding Franco, he wrote:

He takes no lead in the repression, in the savage terror of the rearguard. He lets others get on with it. The repression in the rearguard is left to a venomous and malicious monster of perversity, General Mola . . . I said, and Franco repeated it, that what has to be saved in Spain is Western Christian civilization under threat from

Bolshevism, but the methods they are using are not civilized, nor Western, but rather African, certainly not Christian. The crude traditionalist Spanish Catholicism has very little that is Christian. What we have here is pagan, imperialist, African militarization. In this way there will never be real peace. They will win but they will not convince; they will conquer but they will not convert.

Unamuno died at the end of December 1936.

As chief of propaganda, Millán Astray encouraged his subordinates regularly to threaten foreign journalists with execution. One such subordinate was Luis Bolín, who had helped organize Franco's transit from the Canary Islands to Morocco. He was later to achieve lasting notoriety for his efforts to prove that the bombing of Guernica had never taken place. Another was the notorious Captain Gonzalo de Aguilera, Conde de Alba y Yeltes, who was responsible for explaining the Francoist position to foreign visitors. Peter Kemp, the British Francoist volunteer, felt that the count did more harm than good:

> Loyal friend, fearless critic and stimulating companion that he was, I sometimes wonder if his qualities really fitted him for the job he was given of interpreting the Nationalist cause to important strangers. For example, he told a distinguished English visitor that on the day the Civil War broke out he lined up the labourers on his estate, selected six of them and shot them in front of the others – '*Pour encourager les autres*, you understand.'
>
> He had some original ideas on the fundamental causes of the Civil War. The principal cause, if I remember rightly, was the introduction of modern drainage.

Captain Aguilera's theory on the evils of urban sanitation was also elaborated to Charles Foltz, Associated Press correspondent during the war:

Sewers caused all our troubles. The masses in this country are not like your Americans, nor even like the British. They are slave stock. They are good for nothing but slaves and only when they are used as slaves are they happy. But we, the decent people, made the mistake of giving them modern housing in the cities where we have our factories. We put sewers in these cities, sewers which extend right down to the workers' quarters. Not content with the work of God, we thus interfere with His will. The result is that the slave stock increases. Had we no sewers in Madrid, Barcelona, and Bilbao, all these Red leaders would have died in their infancy instead of exciting the rabble and causing good Spanish blood to flow. When the war is over, we should destroy the sewers. The perfect birth control for Spain is the birth control God intended us to have. Sewers are a luxury to be reserved for those who deserve them, the leaders of Spain, not the slave stock.

He confided to Peter Kemp his theory that Nationalists had made a major error in failing to have shot Spain's bootblacks. 'My dear fellow, it only stands to reason! A chap who squats down on his knees to clean your boots at a café or in the street is bound to be a Communist, so why not shoot him right away and be done with it? No need for a trial – his guilt is self-evident in his profession.'

Millán Astray, Bolín and Aguilera were at the extreme margins of Nationalist propaganda. Altogether more effective in international terms was the legitimization of the Francoist cause provided by the Catholic Church. Long hostile to rationalism, freemasonry, liberalism, socialism and communism, the Church played a central role in the political life of the Nationalist zone. With the exception of the Basque clergy, most Spanish priests and religious sided with the Nationalists. They denounced the 'reds' from their pulpits. They blessed the flags of Nationalist regiments and some – especially Navarrese priests – even fought in their ranks. Clerics took up the Fascist salute. As early as mid-August 1936, Bishop Marcelino Olaechea Loizago of Pamplona had already denounced the Republicans as 'the enemies of God and Spain'. In the last week of August, Bishop Olaechea and two Archbishops, Rigoberto Doménech of Zaragoza and Tomás Muniz Pablos of Santiago de Compostela, declared the rebel war effort to be a religious crusade. Catholic Action declared its enthusiasm for the *alzamiento* at its congress in Burgos in September 1936.

At the beginning of September, José Álvarez Miranda, the Bishop of León, associated the Republic with 'Soviet Jewish–Masonic laicism'. The Jesuit provincial of León wrote to Rome on 1 September to warn against any peace initiatives by the Vatican: 'Catholics see this war as a veritable religious crusade against atheism, and regard it as totally inevitable. Either it is won or Catholicism will disappear from Spain.' The most widely celebrated designation of the military rebellion as a crusade came from the pen of Enrique Plá y Deniel, Bishop of Salamanca. On 28 September, he issued a long and scholarly pastoral letter entitled 'The Two Cities', based on St Augustine's notion of the cities of God and of the Devil. It declared that 'on the soil of Spain a bloody conflict is being waged between two conceptions of life, two forces preparing for universal conflict in every country of the earth . . . Communists and Anarchists are sons of Cain, fratricides, assassins of those whom they envy and martyr merely for cultivating virtue . . . It [the war] takes the external form of a civil war, but in reality it is a Crusade.'

On the same day, Cardinal Isidro Gomá, Archbishop of Toledo and Primate of All Spain, broadcasting on Radio Navarra to the defenders of the Alcázar, rejoiced in their liberation and 'of the city of the most Christian Spanish empire'. For him the rebel victory was the high point of the war, of the 'clash of civilization with barbarism, of the inferno against

Christ'. He thundered against 'the bastard soul of the sons of Moscow', 'Jews and the freemasons who poisoned the nation's soul with absurd doctrines, Tartar and Mongol tales dressed up as a political and social system in the dark societies controlled by the Semite International'. As a young priest, Vicente Enrique y Tarancón, who as a Cardinal forty years later was to put the Church's weight behind the democratization of Spain, was perplexed by the militancy of senior churchmen. On a visit to Burgos, he attended a Te Deum in the Cathedral to celebrate the Nationalist capture of a provincial capital. When the Captain-General and the Archbishop of Burgos spoke to the crowd afterwards, Tarancón was astonished to hear the general speak in exclusively military terms while the Archbishop delivered an aggressive military harangue. Ecclesiastical militancy was rewarded with overflowing churches. Not to attend mass in the Nationalist zone could lose a man his job or put him under political suspicion.

For Cardinal Gomá, Franco's cause was God's cause. After the destruction of Guernica, when many Catholics began to question the sanctity of the Francoist cause, he rendered the Caudillo an inestimable service. In response to a request for public affirmation of the hierarchy's support, he organized a collective letter 'To the Bishops of the Whole World'. The text described the 'crusade' as 'an armed plebiscite' and rejoiced that on their executions the Nationalists' enemies had become reconciled to the Church. It was signed by two Cardinals, six Archbishops, thirty-five bishops and five vicars-general. It was not signed by Cardinal Francesc Vidal i Barraquer, Archbishop of Tarragona in Catalonia, nor by Monsignor Mateo Múgica, Bishop of Vitoria in the Basque Country. Múgica was especially distressed by the execution by Nationalist firing squad of fourteen Basque priests at the end of October 1936. This should, in Canon Law, have led to the excommunication of those responsible, but neither the Vatican nor the Spanish hierarchy condemned the executions. Múgica, however, was told that his safety could not be guaranteed in the Nationalist zone and he remained in exile.

Throughout the world, Catholics rallied to the Francoist cause. The German bishops had issued a collective pastoral on 19 August 1936 to endorse Hitler's support for Franco. In the United States, the efforts of militant Catholics, and especially those of the 'Radio Priest', Father Charles Coughlin, were probably instrumental in blocking aid to the Republic. A campaign in Britain, Ireland and elsewhere to brand the Republic as the bloody executioner of priests and nuns was given greater authority by the decision of the Pope to make those who had been murdered officially martyrs. The Vatican effectively recognized Franco on 28 August 1937 and supplied an Apostolic Delegate, Monsignor Ildebrando Antoniutti, on 7 October. *De jure* recognition came on 18 May 1938 when Archbishop Gaetano Cicognani was made Apostolic Nuncio and Franco sent an Ambassador to the Holy See. The attitude to Franco of international Catholicism was summed up in a letter sent to Franco on 28 March 1939 by the Archbishop of Westminster, Cardinal Arthur Hinsley, thanking him for a signed photograph: 'I look upon you as the great defender of the true Spain, the country of Catholic principles where Catholic social justice and charity will be applied for the common good under a firm peace-loving government.' The newly elevated Pope Pius XII greeted Franco's ultimate victory with a message beginning, 'With immense joy'. The Church was rewarded for its efforts on the Nationalists' behalf by being given exclusive control over education in the post-war state.

Catholicism was only one element of the Nationalist ideological armoury. The images of the *Reconquista* of Spain from the Moors were used to exalt and reinforce the notion of their war effort as a 'crusade' which was 'liberating' Spain from the godless hordes of Moscow. *Imperio* (empire) became an ideological watchword. The Francoists latched onto the statement by the Carlist Victor Pradera that 'the New State is no more than the Spanish State of the Catholic Kings'. However, the imperial verbiage and the references to Ferdinand and Isabella were balanced by more modern borrowings from fascism and Nazism. The Falangist symbol of the yoke and the arrows, like the swastika and the fascio, married the ancient and the modern. Theorists of the regime attempted to elaborate its own *Führerprinzip*, the so-called *teoría del caudillaje*, which borrowed from the doctrines of the German National Socialist Carl Schmitt. Parliamentary democracy and the rule of law were dismissed as antiquated survivals of the liberal age. All this was designed to ensure that real power would lie exclusively in the hands of General Franco. He would prove to be a jealous guardian of that power.

Perhaps out of a cynical desire to maintain the goodwill of his benefactors, the Caudillo was unrestrained in his praise for Nazism. He told German journalists 'what the German nation has already achieved with its struggle for liberation constitutes a model which we will always keep before us'. He exchanged fulsome telegrams with Mussolini. The first three recipients of the Grand Imperial Order of the Yoke and Arrows, the highest decoration in the New State, were King Vittorio Emmanuele, Benito Mussolini and Adolf Hitler. After the April 1937 unification, all Nationalist newspapers had to carry the slogan 'One Fatherland, One State, One Caudillo'. Germanic borrowings could also be discerned in the emergence of anti-semitism. *The Protocols of the Elders of Zion* was reprinted in large, cheap editions. Falangists were told, 'Comrade, it is your duty to root out Judaism, along with freemasonry, Marxism and separatism.' The Catalan magnate Francesc Cambó, who had gone into exile whence he had contributed significantly to the funding of the Nationalist war effort, was denounced as 'the wandering Jew'. Fundraising campaigns for the Nationalist war effort used slogans like 'He is a Jew who hides his gold when the Fatherland needs it'. When the distinguished French Catholic philosopher Jacques Maritain criticized the Nationalist bombing raids on Barcelona, he was denounced by Ramón Serrano Suñer as 'this converted Jew'. Claiming that the words of Maritain echoed those of the Elders of Zion, he described him as the darling of masonic lodges and synagogues.

The 'New State' over which Franco ruled was an ideological amalgam more or less satisfactory to all the component groups of the Nationalist side. Aristocrats and army officers shuddered with patrician disdain when addressed by Falangists as 'comrade' using the familiar *tu* form. Acid comments about the 'FAllange' reflected disquiet about the way ex-leftists were flooding the ranks of the *Movimiento* to escape the repression. Drapery establishments in the Nationalist zone ran out of blue cloth as orders flooded in for the *camisa azul* (blue shirt). It came to be known as the *salvavidas* (life jacket) and decrees were passed forbidding the sale of blue cloth without written authorization from Falange headquarters. The more conservative among the Francoist forces regarded the Falange with distaste but knew that it was a necessary evil. They could console themselves with the thought that, superficial appearances aside, the New State was nearer to their vision of the political future than to that of the more radical elements in the Falange.

The 'legal' formula on which the Nationalist state was based derived from the ideas of the monarchist group, Renovación Española. It justified the *Movimiento* and Franco's rule as a kind of military interregnum which would eradicate the liberal and leftist poison from Spain. When this was done, the monarchy would not be restored but 'installed' to emphasize the break in continuity with the past. The Francoist institutions, and particularly the 'Vertical' Syndicates, or state-run, non-representative and non-confrontational trade unions, were based on Italian Fascist models and a sop to the Falangists who found that their role was less than they had hoped. The wartime regime sported an ultra-Catholic, Nationalist and centralist rhetoric which was pleasing to all sections of the right.

Basque and Catalan names were banned from baptismal ceremonies. The use of the local languages, Catalan and Euskera,
was turned into a clandestine activity. When the Francoist
forces reached Tarragona in mid-January 1939, an elaborate
ceremony was held in the cathedral involving a company of
infantry. The officiating priest, a canon of the Cathedral of
Salamanca, José Artero, got so carried away during his sermon
that he shouted 'Catalan dogs! You are not worthy of the sun
which shines on you!' There was nothing in the Republican
zone to compare with the ideological cohesion or clarity of
purpose provided by the Catholic Church and the unified
Movimiento.

The dominant values of everyday life in the Nationalist zone
were Catholic, hierarchical and somewhat puritanical. To eat
in a restaurant without a jacket was frowned upon. Women
were encouraged to dress with protective modesty and not to
smoke or use make-up. Sleeves were expected to reach the
wrist; necklines to stay at the neck; skirts to be full and long.
Children over the age of two were obliged to wear bathing
suits at the beach. In the wartime conditions of social upheaval,
uncertainty and bereavement, however, there was a degree
of sexual licence which horrified the authorities. Moreover,
economic necessity and the demands of troops on leave led to
a massive prostitution boom and decrees were passed against
'carnal traffic'.

In the reactionary atmosphere of the rebel Nationalist zone,
there was nothing comparable to the Republican emancipation
of women. An image of Nationalist women as virgins or good
mothers – unblemished, passive, submissive and pious guard-
ians of the moral order – was propagated through the Church
and the Falange's women's organization, the *Sección Femenina*.
This was in sharp contrast to the imagery directed against
'red whores'. In general, Nationalist women were expected to
contribute to the war effort by joining various social services
run by the *Sección Femenina*. There, within the Francoist medical

services and the relief organization Auxilio Social, women were enabled to have a public existence hitherto denied them although it was to be short-lived. The ideological thrust of Franco's emergent regime was to stress women's role as home-makers and mothers for Falangist warriors. Ironically, the propagation of this message was put in the hands of indepen-dent single women.

Intellectual life was stultifying in the extreme. Ritualistic book burnings eliminated any remnants of liberal culture and a lot more besides. Books printed in the Nationalist zone usu-ally had a *nihil obstat* and were dated I, II or III Triumphal year rather than by the calendar. The bestsellers were lurid descriptions of red atrocities, eulogies of Nationalist military victories or else glutinous works of Falangist theory. Art was doggedly representational and music virtually non-existent. The political debate of the Republican zone had no equivalent. Propaganda was dreary and ubiquitous. A typical slogan to be found stencilled on walls all over the Nationalist zone was 'Honour – Franco, Faith – Franco, Authority – Franco, Justice – Franco, Efficacy – Franco, Intelligence – Franco, Will – Franco, Austerity – Franco'. Beneath a surface of religious and patriotic exaltation, there was core of cheap and prurient scur-rillity. Azaña was described as a monster created by Frankenstein rather than born of woman. Other Republican leaders were described as sexual perverts. Some of the more absurd asser-tions came from the pen of Ernesto Giménez Caballero, whose early novels have led to his being regarded nowadays as the father of Spanish surrealism. His views on the causes of the war were on a par with those of Captain Aguilera: 'If French women had not shown their thighs in the vaudevilles and swim-ming pools of Paris where our Republicans were educated, if there had not been so much tennis played by the American women who have filled our cinema screens for years, if Nordic women had not thrown themselves into the cult of the sun, perhaps our horrible Spanish Civil War would not have broken out.' Amongst his more demented inventions, he nurtured ambitions of creating a new Fascist dynasty by mating the Nordic Hitler with a Spanish woman, the prim and unsuspecting Pilar Primo de Rivera, sister of José Antonio.

Representative of the atmosphere in the Nationalist zone was the way in which the bellicose and triumphal tone of official propaganda crept into commerce. The sherry producers Gonzáles Byass cashed in on the liberation of the Alcázar by naming one of their brands *Imperial Toledano* and having it endorsed by General Moscardó. Hatters pointed out that the reds went bare-headed. Newspapers were full of advertisements which both contributed to and exploited the war effort. A Málaga pharmaceutical laboratory announced 'now that the city has been liberated from the Marxist hordes, its products are available at all good pharmacies in Seville'. The Firestone company expressed its confidence in Franco with a publicity campaign which blatantly identified its product with the war effort: 'Victory smiles on the best. The glorious Nationalist army always wins on the field of battle. Firestone Tyres has had its nineteenth consecutive victory in the Indianapolis 500.' The tone of mutual uplift and support was most aptly and graphically expressed in the advertisement which ran 'Araceli [brassières and corsets] salutes the Nationalist army. ¡Viva Franco! ¡Arriba España!'.

Daily life in the Nationalist zone was rather more agreeable than in the Republican half of the country, provided you had money and were in agreement with the prevailing political atmosphere. Food was plentiful, restaurants brightly lit and crowded. Hardly representative, but somehow indicative of the dramatic difference between patrician San Sebastián and the dourly serious and dispirited atmosphere of besieged Madrid, is the account given by Juan Antonio Ansaldo of his typical day during the campaign in the north. It will be recalled that Ansaldo was the pilot at the controls when Sanjurjo died. His arduous day of combat went as follows:

8.30   Breakfast with the family.

9.30   Takeoff for the front; bombard enemy batteries; machine-gun convoys and trenches.

11.00   Rudimentary golf in the club at Lasarte, next to the airport and partially usable.

12.30   Sunbathing on the Ondarreta beach and quick splash in the calm sea.

13.30   Shellfish, beer and a chat in a café in the Avenue.

14.00   Lunch at home.

15.00   Short siesta.

16.00   Second sortie, similar to this morning's.

18.30   Cinema. Old, but wonderful, movie with Katharine Hepburn.

21.00   Aperitif in the Bar Basque. Good 'Scotch', animated atmosphere.

22.15   Dinner at the Nicolasa Restaurant, war songs, camaraderie, enthusiasm.

It was a far cry from the daily rations of 'Dr Negrín's victory pills', the lentils on which the bulk of the Madrid population had to depend.

EIGHT

Politics behind the Lines: Revolution and Terror in the City of the Devil

The Republicans suffered from numerous problems which were virtually unknown to the Nationalists. They were never able to achieve anything like the singleness of purpose enjoyed in Salamanca. Political rivalries in the loyalist zone were possible precisely because the Republic remained a democracy, even in wartime conditions. Such rivalries were exacerbated by, and closely linked to, the question of foreign aid and Republican dependency on the Soviet Union. Another acute problem which afflicted the Republic, and not the Nationalists, was the questionable loyalty of its military personnel. Estimates of how many army officers remained loyal to the Republic vary. Much has been made by Francoist military historians of the fact that 'the army' as a whole did not rebel. Certainly, it has now been established that fewer senior generals rebelled than once was thought to be the case. About 70 per cent of generals and a small majority of colonels remained ostensibly loyal. However, the balance of military advantage still lay decisively with the Nationalists. Apart from total control of the best operational unit, the Army of Africa, they had a clear majority of field officers, majors, captains and lieutenants and an adequate number of the best generals to command them.

More importantly, the officers who opted for the Nationalists were committed to the cause and were immediately usable. Those who remained loyal to the Republic were not. They were mistrusted because of the simple fact that so many of their brothers-in-arms had already rebelled. Thus, it was feared that they were often loyal to the Republic only out of an expediency based on the geographical accident of where they happened to find themselves on 18 July. The deceptions practised by Queipo de Llano in Seville, by Aranda in Oviedo or by the officers who took Vigo and La Coruña did nothing to enhance the idea that army officers were honourable or trustworthy. With the war under way, there were numerous examples in the Republican zone of treachery, sabotage, deliberate incompetence and desertion. Artillery officers had their batteries aimed to miss their targets or 'accidentally' to rain shells on Republican troops. At the first opportunity, others crossed the lines with their units taking with them Republican battle plans. The suspicion with which regular army officers were regarded by the forces of the left was entirely comprehensible. In consequence, even competent and loyal officers were often not used to their fullest capabilities. A committee was set up under the fanatical Communist Major Eleuterio Díaz Tendero to classify officers as *faccioso* (rebel), indifferent or Republican. From his efforts emerged the nucleus of what was to be the Popular Army.

Just as the military rising had effectively denuded the Spanish Republic of a significant portion of its armed forces, so too did it leave the regime bereft of forces of law and order. In the short term, the lack of military units was spontaneously, albeit inadequately, made good by untrained militia units. The problem of the Civil Guard and the armed police known as the Assault Guards was less easily resolved. In the areas where the Civil Guard and the Assault Guards remained loyal, like Barcelona or Málaga, they held them for the Republic. However, in the main, their loyalties lay with the insurgents and even where they did not, the old forces of order were the object of understandable mistrust. The revolutionary enthusiasm which took workers to the front did not serve to make them volunteer to become policemen. As a result, the first two months of the war saw a breakdown of law and order in the Republican zone.

The Republican authorities made every effort to control the 'uncontrolled' elements. The official response was typified by a broadcast made by Indalecio Prieto. Although he held no official post, Prieto was effectively Prime Minister in the shadows while apparently serving merely as adviser to Giral's cabinet from 20 July to 4 September. From a large office in the Ministerio de la Marina, he worked untiringly to impose order and direction on the shambles that was the government. On 8 August 1936, he declared in a radio broadcast:

> Even if the terrible and tragic reports about what has happened and is happening in areas dominated by our enemies are true, even if day after day we receive lists of the names of comrades, of beloved friends, whose attachment to an ideal was enough to ensure them a treacherous death, do not, I beg you, I entreat you, do not imitate their behaviour. Meet their cruelty with your pity, meet their savagery with your mercy, meet the excesses of the enemy with your generous benevolence. Do not imitate them! Do not imitate them! Be better than them in your moral conduct! Be better than them in your generosity. I am not asking you, let it be clear, to lose strength in the struggle, ardour in the battle. I call for toughness in combat, breasts of steel, as some of our brave militias call themselves, breasts of steel, but responsive hearts, capable of shuddering in the face of human suffering, capable of pity and tender feeling, without which is lost the very essence of human greatness.

Julián Zugazagoitia, the editor of the daily *El Socialista* and a loyal supporter of Indalecio Prieto, wrote that 'the power of state lay in the street'. Described by Azaña as a 'taciturn

Basque', Zugazagoitia used his position to campaign for discipline in the rearguard and for respect on the battlefield for the lives of opponents. Typical of the ethical tone adopted by the paper was his editorial of 3 October 1936, headed 'Moral Obligations in War'. He wrote, 'The life of an adversary who surrenders is unassailable; no combatant can dispose of that life. That is not how the rebels behave? It matters not. It is how we should behave.'

Nevertheless, there was widespread terrorism for a brief period, mainly directed against the supporters of right-wing parties and the clergy. This situation was facilitated by the effective disappearance of the police force and the judiciary together with the fact that revolutionary crowds had opened the jails and released the common prisoners. Accordingly, behind a rhetoric of revolutionary justice, acts of violence of all kinds were perpetrated. Some violence was certainly an expression of popular outrage at the very fact of the military coup and its attempt to destroy the advances made by the Republic. Acts of revenge were directed at the sections of society on whose behalf the military was acting. Thus, hatred of an oppressive social system found expression in the murder or humiliation of parish priests who justified it, Civil Guards and policemen who defended it, the wealthy who enjoyed it and the employers and landlords' agents who implemented it. In some cases, the acts had a revolutionary dimension – the burning of property records and land registries. But there were also criminal acts, murder, rape, theft and the settling of personal scores. Courts were replaced by revolutionary tribunals set up by political parties and trade unions.

In the view of Juan García Oliver, the anarchist who was to become Minister of Justice in November 1936, such action was justified: 'Everybody created his own justice and administered it himself. Some used to call this "taking a person for a ride", but I maintain that it was justice administered directly by the people in the complete absence of the regular judicial bodies.'

Much less organized than even the 'tribunals' were the uncontrolled acts of reprisal and revenge for earlier offences real and imagined. The gruesome products of midnight *paseos* (car rides) at the hands of militia patrols or private enterprise hoodlums were the corpses to be found at dawn strewn along roadsides. The government did take steps to put a stop to irregular 'justice'. Under the premiership of José Giral, after the massacre at the Cárcel Modelo in Madrid on 23 August 1936, it set up Popular Tribunals in order to temper the revolutionary excesses. These had only a limited effect in the early weeks of the war.

It was impossible to keep the groundswell of long-repressed anti-rightist feeling entirely in check once the restraints were removed. Churches and convents in the Republican zone were sacked and burned. Many were put to profane use as prisons, garages or warehouses. Acts of desecration – the destruction of works of art, or the use of sacred vestments in satires of religious ceremonies – were usually symbolic and often theatrical. The most reliable study of religious persecution during the Civil War, by Fr Antonio Montero, claims that 6832 members of the clergy and religious orders were murdered or executed. Many others fled abroad. The popular hatred of the Church was the consequence both of its traditional association with the right and the ecclesiastical hierarchy's open legitimation of the military rebellion. About 55,000 civilians were killed in the Republican zone in the course of the war. It is difficult to find a simple explanation. Some, like those who were killed at Paracuellos del Jarama and Torrejón de Ardoz during the siege of Madrid, were victims of decisions based on an assessment of their potential danger to the Republican cause. Some were executed as known fifth columnists. Others died in explosions of mass rage which occurred as news arrived of the savage purges being carried out in the Nationalist zone and especially of atrocities committed by Franco's Moors. Air raids on Republican cities were another obvious trigger of popular fury.

Whatever the reasons behind the violence, it seriously damaged the reputation of the Republic abroad and undermined its efforts to secure international support. Bizarrely, the atrocities in the Nationalist zone did nothing to diminish its standing even in British and French government circles, let alone in Berlin or Rome. Republicans and Socialist like Azaña, Prieto and Negrín, for whom the Republic's legitimacy was based on its democratic norms and its defence of the rule of law, were appalled by the extra-judicial murders. On hearing of the shootings at the Cárcel Modelo in August, Negrín drove to the prison to try and stop the killing. He arrived too late but, in his outrage and frustration, his furious rant against the perpetrators nearly cost him his own life. Thereafter, in Madrid and later in Valencia, he would go out at night, unarmed and without an escort, and confront groups of militiamen who were making illegal arrests.

Even in besieged Madrid, efforts were made by the authorities to keep popular rage in check. On 14 November, the General Staff, via the press and the radio, issued an order that any enemy airmen who either crash-landed or parachuted from their planes were to be well treated. 'We understand only too well the feelings of anger and fury that overcome *milicianos* when they see the Fascists who destroy our houses. But principles of a military nature oblige us to demand that all units treat captured airmen scrupulously. A pilot who has come down in a parachute is *hors de combat*, and at the same time, is also a valuable source of information. The military authorities trust that this order will be obeyed, not because of possible sanctions, but because of the decency of Republican fighters.'

On the previous day a Russian pilot who had baled out of his aircraft was wounded as he dangled from his parachute, shot by loyalists on the ground. When he landed, he was assumed to be a German and beaten. Finally recognized as a Russian and taken to hospital, he died from his wounds. The General Staff order was aimed at preventing a repetition. The dangers to downed pilots were, however, much greater on the other side. On the same day that the Republican order was published, 14 November, after an aerial dogfight over Madrid, a Republican fighter came down behind the Nationalist lines. The pilot was captured and hacked to pieces. On the following day, the dismembered corpse was carefully wrapped and placed in a wooden box which was then parachuted into the centre of Madrid labelled 'For the Junta de Defensa'.

The delay in reimposing law and order and in organizing the war effort was a direct consequence of the confused relationship between the institutions of the state and the power which had passed into the hands of the people. The ambiguity was most acute in Barcelona and had been overtly recognized by the President of the Generalitat, Lluis Companys, leader of the bourgeois Republican party, the Esquerra. On 20 July 1936, immediately after the rising had been defeated, he was visited by a delegation from the CNT consisting of Buenaventura Durruti, Ricardo Sanz and Juan García Oliver. With astonishing candour, and not a little cunning, he told them, 'Today you are masters of the city and of Catalonia ... You have conquered and everything is in your power; if you do not need or want me as President of Catalonia, tell me now. If, on the other hand, you believe that in my post, with the men of my party, my name and my prestige, I can be useful in the struggle ... you can count on me and on my loyalty as a man and a politician.' Taken by surprise, the anarchist delegation asked Companys to stay on. They were then persuaded to join with the members of the Popular Front, to which the CNT did not officially belong, and create an Anti-Fascist Militia Committee to organize both the social revolution and its military defence.

Even after full consultation, the CNT leadership went along with the spontaneous decision of Durruti, Sanz and García Oliver. A combination of an apolitical anti-statist ideology and years of involvement in the day-to-day trade union activities of the CNT had left the anarcho-syndicalists ill-prepared to improvise the institutions necessary to handle the simultaneous organization of a revolution and a war. The Anti-Fascist Militia Committee was a great face-saving device for them. It seemed as if the workers were in control but the CNT acquiesced in the Central Anti-Fascist Militia Committee being simply a sub-committee of the Generalitat. Companys had effectively ensured a continuity of state power even if it was temporarily in the background. The presence in the Committee of both his own liberal Republican party, the Esquerra Republicana de Catalunya, and the Catalan Communist Party, the Partit Socialista Unificat de Catalunya, was a guarantee of this. The PSUC was as committed as Companys and the Esquerra to taming the revolution. Companys had manoeuvred the CNT into accepting responsibility without long-term institutionalized power. It did not occur to the anarchists that their effective authority in the streets could be short-lived. By the end of September, the CNT had agreed to the dissolution of the Anti-Fascist Militia Committee and its own direct participation in the Generalitat.

In Madrid, the unions dominated the government through their control of transport and communications, but ultimately the state apparatus survived, despite the appearance of a revolutionary takeover. In small towns and villages, Popular Front Committees and Committees of Public Safety were set up. In a frenetic atmosphere of revolutionary enthusiasm, the question of state power seemed irrelevant. Lorry loads of trade unionists set off for the front accompanied by hastily improvised armoured cars. The luxury hotels of Madrid and Barcelona were commandeered, their dining rooms converted into militia canteens. Symbols of middle-class respectability disappeared overnight. Hats, ties, tipping in restaurants, the polite *Usted* form of address all became things of the past. In Barcelona, brothels and cabarets were closed down. For two months, the trade unions were in control. They euphorically believed that the seizure of the means of production *was* the revolution. The advances of Franco's Army of Africa and Mola's northern army, however, pointed unavoidably to the need for military and economic coordination. By the end of September, the Militia Committee was dissolved and the CNT joined the Generalitat, along with the PSUC and the Esquerra.

The co-existence of the traditional institutions of the state and the spontaneous revolutionary committees of the workers was the clearest symptom of the Republic's most dramatic difficulty. This was born of the contradictory ambitions of the various component groups of the Popular Front. The ultimate issue was to do with the primacy of war or revolution. The view argued by the Communist Party, the right-wing of the Socialist Party and the bourgeois Republican politicians was that the war must be won first in order to give the revolution any possibility of triumphing later. With the possible exception of the Prieto wing of the PSOE, this was a not entirely disinterested argument. For the anarcho-syndicalist CNT, the more or less Trotskyist POUM and the left wing of the PSOE, proletarian revolution was itself the essential precondition for the defeat of fascism. The revolutionary viewpoint is best summed up in the aphorism that 'the people in arms won the revolution; the People's army lost the war'. However, neither the popular victories over the insurgents in Barcelona and Madrid in the first few days of the war nor the ultimate defeat of the Communist-organized Popular Army can definitively resolve the argument. After all, the Republic lost far more territory in the first ten months of the war before the Communists had finally established their hegemony than it did in the subsequent twenty-three months during which they dominated the war effort.

After 1939, Spanish Republicans engaged in bitter polemics about the responsibility for their defeat. The position put forward by the Communists and their allies was that the Spanish Civil War was fought between fascism and a popular, democratic anti-Fascist Republic. In this view, popular revolutionary movements were an obstacle which not only hindered the central task of creating an efficient army to win the war but also threatened to bring down on the head of the Republic an alliance of the conservative Western democracies with the Axis powers. The contrary position was best expressed in the words of the Italian anarchist Camilo Berneri who was murdered in murky circumstances in Barcelona in May 1937, either by Russian agents or Italian secret policemen: 'the dilemma, war *or* revolution, has no meaning. The only dilemma is this – either victory over Franco through revolutionary war *or* defeat.' In other words, only a full-scale proletarian revolution could destroy the capitalism which spawned fascism. This had been recognized by the vacillating Republican authorities who had hesitated to arm the workers on 18 July. They rightly feared that by arming the workers to defeat the military uprising, they risked unleashing proletarian revolution.

The two diametrically opposed positions are each based on a partial view of the war. In denouncing the revolutionaries as wreckers and the objective enemies of the popular cause, the Communists ignored the fact that the one great and unique weapon which the Republic possessed was popular enthusiasm. That weapon was destroyed when revolutionary structures were dismantled by ruthless methods. The revolutionary position tends to ignore both the international situation and the scale of conventional military might confronting the Republic. It is unlikely that Chamberlain's Britain or even Blum's divided France would stand idly by and watch a full-blown revolutionary society being built at the mouth of the Mediterranean. The Communist argument implies that the final outcome of the Civil War was inevitable. The revolutionary argument avoids that trap only at the expense of falling into another, the counter-factual proposition that 'if revolutionary war had been unleashed, then Franco would have been defeated'.

The entire debate was revived in 1969 by Noam Chomsky, who tried to link the Spanish struggle with the popular liberation movements then active in South East Asia. In doing so, Chomsky provided valuable insights into the power of popular revolutionary enthusiasm. On the other hand, his analogies fell down on the fact that neither Largo Caballero nor even Durruti were Ho Chi Minh and, more crucially, on the fact that there was no Ho Chi Minh trail weaving its way across the Pyrenees to a strong ally. The attractiveness of Chomsky's views is threefold. In the first place, the Communist destruction of the popular revolution seems a tragic waste to genuine supporters of the Spanish people's struggle against the most reactionary elements in Spanish society and their foreign Fascist allies. At the same time, many conservative historians have delighted in being able to condemn Communist atrocities in Spain against revolutionary groups with which they would otherwise have no sympathy. Finally, since the Communist proposition of the primacy of war over revolution was tried and found wanting, it is easy to clutch at the counter-factual straw that, had it not been for the Communists, the Republic would have won the Civil War. Against all of this stands the indisputable perception of the Communists, the bourgeois Republicans and the moderate Socialists that once the uprising had developed into a civil war, then the first priority had to be to win that war.

However, the reality of the revolutionary developments which took place in the first few days of the war could not simply be ignored. It had sweeping implications both in terms of the attitude of the masses to the loyalist war effort and of the international context in which the Republic had to exist. In all of Spain before July 1936, various class wars were being fought out. In the Nationalist zone, they were snuffed out by draconian repression. Not only working-class organizations and their members were crushed but a similar fate was also meted out to the adherents of the bourgeois Republican parties. This brutal resolution of the class problem was not emulated in the Republican zone. There were cases of factory owners and landlords being killed and the means of production passed to the urban and rural working classes. However, the contradictions between the bourgeois democratic Republicans and the moderate Socialists on the one hand and the revolutionary proletarian groups on the other remained a burning issue. The defeat of the rising by the workers brought about the situation of dual power epitomized by Companys' meeting with the CNT leaders. The Republican government in Madrid and the Generalitat in Catalonia theoretically ran the country but effective authority had passed, albeit very briefly, to the anarcho-syndicalist workers in Barcelona and to the UGT in Madrid.

The CNT delegation's decision to let Companys stay on meant a tacit acceptance that the libertarian revolution should take a back seat to the more immediate task of defeating the common enemy. However, impelled by their rank and file, the individual CNT unions ignored the leadership and ensured that a revolutionary takeover did indeed occur. Wholesale collectivization took place in industry and commerce, involving not just large enterprises, but also small workshops and businesses. This was sufficiently dramatic to impress even Communists. One, Narciso Julián, a railway worker who had arrived in Barcelona the night before the rising, told the British oral historian Ronald Fraser, 'it was incredible, the proof in practice of what one knows in theory: the power and strength of the masses when they take to the streets. Suddenly you feel their creative power; you can't imagine how rapidly the masses are capable of organizing themselves. The forms they invent go far beyond anything you've dreamt of, read in books.'

However, Barcelona was not representative of the whole of Republican Spain. The revolutionary takeover of lands and industry occurred to differing degrees according to the area in question. The only common features were the disorder and chaos that marked the first months of the war in the Republican zone. Moreover, few other cities experienced the revolutionary fervour felt in Barcelona. In Madrid, where there was far less industry anyhow, the atmosphere was more sombre and warlike than revolutionary. Valencia experienced no social cataclysm on a scale comparable to Barcelona, while in San Sebastián and Bilbao affairs carried on much as they had before 18 July. Throughout rural Spain, above all in the areas of *latifundio* estates and poor soil, the peasants quickly resolved the land question by collectivization. In Andalusia, there was socialized austerity of an impressive kind. The 'tyranny of property' was abolished and with it vices such as the consumption of coffee and alcohol. In parts of Aragón, the same was true although the spontaneity and revolutionary nature of much of the collectivization that took place has been exaggerated. In parts of Republican-held Castile, poverty overcame the instinctive individualism of the smallholders. The prosperous farmers of Catalonia, the Levante and Asturias, however, were anything but enthusiastic.

The collectives varied enormously in the way they were set up and run. Moreover, they were not all organized by the CNT. In the Levante, for instance, there occurred situations in which one small *pueblo* would have three collectives, one controlled by the CNT, one by the UGT and one by left Republicans. Not all the land that was expropriated was collectivized, and the amount of land seized varied according to the region. For instance, the recent study by Professor Aurora Bosch has shown that, while in Jaén 65 per cent of the useful land surface was expropriated, and 80 per cent of that land collectivized, in Valencia only 13.8 per cent of the land surface was seized, of which a mere 31.58 per cent was turned over to collectives. In general, however, in all Republican areas collectivization was most intense where the CNT was strongest. This was particularly evident in Aragón. There, the areas with the greatest UGT strength were in the west of the region and had fallen to the insurgents. The PCE, meanwhile, was very weak in Aragón, while the Republicans did not have sufficiently compact local organizations to command power. This left the field open to the CNT, even though its only real centre of strength was in the province of Zaragoza. The Aragónese anarcho-syndicalist collectivizers were bolstered by the military assistance granted by their Catalan comrades.

Indeed, the initial predominance of the CNT in the revolutionary committees of Aragón has been seen as largely the result of the influence of the Catalan militia. After the failure of the military uprising in the east of Aragón, Catalan CNT militia columns played a fundamental role in creating the 'climate' for social revolution. According to the Communists, this was done at the point of a gun. In much of the region, the collectives, far from being the spontaneous creation of peasants, were imposed by force. Moreover, whether genuinely spontaneous or forcibly created, they all faced the problem of putting into practice what had been up to that point only abstract theory. In the view of Juan Zafón, a Catalan militant of the CNT, who later wrote a book about his experiences as propaganda counsellor on the Revolutionary Council of Aragón, 'We were attempting to put into practice a libertarian communism about which, it's sad to say, none of us really knew anything.'

The Council of Aragón had been established in early October 1936 in an attempt to fill the political void created by the military rising and the widescale collectivization. As the fief of the CNT, the Council was from the first the target of hostile reaction from Communists, Socialists and Republicans alike. It was granted recognition by the central government of Largo Caballero in December. This entailed the creation of municipal councils, and the inclusion in the Council of representatives of the other Popular Front parties. The Council soon found itself caught in the dilemma of trying to provide a coherent structure to a highly disorganized series of local bodies without impinging upon their 'spontaneity'. In the event, it was forced to engage in economic centralization and thereby abandon the anarchist principle of autonomous local government. Indeed, the Council of Aragón was attacked by other Popular Front organizations for its interventionism, particularly in the sugar-producing factory at Monzón, and it was even accused of 'counter-revolutionary activity' within the CNT. This did not prevent the Communists denouncing the Council for imposing the 'tyranny of gangsters'.

Much the same story was true of Valencia where there were few clear ideas as to how to run collectives in practice. Moreover, the local provincial delegates of the government's Institute of Agrarian Reform were quite unable to impose any kind of order. In consequence, the Valencian agricultural collectives were permitted to operate with complete independence and autonomy. This, together with the violence which accompanied much of the collectivization, had a disastrous effect on the Valencian agricultural economy. Production was disrupted of the Valencian export crops of rice and oranges, a crucial source of foreign currency for the Republic. The extent of the economic chaos was so great that even the provincial revolutionary powers recognized the need to institute some unitary norm. However, although a Consejo de Economia de Valencia was set up, it had little or no effect. In fact, the instances in Valencia of total collectivization and the proclamation of libertarian communism were few and short-lived. War was hardly the best context for massive economic experiments. Collectivization tended to disrupt both the continuity of production and market mechanisms at precisely the time when planning and coordination were most urgently needed.

As a general rule, rural collectivization was accepted wholeheartedly by the landless *braceros* but resented by smallholders who saw the labour market drained, the threat of competition from units large enough to enjoy economies of scale and the ultimate possibility of their own expropriation. At the risk of simplification, it could be said that the Republican countryside witnessed a potential conflict between the rural proletariat gathered in the collectives and the smallholding rural middle classes. Similarly, in industrial towns, small businessmen, who might in fact be Republican voters, awaited warily the process of collectivization. These two conflicting groups in town and country looked to different national authorities: the collectivizers to the CNT and the UGT, the smallholders and businessmen to the Republican government. The overwhelming power of the proletariat might have been expected to prevail had there not been a war to be fought against Franco, Hitler and Mussolini. However, the need for foreign aid and the fact that the Soviet Union provided it soon altered the relation of forces within the Republican zone. The Communist Party was pushed from its relative obscurity to be, as the channel through which Russian aid passed, the arbiter of Republican politics.

Soviet policy on Spain was constrained by Stalin's search for Western allies against Hitler. Accordingly, Russian help had to ensure that political and social developments in Spain would stop short at the maximum which French and British policy-makers would tolerate. This meant guaranteeing that the Spanish Republic remained a bourgeois democratic parliamentary regime. In any case, the Spanish Communists were convinced that Spain was obliged by an iron historical destiny to pass through a bourgeois democratic stage on its road to socialism. They failed to perceive that in legal and economic terms Spain had already passed through a bourgeois revolution, albeit without a democratic political revolution, in the nineteenth century. Soviet directives and its own erroneous analysis of Spanish history thus meant that, in the potential class conflicts of the loyalist zone, the newly powerful PCE would throw its weight behind the bourgeois Republican forces. The consequent hostility between the Communists and the forces of revolution was bitter and violent. It would be intensified in 1937 by the determination of the Soviet advisers in Spain to emulate the Moscow purge trials and Stalin's witch hunt against Trotskyists.

However, it would be misleading to dwell only on divisions between the left-wing organizations. In the bleak world of the Depression, the Republican experiment inspired many Spaniards and foreigners with hopes of an egalitarian future. Despite the inexorable deterioration of wartime conditions – shortages, rationing, privations of all kinds – the sense of the Republic being worth fighting for survived well into 1938. One major area of change that symbolized this was the invasion by women of hitherto forbidden areas of politics, economics and society. The need to mobilize society for total war gave women in both zones a dramatically new participation in the functions of both government and society. As in all modern wars, the almost exclusively male preoccupation with violence created the necessity for women to take over the economic and welfare infrastructure. In the Republican zone, working-class women played key roles in war production, as nurses, even as soldiers, as farm labourers and as factory workers, often in appalling conditions of toxicity, running buses and trams in towns, as teachers in literacy campaigns at the front – as well as continuing to provide food and laundry for men. Women not only played a crucial role in industrial production but also assumed important positions in the political, and even military, establishment.

This was not without its complications. The young politically committed women who took up arms and went to fight as militiawomen fought with great courage when they were allowed to do so. However, it was widely assumed by their male comrades that they would be best employed cooking and washing. They were also subjected to considerable sexual pressure and, whether they succumbed to it or not, to the assumption that they were whores. Behind the lines, women ran public services in transport, welfare and health. That, together with the assumption of the role of principal breadwinner, had a dramatic effect on traditional gender relations. It was, however, short-lived and confined to the public sphere.

Domestic life was rarely democratized and women continued to take principal responsibility for cooking, cleaning and child-care even as they organized the sinews of war.

The revolutionary euphoria was also short-lived in many respects. By August 1936, the Communists were working to ensure that the war effort would have as its central objective the defence of the legitimately elected bourgeois democratic Republic. At first, they gave their backing to the Giral government. This brought them into conflict with the reality of the revolution in the fields and the factories. However, the PCE had a certain advantage in its control of Soviet aid which would be cut off unless certain adjustments were made. Thus, in late August, when it became obvious that the Giral government had to be replaced, the Comintern sent the French Communists André Marty and Jacques Duclos to persuade Largo Caballero that his preference for a revolutionary Junta of the PSOE–UGT, the CNT–FAI and the PCE was dangerously irresponsible. The Russian view was that the Western powers would not tolerate a workers' government within their sphere of influence. Far from trying to take over themselves, they were committed to ensuring that the Republic maintained a more broadly based government. According to the diaries of Georgi Dimitrov, the head of the Comintern, a Politburo meeting in the Kremlin agreed, with Stalin's telephoned approval, 'to seek the transformation of the Giral government into a government of national defence, headed by Giral with a majority of Republicans, participation of Socialists and two Communists, as well as representatives of the Catalans and Basques'.

The Communists were anxious that the new government should not be headed by a Socialist, particularly by Largo Caballero. When they were unable to prevent this happening, in reporting their failure to Moscow they cited the continued presence of Giral as Minister without Portfolio in mitigation. The government formed by Largo Caballero on 4 September included Republicans as well as representatives of the workers' parties. Largo Caballero's undeserved reputation as the 'Spanish Lenin' served as a sop to the workers although it also confirmed the prejudices of diplomats in London and Paris. However, Azaña and Prieto, who rather despised Largo Caballero, looked to the Communists as a guarantee that the bourgeois Republic was intact.

The position of the Communists posed a terrible dilemma for the anarchists. If the rebels should win the war, the anarchist experiment would definitely be brought to an end. For the Republic to win, the active cooperation of the anarchists was essential. The issue hinged on what form that cooperation should take, and what price should be paid in terms of sacrificing revolutionary gains. The Communists had no doubt that the CNT–FAI should join the central government both in order to create a solid political front and to implicate them in the destruction of their autonomous revolutionary powers. It was the Communists who, according to Largo Caballero, 'asked that everything possible should be done in order that the CNT should be represented in the government, and I promised it'. Pressure was brought to bear upon the CNT and on 3 November 1936 negotiations were finalized. On the following day, their four representatives joined the cabinet in besieged Madrid. Inevitably, the decision created tensions and frictions within the anarchist movement. Even for those in favour of participation, it was a painful decision. Joining the cabinet reflected a recognition that if the CNT remained outside, it would be that much easier for the Communists to control the key decision-making apparatus.

The anarchist ministers quickly found themselves confronted with the PCE assertion of the need to postpone revolutionary action until the bourgeois Republic had been consolidated against Fascist attack. They were slow to perceive the strength of the tacit alliance created between the PCE on the one hand and Azaña and Prieto on the other. They hoped to use the Communists to control the revolutionary masses of the UGT and the CNT. The central government began a policy of bureaucratic harassment of collectivized industry and agriculture. This could be justified by the fact that production had to be integrated into a centralized war effort. However, deliberately manipulated credit shortages created major difficulties for many collectives. At the same time as the achievements of the popular revolution were being whittled away, the Communists aligned themselves with the petty bourgeois forces within Republican society. For a large sector of the rural and urban middle classes, the Communist position came as an immense relief. Profoundly disheartened by the trend to collectivization, they had been driven to despair by the seeming inability of their own Republican leaders to control events. The Communists consciously set out to win the support of the threatened small-property owners. They began to pick up members among army officers, state bureaucrats and middle-class professionals, attracted by their efficiency, as well as smallholders and small businessmen, attracted by their hostility to collectivization.

PCE party offices carried signs which read 'Respect the property of the small peasant' and 'Respect the property of the small industrialist'. Vicente Uribe, the Communist Minister of Agriculture in the government of Largo Caballero, legalized the expropriation of lands belonging to Francoists – but not of other collectivized land, much of which was now returned to its owners. He stated that 'the property of the small farmer is sacred and that those who attack or attempt to attack that property must be regarded as enemies of the regime'. It was all part of a policy of dismantling the revolution. Stalin wrote to Largo Caballero on 21 December 1936, 'the urban petty and middle bourgeoisie must be attracted to the government side ... The leaders of the Republican party should not be repulsed; on the contrary they should be drawn in, persuaded to get down to the job in harness with the government ...

This is necessary in order to prevent the enemies of Spain from presenting it as a Communist Republic, and thus to avert their open intervention, which represents the greatest danger to Republican Spain.'

The policies advocated by Stalin and pursued by the Largo Caballero government were based on a realistic assessment of the attitudes of the great powers. Unfortunately, since the five years of the Republic had stripped the Spanish working class of any illusions about the capacity for reform of bourgeois democracy, those policies dramatically damaged working-class morale in the Republican zone.

In a similar way, the dissolution on 30 September 1936 of the spontaneous revolutionary militia and their replacement by regular army units diminished the revolutionary élan of the masses. However, after the uninterrupted defeats at the hands of the Army of Africa in the early months of the war, it seemed an elementary military requirement. It is a romantic view which sees the creation of the Popular Army as a backward step. Indeed, it is difficult to deny the military achievements of the Communists. The Spanish Communists, advised by the delegates of the Comintern and Soviet military technicians, were the first to appreciate that, if the Republic was to avoid being swept aside by the Nationalists, it must have properly trained regular troops carrying out the orders of a unified and coherent command. The Communists, by dint of their organizational structure, their fetish for rigid discipline and their access to Soviet aid, were in an immediate position to organize the Popular Army. Largo Caballero was persuaded of the logic of the Communist position through the combined efforts of Mikhail Koltsov, the Soviet journalist, and Julio Alvarez del Vayo, the Socialist Foreign Minister who had developed very close ties with the Communists. In any case, the defects of the militia system were glaringly obvious. Their attempt to maintain full democracy in the field had led to costly inefficiency. Vital hours would often be lost in discussions and deliberations amongst committee members. Discipline was almost impossible to enforce. There had even been cases of militiamen going home for the weekend while on active service.

The Communists, in contrast, demanded 'Discipline, Hierarchy, and Organization'. These three virtues reached their apogee in the Communists' own Fifth Regiment, which was to form the core of the Popular Army. Modelled on the Red Army of the Russian Civil War, the Fifth Regiment was led by a series of outstanding Communist officers: Enrique Castro Delgado, Enrique Lister and Juan Modesto. The efficiency of the Fifth Regiment attracted thousands to its ranks. According to José Martín Blázquez, a Republican army officer, 'The Communist Party must be granted the credit of having set the example in accepting discipline. By doing so it enormously increased not only its prestige, but its numbers. Innumerable men who wished to enlist and fight for their country joined the Communist Party.' The Fifth Regiment also enjoyed the advantage of being favoured in the distribution of Soviet arms.

It was precisely over the Republican army that the Communists ultimately clashed with Largo Caballero. It was to lead to his downfall as Prime Minister. The Communists were anxious for the removal of General José Asensio, Largo Caballero's appointee as Under-Secretary for War, whom they saw as an obstacle to their plans to gain hegemony over the Republican war effort. The crude and blatant way in which the Soviet Ambassador, Marcel Rosenberg, attempted to impose his viewpoint caused intense friction. Eventually, Rosenberg's intrusions led to a famous incident in which Largo Caballero rounded on him, and on the Minister of Foreign Affairs, Julio Alvarez del Vayo, who had demanded Asensio's dismissal. Apparently, the Soviet Ambassador spent several hours every day in the office of the Prime Minister. Largo Caballero's friend and adviser Luis Araquistain wrote later:

More than an ambassador, [Rosenberg] acted like a Russian viceroy in Spain. He paid daily visits to Largo Caballero, sometimes accompanied by Russians of high rank, military or civilian. During the visits, which lasted hours on end, Rosenberg tried to give the head of the Spanish government instructions as to what he should do in order to direct the war successfully. His suggestions, which were practically orders, related mainly to army officers. Such and such generals and colonels should be dismissed and others appointed in their place. These recommendations were based, not on the competence of the officers, but on their political affiliations and on the degree of their amenability to the Communists.

Rosenberg was usually accompanied on these visits by the most elevated interpreter imaginable, Alvarez del Vayo himself. On the morning of the confrontation, a two-hour meeting ended when Largo Caballero was heard shouting. According to the Socialist deputy Ginés Ganga, Caballero's shouting increased in intensity. Then, all of a sudden, the door opened, and the aged premier of Spain, standing in front of his table, his arms outstretched and his shaking finger pointing at the door, was heard saying in a voice tremulous with emotion: 'Get out! Get out! You will have to learn, Señor Ambassador, that although we Spaniards are very poor and need help from abroad very much, we are too proud to let a foreign ambassador attempt to impose his will on the head of the government of Spain! And as for you, Vayo, it would be better to remember that you are a Spaniard and Minister of Foreign Affairs of the Republic and that you should not combine with a foreign diplomat in putting pressure on your Prime Minister.'

Relations between Largo Caballero and the Communists rapidly deteriorated. He had belatedly realized that the massive Communist contribution to Republican resistance was unfortunately linked to a sectarian view of society and a set of dictatorial methods which could only lead to conflict with other groups which were also making a great sacrifice in the fight against Franco. After the débâcle at Málaga, in which all the shortcomings of the militia system were starkly revealed, Asensio was dismissed. Largo Caballero now began to try to reduce the dominance of the Communists in the army, without really having a coherent alternative strategy. By the time he tried to take them on, however, it was too late. Soviet arms supplies, and the ordered efficiency of the Communists, left the Spanish Prime Minister with little hope of success. His sympathies lay with the revolutionary elements of the left that had set about collectivizing industry and agriculture without showing too much concern for the war effort. The efforts of the Communists, on the other hand, were supported by substantial sectors of the PSOE and by the bourgeois Republican parties which realized that priority had to be given to the war effort.

Events came to a head in May 1937 in Barcelona where both social and political tensions had been mounting for some months. By this stage the 'proletarian content' of the initial revolutionary stages of the struggle had been severely emasculated. Increasingly, the PCE, the Republicans and the reformist Socialists were taking command of the political and military structures of the Republic. In Catalonia, the regional government, the Generalitat, was systematically recovering the powers lost when the military coup undermined the apparatus of the state. In Spain as a whole, the trend towards the creation of a conventional state capable of fighting a conventional war effort constituted a challenge to the left Socialist followers of Largo Caballero, the anarchists and the POUM. Until ousted by Communists in December 1936, the POUM leader, Andreu Nin, had been Minister of Justice (Conseller de Justicia) in the Generalitat. The CNT and the POUM had come to feel that the sacrifices (such as the removal of Nin) demanded by the Communists in favour of a bourgeois Republic were simply not influencing the Western powers, who were in the last analysis fully aware that Franco was a better bet for Western capitalism than the Republic could ever be. For the POUM, which had its main strength in Lérida and Barcelona, the war and revolution were inseparable.

The Generalitat's efforts to claw back its powers from the revolutionary unions were already creating considerable tension. This was dramatically exacerbated by the context of economic and social distress caused by the war. The population of Barcelona had been swelled by 10 per cent by the arrival of 350,000 refugees. Shortages and inflation were kept under control in the short term by the CNT's supply committees which requisitioned food in the countryside and distributed it to the urban poor. Inevitably, the actions of the CNT in imposing low prices led to peasants hoarding food. The consequent shortages and food price inflation led to bread riots in Barcelona. Companys was already on a collision course with the CNT. Determined to put an end to anarchists' excesses, he had already re-established conventional police forces in October. Moreover, in the interests of the war effort, Companys was anxious to establish central control of industry. On 9 December 1936, he told the press, 'We all want to rescue the honour and glory of the revolution and win the war and stop the murderers. We don't need juntas large or small, commissions and committees and this and that initiative. There are at least a dozen reasons which make it necessary to constitute a strong government to impose its authority with full powers.'

Companys's stance on all these issues was strongly supported by the PSUC which, for a variety of reasons, was already campaigning for the removal of the POUM from the Catalan government. Like Companys, the PSUC leadership believed that the POUM's denunciation of the Generalitat as counter-revolutionary and its call for a revolutionary workers' front with the CNT were undermining the war effort. Moreover, at a dinner on 12 December with Companys, the Russian Consul

General in Barcelona, Vladimir Antonov-Ovseenko, stressed that continued Soviet aid required evidence that obstacles to a unified war effort were being removed. On 16 December, Companys reshuffled his cabinet. He put Joan Comorera of the PSUC in charge of supply as the first step towards a return to the free market. Conflict between the Esquerra and the PSUC on the one hand and the CNT committees on the other was only a matter of time.

The POUM was being singled out for the enmity of the Communists precisely because of views which, while not strictly Trotskyist, given its founder Nin's complex relationship with Trotsky himself, could easily be presented as such. The party had made itself even more of a target by dint of its outspoken public criticisms of the trial and execution of the old Bolsheviks Kamenev and Zinoviev. Their Bolshevik analysis of the PCE's betrayal of the revolution in Spain was especially wounding to the Communists. Encouraged by Antonov-Ovseenko, the PCE began to call for the extermination of the POUM and to denounce as enemies of the USSR, 'Fascist spies' and 'Trotskyist agents' those who criticized the Moscow trials. Blindly following the Soviet leadership, the Spanish Communists were convinced that the trials were genuinely directed against 'enemies of the people'. Moreover, after the Republican defeat at Málaga, the Russians, and particularly the newly arrived Comintern delegate, 'Boris Stepanov', became obsessed with the notion that there had been sabotage and treachery. Inevitably, this put the spotlight on the local 'Trotskyists', the POUM.

However, the notorious persecution of the POUM has to be seen in the context of the Russians' concern, shared by Spanish Republicans and Socialists, as well as Communists, that the war effort needed to be more disciplined and centralized. The Russians used their influence to insist that 'experiments in industry and especially among the peasantry' were abandoned. In the context of the time, and in the light of the

POUM's provocatively subversive criticisms of the Generalitat, it was almost inevitable that POUM militia units were starved of arms. Orwell and others complained that POUM units at the front had to make do with tattered uniforms, bad equipment and inadequate supplies of food and ammunition. In contrast, the Communist units in Barcelona which spent their time harrassing the POUM were well equipped. As Orwell put it, 'a government which sends boys of fifteen to the front with rifles forty years old and keeps the biggest men and the newest weapons in the rear is manifestly more afraid of the revolution than of the fascists'.

However, Orwell, inevitably given his lowly position in a POUM militia, was not seeing the bigger picture. The growing tide of refugees into Catalonia was putting increasing pressure on food supplies. Comorera's liberalization of the market permitted rural producers to raise their prices but that didn't resolve the issue since Catalonia needed to import food and simply did not have the foreign currency to do so. Despite rationing, shortages, inflation, speculation and the growth of a black market caused bitter social tension. At the same time, the Generalitat and the PSUC were in conflict with the CNT and the POUM over control of war industries and armaments, rural and industrial collectivizations, the militarization of the militias and public order. Both sides claimed that violent mass demonstrations by women against rising food and fuel prices supported their case. Tension was heightened from mid-March when the Generalitat made a definitive push to take control of public order, dissolving the CNT's security patrols and demanding that all workers' organizations surrender their arms. The CNT withdrew from the government of the Generalitat.

Tension was screwed even higher when one of the many consequent clashes saw, on 25 April, the assassination of Roldán Cortada, a member of the PSUC and secretary to Rafael Vidiella, Minister for Labour and Public Works for the

Generalitat. A few days later the leader of the local CNT committee in Puigcerdá, Antonio Martín, known as '*el cojo de Málaga*' (the cripple from Málaga), and two other anarchists died in a shootout with a detachment of *carabineros*, the frontier guards who were under the jurisdiction of the Minister of Finance, Dr Negrín. The collectives were being brought under government control. There were clashes between the CNT patrols and the security patrols. Communist secret police units began to pick up POUM militants. By April 1937 tension in Catalonia was reaching extreme levels. In consequence, the Generalitat decreed the prohibition of the traditional May Day rallies. This was perceived as a provocation by the CNT rank and file. In early May, the crisis exploded.

The immediate catalyst of the May Days was the raid on the CNT-controlled central telephone exchange in Barcelona ordered on 3 May by Eusebio Rodríguez Salas, PSUC police commissioner for Catalonia. Coming in the wake of deteriorating conditions and police heavy-handedness over the previous three months, this led to the outbreak of street fighting – a small-scale civil war within the Civil War. This could have been averted had the Generalitat pulled back the forces surrounding the telephone building but Companys took the opportunity to continue the offensive against the CNT. He told the press, 'there are armed groups on the streets and there is no choice but to disperse them'. He underestimated the scale of popular resistance to the campaign to re-assert the power of the state. Barricades went up in the centre of Barcelona. The CNT, the POUM and the extreme anarchist group, the Friends of Durruti, confronted the forces of the Generalitat and the PSUC for several days. Working-class districts and the industrial suburbs were in the hands of the anarchist masses but their lack of coordination gave the initiative back to Companys.

Although the origins of the May Days lay deep in the wartime circumstances of Catalonia and their impact on the poorest members of society, the central government, the

Generalitat and the PSUC were not slow to seize opportunities to advance their own agendas. The Communists and Prieto were delighted to have a chance to break the power of the CNT and limit that of the Generalitat. The fighting exposed the central dilemma of the CNT. The anarchists could win in Barcelona and other Catalan cities only at the cost of bloodshed which would effectively lose the war for the Republic. They could hold on only by recalling their troops from Aragón and having then to fight both the central Republican government and the Francoists. Accordingly, Juan García Oliver, the Minister of Justice, made a broadcast from the Generalitat on behalf of the CNT leadership calling on the incredulous militants to lay down their arms. The government in Valencia provided the decisive police reinforcements on 7 May which finally decided the outcome. It did so only in return for the Generalitat surrendering autonomous control of the Army of Catalonia and responsibility for public order. Several hundred members of the CNT and the POUM were arrested, although the need to get the war industries working again limited the scale of the repression. All this was happening as the Basque Country was falling to Franco.

This left the POUM as the sacrificial goat. Andreu Nin and the rest of the POUM leadership had far exceeded the CNT in the militancy of their revolutionary pronouncements during the crisis. In victory, the Communists were anything but magnanimous. They would settle for nothing less than the complete destruction of the POUM. Orwell noted that 'there was a peculiar evil feeling in the air – an atmosphere of suspicion, fear, uncertainty and veiled hatred'. Immediately the fighting in Barcelona was over, the Communists demanded that the Largo Caballero government dissolve the POUM and arrest its leadership. Largo Caballero refused. For the Communists, this confirmed their belief that he must go. In fact, the decision had already been taken in March at a fiery meeting of the Spanish Politburo, a meeting at which there were more foreigners than Spaniards. The Comintern advisers, particularly André Marty and 'Boris Stepanov', had insisted on the removal of Largo Caballero and clashed violently with the PCE leaders, José Díaz and Jesús Hernández. When the Prime Minister's fate was put to the vote, theirs had been the only two votes in his favour. By blocking Largo Caballero's plans for an offensive in Extremadura, the Communists provoked a cabinet crisis. Largo Caballero was left without support. Indalecio Prieto, the moderate Socialist, nurtured a long-smouldering resentment against the dour Prime Minister, and his supporters in the PSOE were glad of the chance to oust the Caballerists. They particularly felt that he and his Minister of the Interior, Ángel Galarza Gago, had not shown sufficient energy in reimposing public order. Azaña, meanwhile, would not forgive Largo Caballero for the delay in getting him out of Barcelona during the May Days. Thus, Largo Caballero was forced to resign, and the government was offered to Dr Juan Negrín. In a sense, this marked an end to the power struggle between the revolutionists and the Communists. From this point on, the revolutionary achievements of the initial stages of the struggle would be steadily dismantled, leaving the war to follow the direction dictated by the Republicans and moderate Socialists who had taken over the key ministries in the government.

When Azaña asked the PSOE executive to propose a new Prime Minister, he had assumed that Prieto would be their choice. Certainly, Prieto's comrades were unanimous in wanting to put forward his name. However, he categorically refused, claiming both that he lacked support from the anarcho-syndicalists and the Caballeristas and that, decisively, the Communists wanted Negrín. His inclination was to remain working in the shadows. Accordingly, he took overall charge of the war effort in a new Ministry of National Defence created by the merger of two crucial ministries, those of War and of Navy and Air. Azaña was not displeased to have to invite Negrín to form a government: 'As Prime Minister, the ups and downs of Prieto's moods, his sudden impulses, might have been a real disadvantage.'

In the new cabinet, Prieto used his influence with Negrín to press for the appointment as the Minister of the Interior of Julián Zugazagoitia because of his firm commitment to the re-establishment of law and order. Together with the choice of another Basque, Manuel Irujo, as Minister of Justice, this ensured that there would be no Moscow trials in Spain despite the Communist persecution of the POUM. Irujo, on taking up his post, declared, 'I raise my voice to say that the "*paseos*" are a thing of the past. There were days when the government did not control the apparatus of power and found itself powerless to oppose social outrages. Those times are behind us. Now it is crucial that the example of the enemy's monstrous brutality not be used to excuse the repugnant crimes committed nearer to home.'

One of the first things that Irujo did was to professionalize the prison service. The corps of prison guards was reformed and strengthened to ensure no repetition of the atrocities of November 1936. The prison regime was relaxed in a way unimaginable in the Nationalist zone. Catholic clergy and religious were released. The Red Cross was allowed full access to prisons. Many civilian prisoners were allowed out on parole for the births, marriages, illnesses or deaths of family members. As a result of these measures, Irujo was for a time denounced by the anarchist press as a Vaticanist caveman and a bourgeois reactionary but, eventually, he was to be congratulated by an anarchist delegation for his work. In the Ministry of the Interior, Zugazagoitia would use his position to save many lives of prominent Falangists in Republican custody. His conduct did not save him after the Civil War, however. Zugazagoitia was exiled to France, where he was captured by the Gestapo who handed him over to the Francoist authorities. He was executed by firing squad on 9 November 1940.

Dr Negrín was certainly concerned to finish the job of re-establishing discipline but, unlike Azaña, who hoped that this would be the first step towards seeking international mediation to end the war, he knew that the policy had to be to fight on. He was convinced that the only chance for the Republic lay in close cooperation with the Soviets. Juan Negrín remains an enigma. In personal terms, he was a complete opposite of the puritanical Largo Caballero: charming, engaging, cosmopolitan, multi-lingual, a gourmet and apparently a voracious sexual athlete, despite his portly figure. A brilliant medical researcher, he had worked in Germany for several years then gained, in 1922 at the age of thirty, the Chair of Physiology at the University of Madrid. He had joined the PSOE in 1929, and had been elected in 1931 as a moderate Socialist deputy for his native Las Palmas, in the Canary Islands. During the years of the Republic, his prodigious energy had been put at the service of the creation of Madrid's University City, which was to be the scene of so many battles in the Civil War. He was considered to be an ally of Indalecio Prieto. By the time that he assumed the premiership, however, the relations between the two were deteriorating as a result of their differing attitudes to the Communists. In the view of Burnett Bolloten, 'he more than any other Spaniard was responsible for the success of Communist policy during the last year of the Civil War'. Given that the Communists were committed to the defeat of fascism in Spain, that is perhaps not as heinous a crime as Bolloten made it sound. Certainly, Negrín's policy rested on the firm conviction that victory depended upon discipline within the armed forces, and on the continued supply of arms from the Soviet Union. As in the case of the transfer of Spanish gold reserves to Moscow, it is difficult to see what options other than currying Communist favour were open to Negrín. His government was more united than any of its predecessors. However, its unity had been bought at the price of liquidating the revolution. It was the logical conclusion and the most concrete realization of the Popular Front option, a government which enshrined the Communist alliance with bourgeois democratic forces in the interests of Russian relations with the bourgeois democracies.

Negrín was not alone in believing that the democratic powers in Europe must come to the Republic's aid if they could be persuaded of the non-revolutionary nature of the Republican struggle. His close collaboration with the Communists is therefore entirely understandable. For the Communists, once Negrín had been installed as premier, their main objectives were to continue the process of centralization by ensuring the destruction of the POUM. In the long term, they would also turn against Indalecio Prieto, as his defeatism became more manifest. Under pressure from the various Russian advisers, their assault against the POUM was intensified. The party was declared illegal in mid-June 1937, its executive committee arrested and accused of wartime sedition for its part in the May Days.

In a horrific escalation of the assault on the POUM, its leader, Andreu Nin, was kidnapped in Barcelona by Russian agents. They took him to a house in Alcalá de Henares, where he was interrogated and brutally tortured. When he refused to 'confess' to being a Nazi agent, he was taken out and executed. Clumsy Communist propaganda efforts to pretend that Nin had been spirited away by a Nazi rescue squad could not prevent ongoing speculation that his murder was the work of the NKVD, the Soviet secret police. In fact, it was almost certainly masterminded by the chief NKVD rezident in Spain, Colonel Alexander Orlov (Leiba Lazarevich Feldbin). He had been sent to Spain in late August 1936, ostensibly as a political attaché with the exclusive task of combating Trotskyism. At the same time as Nin disappeared, so too did a number of foreign Trotskyists, including the Austrian writer Kurt Landau and José Robles Pazos, a friend of the influential American novelist John Dos Passos.

Irujo initiated a judicial investigation. Zugazagoitia dismissed the Director General of Security, the Communist Colonel Antonio Ortega, because of his inability to explain his role in the disappearance of Nin. The Communists were furious but backed down when Zugazagoitia, Irujo and Prieto threatened to leave the government. Negrín, though he supported the sacking of Ortega, was not prepared to see further revelations undermine the unity of the cabinet and ordered the suspension of the investigation. An incandescent 'Boris Stepanov' reported to Moscow that Zugazagoitia was 'a Trotskyist in disguise and Irujo 'a Jesuit', 'a Fascist'. The Nin affair caused considerable friction between Negrín on the one hand and Zugazagoitia and Irujo on the other. Unappeased and outraged by the murder, Largo Caballero, still smarting from his removal, and the anarchists who had been in his cabinet went to see Azaña and denounced Negrín as a traitor. However, the President of the Republic shared Negrín's view that rebellion in wartime could not be tolerated. Azaña had no more sympathy than Negrín with the POUM advocacy of a revolutionary workers' and peasants' government and so ignored their request that he should dismiss the Prime Minister. Curiously, Azaña's view was shared by the man who founded the POUM with Nin, Joaquín Maurín, who had spent the May Days in a Francoist prison. Many years later, he wrote the epitaph for his own movement: 'The POUM executive never understood that the first priority had to be to win the war. They put the revolution before the war effort and they lost the war and the revolution, and they lost themselves in the process.' Nevertheless, the disappearance and murder of Nin, Landau, Robles and others did enormous damage to the credibility of the Negrín government both at the time and long after.

In the event, the rest of the POUM executive did not share the fate of their leader. There were no subsequent executions. Indeed, Manuel Irujo ensured that Nin would be the last

Trotskyist to be murdered. For the repression of the POUM, the government had created a Special Court for Espionage and High Treason but Irujo ensured that it would be made up of judges of the highest impartiality and probity. Large numbers of rank-and-file POUM militants were in prison, infuriated at being held alongside Fascists and saboteurs and still not formally charged. Kurt Landau's wife, Katia, still unware of her husband's precise fate, began a hunger strike which spread quickly through the penitentiaries of Barcelona and Valencia. Irujo visited her in hospital and persuaded her that the trials would be fair. She was sufficiently impressed to call off the strike. When Irujo sent prosecutors and judges into each prison with the appropriate paperwork, they were applauded by the prisoners who saw them as guarantors against Stalinist illegalities.

The seriousness of Irujo's commitment to restoring full Republican legality can be deduced from the fact that, in the autumn of 1937, he initiated investigations into what had happened at Paracuellos in November 1936. To the outrage of 'Boris Stepanov', he ordered a judicial enquiry into the role of Carrillo. By the time the trial of the POUM executive took place in October 1938, Irujo was no longer Minister of Justice. He had resigned at the end of November 1937 in disagreement with Negrín's proposals for special courts with emergency powers and was replaced by the Republican Mariano Ansó. Irujo stayed on as Minister without Portfolio, having ensured that any death penalties imposed by the special courts would have to be ratified by the cabinet. The trial eventually of the seven POUM executive committee members proceeded in the heightened atmosphere during the tense final stages of the decisive battle of the Ebro. Nevertheless, it was conducted, as Irujo had promised Katia Landau, with full judicial guarantees. Two of the accused were absolved and five given prison sentences. All escaped from Spain at the end of the war.

Meanwhile, the Communists had continued to press for

fuller centralization. Thus, the Council of Aragón was dissolved. However, in enacting the Decree of Dissolution of 11 August 1937, Enrique Lister, the Communist commander, went well beyond the decree's provisions. In an unnecessarily brutal repression, the Council was dismantled and many CNT members were arrested. The effects on both morale and agricultural efficiency were devastating. After Aragón, the Communists moved against the collectives of Catalonia, and by 1938 there remained little of the autonomy granted by the Popular Front. Other centralizing measures included the use of the secret police known as the Servicio de Investigación Militar (SIM), which had been increasingly infiltrated by Communists, to purge opponents. Gustav Regler referred to the Comintern's obsession with spies and traitors as the 'Russian syphilis'. The crushing of the collectives and the use of secret police ensured that the last two years of the Civil War in the Republican zone were very different from the first. Without the sense of a new world to fight for, the sacrifices and the hunger were that much harder to bear.

The PCE was in an ironic sense also a loser. The Communists had backed the bourgeois Republicans and the moderate Socialists and in the latter stages of the war those groups were suffused with defeatism. Even within the PCE doubts were expressed about the choices that had been made, especially after Munich seemed to suggest a rapprochement between the Western powers and the Axis. The major obstacle remaining for the PCE was the continued presence in the cabinet of the increasingly anti-Communist Indalecio Prieto as Minister of Defence. Although Prieto and the PCE had been united by their opposition to the revolutionism of Largo Caballero and the anarchists, each saw in the other the means to further their own particular interests. Prieto had always been suspicious of the Communists. Once Largo Caballero had been removed, the marriage of convenience was bound to break down. Prieto, whose natural tendency to pessimism and discouragement found an echo in Azaña's traumatized state of despair, sought to reduce the prominence of the Communists. This put the PCE in an awkward position. Having placed such stress on the need to defend a moderate bourgeois Republic, they could hardly move openly against its foremost representatives, Azaña and Prieto.

Ironically, then, Communist efforts against the revolutionists had in some senses let their own control of the war effort slip. Unfortunately, the methods that they used to impose their views were to lead, in early 1939, to a second civil war within the Civil War. It has been plausibly argued by the Spanish Marxist Fernando Claudin and by Ronald Fraser that, if the Communists had been able to find some way to harness the revolutionary enthusiasm of the first months, instead of simply crushing it, the war might have been won. This would have involved a revolutionary guerrilla war in the zones occupied by the Nationalists. It would have required a genuine revolutionary policy in the loyalist zone. Given the sectarian tendencies of the Communists, that is unlikely to have produced a policy acceptable to the CNT and the POUM. Moreover, in the light of the international situation between 1936 and 1937, and Stalin's perception of it, Communist sponsorship of revolution was virtually inconceivable. As it was, the Communist Party, for all its crimes and its errors, played a major role in keeping Republican resistance alive as long as it did.

NINE

Defeat by Instalments

It was hardly surprising, given the divisions which wracked the Republicans, that even after the defeat of Guadalajara, in which the Italian Corpe Troppe Voluntarie had been routed, the Nationalists continued to hold the initiative. This was starkly demonstrated by the ease with which they swept through the north in the spring and summer of 1937. In March, Mola had gathered nearly forty thousand troops for an assault on the Basque Country, and he opened his campaign at the end of the month with a widely publicized threat: 'If submission is not immediate, I will raze all Vizcaya to the ground, beginning with the industries of war. I have the means to do so.' However, despite Mola's evident desire for a quick victory, the campaign was slower than either the rebels or their German allies cared for. Steep, wooded hills and poor roads held up the advance and the dogged Basque retreat also exacted a high price from the attacking forces. Skilful use of tank traps and barbed-wire entanglements seemed merely a prelude to what would happen at the much-vaunted 'iron ring' of defences of Bilbao, which had been known as the great 'city of sieges' during the Carlist wars of the nineteenth century.

Mola enjoyed the air support of the German Condor Legion, whose Chief of Staff and later leader was Lieutenant Colonel Wolfram von Richthofen, cousin of the 'Red Baron'. Von Richthofen, who was later to mastermind the Nazi invasion of Poland, used the Condor Legion to practise the techniques of coordinated ground and air attacks, dive-bombing and saturation bombing, which were later to be incorporated into the Second World War *Blitzkrieg*. An exigent and cold-bloodedly professional commander, von Richthofen was firmly committed to the use of terror. He advised Mola that 'nothing is unreasonable that can further destroy enemy morale and quickly'. On the night of 25 April, Mola had the rebel radio at Salamanca broadcast the following warning to the Basque people: 'Franco is about to deliver a mighty blow against which all resistance is useless. Basques! Surrender now and your lives will be spared.'

On the following afternoon, 26 April, which was a Monday and market day in the small town of Guernica, the Condor Legion struck. Guernica, which was of deep symbolic importance to the Basque people, was destroyed in one awful afternoon of sustained bomb attacks. The scale of the atrocity was compounded by subsequent efforts on the part of the Nationalists to deny any responsibilty. George Steer, correspondent of *The Times*, was one of the first journalists to arrive at the scene. With some misgiving, the editor of *The Times*, Geoffrey Dawson, published the following report by Steer on 28 April:

> Guernica, the most ancient town of the Basques and the centre of their cultural tradition, was completely destroyed by insurgent air raiders. The bombardment of this open town far behind the lines occupied precisely three hours and a quarter, during which a powerful fleet of aeroplanes consisting of three German types, Junkers and Heinkel bombers and Heinkel fighters, did not cease unloading on the town bombs weighing from 1,000 lb downwards and, it is calculated, more than 3,000 two-pounder aluminium incendiary projectiles. The fighters, meanwhile, plunged low from above the centre of the town to machine-gun those of the civilian population who had taken refuge.

Dawson later wrote, 'I did my best, night after night, to keep out of the paper anything that might hurt [German] susceptibilities.' Steer was a first-class war correspondent. The Francoists, in an effort to discredit his report, went to great lengths to denigrate his personal and professional integrity.

Franco's foreign press service, under the direction of Luis Bolín, immediately got to work denying that the bombing had taken place. For Bolín, once London correspondent of the monarchist daily *ABC*, the cover-up was inspired in large measure by his worries about the possible reaction of the English Catholic Church. When it quickly became obvious that outright denial of the atrocity was no longer tenable, the Nationalists claimed that Guernica had been dynamited by the Basques themselves in order to fabricate an atrocity for propaganda purposes. This story was maintained by some even up to the 1970s. Unfortunately for Bolín, though, there were too many reliable witnesses. Father Alberto Onaindia, unofficial diplomatic agent of the Basque Country in Paris, reached the town on the day of the German attack:

> I arrived at Guernica on April 26, at 4.40 p.m. I had hardly left the car when the bombardments began. The people were terrified. They fled, abandoning their livestock in the market place. The bombardment lasted until 7.45. During that time, five minutes did not elapse without the sky's being black with German planes. The planes descended very low, the machine-gun fire tearing up the woods and roads, in whose gutters, huddled together, lay old men, women and children. Before long it was impossible to see as far as five hundred yards, owing to the heavy smoke. Fire enveloped the whole city. Screams of lamentation were heard everywhere, and the people, filled with terror, knelt, lifting their hands to heaven as if to implore divine protection . . . As a Catholic priest, I state that no worse outrage could be inflicted on religion

than the Te Deum to be sung to the glory of Franco in the church at Guernica, which was miraculously saved by the heroism of firemen from Bilbao.

Not all Nationalists attempted to deny the bombing of Guernica. Virginia Cowles, an American reporter, travelled extensively through rebel Spain in the company of Captain Gonzalo de Aguilera, the eccentric aristocrat who blamed the outbreak of the war on sewers. On meeting German soldiers in the north, he remarked to her, 'Nice chaps, the Germans, but a bit too serious; they never seem to have any women around, but I suppose they didn't come for that. If they kill enough Reds, we can forgive them anything.' She visited the remains of Guernica in the company of another Nationalist press officer, Ignacio Rosalles.

We arrived in Guernica to find it a lonely chaos of timber and brick, like an ancient civilization in process of being excavated. There were only three or four people in the streets. An old man was clearing away debris. Accompanied by Rosalles, my official escort, I went up to him and asked if he had been in the town during the destruction. He nodded his head and, when I asked what had happened, waved his arms in the air and declared that the sky had been black with planes – '*Aviones*,' he said: '*Italianos y alemanes*.' Rosalles was astonished. 'Guernica was burned,' he contradicted heatedly. The old man, however, stuck to his point, insisting that after a four-hour bombardment there was little left to burn. Rosalles moved me away. 'He's a red,' he explained indignantly. A couple of days later, we were talking to some staff officers. Rosalles described our drive along the coast and told them of the incident at Guernica. 'The town was full of reds,' he said. 'They tried to tell us it was bombed, not burnt.' The tall staff officer replied: 'But of course it was bombed. We bombed it and bombed it and bombed it, and *bueno*, why not?' Rosalles looked astonished, and when we were back in the car again he said, 'I don't think I would write about that if I were you.'

Such attempts at intimidation, if not particularly effective, were nevertheless not uncommon. Luis Bolín, in particular, having already threatened the French cameraman René Brut with execution for filming the Badajoz massacre, was used to the press submitting to his wishes. In the last resort, though, the myth of the Basque dynamiters was counter-productive. Had the Nationalist authorities taken the same line as the nonchalant staff officer, then the bombing could have been dismissed as a regrettable consequence of war. As it was, the controversy made it a central symbol of the war, immortalized in the painting by Pablo Picasso. That Guernica was destroyed by the German Condor Legion is no longer open to any doubt. Moreover, it is this fact which gives the event its military significance, for the town was the first in the world's history to have been entirely destroyed by aerial bombing. The only controversy which remains in relation to the atrocity is whether it was carried out at the behest of the Nationalist high command, or on the initiative of the Nazis. The late Dr Herbert Southworth, the world authority on the destruction of Guernica, reached the unequivocal conclusion that Guernica was destroyed by explosive and incendiary bombs dropped from aircraft of the Condor Legion piloted by Germans. The bombing was undertaken at the request of the Nationalist high command in order to destroy Basque morale and preclude the defence of Bilbao.

The devastation of Guernica certainly shattered Basque morale. The meetings between General Mola and Lieutenant Colonel von Richthofen on the evening of 25 April and the morning of 26 April suggest that this was precisely why it had been bombed. If that was not the case, then the most plausible tactical objective would have been to knock out the Renteria bridge across the river Mundaca across which Basque troops could retreat. However, light incendiary bombs were an odd choice of projectile for use against a stone bridge. Besides, von Richthofen, an austerely efficient man, had access to the new Stuka dive bomber, by far the most suitable aircraft in existence for small-scale precision bombing. Yet he chose not to use it. Even so, eyewitnesses have testified to the fact that the conventional bombers which he did use were low enough to have been able to drop bombs with some accuracy. However, they flew too wide apart for them to have been concentrating on a given target. In fact, it seems that by far the safest place to be in Guernica during the bombing was under the Renteria bridge.

The key to the defence of Bilbao, the 'iron ring' of fortifications, had been betrayed by a Basque officer, Major Alejandro Goicoechea, who had deserted with the blueprints in March. By late May, Mola's troops had Bilbao surrounded. The orders of Prieto, Minister for Defence, to destroy all industrial installations, were ignored by the Basque President, José Antonio Aguirre. Constant air attacks by the Nationalists enabled them to break through the defensive lines on 12 June. A week later Bilbao fell. The newly imposed rebel mayor, the Basque Falangist José María de Areilza, in an effort to minimize the advantage enjoyed by the Nationalists on account of the leaked information, exalted the victory in the following terms:

Bilbao was conquered by arms. No deals and posthumous back-scratching. The rules of war – harsh, virile and inexorable. The revolting, sinister, heinous nightmare known as Euskadi [the Basque Country] has fallen for ever. You have fallen forever, self-seeking, bickering, worthless, Basque Nationalist toady, President Aguirre. You, who cut an elegant figure during eleven months of crime and robbery while the poor Basque soldiers were being hunted down in the villages with lassoes like quadrupeds, leaving their pelts scattered over the length and breadth of the Biscayan mountains. As for Basque nationalism, there exists as from now an argument which supersedes all historical sophistry and legalistic manoeuvres. This argument, written in the blood spilt in Vizcaya, is that it has become once again a part of Spain purely and simply by conquest of arms. Spain has recovered the full independence of her sovereignty. And she is using it to proclaim her friendship for the great European nations who have befriended her in these tragic times of national crusade. I refer to the Germany of Hitler, the Italy of Mussolini, and the Portugal of Oliveira Salazar.

Thirty years later, after a distinguished career in Franco's service, Areilza was to repent his past and joined the moderate opposition to the dictatorship.

For Indalecio Prieto, who had taken over as Minister of War only two weeks earlier, it was a devastating blow. His manic energy had been to no avail. He was inconsolable and told Zugazagoitia: 'I have been so embittered and I have judged myself so severely for my own responsibility that, not only did I send the Prime Minister a letter of resignation, but I also contemplated suicide. I became obsessed with the idea and I had my pistol ready.' Negrín insisted that he remain at the Ministry of National Defence.

After the fall of Bilbao, the Nationalists' northern campaign met few obstacles. An army of sixty thousand men, amply supplied with Italian troops and equipment, easily dealt with disorganised Republican militia and entered the elegant coastal resort of Santander on 26 August. The Italians claimed this as a great triumph, and their troops paraded through Santander holding aloft giant portraits of Mussolini. In Italy, the press gloried in this revenge for Guadalajara even though in reality the Italian troops had faced virtually no resistance. By this stage, the Basques defending Castilian Santander were thoroughly dispirited after the capture of their homeland. Fearful of the vengeful attitude of the Nationalists, they had tried to sue for peace with the Italian General, Ettore Bastico. The Nationalists, however, got wind of the plan and sent troops to curtail negotiations. Thereafter, the remainder of the north was quickly mopped up during September and October. To the despair of Prieto, who again offered his resignation to Negrín, Gijón and Avilés in Asturias fell on 21 October, and by the end of the month northern industry was at the service of the rebels. This gave them a decisive advantage. Already better off in terms of tanks and aeroplanes, the Nationalists were now able to consolidate their military superiority through control of the production of iron ore. Moreover, conscription had been introduced in the rebel zone, giving the Nationalists an advantage of something in the region of two hundred thousand troops over the Republicans.

At the beginning of the war, the Nationalist forces had eighty thousand men. By the end of the campaigns in the north between the spring and autumn of 1937, Franco's armed forces had grown substantially. In the north, he had ten divisions consisting of 140,000 men and, over the next months, a further one hundred thousand were incorporated from Republican prisoners of war. Initially, the prisoners were placed in improvised concentration camps and subjected to interrogation and purges. Officers and political commissars were summarily executed. Those who had volunteered for service were use in forced labour battalions in front-line positions. Conscripts were considered sufficiently apolitical to be absorbed into the Nationalist ranks. Many of these were hardened veterans whom the Republican army could replace only by raw recruits. In addition to his northern army, Franco's forces consisted of the armies of the Centre and of the South, both with ample reserves. By December 1937, Franco had called up eleven years' worth of conscripts, those from 1929 to 1939, consisting of 413,500 men. Together with volunteers and Republican deserters and prisoners, by the end of 1937 he had 772,000 men in arms.

Franco had neither the intention, nor probably the skill, to use this numerical superiority in swift strategic strikes which he considered to be appropriate only in war against a foreign enemy. Having a huge army and little concern for his own men simply offered Franco the possibility of grinding down the Republic in a long war of attrition. His intention was to crush the Republican army completely, a project which, along with the repression in the captured areas, aimed to lay the foundations for an enduring dictatorship. He explained this project to Mussolini's Ambassador, Roberto Cantalupo, on 4 April 1937. Speaking of 'the cities and in the countryside which I have already occupied but which are still not redeemed', he declared ominously that 'we must carry out the necessarily slow task of redemption and pacification, without which the military occupation will be largely useless. The moral redemption of the occupied zones will be long and difficult because in Spain the roots of anarchism are old and deep.' Redemption meant bloody political purges such as those which had followed the capture of Badajoz and Málaga:

> I will occupy Spain town by town, village by village, railway by railway ... Nothing will make me abandon this gradual programme. It will bring me less glory but greater internal peace. That being the case, this civil war could still last another year, two, perhaps three. Dear ambassador, I can assure that I am not interested in territory but in inhabitants. The reconquest of the territory is the means, the redemption of the inhabitants the end. I cannot shorten the war by even one day ... It could even be dangerous for me to reach Madrid with a stylish military operation. I will take the capital not an hour before it is necessary: first I must have the certainty of being able to found a regime.

During the summer, the Republicans had tried to halt the seemingly inexorable process by which their territory was being whittled away. On 6 July, at Brunete, in arid scrubland fifteen miles west of Madrid, a well-planned diversionary offensive achieved initial surprise. The attack was conceived by Colonel Vicente Rojo, the shrewd Republican Chief of Staff. His idea was to break through the Nationalist lines at their weakest point. Nearly fifty thousand troops smashed through enemy lines, but in conditions of extreme heat and great confusion Republican discipline broke down. Political rivalries hampered the effective prosecution of the campaign, and within two days General Varela was able to call up enough reinforcements to plug the gap. Despite the strategic irrelevance of Brunete, Franco delayed his northern campaign. As he was later to show at Teruel and the Ebro, Franco's notion of a war of moral redemption by terror did not permit him to give up an inch of once captured territory nor to turn aside from any opportunity to hammer home the message of his invincibility in Republican blood – whatever the human cost to his own side. Brunete offered an irresistable temptation to annihilate large numbers of Republican troops.

For ten days, in one of the most ferocious encounters of the war, the Republicans defended the salient they had gained against overwhelming air and artillery attacks. The Nationalists were hugely aided by the introduction at the battle of Brunete of the new German fighter, the Messerschmitt Bf 109, which was to play such an important role in the Second World War. In conditions of total chaos, with both sides mistakenly dropping shells on their own troops, the Nationalists gradually forced the attackers back to their starting point. Franco's decision to accept the challenge of Brunete was considered by his allies to be a strategic error. He did not agree because it ensured that, in one of the bloodiest slogging matches of the war, the Republic delayed the fall of Santander by only about five weeks but lost much valuable equipment and twenty thousand of its best troops, an objective on which he placed the highest value. More remarkable than the decision to abandon the northern campaign in order to fight at Brunete was Franco's response to Varela's success. The road to Madrid was open and Varela was keen to pursue the Republicans back to the capital. He was flabbergasted when Franco ordered him to dig in, saying that it was important to renew the war in the north before fog and snow impeded the Nationalist advance there. Franco had no interest either in the early capture of Madrid or in risking his advance in the north. The collapse of Madrid would probably have ended the war. Franco, however, did not want victory until every square inch of Spain had been cleansed of leftists and liberals.

Despite the cost of Brunete, the Republicans maintained their efforts to take the initiative. In August 1937, an offensive was made on the Aragón front – chosen in part because of the government's desire to end the anarchists' control of the lines there. Again the brainchild of Colonel Rojo, the objective was to approach Zaragoza through a bold pincer movement. However, difficulty was experienced in capturing small towns along the way, like Belchite, and the offensive ground to a halt by mid-September. The story at Belchite was similar to that at Brunete. The Republicans gained an initial advantage, but then got bogged down thanks to a combination of the intense mid-summer heat and poor communications. In particular, the strategy of the Russian tank commander came to grief largely as a result of his insistence on giving orders in Russian. Once more, fierce resistance led to very heavy casualties, and the Republican offensive was again hampered by political conflicts. The Communists' determination to dominate the Republican war effort meant that the CNT militia were denied adequate weaponry. The Republican attacking force as a whole suffered from its internal political divisions, despite the Popular Army's discipline. At its side fought both units of the International Brigades and the remains of the former anarchist militia columns, which were still smarting under their forced militarization.

The Republican army required substantial reconstruction after every major defeat. The Nationalists had ample reserves so they could rotate troops and allow them time for rest and recuperation, while this was rarely the case with the Republicans. The troops of the Popular Army, and the International Brigades in particular, went for long periods without being withdrawn from the front. By the end of 1937, the Republic had called up ten years' worth of conscripts (the *reemplazos* of 1930–39), which provided an army of approximately eight hundred thousand men, with low morale. Many officers were drawn directly from the militias. Although some were outstandingly talented, the majority were simply insufficiently trained. Defeats at the front and low morale in the rearguard provoked considerable desertions despite fierce disciplinary measures, which could see deserters sentenced to the firing squad without trial or punishments inflicted on their families.

The disappointments of the Brunete and Aragón campaigns intensified divisive recriminations within the Republican camp. Largo Caballero had long been in favour of an offensive in Extremadura aimed at cutting Andalusia off from the rest of the rebel zone, but the opposition of the Communists, and particularly of Miaja, scuppered his plan. Now Indalecio Prieto, the Minister of Defence, attacked the Communists' handling of the Aragón offensive. This confirmed the increasingly pessimistic Socialist leader as the main enemy of the Communists in the government. Prieto also came under attack from the anarchists for his role in sanctioning the dissolution of the Council of Aragón in August 1937. However, he always denied having also authorized the brutal destruction of the anarchist collectives by the heavy-handed Stalinist Colonel Enrique Lister. It was clear that morale in the Republican zone was increasingly being undermined by political disputes.

In the Nationalist zone there were no such divisions. General

Mola's death on 3 June allowed Franco to run the war effort without interference. Franco was able to direct the Nationalist forces unhindered by problems of insubordination and indiscipline. Nonetheless, the rebel leader was profligate with the lives of his troops in a series of decisions of questionable strategic wisdom. Having squandered his opportunity to take Madrid by his insistence on relieving the Alcázar of Toledo, he now committed his men to costly counter-offensives, particularly at Brunete. Franco's battle tactics reflected his political vision as well as his character: he was cruel, unforgiving, and vengeful but he also wanted to smash republicanism for ever. His long-term vision, patience and coldness were of inestimable value in allowing him to impose his will upon the rebel zone. With his major potential rivals all dead, Franco was free to control not just the military, but also the political direction of the Nationalists.

The Caudillo's political dominance was confirmed at the start of 1938. On 30 January, he formed his first regular ministry. Thus, the rule of the Burgos Junta of generals was brought to an end. Ramón Serrano Suñer, the *cuñadísimo*, was made Minister of the Interior, and other posts went to a carefully balanced selection of soldiers, monarchists, Carlists and Falangists. The dominant tone, however, was military. The Ministries of Defence, Public Order and Foreign Affairs all went to generals. The New State, as it was known, was formalized through the *Ley de Administración Central del Estado*. According to this, 'The organization which has been created will be subject to the constant influence of the National Movement. The administration of the New State must be imbued with the spirit of its origin: noble and impartial, strong and austere, deeply Spanish down to the marrow.' The Falange was awarded control of the labour movement and with it a hugely lucrative fount of patronage. The Church too was rewarded for its services by the concession of sole authority over education. This was in part reward for the Vatican's formal recognition of Franco in August 1937. The ideology of the New State was wholly backward-looking, concerned above all with the destruction of symbols of progress such as parliamentary democracy and trade unionism. Its political purpose was to rebuild Spain in the image of an imperial past. The only novelty was to be found in the rallies and other trimmings adopted to facilitate its incorporation into the Fascist world order envisaged by Hitler and Mussolini.

That Franco was able to give time to his political future was a sign of the way the military balance was pointing to his ultimate victory. After the Republicans' Aragón offensive, there had been a lull in fighting. Towards the end of 1937, though, Franco decided to launch another attack on what had now become virtually his obsession – Madrid. His plan was to break through the Guadalajara front and move in for the kill on the Spanish capital. However, the Republicans were able to mount a successful spying mission and discover Franco's battle tactics. According to the Francoist historian Ricardo de la Cierva, this was done by the anarchist commander of the Republic's IV Corps, Cipriano Mera, crossing the lines disguised as a shepherd. In his own memoirs, however, Mera makes it clear that he knew little of what was going on. Whoever deserves the credit, the information gathered led the Republicans to decide in December to launch their own pre-emptive attack in the hope of turning Franco away from Madrid. It was to be directed against Teruel, capital of the bleakest of the Aragónese provinces. The Nationalist lines there were weakly held and the city was already virtually surrounded by Republican forces.

Once more, the strategy had been skilfully elaborated by Vicente Rojo. On 22 September 1937, the governent had promoted him to general. The initiative had come from Indalecio Prieto, who had told him nothing for fear that the notoriously modest Rojo would refuse. He learned of his promotion in the papers. As with previous offensives masterminded by Rojo, complete surprise was achieved. The campaign took place in

the midst of one of the cruellest winters Spain had ever suffered, the bitter cold intensified by the rocky terrain around
Teruel. The Nationalists, caught unawares, discovered that
their German and Italian aeroplanes were grounded by the
weather. Their truckloads of reinforcements were delayed by
snow and ice-bound roads. This allowed the Republican forces,
principally composed of units of the Popular Army, to press
home their initial advantage. The rebels thus had to postpone
their planned advance on Madrid and switch their forces to the
east. However, the Nationalist counter-attack, headed by Generals Varela and Aranda, was slowed by the appalling weather
conditions. Although the snow stopped on 29 December, two
days later the lowest temperature of the century was recorded.
In such conditions, the only feasible strategy for either side
was one of attrition, in which the Nationalists enjoyed a distinct
advantage. With more weapons and men at their command,
and driven by Franco's ruthless determination to recapture all
lost territory, the rebels were always likely to be able to outlast
the loyalist troops.

After bloody house-to-house fighting, the Republicans
managed to capture the Nationalist garrison on 8 January;
they were then subjected to a heavy battering by artillery
and bombers. In the freezing conditions, morale was sapped.
Deaths from the cold were high on both sides, many troops
dying in their sleep as the effects of the alcohol they had
consumed to stay warm wore off. Inevitably, political conflicts
broke out once more. Indalecio Prieto visited the front and
made scathing remarks about the inefficiency of the operation.
Costly rivalries flared up between the commanders. Valentín
González, 'El Campesino', the illiterate and fiery Communist
commander, claimed later that during the Nationalist offensive
against Teruel 'the advanced positions were lost, and I quickly
found my force of 16,000 men surrounded. Outside the town,
Lister and Modesto commanded six brigades and two battalions. They could have helped me. They did nothing of the

kind. Even worse, when Captain Valdepeñas wanted to come to my rescue, they prevented him from doing so.' According to 'El Campesino', his division escaped only by dint of a desperate breakout. However, other eyewitnesses claimed that he had fled in panic, leaving his men to their fate. Some brigades refused to obey orders. Lister and 'El Campesino' got away with it. Forty-six CNT mutineers, however, were executed. 'El Campesino' was later to make the entirely bizarre claim that the Communists deliberately sabotaged the capture of Teruel in order to prevent Prieto's position being unduly strengthened. There is no foundation for such a claim not made until 1950, at the height of the Cold War, by which time 'El Campesino' was being used by the American Congress for Cultural Freedom to denigrate the role of the Communists during the Spanish Civil War.

After another costly defence of a small advance, the Republicans had to retreat on 21 February 1938, when Teruel was on the point of being encircled. The casualties on both sides had been enormous, the Nationalists losing more than fifty thousand men and the Republicans more than sixty thousand. What the successive breakdown of the three Republican offensives at Brunete, Belchite and Teruel demonstrated was that the sheer material superiority of the rebel forces could always prevail over the courage of the loyalist troops. Each time, the Republicans had been unable to follow up their initial advantage. In part, this reflected political conflicts within the Republican zone. However, it was also a consequence of the fact that by early 1938 Franco had an overwhelming advantage in terms of men and equipment. His exploitation of that superiority in regaining Teruel made it the military turning point of the Civil War.

As a result of these major losses, the Republican government was now obliged to call up a further nine years' worth of conscripts (the *reemplazos* of 1923–9 and 1940–41). Accordingly, the Republican army was having to train and rely on both older and younger men. In the great final battle of the war, at the Ebro, many Republican soldiers would be adolescents of seventeen. In contrast, by the end of 1938, Franco had called up only an additional three years of conscripts, those of 1927 and 1928, 1940 and the first nine months of 1941. In consequence, together with volunteers and Republican deserters and prisoners, before the battle of the Ebro his army consisted of 879,000 men in arms. The contrast was stark. During the battle, Franco's General Staff reported that many prisoners were captured the day after leaving Barcelona, where they had received only five days training.

It was thus with marked numerical and material superiority that the Nationalists now prepared to consolidate their victory with a massive offensive through Aragón and Castellón towards the sea. One hundred thousand troops, well covered by two hundred tanks and nearly a thousand German and Italian aircraft, began their advance on 7 March 1938. Colonel Wilhelm von Thoma, in command of the Condor Legion's fast tank units, wanted to use *Blitzkrieg* tactics and came into conflict with Franco's conservative instincts. In the style of First World War generals, Franco planned to use them as infantry support. Von Thoma made his point but it hardly mattered. After an opening artillery and aerial bombardment, the Nationalists found their Republican opponents exhausted, short of guns and ammunition and generally unprepared. Demoralization after the defeat of Teruel was compounded by organizational confusion. By the last week of March, the river Ebro had been crossed. The population fled in terror before the advancing Nationalists. With their furniture piled on carts and their animals tied behind, they were straffed from the air. By early April, the rebels had reached Lérida, which fell after a brave defence by the division led by 'El Campesino'. They then moved down the Ebro valley cutting off Catalonia from the rest of the Republic. The Republican retreat was covered valiantly by Colonel Gustavo Durán's Mountain Group, which had been formed from remnants of other units at Morella in the harsh and arid hills of the Maestrazgo between Aragón and Castellón. By 15 April, the Nationalists had reached the sea at the fishing village of Vinaroz. On the beach at Benicasim, joyful Carlist soldiers cavorted in the waves. Serrano Suñer declared that the war was approaching its close. In fact, because of Franco's determination to annihilate the Republic, fighting would go on for another year.

As the advance continued, the major urban centres of the Republican zone were flooded with refugees. Inevitably, hunger took its toll on morale and solidarity. Suffering was intensified by the steady rhythm of air raids on towns with little anti-aircraft artillery and infrequent fighter cover. These problems were most severe in Catalonia. The autumn of 1936 had seen the constant bombing of Madrid and, in the winter 1937, the saturation bombing of Barcelona. However, on 16 March 1938, Mussolini ordered a new bombing technique: repeated waves of attacks which would render irrelevant the air-raid alarm system since it would no longer be clear if the sirens were announcing the beginning or the end of an attack. On the night of 18 March, the working-class districts where the refugees huddled were badly hit, leaving nearly one thousand dead. People fled into the countryside. Since Italian aircraft flew from Mallorca with Spanish markings, they could act with impunity. Throughout 1938, the bombing raids would continue and be extended to the port cities of the Levante coast – Valencia, Gandia, Alcoy and Alicante.

Divided in two, demoralized by the bombing and suffering badly from serious lack of food, the Republic was in dire straits. The Soviet Union had begun to ease off deliveries of armaments. Indeed, so bleak did the prospects seem that the unhappy Indalecio Prieto had come to share Azaña's long-held conviction that all was lost and that a negotiated peace was necessary to avoid the senseless loss of more lives. This gave the Communists the opportunity they were looking for to oust the Minister of Defence. After a tense cabinet meeting on 16 March 1938 at the Palacio de Pedralbes in Barcelona, with demonstrators (orchestrated by PCE) chanting against defeatists, Prieto supported Azaña in proposing a request to the French government to mediate to end the war. Negrín, this time with Zugazagoitia on his side, reasserted his conviction that the war should go on. Two weeks later, on 29 March, at another cabinet meeting, Prieto declared that the war effort could not be sustained with Franco's forces about to reach the Mediterranean and cut the Republic in two. Negrín was appalled, commenting that Prieto's words 'completely demoralized our government colleagues by describing events in a tone of bleak despair and presenting them as fatal'.

Negrín then asked Zugazagoitia to persuade Prieto to accept the post of Minister in charge of public works and railways in a cabinet reshuffle. Prieto refused and was thus provoked into resignation from the cabinet on 5 April, despite appeals to remain from the PSOE executive and a delegation of CNT leaders. Negrín told Prieto that he could not afford to have a pessimist in the Ministry of Defence. Prieto was irritated by his own pessimism, as a friend commented, 'as much as the hump irritates the hunchback', but he believed that it did not inhibit his efficacy. He was prepared to accept the Ministry of Finance, in order to pave the way for what he regarded as the inevitable Republican exile. Negrín rejected the suggestion because he regarded the purpose of the Ministry as the financing of arms purchases. Deeply humiliated, Prieto told Zugazagoitia, 'they've thrown me out with a kick in the . . .'. Prieto chose to ignore the role of his own defeatism in the cabinet reshuffle and to interpret it as a plot against him by the Communists with Negrín as their willing puppet. He neatly forgot that he himself had been a willing accomplice in placing Communists in important positions.

His bitterness was intensified when he discovered that Zugazagoitia had renounced the Ministry of the Interior in order to become Secretary General of the Ministry of Defence under Negrín himself. Zugazagoitia thought that he would be the effective minister with Negrín as mere figurehead. However, given Negrín's boundless energy, it was Zugazagoitia who found himself with virtually nothing to do. Prieto would take his revenge on Negrín at a meeting of the National Committee of the PSOE held on 9 August 1938 to discuss the cabinet crisis of the previous April. Negrín repeated his view that it had been impossible for a defeatist Prieto to stay in the Ministry of Defence. Prieto replied with a savage three-hour-long diatribe accusing Negrín of obeying the orders of the Communists. The consequent feud between them was to guarantee a legacy of harsh and sterile division within the Socialist movement long after the Civil War.

Franco was as convinced as Prieto that the end was nigh. He cautiously suggested that the Germans might recall their troops as a sop to British and French sensibilities. Hitler, in turn, had decided by this stage that there was nothing more for the German technicians to learn from the Spanish conflict. However, the two Fascist leaders had not reckoned with the tenacity of Republican resistance. The Nationalists found that they could not yet afford to dispense with the Condor Legion. The opening of the French frontier in March brought supplies and renewed hope to the defenders of the Spanish Second Republic.

The arms that the Republic were able to secure as a result of the reopening of the border with France led to the halting of the Nationalist advance, or at least to its slowing into a painful crawl. In fact, weighed down by the atmosphere of stalemate and war weariness, Negrín was looking for a compromise peace but Franco was set on exacting nothing less than unconditional surrender. That was, after all, why he had been pursuing a war of annihilation against the Republic. For him there could be no understanding with the Republic. Had he mounted an offensive against Catalonia, where the Republic's remaining war industry lay, he could probably have brought the war to a speedier conclusion. He had no interest in a swift end to the war and an armistice by which some consideration would have to be given to the defeated. Instead, in July he launched a major attack on Valencia.

Franco's decision was in part motivated by the fear that, following the German *Anschluss* in Austria in March, the French would intervene on the side of the Republic in Catalonia. Moreover, Hitler was now worried about possible repercussions should the Nationalists achieve an outright victory so soon after the annexation of Austria. In Hitler's opinion, expressed in November 1937, 'a 100 per cent victory for Franco' was undesirable 'from the German point of view' given that Germany's 'interest lay rather in a continuance of the war and the keeping up of the tension in the Mediterranean'. In fact, the Führer's worries were misplaced. Blum's second administration, which in any case had been hamstrung by the lack of a clear-cut majority, lasted just over a month before Daladier took over in April. He closed the border with Spain again on 13 June. Britain, meanwhile, was going ever further down Chamberlain's road of appeasement at any price. A treaty had been signed with Italy in April, thereby tacitly condoning Italian intervention in Spain. Worse was to follow with the British reaction to the Czechoslovakian crisis during the summer. Rather than risk war with Hitler, Czechoslovakia was effectively surrendered to the Nazis at the Munich Agreement of 29 September. The Republicans awaited the outcome of the Munich meeting in painful suspense. Negrín's naïve hopes of a European war in which a Republican Spain would be a vital ally to the Western democracies were dashed by the cynicism of the democracies. As Prieto stated, Europe had betrayed Spain.

Negrín's immediate response to the Anglo–Italian treaty had been to launch a diplomatic offensive of his own. In a bid to find a formula for peace negotiations, he had issued his 'Thirteen

Al portador de este carnet
Sr. D. *Carsten von Harling*

se autoriza libre circulación por todo el territorio ocupado por el Ejército Nacional. Se ruega a todas las autoridades civiles y militares le presten toda clase de facilidades, manifestándose al mismo tiempo que dicho señor está autorizado a llevar armas.

De orden de S.E.
El Tt. Coronel de E.M.

Firma del interesado:

Unidad: *Escuadrilla Caníbila*

27. Nationalist Safe-conduct issued to a German pilot of the Condor Legion.

28. An ambulance bought by black Americans. In Spain, black soldiers served without suffering racial discrimination. One of their number, Oliver Law, a leader of the unemployment movement during the depression, as commander of the Lincoln Battalion was the first black man to have field command over white Americans.

FROM THE
NEGRO PEOPLE OF AMERICA
TO THE PEOPLE OF REPUBLICAN SPAIN

29. The glorification of Franco, stressing the links between the imperial past and contemporary fascism.

30. The support of the Catholic church for the Nationalist 'crusade' offered invaluable legitimation of the military rebellion. On 5 December 1938, at Santiago de Compostela, Franco, his wife, the Archbishop of Santiago and other Church dignitaries give the fascist salute with varying degrees of enthusiasm.

31. *Above*: A priest says mass for
Nationalist troops in the village
square of Posada (Santander).

32. *Right*: Manuel Hedilla, the
successor to José Antonio Primo de
Rivera, whose political ambitions
were swept aside by Franco's fusion
of the Falange with other rightist
groups in April 1937.

33. *Below*: The Communist orator,
Dolores Ibárruri, 'La Pasionaria';
with Santiago Alvarez, a Communist
political commissar.

34. The Communist Colonel Enrique Líster (*right*) consults with his comrade Juan Modesto (*centre*).

35. Franco, Serrano Suñer and Mola in Burgos, May 1937 – their last meeting before Mola's death some weeks later.

36. Belchite, near Zaragoza, was the site of a Republican counter-offensive in August and September 1937. The ruins of the village were left untouched after the war as a monument to the Nationalist dead.

37. Italian troops enter Santander on 26 August 1937.

38. The Fascist press claims the capture of Santander for Mussolini and reports Franco's praise for the Italian troops.

OPPOSITE:
39. *Top*: Republican troops during the street-fighting in Teruel in January 1938.

40. *Centre*: On 15 April 1938, Nationalist troops sing the fascist anthem on reaching the Mediterranean and thus dividing the Republican zone in two.

41. *Bottom*: The Republic's last gamble: a boat being trundled to the banks of the Ebro for the crossing on 24 July 1938.

42. 'You are history, you are legend.' The farewell parade in Barcelona for the departing International Brigades on 29 October 1938.

43. General Juan Yagüe (*centre with stick*) leads his occupying troops into Barcelona on 26 January 1939.

44. Republican refugees are herded into an unsheltered camp in France.

45. The republican Prime Minister, Dr Juan Negrín (left), with General Vincente Rojo.

46. The moderate Socialist, Julián Besteiro, reads a manifesto of the Junta created by Colonel Segismundo Casado (*left*, *bespectacled*) to seek a negotiated peace.

47. Middle-class women rejoice at Franco's capture of Madrid in March 1939.

48. Bill Alexander, Commander of the British Battalion of the International Brigades in 1938.

49. Bill Alexander, now President of the International Brigade Association at the unveiling in London's Jubilee Gardens of the monument to the Brigades on 5 October 1985.

50. This banner was presented by the women of Barcelona to the British Battalion at the farewell parade on 29 October 1938.

51. 'Volunteers for Liberty'. The medal awarded to all International Brigaders by the Spanish Republican Government.

Points', inspired by Ivor Montagu, the British Communist film producer, in which he promised a Spain free of foreign interference, with free elections and full civil rights. The Western democracies were unmoved by his moderate package. In the United States, hopes that the arms sale embargo would be lifted crashed against the power of the Catholic lobby. A telegram from the reactionary Ambassador in London, Joseph Kennedy, claimed that to drop the arms embargo would be to risk the spread of the war beyond Spain's borders. Father Coughlin broadcast an appeal for Catholics to flood the White House with telegrams. They raised a spectre which frightened President Roosevelt. He told his Secretary of the Interior, Harold Ickes, that he feared 'the loss of every Catholic vote next fall'. The President ordered that the embargo be maintained. His wife Eleanor, who sympathized with the Republic, considered this to be 'a tragic error' and regretted that she had not 'pushed him harder'. On 11 May, Portugal granted diplomatic recognition to the Franco regime. Two days later Alvarez del Vayo's pleas to the League of Nations to end the policy of Non-intervention fell on deaf ears. The Republic appeared to be doomed.

However, Franco's offensive against Valencia had not gone as planned. Once more the Republicans demonstrated their heroic determination in defence, and the Nationalist Generals José Varela, Antonio Aranda and Rafael García Valiño found progress through the rocky terrain of the Maestrazgo towards the coast slow and exhausting. Indeed, the Republicans' achievement in holding up Franco's troops has been much underplayed. Brilliantly marshalled by General Leopoldo Menéndez López and Colonel Durán, the Republicans defended with dogged determination. Through the use of well-planned trenches, and properly protected lines of communication, they were able to inflict heavy casualties on the Nationalists while suffering relatively few themselves. Nonetheless, the progress of the rebels was inexorable, if painfully slow. By 23 July 1938,

Valencia was under direct threat, with the Nationalists less than forty kilometres away. If Valencia fell, the war would effectively be over. In response, Negrín decided to mount a spectacular diversion in the form of a counter-offensive to stem the continual erosion of Republican territory.

Negrín was fully aware of the savage repression imposed by the Francoists as Republican territory was conquered. He told his friend Juan Simeón Vidarte, 'I will not hand over without protection hundreds of Spaniards who are fighting on heroically just so that Franco can have the pleasure of shooting them as he has done in his own Galicia, in Andalusia, in the Basque Country and everywhere that Attila's horse has trod.' Accordingly, he hoped that, if the Republic could fight on for another year, it would find salvation in the general war which he believed to be inevitable.

In an attempt to restore contact with Catalonia, an assault across the river Ebro was conceived and planned by the ever-thoughtful General Vicente Rojo. It turned out to be the most hard-fought battle of the entire war. A special Army of the Ebro was formed for the offensive, which was placed under the command of General Juan Modesto, the domineering Communist. All the division commanders were also Communists, even though some of them, such as Lister, had fallen out with Modesto. The XV Corps was commanded by Lieutenant Colonel Manuel Tagüeña, at twenty-five already an outstanding leader. At the beginning of the war, Tagüeña had been at university studying mathematics and physics. Joining the militia of the Juventudes Socialistas Unificadas, he rose through the ranks, successively commanding a company, a battalion, a brigade, a division and finally an entire army corps. As in previous offensives, the best of the arms went to the Communists. The Nationalists placed the onus of defence on the blunt and outspoken General Juan Yagüe, but once again, through a combination of overconfidence and poor intelligence, the scope and scale of the Republican attack was misjudged.

A huge concentration of men, numbering some eighty thousand, was secretly transported to the river banks. Using boats, the first units of Modesto's army crossed the river on the night of 24–25 July. The remainder crossed on pontoon bridges the following day. The advance covered an immense curve in the Ebro from Flix in the north to Miravet in the south. They surprised the thinly held Nationalist lines. The Popular Army was able to inflict serious casualties on Yagüe's troops, although the 14th International Brigade sustained heavy losses and was forced to withdraw. Further upstream, however, the Republican forces succeeded in establishing a massive bridgehead within the broad bend in the river. By 1 August, they had reached Gandesa, forty kilometres from their starting point, but there they were bogged down. Franco's staff were initially demoralized by the Republicans' strategic success. As usual, Franco showed little emotion. He ordered reinforcements, including the Condor Legion, to be rushed in to contain the advance and a desperate and ultimately meaningless battle began for the territory which had been taken.

Franco's apparent lack of urgency caused his Italian backers doubts. Mussolini became pessimistic about Spain and told Ciano, 'Put on record in your diary that today, 29 August, I prophesy the defeat of Franco . . . The reds are fighters, Franco is not.' The battle of the Ebro was to last for over three months. Despite its strategic irrelevance, Franco was determined to recover the lost ground irrespective of the cost. He seems to have been pleased with the opportunity that was opening up to catch the Republicans in a trap, encircle and destroy them. He could have contained the Republican advance and advanced against a near-helpless Barcelona. Instead, he preferred, regardless of the human cost, to turn Gandesa into the graveyard of the Republican army. With nearly one million men now under arms, he could afford to be careless of their lives. His background in the African wars did not incline him to behave otherwise.

Negrín was pinning his hopes on an escalation of European tension that would alert the Western democracies to the dangers facing them from the Axis. Franco was fully aware that the outbreak of a general European war would jeopardize Nationalist victory. He knew that the Republic would align itself with France and Russia against Germany and feared that, with supplies flooding into the Republicans, the Nationalists would be virtually cut off from the Axis powers and threatened by the French army. Accordingly, he was deeply relieved when the Republic was virtually sentenced to death by the British reaction to the Czechoslovakian crisis.

Opening the dams on the Pyreneean tributaries of the Ebro, the Nationalists managed to cut off the Republican forces which were trapped in hilly country with little cover and short of supplies. Under orders not to retreat, the Republicans doggedly clung on despite fierce artillery bombardment. Five hundred cannon fired more than 13,500 rounds at them every day for nearly four months. In sweltering heat, with little or no water, shelled from dawn to dusk, they held on. Aware that Munich had shattered Negrín's last chance of salvation in a European war, and ever more determined to annihilate the Republican army, Franco gathered over thirty thousand fresh troops. To secure substantial deliveries of new German equipment with which to arm them, he made considerable concessions to the Third Reich in terms of increased participation in Spanish mainland and Spanish Moroccan mining enterprises. It was a surrender of Spanish sovereignty far beyond anything given by the Republic to the USSR. Franco's Foreign Minister, the Conde de Jordana, informed the German Ambassador of 'the firm intention of Nationalist Spain to continue to orient itself towards Germany politically and economically after the end of the war'. With the French frontier now closed and help for the Republic from the Soviet Union dwindling, the German equipment thus secured gave him the crucial advantage for the final push.

The Nationalists relied on the tactic of concentrating air and artillery attacks on selected small areas, and then following these up with regular battalion attacks. It was, incidentally, at the battle of the Ebro that Captain Werner Mölders, the German air ace, conceived aerial fighter tactics which were to become standard practice thereafter. By mid-November, at horrendous cost in casualties, the Francoists had pushed the Republicans out of the territory captured in July. The remants of the Republican army, led by Manuel Tagüeña, abandoned the right bank of the Ebro late at night on 15 November 1938, crossing the iron bridge at Flix, which was then blown up. Many had to swim across the river to safety.

Over a period of 113 days, nearly 250,000 men had clashed in a hilly terrain of approximately five hundred square kilometres. Both sides suffered heavily during the battle of the Ebro, although there is still considerable difficulty in ascertaining the exact numbers of casualties. An approximate total of 13,250 Spaniards and foreigners were killed, 6100 (47 per cent) of them Francoists, and 7150 (55 per cent) Republicans. In roughly similar proportions, about 110,000 suffered wounds or mutilation. The richly fertile Terra Alta became a massive cemetery – tens of thousands of men were buried quickly, many left where they lay, and others drowned in the river. To this day, human remains are regularly found in the area. The battle itself ruined the harvest of wheat and barley in July, of almonds in August, of grapes in September and of olives in November. The retreating Republicans left behind them many dead and much precious matériel. Immediately after the war was over, Republican prisoners forced to work for the new regime's Servicios de Recuperación would collect 75,000 tons of disused war matériel and shells. For years thereafter the inhabitants of the region would make a living combing the area for shrapnel and other scrap metal. In the process, many civilians were killed by unexploded shells.

The Republic had lost its army. The last despairing effort

had seen the Nationalists gain a decisive victory. The Republic would never recover and the Francoists would soon sweep into Catalonia. And yet Vicente Rojo had secured several of his objectives, preventing the offensive against Valencia and tempting the principal Francoist forces to engage in a battle in a terrain which prevented their material and numerical superiority having their expected impact. Great losses had been inflicted on the enemy, albeit at a huge cost, and the war had been prolonged in accordance with Negrín's hope of seeing the democracies wake up to the Axis's aggressive ambitions. It was Munich that fully turned the Ebro into a resounding defeat.

Effectively, the Republic was defeated, yet it simply refused to accept the fact. Madrid and Barcelona were swelled with refugees and their populations on the verge of starvation. Negrín again began to search for a possible formula to allow a compromise peace. As a gesture of sincerity, the Republic proposed the withdrawal of foreign volunteers. Fernando de los Ríos, the Republican Ambassador to the United States, outlined the government's view: 'Spain, from the beginning, has been in favour of the withdrawal of all foreign elements, for two reasons. First, because it is wrong to have foreign elements interfere in a purely domestic struggle. And second, because we are sure that the moment these foreign elements are withdrawn, the end of the civil war will be very near.' Republican propaganda increasingly presented the war as a patriotic struggle to rid Spain of foreign invaders. Along with the liquidation of the last remnants of revolution and the reopening of churches, it was part of a vain effort to pave the way for a possible negotiated peace.

A farewell parade was held in Barcelona for the International Brigades on 29 October, 1938. In the presence of many thousands of tearful, but cheering, Spaniards, the Communist leader Dolores Ibárruri, 'Pasionaria', gave an emotional and moving speech: 'Comrades of the International Brigades!

Political reasons, reasons of state, the good of that same cause for which you offered your blood with limitless generosity, send some of you back to your countries and some to forced exile. You can go with pride. You are history. You are legend. You are the heroic example of the solidarity and the universality of democracy ... We will not forget you; and, when the olive tree of peace puts forth its leaves, entwined with the laurels of the Spanish Republic's victory, come back! Come back to us and here you will find a homeland.' Under the mournful gaze of President Azaña, the brigaders then marched past as the onlookers threw flowers.

It is difficult to calculate exactly the total number of volunteers. Figures vary from a minimum of forty thousand to a maximum of sixty thousand who came from fifty different countries to fight against fascism in Spain. Nearly 20 per cent of them had died and most suffered wounds of varying degrees of severity. In October 1938, 12,673 were still in Spain. They began the slow trek home or back into exile, often to fates more appalling than anything they had yet suffered. Many fell into Nazi hands when France collapsed and many from the East died in Stalin's purges, guilty of having seen the West. Those who survived were not to return to Spain until after the death of Franco thirty-seven years later. However, part of Dolores Ibárruri's prophecy was fulfilled in late 1995 when the Socialist government of Felipe González granted Spanish citizenship to the remaining brigaders.

The departure of the International Brigades left the Republican population with no doubt that defeat was imminent. The war effort was kept alive only by the fear born of Franco's much publicized determination to annihilate liberalism, socialism and communism in Spain. On 7 November, Franco told the vice-president of the United Press, James Miller, 'There will be no mediation because criminals and their victims cannot live together.' He went on threateningly, 'We have catalogued in our files more than two million names with proof of their crimes.' Baron von Stohrer wrote to the Wilhelmstrasse on 19 November 1938, 'the main factors which still separate the belligerent parties are mistrust, fear and hatred. The first of these exists especially among the whites, the second among the Reds, while hatred and a desire for revenge are present on both sides in almost the same degree.' Franco dismissed any possibility of an amnesty for the Republicans. He was committed to a policy of institutionalized revenge. In Salamanca, the political files and documentation captured as each town had fallen to the Nationalists was gathered. Carefully sifted, it provided the basis for a massive card index of members of political parties, trade unions and masonic lodges. It was hardly surprising that the Republican zone was kept on a war footing by fear of Nationalist reprisals.

On 23 December 1938, Franco launched his final offensive. He had new German equipment and sufficient troops to be able to relieve them every two days. The shattered Republicans could put up only token resistance. At the beginning of 1939, Barcelona was a city bursting at the seams with tens of thousands of hungry refugees from all over Spain. Their respite from the relentless pursuit by the troops of General Franco was short-lived. The Republican government, which had moved from Valencia to Barcelona in October 1938, fled northwards to Gerona on 25 January 1939. The following day, the rebels entered the starving Catalan capital. The streets were deserted. The ever-obnoxious Luis Bolín commented, 'the stench was awful. Unswept for years, the streets were full of autumn leaves and garbage, part of the accumulated filth which the Reds bequeathed to every town that they occupied . . . The dust at the Ritz, the best hotel in the town, was inches thick.' While Bolín was rustling up charladies, nearly half a million refugees were trudging north.

When news came on 23 January that the Nationalists had reached the Llobregat river a few kilometres to the south of Barcelona, a colossal exodus began. Hundreds of thousands of terrified women, children, old men and defeated soldiers began to trek towards France. Through bitterly cold sleet and snow, on roads bombed and strafed by Nationalist aircraft, many walked, wrapped in blankets and clutching a few possessions, some carrying infants. Women gave birth at the roadside. Babies died of the cold, children were trampled to death. Those who could squeezed into every kind of transport imaginable. From 28 January, a reluctant French government allowed the first refugees across the border. The retreat of the wretched human mass moving slowly north was covered by the desperate heroism of the remnants of the Republican army.

The rump of the Republican Cortes held its last meeting at Figueras near the French border. On Sunday 6 February, after Negrín had tried to persuade him to return to Madrid, the President of the Republic, Manuel Azaña, chose exile. The manner of his departure, described some months later in a letter to his friend Angel Ossorio, symbolized the plight of the Republic. He was to leave at dawn, with the President of the Cortes, Diego Martínez Barrio, in a small convoy of police cars. Martínez Barrio's car broke down and Negrín, who was present, tried to push it out of the way. The President had to cross the frontier on foot. He was followed three days later by Prime Minister Negrín and General Rojo. Miaja was left in authority over the remaining Republican forces. At the end of February, Azaña resigned, and his constitutionally designated successor, Diego Martínez Barrio, refused to return to Spain. With Britain and France having announced their recognition of Franco's government, the Republic was left in a constitutional shambles: the legal validity of Negrín's government was unclear.

Nevertheless, a huge area of about 30 per cent of Spanish territory still remained to the Republic. The overall command of this central zone lay with General Miaja, although he spent most of his time in Valencia. Negrín and Alvarez del Vayo flew from France to Alicante on 9 February. Negrín still nurtured the vain hope of hanging on until a European war started and the democracies realized that the Republic had all along been fighting their fight. Even if further military resistance was impossible, the Communists were determined to hold on to the bitter end in order to be able to derive political capital out of the 'desertion' of their rivals. Non-Communist elements, however, wanted to make peace on the best possible terms. Such hopes seemed vain in the light of Franco's *Law of Responsibilities*, published on 13 February, by which supporters of the Republic were effectively guilty of a crime, that of military rebellion, which in Franco's topsy-turvy moral world meant opposing his military coup. Whether or not Negrín was still convinced that the Republic would be saved if a European war were to break out, there seemed little option but to fight on. Hence, he returned to Spain and called on his commanders to continue resisting the rebels. Only the Communists supported him.

On 4 March, the ascetic Colonel Segismundo Casado, commander of the Republican Army of the Centre and Miaja's effective substitute, decided to put a stop to what was increasingly senseless slaughter. Together with disillusioned anarchist leaders and the distinguished Socialist law professor Julián Besteiro, Casado formed an anti-Negrín National Defence Junta (Consejo Nacional de Defensa) in the hope that his contacts in Burgos would facilitate negotiation with Franco. He may also have hoped that by inspiring a military uprising 'to save Spain from Communism', he would somehow endear himself to Franco. It has been suggested that Casado was a British agent. This is unlikely but he was in touch with British representatives in Madrid who probably encouraged him in his efforts to end the war. Personally unambitious and a capable soldier, Casado was motivated by disgust that Negrín and the Communists talked of resistance to the bitter end while simultaneously arranging to get funds out of Spain and organizing aircraft for their flight into exile. The Casado revolt against the Republican government sparked off what was effectively the second civil war within the civil war in the Republican zone.

The Casado action received unexpectedly wide support because it tapped into deep seams of war weariness. Hunger and demoralization were rife in the central zone where anarchist and Socialist hostility to the Communists and their policy of resistance to the end just reflected a desire for the war to be over. Besteiro's contribution was of crucial importance. Having a carefully nurtured reputation for rectitude, his participation gave the Casado Junta a moral legitimacy which it would not otherwise have had. What Casado and Besteiro were doing was to render pointless the bloodshed and the sacrifices of the previous three years by emulating the military coup of 18 July 1936 against an alleged Communist danger. Casado was naïve in thinking that Franco would contemplate any form of armistice and Besteiro culpably ignorant in playing down the likely post-war repression. Already in contact with the Francoist fifth column, he seems to have believed that he could be the moral barrier between the victors and the vanquished. Like many less sophisticated and less well educated than himself in towns all over Spain, he accepted the Francoist claim that all of those who were guiltless of common crimes had nothing to fear in terms of life and liberty.

What was happening in Madrid had echoes elsewhere. In Valencia, the military governor General José Aranguren refused to hand over to the loutish Enrique Líster. At the Cartagena naval base, a bizarre set of events was sparked off when Negrín sent the Communist Major Francisco Galán to take over command. A number of artillery officers, with views similar to those of Casado, rose against Galán. They were embarrassed to find their action seconded by secret Nationalist sympathizers, retired rightists and local Falangists. The Falangists seized the local radio station. Sporadic fighting broke out between Galán, the anti-Communist Republican artillery officers and the Nationalists. After coastal batteries had fired on the fleet, the pro-Negrín forces re-established their control.

Meanwhile, in Madrid, arrests of Communists had begun on 6 March. General Miaja reluctantly agreed to join the Junta and took over its presidency. Most of the PCE leadership had already left Spain. From France, they denounced the Casado Junta in the most virulent terms. On 7 March, Luis Barceló, commander of the I Corps of the Army of the Centre, decided to take more direct action. His troops surrounded Madrid, and for several days there was fierce fighting in the Spanish capital. The IV Corps, commanded by the anarchist Cipriano Mera, managed to gain the upper hand, and a ceasefire was arranged on 10 March. Barceló, together with some other Communist officers, was arrested and executed. This marked the end of the dominance of the Communist Party in the central zone. Indeed, the relative ease with which the Casado Junta took over demonstrates just how misplaced are the accusations that the Republic was in the grip of a Soviet stranglehold. In the meantime, Casado was attempting to negotiate terms with Franco. Not surprisingly, the Caudillo remained interested only in unconditional surrender. His determination not to compromise was reflected after the war in the labour camps, the five hundred thousand prisoners, and the 150,000 executions on which his dictatorship was built. Casado and all the members of the Defence Junta, except Besteiro, went into exile. He stayed in Madrid, believing he could help others escape yet blithely unaware of the fact that the Casado coup had in itself severely sabotaged any chance of a properly organized evacuation of those in danger. Charged with 'military rebellion', he would face a court martial of rebel generals, be sentenced to thirty years imprisonment and die in captivity.

With the bankruptcy of Casado's plans brutally exposed, troops all along the line were surrendering or simply going home, although some took to the hills from where they kept up a guerrilla resistance until 1951. On 26 March, a gigantic and virtually unopposed advance was launched along a wide front. The Nationalists entered an eerily silent Madrid on 27 March. Luis Bolín was as scathing as he had been in Barcelona about the bewildered and shabbily dressed bystanders and the fact that the city was 'evil-smelling and dirty'. By 31 March 1939, all Spain was in Nationalist hands. A final bulletin was issued by Franco's headquarters on 1 April 1939 which ran, 'Today, with the Red Army captive and disarmed, our victorious troops have achieved their objectives'. Franco had the gratification of a telegram from the Pope thanking him for the immense joy which Spain's 'Catholic victory' had brought him. It was a victory which had cost well over half a million lives, and which was yet to cost many more. Those Republicans who could get transport had made a desperate bid to get to the Mediterranean ports. After waiting vainly in Alicante harbour for evacuation, some committed suicide rather than allow themselves to fall into the hands of the Falange. Those who had reached the French frontier were subjected to careless humiliation before being herded into concentration camps. The women, children and the old were shepherded into transit camps. The soldiers were disarmed and escorted to unsanitary camps on the coast, rapidly improvised by marking out sections of beach with barbed wire. Under the empty gaze of Senegalese guards, the men improvised shelters by burrowing into the wet sand.

Gustav Regler, a German Communist commissar with the International Brigades, had been at the French frontier looking for some of his men. He wrote later of the harrowing sights that he had witnessed:

That afternoon the Republican troops came. They were received as though they were tramps ... The Spaniards were asked what was in the haversacks and ditty-bags they carried, and they answered that in surrendering their rifles they had given up all the arms they possessed. But the French tapped disdainfully on the haversacks and demanded that they should be opened. The Spaniards did not understand. Until the last moment they persisted in the tragic error of believing in international solidarity ... The dirty road on which the disarmed men stood was not merely the frontier between two countries, it was an abyss between two worlds. Under the eyes of the Prefect and the generals, the men of the *Garde Mobile* took away the bags and bundles containing the Spaniards' personal belongings and emptied their contents into a ditch filled with chloride of lime. I have never seen eyes of such anger and helplessness as those of the Spaniards. They stood as though turned to stone, and they did not understand.

TEN

Franco's Peace

To quantify the number of deaths which occurred as a result of the post-war repression, it is necessary to recognize that 'after the civil war' means different things in different parts of Spain. In Old Castile, Seville, Granada, Córdoba, Huelva, Cádiz, Cáceres, Galicia and Zaragoza, the 'war' was over within hours or days of the military coup. Accordingly, the figures that matter are those regarding deaths at the hands of those who had untrammelled control of each area. Deaths in the Republican zone were carefully registered. They were fully investigated by the machinery of the state as one-time Republican areas fell to the Francoists. Detailed research has produced figures of approximately fifty thousand dead as a result of political repression or uncontrolled violence within the Republican zone.

Deaths in the Nationalist zone were not similarly registered other than in those cases where the deaths were as a result of summary (and, of course, totally illegal) courts martial. Accordingly, there are thousands more dead who just disappeared. Most deaths were not registered and many were simply buried in collective common graves. Since the death of Franco, huge efforts have been made by local historians to recover surviving documentation, more thoroughly in some areas than in others. It is on this basis that serious estimates of the figures involved can now be made and they suggest that the assassinations in the Nationalist zone were between three and four times those committed in Republican territory.

Apart from those killed on the battlefields, tens of thousands were officially executed, judicially murdered, between 1936 and 1945, when the Axis defeat imposed some caution on the Caudillo. Some were thrown alive from cliffs into the sea, or from high bridges into deep rivers. Others were shot against the walls of a cemetery or by a roadside and buried in shallow graves where they fell or were thrown into disused mineshafts. For decades, their families lived in terror, unable to grieve properly, unsure of the fate of their mothers or fathers, their husbands or sons.

An indication of the scale of the repression is given by the fact that researchers in the thirty-six of Spain's fifty provinces that had been fully or partially investigated by 2005 had dis-covered the names of 92,462 persons judicially murdered. Extrapolating the likely results from the provinces still to be investigated, this suggests that, in terms of the identifiable dead, those mainly the victims of 'judicial executions', the final figure may be in the region of 130,000. However, there were others, probably at least another fifty thousand, who were killed without even the simulacrum of a trial. Those whose names have been identified are those who were either executed after a pseudo trial and/or buried in a cemetery where records were kept. To them must be added those murdered whose names cannot be known. It may never be possible to calculate the exact numbers killed along the road travelled by the African columns that raped, looted and murdered their way from Seville to Madrid. What of those killed in the open fields by the patrols of mounted Falangists and Carlists who 'cleaned up' the countryside when the columns had moved on? What of those who, having fled from their own towns and villages, were murdered elsewhere with no one to recognize their corpses?

To give an idea of the scale of the still unknown dead, it is possible to look the case of Valladolid, known at the time as 'the capital of the uprising', partly because the military coup succeeded there so quickly. After three years of exhaustive research, a twenty-five-person team from the Asociación para la Recuperación de la Memoria Histórica of Valladolid found evidence of two thousand people killed in the province in addition to 1300 known to have been judicially murdered. They estimated in 2005 that the total numbers for Valladolid are likely to be around five thousand.

A different idea of the complications is provided by the province of Jaén. The official Francoist investigation, the Causa General, reached a figure of 1875 rightists killed while the province was in Republican hands. The later Francoist study by General Ramón Salas Larrazábal inflated the figures of rightists killed to 3049 and produced a figure of 857 leftists killed in the repression, 606 in the part held by the Francoists during the war and 251 in the entire province thereafter. Subsequent research in the province reduced the number of identifiable right-wing victims to 1368. However, the painstaking village-by-village research of the local historian Luis Miguel Sánchez Tostado has altered the picture yet again. By 2005, he had unearthed details of 1859 rightists murdered or dead in prison, as against 3278 victims of the Francoist repression.

All over Spain, archaeological activity is producing evidence of the horrors of the Civil War. A typical example was what happened between July 1936 and December 1937 near the village of Concud in the province of Teruel. Into *los pozos de Caudé*, a pit six feet wide and 250 feet deep, were hurled the bodies of 1005 men and women, including adolescent boys and girls. Few of them were political militants. Their crime was simply to be considered critical of the military coup, related to someone who had fled, to have owned a radio or have read liberal newspapers before the war. Some were shot by Civil Guards, others by local Falangists. It took sixty-eight years for their families to find out the truth. Fear prevented anyone from even going near the pit although occasionally at night bunches of flowers would be left nearby. Once the Socialists were in power, people began openly to leave floral tributes. Then, in

1983, a local farmer came forward and said that he had kept a notebook with the numbers of *coups de grâce* that he heard each night throughout the Spanish Civil War. They came to more than one thousand.

Media interest in Caudé and other common graves intensified after the year 2000, when a young Navarrese sociologist, Emilio Silva-Barrera, began to investigate the fate of his grandfather who had disappeared in León in the first months of the war. Overcoming the wall of silence and fear built by the Franco regime, which survived the transition to democracy, Silva discovered the truth. At dawn on 16 October 1936, his grandfather, with twelve other Republicans, was murdered by Falangist gunmen on the outskirts of Priaranza del Bierzo, near Ponferrada. Their bodies were buried in a field next to the roadside where they fell. A shopkeeper, Emilio Silva-Faba, was the father of six children aged between three months and nine years, his offence his membership in the centre-left party, Izquierda Republicana. His grandson then located the burial place and persuaded a group of archaeologists and forensic medical experts to take part in exploratory digs. DNA tests of the exhumed bones identified Emilio Silva-Faba.

As a result of that 'success', all over Spain there have emerged branches of the Association for the Recovery of Historical Memory, which have received thousands of requests for help in locating the remains of relatives. It is impossible to calculate with certainty the number of bodies lying in shallow graves across Spain. There exist gigantic common graves, in Extremadura, where mass killings took place at the concentration camp of Castuera; in Asturias, in both Oviedo with 1600 and Gijón with 2000; and in various parts of Andalusia. In Catalonia the regional government has located fifty-four such graves with four thousand corpses in Barcelona alone. There are graves in every part of Spain. As they are excavated, relatives stand nervously, like those awaiting rescue parties in mining disasters or earthquakes. Those who never knew what happened to their loved ones, even though they are certain that they were murdered, still await the definitive confirmation with horror and trepidation. When it comes, as sometimes it does, it permits the shuddering release of pent-up and unacknowledged grief.

It was a Spanish investigating judge, Baltasar Garzón, who pursued General Pinochet in 1998 on behalf of the 'disappeared' in Chile. Yet in Spain, where there are more than ten times as many cases, despite the private initiative of Emilio Silva-Barrera who took the case to the United Nations, the government of the Partido Popular refused to put resources into the search. Under the PSOE, that began to change. Nevertheless, there is still no nationwide census of the dead, no team of historians working on the problem, no funds for DNA testing. The government does, however, contribute to the upkeep of the graves of Falangist volunteers who fought with the Germans on the Eastern Front. Moreover, right-wing historians have been responding to the work of the Association with a resurrection of the Francoist propaganda, which implies that the 'reds' simply got what they deserved. With the most virulent of their number regularly riding high in the bestseller lists, the Spanish Civil War is being fought all over again on paper.

To his dying day, Franco vengefully kept Spain divided between the victors and the vanquished of 1939. This benevolent father of his nation regarded the civil war as 'the struggle of the *Patria* [the fatherland] against the *anti-Patria*' and the defeated as the '*canalla* [scum] of the Jewish–Masonic–Communist conspiracy'. The view of Franco as a magnanimous patriot is difficult to reconcile with the psycho-pathological language used by Francoists to depict their left-wing compatriots as subhuman – dirty, filthy, stinking depraved scum, slime, whores and criminals. This language justified the need for 'purification', a euphemism for the most sweeping physical, economic and psychological repression. The cost in blood of saving a nation's soul mattered little to the victors. Like the Nazi *Volksgemeinschaft* and the Soviet gulags, the Franco dictatorship also embarked on a process of national 'reconstruction' through the execution, forced exile, imprisonment, torture and economic and social humiliation of hundreds of thousands of Spaniards defeated in the Civil War of 1936–9. The persecution of the compatriots deemed to belong to the 'anti-Spain' (leftists or liberals and their extended families, all of whom became non-persons without civil rights) affected millions.

From the very first days of the war, terror had been a crucial instrument of the military rebels but to this Franco added a determination to annihilate as many Republicans as possible. Despite the German and Italian hopes for a rapid Nationalist victory, Franco's objective was the gradual and thorough occupation and purging of Republican territory. As early as 4 April 1937, at the beginning of the campaign against the Basque Country, he had explained to the Italian Ambassador Roberto Cantalupo his commitment to 'the necessarily slow task of redemption and pacification.' What he meant by moral redemption would be demonstrated by the massacres which followed the capture of town after town, of Badajoz, of Talavera de la Reina, of Toledo, of Málaga, of Gijón, of Santander, of Teruel, of Barcelona. Franco's determination to move slowly derived from his belief that would guarantee that there would never be any turning back, not only through the physical elimination of thousands of liberals and leftists but also in the long-term terrorizing of others into political support or apathy. Franco was fully conscious of the extent to which the repression not only terrified the enemy but also inextricably tied those involved in its implementation to his own survival. Their complicity ensured that they would cling to him as the only bulwark against the possible revenge of their victims.

The horrors were perhaps greatest in the south, where a colonial army applied against the civilian population the techniques of terror used in the African wars. The ferocity of the terror was unrelated to the strength of working-class resistance. In the case of Badajoz, where the resistance was fierce, nearly four thousand people were killed in one week. The repression was also bloody in the working-class districts of Seville, where the workers opposed the coup, but in Huelva, where the right took over relatively easily, the repression took more than six thousand lives. What happened in Huelva was representative of what took place in all parts of rebel-held territory, not just those places that had to be conquered by military force. Systematic terror was also applied where the military rebels succeeded immediately and where there was virtually no resistance. This was not the work of uncontrolled elements as happened in the Republican zone where the military rebellion had triggered the total collapse of the entire apparatus of law and order. The Falangists and others carrying out the systematic killings could at any time have been restrained by the military authorities. Yet the military actively encouraged thousands of civilian vigilantes to carry out a dirty war.

It was common for the widows and the wives of prisoners to be raped. The conquerors regularly used their position to exact sexual gratification. There exist various testimonies about one of the most notorious examples of this, the man appointed by Queipo de Llano to supervise the repression in Seville, Captain Manuel Díaz Criado. Queipo's propaganda chief, Antonio Bahamonde, wrote later, 'only young women were allowed into his office. I know cases of women who saved their loved ones by submitting to his demands.' The sufferings of female survivors of the repression did not end with widowhood or sexual abuse. Houses were requisitioned, furniture, sewing machines and anything portable simply confiscated. It was not just a question of ordinary soldiers looting watches and jewellery. Farms and entire businesses were stolen. In some cases, substantial fortunes were made by the conquerors. When Major Gregorio Haro Lumbreras was dismissed as civil governor of Huelva, it was alleged that his personal effects occupied three lorries. Many women were forced to live in total poverty and frequently, out of desperation, to sell themselves on the streets. The increase in prostitution both benefited Francoist men who thereby slaked their lust and also reassured them that 'red' women were a fount of dirt and corruption.

As each area of Spain was conquered, there began a process of political and social purge. This was often justified in terms of left-wing atrocities despite the fact that, in many places, the military coup had succeeded within days, if not hours, and there had been no such atrocities. There were successive, and massive, increases in the numbers of prisoners after the conquest of the north in 1937, the occupation of eastern Aragón in the spring of 1938, the battle of the Ebro, the fall of Catalonia, and, massively, the end of the war. The Francoist prison system was chaotic, improvised and utterly arbitrary. Hundreds of thousands who escaped the random killing were kept in conditions of extreme degradation in prisons and concentration camps. The situation in the camps was not merely a reaction to the problem presented by the volume of prisoners of war but was also a fundamental pillar of the Franco state's policy of dividing victors and vanquished. The defeated were being branded as permanent enemies, separated from society because they did not share the values on which the Francoist state was being built. The camps provided an apparatus for the mass application of punishment and the subsequent social, moral, ideological and political reconstruction of the Republicans.

Initially, there were nearly two hundred camps, some provisional, as the victorious Francoists set up detention centres to intern and classify prisoners of war. The first function of the camps was to divide prisoners into those who were regarded as 'recoverable' after re-education and those who were not. The non-recoverable were shot. The next category was reintegrated through forced labour through the Patronato para la Redención de Penas por el Trabajo. The idea underlying this Board for the Redemption/Remission of Sentences through

Labour was heavily religious and part of the process of humiliating the prisoners, who had to find 'redemption' for their sins by work, just as others were forced to find redemption in their executions. More than one hundred camps remained in existence well into the 1940s as centres of coercion, humiliation and exploitation. The last one, at Miranda del Ebro, was not closed until 1947. More than four hundred thousand prisoners passed through them. After classification, many of those who were not executed were sent to work in one of a confusing network of overlapping entities, the Colonias Penitenciarias Militarizadas (militarized penal colonies), Destacamentos Penales (penal detachments) or Trabajos de Regiones Devastadas (reconstruction of devastated regions). Many Republican prisoners awaiting classification were sent to Batallones Disciplinarios de Soldados Trabajadores (disciplinary battalions of worker-soldiers), where they were treated as slave labour. Despite regarding the prisoners as non-Spanish, the Francoist authorities showed no respect whatsoever for the Geneva Convention and most prisoners, not just prisoners of war, but other political prisoners, were systematically mistreated, tortured and forced to work.

The existence of these camps was the cause of considerable opprobrium for the Franco regime. In an effort to prove that the regime's record was spotless, at the end of 1950 the Spanish Ambassador in Paris, Manuel Aguirre de Carcer, sent a dispatch to the Minister of Foreign Affairs in Madrid, Alberto Martín Artajo, requesting permission to invite the Commission International contre le régime concentrationaire (the International Commission against Concentration Camps) to Spain. The Commission had been set up after the Second World War by representatives of survivors of Nazi concentration camps from seven European 'countries' – Germany, Belgium, France, Holland, Norway, the Saarland and the Spanish Republic in exile. After the Minister delayed for two years, in 1952 permission was astonishingly granted for the Commission to go to Spain to inspect some 'centres in which there are applied the modern and humanitarian doctrines established by our regime and inspired by the Christian principles of redemption through work'. The Commission's investigation, despite the enormous limitations placed on its freedom of movement, produced startling conclusions about the arbitrary nature of mass imprisonment and intense overcrowding. Its report was denounced as lies by regime, which claimed that the 'forced labour' discovered by the Commission was actually a benevolent regime of 'Christian redemption'.

Torture accounted for large numbers of suicides in prison, and the authorities, feeling cheated by these 'escapes' from their justice, often reacted by executing a relative of the prisoner. Central to the repression was the systematic economic exploitation of both the rural and industrial working classes. Many thousands were forced to work – and die – in inhuman conditions in penal detachments and work battalions. The threat of imprisonment forced millions of workers to accept starvation wages.

The social humiliation and exploitation of the defeated was justified in religious terms as the necessary expiation of their sins and also in social-Darwinist terms. The defeated were denounced as degenerate, their children were taken away and military psychiatrists carried out experiments on women prisoners in search of the 'red gene'. In prisons, massive efforts were made to break not only the bodies of prisoners but also their minds. The man who supervised the process was Major Antonio Vallejo-Nájera, the head of the Psychiatric Services of the Nationalist Army. He set up the Laboratory of Psychological Investigations to engage in psychological studies of prisoners in concentration camps to establish 'the bio-psychic roots of Marxism'. The results of his investigations provided the delighted military high command with the 'scientific' arguments to justify their views on the subhuman nature of their adversaries for which he was promoted to colonel.

A good example of what redemption by Franco really meant could be found in the experience of Catalonia after the region's capture in January 1939. The formal parade into Barcelona was headed by the Army Corps of Navarre, led by General Andrés Solchaga. They were accorded this honour, according to a British officer attached to Franco's headquarters, 'not because they have fought better, but because they hate better. That is to say, when the object of this hate is Catalonia or a Catalan.' A close friend of Franco, Víctor Ruiz Albeniz ('El Tebib Arrumi'), published an article demanding that Catalonia needed 'a biblical punishment [Sodom, Gomorrah] to purify the red city, seat of anarchism and separatism as the only remedy to extirpate these two cancers by implacable thermo-cauterization'. For Ramón Serrano Suñer, Franco's brother-in-law and Minister of the Interior, Catalan nationalism was a sickness that had to be exterminated. The man he appointed as civil governor of Barcelona, Wenceslao González Oliveros, claimed that the Civil War had been fought with greater ferocity against the regions than against communism and that any toleration of regionalism would lead once more to 'the putrefaction represented by Marxism and separatism that we have just surgically eradicated'.

Occupied Catalonia experienced an all-pervading terror in a period when merely to stay alive was a major achievement for many. Research into daily life for the defeated in rural Catalonia in the 1940s is deeply shocking, revealing an appalling catalogue of hunger and illness, arbitrary repression and fear – fear of arrest, fear of denunciation by a neighbour or by a priest. The entire process was underpinned by the complicity of thousands of people who for many reasons – fear, politics, greed, jealousy – became informers and denounced their neighbours. The sheer misery of life for the defeated in Franco's Spain accounts for the notable rise in the suicide rate, which was often the consequence of economic and sexual extortion by the powerful. In Catalonia, as elsewhere, considerable cruelty was visited upon women under the rhetorical Francoist umbrella of 'redemption' – rape, imprisonment as retribution for the behaviour of a son or husband and confiscation of goods. Soldiers billeted on poor families often took advantage of the unprotected women of the household. There was no shortage of priests ready to defend the honour of male parishioners and to denounce their female victims as 'reds'.

Violence against the defeated was not limited to prison, torture and execution but extended to the psychological humiliation and economic exploitation of the survivors. Franco's policy of economic self-sufficiency or autarky contributed to the repression and humiliation of the defeated and to capital accumulation although its rigidity also delayed eventual growth. Considering himself to be an economist of genius, Franco embraced autarky oblivious to the fact that Spain lacked the technological and industrial base which had made such a policy feasible for the Third Reich. Autarky in Spain brought economic and social disaster – the shortages consequent upon closing Spain to the world provoked the emergence of a black market, the *estraperlo*, which exacerbated the differences between rich and poor. Inevitably, it was those close to the regime who benefited and the defeated who suffered. State interventionism in every aspect of the planting, harvesting, processing, sale and distribution of wheat was so corrupt that it made fortunes for officials while creating shortages that saw food prices rocket. Access to work and ration cards meant getting identity cards and safe conducts, which involved certificates of 'good behaviour' from local Falangist officials and parish priests. Inevitably, the defeated suffered materially and were further humiliated while the victors' sense of wellbeing was enhanced.

The social consequences of autarky and the workings of the black market fitted well with the Caudillo's rhetorical insistence that the defeated could find redemption only through sacrifice. There was a clear link between the repression and the capital accumulation that made possible the economic boom of the 1960s. The destruction of trade unions and the repression of the working class ensured starvation wages that permitted banks, industry and the landholding classes to record spectacular increases in profits. Moreover, the organization which enabled prisoners to redeem their sentences by work, the Patronato para la Redención de Penas, effectively forced thousands of Republican prisoners into slave labour. The penal detachments provided forced labour for mines, railway building and the reconstruction of the so-called 'devastated regions'. The military penal colonies were set up for long-term public work projects such as the Guadalquivir Canal, dug out over 180 kilometres and twenty years.

The greatest symbol of the exploitation of Republican prisoners was Franco's personal caprice, the gigantic basilica and towering cross of the mausoleum of the Valle de los Caídos. Twenty thousand were employed, and several were killed or badly injured, in its construction, a gigantic mausoleum for Franco and a monument to those who fell in his cause. The Valle de los Caídos was merely one of several enterprises in which Republican prisoners were forced to work to perpetuate the memory of the Francoist victory in permanent form. The ruined Alcázar of Toledo was rebuilt as a symbol of the Nationalist heroism displayed during its three-month siege. In Madrid, the entrance to the University City, the site of the savage battle for the capital, was marked by a gigantic Arch of Victory. The Valle de los Caídos, however, dwarfed them all. The human cost of forced labour, the deaths and the suffering of the workers and their families were matched by the fortunes made by the private companies and the public enterprises that exploited them.

After years in which the atrocities of Francoism were silenced in the interests of the consolidation of democracy, it is now possible to put together the overall picture of the Spanish holocaust. Mass graves are one of the most horrendous legacies of the way in which Franco established his power. The true extent of the appalling conditions of the Francoist prison regime is only now beginning to emerge. The daily conditions of starvation and torture and the terror of waiting for the firing squad are things that have long been familiar through the memoirs of survivors. Yet it is only recently that the stories are beginning to be heard about what happened to the women and children forced into Franco's prisons at the end of the Civil War. Many of the thousands of women imprisoned by the regime at the end of the Civil War were young, some with very young children, some pregnant, some raped and made pregnant by their guards. The consequence was a substantial prison population of children who were punished for the perceived crimes of their mothers. Many died in the goods trains into which they were packed to be moved from one prison to another. Many died of hunger, of cold or of disease. In the provincial prison of Zaragoza, forty-two newborn babies died in one week. Many children were mistreated, locked up in dark rooms and forced to eat their own vomit. Thousands were forcibly taken from their mothers and handed over to Francoist families for adoption or sent away to be brought up in religious establishments. Usually, albeit not always, the removal of a child signified that the mother was about to be shot. Pregnancy did not save a young woman from execution, one judge commenting, 'We cannot wait seven months to execute a woman.'

An important part of the story of the Civil War concerns the Spaniards who were victims of Nazism as a result of actions taken by the Franco regime. For many Republicans, forced into exile by the regime, there was no escape from the Nazi war and terror machine. Thousands of exiled Spaniards found themselves among the millions of non-German forced labourers obliged to work for the German war effort. Nearly 15,000 Spaniards were forced to work in the construction of the Atlantic Wall in 1940–41 while approximately four thousand were deported to the German-occupied Channel Islands.

From October 1941, these 'Spanish Communists', as Hitler described them, were forced to build strong points on the various islands. Only fifty-nine survived.

In addition to those forced to work for the Nazis, there were many Spaniards who ended up in German concentration camps. The most detailed examination of the fate of the Spaniards who ended up in Mauthausen in Austria concluded that, of the more than thirty thousand Spanish refugees who were deported from France to Germany, nearly 15,000 were imprisoned in Nazi camps. Of these by far the largest contingent, around 50 per cent, ended up in Mauthausen (making up the second largest contingent of prisoners there), with other groups transported to Auschwitz, Buchenwald, Dachau and other parts of the Nazi camp system. Around half of the Spaniards that were deported were killed. Although the number of Spanish victims of the Nazi terror machine pales into relative insignificance compared to the total number of victims, it is significant that the Franco regime not only did nothing to prevent Spaniards suffering the fate of other Europeans, but actively encouraged the Germans to detain and deport exiled Republicans.

It was not just exiled leftists who, thanks to the Franco regime, fell into the clutches of the Nazis. A major propaganda operation was mounted to deceive large numbers of Spanish workers, driven by hunger, to work in the Third Reich. Franco owed Hitler a considerable debt and the need of the German war industry for labour provided a method of payment. A visit to Germany by Gerardo Salvador Merino of the Falangist union organization resulted in propaganda about the high standards of living in Germany, high wages and possibilities for saving. No mention was made of the fact that the money earned by Spanish workers would go towards payment of the Civil War debt. Within weeks of the German invasion of the Soviet Union, the Blue Division of Falangist volunteers was on its way to fight in Russia. In addition to the combatants, an agreement was made on 21 August 1941 between the *Deutsche Arbeitsfront* (German Labour Front) and the Falange for one hundred thousand Spanish workers to be sent to Germany. In fact, after the first batch of seven thousand went, their reports of the conditions made it more difficult for the Falange to find volunteers.

The reconstruction of this repression has been rendered difficult by the one-sided destruction of archival material. This begs the question, if Francoism had so much to be proud of, why were the police, judicial and military archives of the 1940s so ruthlessly purged? In the 1960s and 1970s, the archives of provincial police headquarters, of prisons and of the main Francoist local authority, the Civil Governors, disappeared. Conveys of trucks removed the 'judicial' records of the repression. As well as the deliberate destruction of archives, there were also 'inadvertent' losses when some town councils sold their archives by the ton as waste paper for recycling. Despite the losses, enough has survived to permit the reconstruction of the 'legal' repression. The efforts of the Association for the Recovery of Historical Memory, both through their archaeological digs and also by encouraging people to come forward and recount their memories, are contributing to the nationwide reconstruction of the 'unofficial' repression. Finally, it is possible to have a reasonably approximate overview of the human cost of the military coup of 1936. This has been a cumulative process. Since the death of Franco, huge efforts have been made by local historians to recover surviving documentation, more thoroughly in some areas than in others. It is on this basis that serious estimates of the figures involved can now be made.

The responsibility for the crimes committed by the military rebels has to be sought in a huge pyramid of collaborators, built on the eager participation of right-wing army officers, of landowners, village Falangists and priests through to the military commanders of entire provinces, on up to Mola, Queipo de Llano and Franco. At the top of the pyramid was Franco.

The 'legal' or 'constitutional' system that his advisers began to create from 1 October 1936 attributed absolute power to him. Accordingly, his personal responsibility was the greatest, though it was not an issue that caused him pangs of conscience. In his deathbed testament, he wrote, 'with all my heart, I pardon all those who declared themselves my enemies, even if I did not regard them as such. I believe, and I wish it to be the case, that I never had any other than those who were the enemies of Spain.' Clearly, in this regard he was happy to believe his own propaganda. Franco's propagandists presented the repression, the executions, the overflowing prisons, the concentration camps and the slave-labour battalions as the scrupulous yet compassionate justice administered by a wise and benevolent Caudillo. One after another they lined up to sing the praises of the Caudillo's lofty and noble impartiality.

In mid-July 1939, Count Galeazzo Ciano, the Foreign Minister of Fascist Italy, arrived in Barcelona. He was returning the official visit made to Italy one month earlier by Ramón Serrano Suñer, Franco's brother-in-law. Having been an enthusiastic advocate of Franco's cause during the Civil War, he was assured of a warm welcome. However, he was not impressed. Among the entertainments provided for such an illustrious guest was a tour of battlegrounds. Near one of them, he was shown a group of Republican prisoners working. Their condition provoked the bitter commentary, 'They are not prisoners of war, they are slaves of war.' Later, he was received by Franco in the Palace of Ayete in San Sebastián. On his return to Rome, he described Franco to one of his cronies: 'That queer fish of a Caudillo, there in his Ayete palace, in the midst of his Moorish Guard, surrounded by mountains of files of prisoners condemned to death. With his work timetable, he will see about three a day, because that fellow enjoys his siestas.' It certainly seems to be the case that Franco's sleep was never interrupted by any concern for his prisoners nor by any sense of guilt as he signed death sentences.

Epilogue

Although those who escaped across the French border faced internment in unsanitary concentration camps, they were among the lucky ones. After Catalonia was occupied, the Mediterranean coast remained the last escape route. On 27 March 1939, with the Republic crumbling before the unopposed Nationalist advance, Colonel Casado together with some of his Defence Junta colleagues and their staff were taken on board a British ship at Gandía near Valencia. The veteran Socialist leader Julián Besteiro decided that it was his duty to remain with the people of Madrid in the vain hope that he might somehow limit the vengeance of the Nationalists. He was imprisoned and died in the squalid prison of Carmona. Communists left in jail in Madrid by the Casado Defence Junta were shot when Franco entered Madrid. Efforts to organize mass evacuation were inept. Refugees gathered at the Mediterranean ports, where only a small proportion of them managed to avoid being herded into prison camps by the arriving Nationalists. Even those who reached exile were far from safe. Julián Zugazagoitia, Lluis Companys and Juan Peiró were captured by the Gestapo in France, handed over to Franco and shot. Largo Caballero spent four years in the German concentration camp at Mauthausen and died shortly after his release. Negrín, Prieto and other Republican leaders who escaped to Mexico spent the rest of their lives locked in sterile polemic about responsibility for their defeat. Manuel Azaña died in Montauban on 3 November 1940.

From 1939 until Franco's death, Spain was governed as if it were a country occupied by a victorious foreign army. The training, deployment and structure of the Spanish army were such as to prepare it for action against the native population rather than an external enemy. That was entirely in keeping with the Caudillo's view, expressed in 1937, that he had been fighting a 'frontier war'. When Ciano returned to Italy after his ten-day visit to Spain in the summer of 1939, he wrote a long report for Mussolini. It was much less critical than the private remarks quoted in the last chapter, yet still noted that 200 to 250 executions were being carried out daily in Madrid, 150 in Barcelona and 80 in Seville. In May 1939, the *Manchester Guardian* alleged that three hundred people per week were being shot in Barcelona. The British Consul in Madrid reported that by June there were thirty thousand political prisoners in the city and that twelve tribunals were dealing with them at breathtaking speed. In proceedings lasting only minutes, the death penalty was invariably demanded and often passed. British consular sources estimated conservatively that ten thousand people were shot in the first five months after the war. The killings went on well into the 1940s. In November 1939, a torch-lit procession escorted the mortal remains of José Antonio Primo de Rivera from Alicante to the Escorial. Prisons were attacked along the way and Republican prisoners lynched. The military authorities complained that with 70 per cent of barracks turned into jails, army units had to be accommodated in tents. More than four hundred thousand Spaniards, including women, children, the old and infirm, and wounded and mutilated soldiers, were forced to face the horrors of exile.

The Civil War had been won by a rightist coalition which had arisen in response to the reformist challenge of the Second Republic. Franco rarely missed an opportunity to boast that he had eliminated the legacy of the Enlightenment, the French Revolution and other symbols of modernity. Indeed, the strength of Francoist links with the old order made the Second Republic appear to be a mere interlude in the history of Spain. During that parenthesis, an attack had been mounted against the existing balance of social and economic power. The defensive response of the right had been twofold – the violent, or 'catastrophist', and the legalist, or 'accidentalist'. 'Catastrophist' violence had little possibility of success in the first years of the Republic. Indeed, its most spectacular failure, the abortive military coup of General Sanjurjo, merely confirmed the wisdom of entrusting oligarchical interests to the legalist means of the CEDA. However, the success of Gil Robles in building up a mass party, using parliament to block reform and winning the 1933 elections, drove the Socialists to despair. Their optimistic reformism hardened into an aggressive revolutionism.

The consequent rising of October 1934 suggested a leftist determination to resist the legal establishment of an authoritarian corporative state. The repression which followed October united the left and paved the way to the Popular Front electoral victory of 1936. The right was not slow to perceive the impossibility of defending traditional structures by legal means. Given the unmistakable determination of working-class forces to introduce major reforms and the equal readiness of the oligarchy to resist them, the failure of the legalist tactics of Gil Robles could only lead to a resurgence of 'catastrophism' and an attempt to impose a corporative state by force of arms. That attempt, in the form of the Nationalist war effort, was crowned with success. The first objectives of the new regime were the maintenance of the existing structure of landed property and the strict control of the recently defeated working class. These tasks were carried out by an enormous political and military bureaucracy beholden to the Franco regime.

Wages were slashed, strikes were treated as sabotage and made punishable by long prison sentences. The CNT and the UGT were destroyed, their funds, their printing presses and other property seized by the state and the Falange. Travel and the search for jobs were controlled by a system of safe-conducts and certificates of political and religious reliability. This effectively made second-class citizens of those defeated Republicans who escaped imprisonment. The Franco regime was especially committed to the maintenance of the rural social structure which had been threatened by the Republic. Among the smallholders of the north, this was relatively easy given their social and religious conservatism. In the south, however, the regime faced the problem of maintaining a social system that had provoked the rage and militancy of the landless *braceros*. This was done by the creation of a series of institutions which compelled rural labourers to work the soil under conditions even more inhuman than those they had known before 1931. With no social welfare safety net, not to work was to starve. In 1951, wages were still only 60 per cent of 1936 levels. The Civil Guard and armed retainers, or *guardas jurados*, employed by the *latifundistas*, maintained a hostile vigilance of the estates against the pilfering of hungry peasants. The Falangist corporative, *Hermandades de Labradores y Ganaderos* (fraternities of farmers and cattlemen), was based on the myth that labourers and landowners shared 'fraternal' interests. A similar fraud was at the heart of the repressive system of industrial labour relations.

In fact, behind the rhetoric of national and social unity, until the death of Franco every effort was made to maintain the division between the victors and the vanquished. The Falange, as a Fascist organization, might have been expected to attempt to integrate the working class into the regime. However, after a victorious war, the ruling classes had little need for such an operation. Falangist bureaucrats still mouthed anti-capitalist rhetoric but it rang ever more hollow. They dutifully served their masters by disciplining the urban working class within the corporative syndicates and drumming the peasantry into the rural *Hermandades*. The anti-oligarchical aspects of the Nazi and Fascist regimes had no place in Franco's Spain. The post-war state remained the instrument of the traditional oligarchy. The Falangist bureaucrats themselves openly acknowledged the class nature of the regime. José María Areilza declared that the state protected capital from internal as well as external aggressors. In the late 1950s, the head of the Falange, José Solís, admitted that 'when we speak of transformation or reform in the countryside, no one should think that we intend to harm the present owners'. The emptiness of the Falangist rhetoric of revolution was so apparent that it shamed some of José Antonio Primo de Rivera's followers into timidly opposing the regime. They created a tame dissident Falange dedicated to the fulfilment of his heritage.

Francoism was merely the latest in a series of military efforts to block social progress in Spain. However, unlike its predecessors it served not just the Spanish oligarchy but also international capitalism. The abandonment of the Republic by the Western democracies during the Civil War was matched by the feebleness of international action against Franco after 1945. This reflected a recognition that a military dictatorship could defend the economic interests of foreign investors far better than a democratic Republic ever could. Ironically, however, the twin defence of the interests of Spanish and foreign capitalists was to lay the foundations for the ultimate democratization of Spain. The efforts made by Francoism to put back the clock inadvertently created the social and economic conditions for the regime's ultimate transition to democracy.

The repressive labour relations of the 1940s and 1950s contributed to higher profits and the accumulation of native capital. It was also a contribution, along with Franco's much-vaunted anti-communism, to the process of making Spain attractive to foreign investors. Foreign capital flooded in. The boom years of European capitalism saw tourists pouring south as Spanish migrant labourers headed north, from where they would send back their foreign currency earnings. Gradually, within the antiquated political straitjacket of Francoist Spain, there began to grow a new, dynamic, modern society. The pattern of Spanish history was being repeated, with the political framework out of phase with the social and economic reality. By the time of the energy crisis of the 1970s, many of Franco's supporters were beginning to wonder if their own survival did not lie in some sort of accommodation with the forces of the democratic opposition.

The dictator himself had created a complex edifice of laws and institutions that was intended to guarantee the survival of his regime long after his own death. By one of those laws, the Law of Succession of 1947, he had given himself the prerogative of choosing his own royal successor. In 1969, he chose Prince Juan Carlos de Borbón, the grandson of Alfonso XIII, a young man who had been trained since 1948 in 'the principles of the regime'. In his end-of-year message on 30 December 1969, the Caudillo confidently declared that 'all is tied down and well tied down'. However, he was wrong. The Prince realized that his own survival depended on his being 'King of all Spaniards', not just of the Francoists, and that the bulk of the population wanted a return to the democracy that had been destroyed in 1939. By 1977, only two years after his death, Franco's worst nightmares had begun to be realized. Drawing on an overwhelming consensus of right and left, King Juan Carlos had presided over a process whereby the most progressive elements of the Francoist elite and the moderate majority of the democratic opposition worked together in a spirit of compromise to create a democracy for all Spaniards. The cherished Francoist divisions between victors and vanquished were meaningless. Five years later, the Socialists were in power in Madrid.

Underlying the entire process was a great determination never again to suffer a bloody civil war or a repressive dictatorship. It was that desire for a different future which saw the agreement in early 1977 of an amnesty law which effectively granted impunity to those responsible for the abuses of human rights committed by the dictatorship. This was the basis of what came to be known as the 'pact of oblivion'. The political decision not to rake up the past has not inhibited a popular desire to know more about the Civil War and the repression that followed it. In the resulting torrent of books, television documentaries and public events, the Spanish conflict is refought as a war of words.

Principal Characters

ALCALÁ ZAMORA, Niceto – Conservative Republican, first Prime Minister and then first President of the Republic until deposed in May 1936.

ALVAREZ DEL VAYO, Julio – Left Socialist follower of Largo Caballero, became a close ally of the Communists.

AZAÑA, Manuel – Left Republican writer and intellectual, Prime Minister 1931–3 and again in 1936, President 1936–9.

BESTEIRO, Julián – Moderate right-of-centre Socialist, opposed leftward trend of PSOE, joined Casado's Defence Junta in 1939.

BOLÍN, Luis – Right-wing journalist, helped arrange Franco's trip to Morocco in 1936, enthusiastic defender of the Nationalist cause to the international press.

CALVO SOTELO, José – Authoritarian monarchist, leader of Renovación Española, murdered on 13 July 1936.

CASADO, Segismundo – Colonel in command of Republican Army of the Centre, organized coup against Negrín in February 1939.

COMPANYS, Lluis – Leader of Catalan Esquerra and President of the Generalitat, executed by Francoists in 1940.

DURRUTI, Buenaventura – Anarchist militia leader, killed on Madrid front in November 1936.

FRANCO BAHAMONDE, Francisco – Youngest general in Europe; after early hesitation, assumed leadership of Nationalist forces.

GOICOECHEA, Antonio – Leader of Renovación Española before return from exile of Calvo Sotelo.

GIL ROBLES, José María – Leader of legalist right, later shunned by Franco.

KOLTSOV, Mikhail – Russian journalist close to Stalin.

LARGO CABALLERO, Francisco – Minister of Labour 1931–3, became figurehead of Socialist left in 1930s and Prime Minister 4 September 1936 to 17 May 1936.

LERROUX, Alejandro – Founder of Radical Party, became increasingly corrupt and conservative, Prime Minister 1934–5 in coalition with Gil Robles.

MARTÍNEZ BARRIO, Diego – Centre Republican, left Radical Party in 1934, Prime Minister 18–19 July 1936, then President of the Republic 1939.

MIAJA, José – General entrusted with organizing the Madrid Defence Junta in November 1936.

MOLA, Emilio – Director of the military conspiracy in 1936, and general who commanded Nationalist northern armies until killed in a plane crash in 1937.

NEGRÍN, Dr Juan – Moderate Socialist and Professor of Physiology, Finance Minister under Largo Caballero, Prime Minister May 1937 to end of war.

NIN, Andrés – One-time Trotskyist, leader of the POUM, murdered by Communists in May 1937.

PRIETO, Indalecio – Moderate Socialist rival of Largo Caballero, Minister of Finance 1931, Minister of Defence May 1937 to April 1938.

PRIMO DE RIVERA, José Antonio – Founder of the Falange, executed in Alicante in November 1936.

QUEIPO DE LLANO, Gonzalo – Eccentric general who seized Seville and set up rule of terror in Andalusia.

ROJO, General Vicente – Republican Chief of Staff, masterminded Teruel and Ebro offensives.

SANJURJO, José – Right-wing general, organized abortive coup in 1932, killed in air crash in Portugal en route to be the figurehead of 1936 rising.

SERRANO SUÑER, Ramón – Falangist, Franco's brother-in-law, architect of the Nationalist political structure.

VARELA, José Enrique – Carlist sympathizer, general who led attack on Madrid.

YAGÜE, Juan – Falangist sympathizer, field commander of the Army of Africa.

ZUGAZAGOITIA, Julián – Socialist newspaper editor, wartime Minister of the Interior, executed by Franco in 1940.

Glossary

accidentalist – A conservative prepared to work legally within the Republic on the grounds that forms of government were 'accidental' and not fundamental.

Alfonsist – Orthodox monarchist committed to the restoration of King Alfonso XIII who left Spain in 1931.

alzamiento – Military uprising.

bracero – Landless agricultural worker.

bunker – Die-hard Franco supporters who went on fighting for years after his death to maintain Civil War divisions.

cacique – Political boss, usually rural.

caciquismo – System of political corruption and electoral fraud.

Carlist – Extreme reactionary monarchist follower of the rival royal dynasty.

catastrophist – Rightist from the Carlist, Falangist or Alfonsist factions committed to the violent destruction of the Republic.

Caudillo – literally bandit chieftain, more usually military leader, became Franco's equivalent to Führer or Duce.

CMI: Circulo Monárquico Independiente – monarchist organization whose propaganda may have contributed to the church burnings of 10 May 1931.

Cortes – The Spanish parliament.

Esquerra – Catalan regionalist Republican party.

estraperlo – the black market; the name is derived from a major political corruption scandal in 1935 involving three men named Strauss, Perl and Lerroux.

Euskadi – the Basque Country.

faccioso – Military rebel.

Falange – Spanish Fascist party.

Generalitat – Autonomous Catalan government.

Hermandad – State-run union or 'fraternity' encompassing both landlords and rural labourers after the Civil War.

Jefe – Chief, a Spanish equivalent of *Duce* (when applied to Gil

Robles, the leader of the CEDA) or *Capo*, when referring to the rank held by provincial leaders of the Falange.

jornalero – Landless agricultural day labourer.

latifundista – Landlord of a big estate.

Movimiento – General term for the Nationalist war effort; more specifically Franco's single party which united all other rightist groups on 19 April 1937.

pronunciamiento – military coup.

pueblo – Small town or village.

Reconquista – The reconquest of Spain from the Moors in the Middle Ages, used by the right as an allegory for its struggle against the left.

reemplazos – Annual draft of recruits.

Regulares – Brutal Moorish mercenaries who fought with the Army of Africa.

requeté – Carlist militia unit or militiaman.

retranca – Taciturn peasant cunning, supposedly typical of Galicians, particularly General Franco.

sacas – Unofficial removal of prisoners from jail to be executed.

Sanjurjada – Abortive military coup of 10 August 1932.

Sindicato – State-run vertical or corporate trade union after the Civil War.

List of Abbreviations

ACNP: Asociación Católica Nacional de Propagandistas – the elite rightist group founded by Ángel Herrera, which later provided the CEDA high command.

CEDA: Confederación Española de Derechas Autónomas – the largest mass political organization of the legalist right in the Second Republic.

CMI: Circulo Monárquico Independiente – monarchist organization whose propaganda may have contributed to the Church burnings of 10 May 1931.

CNT: Confederación Nacional del Trabajo – giant anarcho-syndicalist trade union.

FAI: Federación Anarquista Ibérica – the insurrectionary vanguard of the Iberian anarchist movement.

FET y de las JONS: Falange Española Tradicionalista y de las Juntas Ofensivas Nacional Sindicalistas – Franco's single party created by the forced merger in April 1937 of the Falange Española, the Comunión Tradicionalista (the Carlists), the CEDA and Renovación Española (the monarchist followers of Alfonso XIII).

FJS: Federación de Juventudes Socialistas – Socialist youth movement.

FNTT: Federación Nacional de Trabajadores de la Tierra – the landworkers' section of the UGT.

HISMA: Hispano-Marroquí de Transportes – the company set up in Morocco on 31 July 1936 to send Spanish goods to Germany in payment for aid received by the Nationalists from the Third Reich.

JAP: Juventud de Acción Popular – the CEDA youth movement.

JSU: Juventudes Socialistas Unificadas – Socialist youth movement created by the unification of the Socialist and Communist youth in 1936.

NKVD: Narodny komissariat vnutrennykh del (People's Commissariat of Internal Affairs), the Russian secret police.

PCE: Partido Comunista de España – the Moscow-orientated Spanish Communist Party.

POUM: Partido Obrero de Unificación Marxista – a combination of anti-Stalinist Communist dissidents and Trotskyists who united in 1935 in an effort to create a bolshevik vanguard party.

PSOE: Partido Socialista Obrera Español – the Spanish Socialist Workers' Party.

ROWAK: Rohstoff-und-Waren-Kompensatsion Handelsgesellschaft – the export agency set up in Germany in October 1936 to channel supplies to Nationalist Spain.

SIM: Servicio de Investigación Militar – secret police in Republican zone.

UGT: Unión General de Trabajadores – the trade union federation linked to the Spanish Socialist Party.

Bibliographical Essay

The Spanish Civil War has given rise to an astonishing wealth of polemical, scholarly and memoir material. At the last exact count, in 1968, there were 15,000 books and pamphlets on the war. In the thirty-eight years since then, that figure has continued to rise steadily. Indeed, since the death of Franco, there has been an incessant flood. Among the thousands of new books, there are works of political, historical and literary importance. There is also a certain amount of rubbish. For obvious reasons, the most extensive bibliography is to be found in Spanish and, to a lesser extent, Catalan. In addition, there are many important books in French, German, Italian, Portuguese and, indeed, in most European languages. However, the English reader need not despair. Some of the best writing has been produced in Britain and the United States. Moreover, many important works have been translated although there remain crucial works available only in languages other than English. The following remarks are not intended as a comprehensive survey of the international literature on the Spanish Civil War but they are intended to serve as a guide to the bibliography in English. Titles available in modern paperback editions are marked with an asterisk. Unless otherwise stated, all were published in London.

Precisely because the Franco dictatorship forbade the objective study of the bloodshed from which it sprang, the literature in Spanish has been heavily weighted towards partisan interpretation. The most crucial losses to the reader without Spanish are the many memoirs by participants. Fortunately, much of what they have to say is reflected in the works of British and American scholars. Since the death of the dictator, and the consequent liberalization of universities and the opening of archives, there has been a revolution in Spanish historiography with regard to the war. However, the central thrust of Spanish scholarship in the last thirty years has been principally in the area of local studies and, to a lesser extent, in the investigation of the international dimension of the war. Province by province, immense detail had been unearthed about collectivization and the revolution in the Republican zone and about repression in the Nationalist zone. Much of that work is filtering only slowly into books published in English. Otherwise, the contribution by Spaniards to the significant changes in perceptions of the war's international context have either been published in English or else had an influence on works available in English.

There are many general works on Spain which place the Civil War in its long-term historical context but those by two English authors are outstanding. Gerald Brenan's *The Spanish Labyrinth* (*Cambridge: Cambridge University Press, 1943) is unsurpassed for its sympathetic 'feel', particularly for all aspects of the agrarian problem. Brenan's analysis of the divisions of the left and of regional nationalism combines shrewd reflection with the immediacy of an eye-witness account. Written in the most delightfully limpid prose, it reflects the long years that Brenan, a Bloomsbury exile, spent in southern Spain between the wars, an experience recounted in the exquisite memoir, Gerald Brenan, *Personal Record 1920–1972* (Jonathan Cape, 1974). Raymond Carr's monumental *Spain 1808–1975* (*Oxford: Clarendon Press, 1982) is a beautifully written account of the failure of the Spanish middle classes to modernize the country, a failure in which can be discerned the long-term origins of the Civil War. It is based on a lifetime's reading, a knowledge of modern Spanish literature and widespread travel. Also worth considering is Salvador de Madariaga's *Spain: A Modern History* (Jonathan Cape, 1972). First published in 1930, it was substantially rewritten after the Spanish Civil War and republished in 1942. Madariaga was a prolific author, a professor in Oxford and protagonist of the politics of the Second Republic, serving as Ambassador to Washington and Paris, representative to the League of Nations and, briefly, as Minister of Education and as Minister of Justice. Full of literary flourishes, his book also reflects his bitterness about the attacks from the left to which he was subjected. On Madariaga, those attacks and his peace-making initiatives during the war, see Paul Preston, *Salvador de Madariaga and the Quest for Liberty in Spain* (Oxford: Clarendon Press, 1987).

There are a few important monographs which illuminate various aspects of the long-term origins of the war. Almost every major political upheaval of an especially turbulent period had its religious back-cloth and a crucial, and usually reactionary, role for the Church hierarchy. Frances Lannon, *Privilege, Persecution, and Prophecy: The Catholic Church in Spain 1875–1975* (Oxford: Clarendon Press, 1987), contains many sharp and subtle insights about the reasons why the Catholic Church opposed the Second Republic and supported Franco. Also of immense value is the judicious study by William J. Callahan, *The Catholic Church in Spain 1875–1998* (Washington, DC: The Catholic University of America Press, 2000). Colin M. Winston, *Workers and the Right in Spain 1900–1936* (Princeton, NJ: Princeton University Press, 1985), is a useful examination of Catholic trade unionism in Catalonia and its links with more overtly Fascist groups.

The reasons for the Spanish army's eagerness to intervene in domestic politics are explained by Stanley G. Payne, *Politics and the Military in Modern Spain* (Stanford, Calif.: Stanford University Press, 1967). On the 'intellectual' basis of military attitudes, it is also worth consulting Geoffrey Jensen, *Irrational Triumph. Cultural Despair, Military Nationalism and the Intellectual Origins of Franco's Spain* (Reno and Las Vegas, Nev.: University of Nevada Press, 2002). The wellsprings of the savagery with which the Spanish Moroccan army behaved during the Civil War are explored in David S. Woolman, *Rebels in the Rif: Abd el Krim and the Rif Rebellion* (Stanford, Calif.: Stanford University Press, 1969). Even more focused on the long-term consequences of the imperial adventure is Sebastian Balfour, *Deadly Embrace: Morocco and the Road to the Spanish Civil War* (Oxford: Oxford University Press, 2002), a subtle and thoughtful account which abounds in insights into the way the colonial mentality was imported into peninsular Spain. The long-term political, social and economic reverberations of the Spanish loss of empire are the subject of another stylish and sophisticated volume by Sebastian Balfour, *The End of the Spanish Empire 1898–1923* (Oxford: Clarendon Press, 1997). He shows how the consequent trauma led to the right seeing dictatorship as the answer to all its ills. Francisco J. Romero Salvadó, *Spain 1914–1918: Between War and Revolution* (Routledge/Cañada Blanch Studies, 1999), is a superb account of the period when Spain missed an opportunity to avoid civil war.

The long-term background to the divisions of the left can be traced in several books. Murray Bookchin, *The Spanish Anarchists: The Heroic Years, 1868–1936* (New York: Free Life Editions, 1977), is a warm-hearted tribute to the idealism of Spanish anarchism but is marred by its partisan style and some factual errors. Not partisan but so riddled by wild inaccuracy as to require warnings as to its use is Robert W. Kern's *Red Years, Black Years: A Political History of Spanish anarchism 1911–1937* (Philadelphia, Pa.: Institute for the Study of Human Issues, 1978). Altogether superior is the sophisticated recent analysis by Chris Ealham, *Class, Culture and Conflict in Barcelona 1898–1937* (Routledge/Cañada Blanch Studies, 2004). Dr Ealham illuminates the real origins of anarchist radicalism in terms of the daily problems of unemployment, high rents and the increase in food prices. That this is a book about real people living in extreme situations is evident throughout, whether in the vivid account of the popular jubilation that greeted the Republic in Barcelona or in the sombre picture of popular resistance to attempts by the Esquerra forcibly to repatriate southern immigrants back to Murcia and Andalusia.

A splendid collection of articles on different aspects of working-class radicalism in Barcelona has been edited by Angel Smith, *Red Barcelona: Social Protest and Labour Mobilization in the Twentieth Century* (Routledge/Cañada Blanch Studies, 2002). An excellent attempt to deal with the entire spectrum of the working-class left is the wide-ranging and judicious study of working-class movements in Spain from early industrialization to 1939 by Benjamin Martin, *The Agony of Modernization: Labor and Industrialization in Spain* (Ithaca, NY: Cornell University Press, 1990). Even better is the elegant account of the internal conflicts within the Socialist movement by Paul Heywood, *Marxism and the Failure of Organised Socialism in Spain 1879–1936* (Cambridge: Cambridge University Press, 1990).

There are a number of essential accounts of the breakdown of the Second Republic. Stanley G. Payne, *Spain's First Democracy: The Second Republic, 1931–1936* (Madison, Wis.: Wisconsin University Press, 1993), is a sober and conservative overview. Other authors have related the Republic's political polarization to the underlying social tensions. Paul Preston, *The Coming of the Spanish Civil War* (2nd fully revised edition, *Routledge, 1994), analyses the way in which the struggles between landless labourers and landowners, and between miners and mine-owners, were transmitted into national politics and fed into a battle for control of the state apparatus between the PSOE and the CEDA. Edward Malefakis, *Agrarian Reform and Peasant Revolution in Spain* (New Haven, Conn.: Yale University Press, 1970), explains the intensity of the social conflict generated by the agrarian problem and the failure of agrarian reform. Adrian Shubert, *The Road* *to Revolution in Spain: The Coal Miners of Asturias 1860–1934* (Urbana and Chicago, Ill.: Illinois University Press 1987), is a sensitive recreation of the lives and politics of the miners. Richard A. H. Robinson, *The Origins of Franco's Spain: The Right, The Republic and Revolution, 1931–1936* (Newton Abbot: David & Charles, 1970), is an interpretation of the political polarization of the Republic which is heavily critical of the Socialists and an apologia for the CEDA. Of crucial importance to our understanding of the CEDA's electoral success is Mary Vincent, *Catholicism in the Second Spanish Republic. Religion and Politics in Salamanca 1930–1936* (Oxford: Clarendon Press, 1996). Sharply and elegantly written, Dr Vincent's book provides an empathetic depiction of how the uncompromising secularism of the Second Republic played into the hands of its right-wing enemies. A thoughtful account of the crucial role of Alejandro Lerroux and the Radical Party is to be found in Nigel Townson, *The Crisis of Democracy in Spain. Centrist Politics under the Second Republic 1931–1936* (Brighton: Sussex Academic Press, 2000).

The role of the extreme right during the Republic and the war can be studied in Martin Blinkhorn, *Carlism and Crisis in Spain 1931–1939* (Cambridge: Cambridge University Press, 1975), a sophisticated and superbly written account of the movement from which all other rightists drew much of their ideology. On the Carlists' allies and rivals, the followers of Alfonso XIII, see the article by Paul Preston, 'Alfonsist Monarchism and the Coming of the Spanish Civil War', *Journal of Contemporary History*, VII, nos 3–4 (1972). On the Falange, the standard work, now beginning to show its age but still well worth reading, is Stanley G. Payne, *Falange: A History of Spanish Fascism* (Stanford, Calif.: Stanford University Press, 1961). A much fuller and substantially updated account can be found in Stanley G. Payne, *Fascism in Spain 1923–1977* (Madison, Wis.: University of Wisconsin Press, 1999). See also the chapters on José Antonio and Pilar Primo de Rivera in Paul Preston, *¡Comrades! Portraits from the Spanish Civil War* (HarperCollins, 1999). The female section of the Falange is dealt with in Kathleen Richmond, *Women and Spanish Fascism. The Women's Section of the Falange 1934–1959* (Routledge/Cañada Blanch Studies, 2003).

A highly critical overview of the left can be found in Stanley G. Payne, *The Spanish Revolution* (Weidenfeld & Nicolson, 1970). The gap in English on the anarchists during the Second Republic and the

Civil War has now been filled by the translation of a major Spanish work, Julián Casanova, *Anarchism, the Republic and Civil War in Spain 1931–1939* (Routledge/Cañada Blanch Studies, 2004). Based on massive research and written with an acerbic intelligence, it is a highly readable critique of anarchist disorganization. There is also an important article on the social background to anarchist hostility to the Republican state by Chris Ealham, ' "From the Summit to the Abyss": The Contradictions of Individualism and Collectivism in Spanish Anarchism', in Paul Preston and Ann Mackenzie, eds, *The Republic Besieged: Civil War in Spain 1936–1939* (Edinburgh: Edinburgh University Press, 1996). There is significantly more on the Socialists. See Preston, *The Coming of the Spanish Civil War*, Heywood, *Failure of Organized Socialism* (see above) and Helen Graham, 'The Eclipse of the Socialist Left: 1934–1937', in Frances Lannon and Paul Preston, eds, *Élites and Power in Twentieth-Century Spain: Essays in Honour of Sir Raymond Carr* (Oxford: Clarendon Press, 1990).

The development of the Popular Front has given rise to a substantial literature. See Michael Seidman, *Workers against Work: Labor in Paris and Barcelona during the Popular Fronts* (Berkeley, Calif.: University of California Press, 1991), and the essays collected in both Martin Alexander and Helen Graham, eds, *The French and Spanish Popular Fronts: Comparative Perspectives* (Cambridge: Cambridge University Press, 1989) and Helen Graham and Paul Preston, eds, *The Popular Front in Europe* (Macmillan, 1987). Sixty years old but well worth seeking out is a fascinating long-term interpretation of the origins of the Civil War from the point of view of a Socialist eyewitness – Antonio Ramos Oliveira, *Politics, Economics and Men of Modern Spain: 1808–1946* (Gollancz, 1946).

There are several books which combine a full-scale account of the politics of the Second Republic with a survey of the Spanish Civil War. Gabriel Jackson, *The Spanish Republic and the Civil War* (*Princeton, NJ: Princeton University Press, 1965), has attained the status of a minor historical classic. It is an elegant and humane account from a liberal standpoint, but unfortunately has never been updated to take account of the massive advances in research over the last forty years. In consequence, it is indeed now rather dated. There are more recent accounts such as the work co-authored by George Esenwein and Adrian Shubert, *Spain at War: The Spanish Civil War in Context 1931–1939* (*Harlow: Longman, 1995). However, that has been superseded by the splendid account by Francisco J. Romero Salvadó, *The Spanish Civil War: Origins, Course and Outcomes* (*Palgrave Macmillan, 2005), which carefully places the war and its causes within both a long-term interpretation of Spanish history and a wider European context. Sandie Holguín, *Creating Spaniards: Culture and National Identity in Republican Spain* (Madison, Wis.: University of Wisconsin Press, 2002) charts the efforts of successive governments to create a sense of national Republican identity among the masses by means of cultural projects that included theatre groups and the *misiones pedagógicas*, literacy squads, both of which toured rural Spain.

General surveys of the war itself also abound. Hugh Thomas's *The Spanish Civil War* 4th edition (*Penguin, 2003) is a long (1115 pages), encyclopaedic and highly readable narrative account. It remains the standard work and is especially good on the military and diplomatic aspects of the war. Raymond Carr's short interpretative account, *The Spanish Tragedy* (Weidenfeld & Nicolson, 1977; reprinted as *The Civil War in Spain*, *1986), is perceptive and vibrant with insights at every turn. Ronald Fraser's *Blood of Spain* (*Allen Lane, 1979), is a work of oral history which weaves together a mass of eyewitness testimonies into something like a great novel. Antony Beevor's *The Spanish Civil War* (Orbis Publishing, 1982) is well written, especially good on the military side and politically sympathetic to the anti-Communist left. The same may be said for his much fuller account, *The Battle for Spain: The Spanish Civil War (1936–1939)* (Weidenfeld & Nicolson, 2006), whose sweeping narrative now challenges Thomas. An unusual anecdotal recreation of the war is provided by Peter Wyden's The Passionate War (New York: Simon & Schuster, 1983) which is at its best on the personal involvement of the Americans who went to Spain. An excellent short introduction is provided by Sheelagh Ellwood, *The Spanish Civil War* (*Oxford: Blackwell, 1991). Best of all is the remarkable little book by Helen Graham, *The Spanish Civil War. A Very Short Introduction* (Oxford: Oxford University Press, 2005). Every sentence of this concise account is packed with thought and meaning. It is provocative and illuminating in equal measure. In an effort to interpret the ethical conflicts of leaders dealing with extreme situations, Paul Preston, *¡Comrades! Portraits from the Spanish Civil War* (HarperCollins, 1999), provides biographies of nine individuals from across the political spectrum, from the deranged General José Millán Astray to the Communist orator Dolores Ibárruri.

A flawed recent attempt at a social history of the war can be found in Michael Seidman, *Republic of Egos: A Social History of the Spanish Civil War* (Madison, Wis.: University of Wisconsin Press, 2002). Seidman has virtually nothing to say about the Nationalist zone and what he has to say about the Republican zone is deeply marred by a static thematic approach that fails to take into account changes imposed by wartime conditions. Thus, the reader is given no notion of the extent to which deteriorating living conditions altered popular perceptions of the Republic. As the work of Helen Graham has shown, wartime hardship, constant defeats, battlefield slaughter, dread of the Francoist repression, a huge refugee crisis and mass hunger had eroded the hope and optimism of the Republican masses. Seidman blithely presents the embittered attitudes of 1938 as if they were illustrative of the popular mood in 1936. For a splendid graphic recreation of the period, there is the lavishly illustrated *Images of the Spanish Civil War*, with an introduction by Raymond Carr (George Allen & Unwin, 1986). The latest international scholarship on a variety of aspects of the war is reflected in the collective volumes edited by Paul Preston, *Revolution and War in Spain 1931–1939* (*Routledge, 1984); by Martin Blinkhorn, *Spain in Conflict 1931–1939: Democracy and its Enemies* (Sage, 1986) and by Paul Preston and Ann Mackenzie, *The Republic Besieged: Civil War in Spain 1936–1939* (Edinburgh: Edinburgh University Press, 1996).

On the politics of the Second Republic and on political and social life in the Republican zone during the war, the definitive account now is surely Helen Graham, *The Spanish Republic at War 1936–1939* (Cambridge: Cambridge University Press, 2002). On the pre-war period, the author's careful and subtle dissection of political disputes is linked to a sensitive awareness of the social history of the period in a text glittering with brilliant *aperçus* about the impact on high politics of mass unemployment in both rural and urban areas. On the war itself, her detailed account of the bewildering shifts and turns of relationships between the various Socialist factions, the Communists, the anarchists and the middle-class Republican liberals is placed in two linked contexts. First, and most valuably, she relates daily politics to the various Republican governments' attempts to deal with the problems of both social revolution and disorder arising from the destruction of the state apparatus by the military rising of 17–18 July 1936. No previous scholar has engaged so fruitfully with the issue of how the Republic could mount a war effort from scratch, which meant attempting to militarize the many disparate militia groups and also to centralize the economy while facing war on several fronts. She explains, with an illuminating clarity attained by no predecessor, the articulation of the process of creating a war economy spread across the competing jurisdictions of the Catalan, Basque and central Spanish Republican governments. This is then linked with a sharply thoughtful account of the impact on Republican leaders of having to make decisions in a deeply hostile international context.

There are several eyewitness recollections which are well worth searching for. Those by the American Ambassador, Claude Bowers, *My Mission to Spain* (Gollancz, 1954), are deeply sympathetic to the Republic. Bowers writes passionately from a position of deep inside knowledge of high-level politics and diplomacy. Those by the British journalist Henry Buckley, *Life and Death of the Spanish Republic* (Hamish Hamilton, 1940), provide personal recollections of meetings with the great politicians of the day and eyewitness accounts of dramatic events. His book recounts the complex experience of the Republic and the Civil War in a vivid prose laced with humour, pity for human suffering and outrage at those whom he considered to be responsible for the tragedy of Spain. The autobiography of Louis Fischer, *Men and Politics: An Autobiography* (Jonathan Cape, 1941), written from a pro-Communist position, teems with insights about the principal political leaders of the Republic. Its portrait of Francisco Largo Caballero is particularly damning.

Inevitably, as Fischer's work shows, the Spanish war aroused intense passion on the left and many books reflect a preference for a particular faction. There is a broadly Trotskyist account by two French historians, Pierre Broué and Emile Témime, *The Revolution and the Civil War in Spain* (Faber & Faber, 1972). Their work is not narrowly partisan, something which cannot be said for Arthur H. Landis, *Spain! The Unfinished Revolution* (Baldwin Park: Camelot, 1972), which is an unashamedly pro-Communist interpretation. A somewhat more sophisticated pro-Communist account is Frank Jellinek's *The Civil War in Spain* (Left Book Club, 1938). The outstanding, and best-informed, pro-Communist and pro-Socialist accounts of the war, the colourful diaries of Mikhail Koltsov, *Diario de la guerra de España* (Paris: Ruedo Ibérico, 1963), and the important memoirs of Julián Zugazagoitia, *Guerra y vicisitudes de los españoles*, 2nd edition,

2 vols (Paris: Librería Española, 1968), have unfortunately not been translated into English. However, there are vivid, if somewhat blinkered works by the Republican Foreign Minister, Julio Alvarez del Vayo, *Freedom's Battle* (Heinemann, 1940), and by a remarkable woman, an aristocrat turned Communist, the early Spanish feminist Constancia de la Mora, *In Place of Splendour* (Michael Joseph, 1940). The indispensable memoirs of the Socialist Arturo Barea, *The Forging of a Rebel* (*Granta, 2001), take the form of a slightly fictionalized and deeply moving trilogy.

The central issue within the Republican zone, and indeed among the exiles after the war, was the debate over the degree of priority to be given to the making of the war effort or the construction of the revolution. In consequence, the 'war or revolution' issue provoked acrimonious debate and a considerable literature. On the demolition of the revolution, the indispensable work is Burnett Bolloten's monumental and devastating assault on the Communists, *The Grand Camouflage* (New York: Praeger, 1968), revised as *The Spanish Revolution* (Chapel Hill, NC: University of North Carolina Press, 1979), and definitively as *The Spanish Civil War: Revolution and Counterrevolution* (Hemel Hempstead: Harvester Wheatsheaf, 1991). Its great flaw is the fact that it denounces Communist methods without seriously examining why they were thought necessary not only by the Communists themselves, but also by the moderate Socialists and the Republicans. In other words, Bolloten decontextualized the internal struggles within the Republican zone from the practical consequences – domestic and international – of the fact that the Republic had to fight a war against Franco and his German and Italian allies. He pays scant attention to the need for centralization in the interests of the war effort. In this regard, the most sustained counter-arguments to those of Burnett Bolloten are found in Helen Graham's *The Republic at War* (see above). For a sweeping critique of Bolloten's methods, see Herbert R. Southworth's 'The Grand Camouflage: Julián Gorkin, Burnett Bolloten and the Spanish Civil War', in Preston and Mackenzie, *The Republic Besieged*.

Along similar interpretative lines to Bolloten are the now very outdated David T. Cattell, *Communism and the Spanish Civil War* (Berkeley, Calif.: California University Press, 1955), and the much more recent Stanley G. Payne, *The Spanish Civil War, the Soviet Union, and Communism* (New Haven, Conn.: Yale University Press, 2004), an interesting anti-Soviet account which draws heavily on the latest scholarship. The documents edited by Ronald Radosh, Mary R. Habeck and Grigory Sevostianov, *Spain Betrayed: The Soviet Union in the Spanish Civil War* (New Haven, Conn.: Yale University Press, 2001), present a picture of the Soviet frustrations in the face of their inability to impose discipline and uniformity on Republican politics. What the documents demonstrate is, however, in outright contradiction to the editors' commentary which interprets them as proving that there was an iron control by the Russians. A much more nuanced account has been produced in Spanish by Daniel Kowalsky, *La Unión Soviética y la guerra civil española. Una revisión crítica* (Barcelona: Editorial Crítica, 2003). Dr Kowalsky's English text, under the title *Stalin and the Spanish Civil War*, is not available as a printed book but rather in a digital form sponsored by both the American Historical Association and Columbia University Press. The Gutenberg-e website is at *http://www.gutenberg-e.org.* on the internet.

Defence of Communist policies is undertaken crudely by Dolores Ibárruri, *They Shall Not Pass* (*Lawrence & Wishart, 1967), and by José Sandoval and Manuel Azcárate, *Spain 1936–1939* (*Lawrence & Wishart, 1963), and with great intelligence and sophistication by Fernando Claudín, *The Communist Movement* (*Peregrine, 1970). An outstanding contribution to the debate with an eloquently argued case for 'the primacy of war' is to be found in the definitive work on the socialists and the war – Helen Graham, *Socialism and War: The Spanish Socialist Party in Power and Crisis, 1936–1939* (Cambridge: Cambridge University Press, 1991). See also her startlingly original article, 'War, Modernity and Reform: The Premiership of Juan Negrín 1937–39', in Preston and Mackenzie, *The Republic Besieged*. On the practical difficulties of building an army, see José Martín Blázquez, *I Helped to Build an Army: Civil War Memoirs of a Spanish Staff Officer* (Secker & Warburg, 1939)

Ironically, the essentially right-wing Cold War account by Bolloten has been taken by some left-wingers as pro-revolutionary although that was clearly not the intention of the author. The most outspoken example of this is Noam Chomsky's polemical article in his *American Power and the New Mandarins* (Chatto & Windus, 1969), a reading of the Spanish Civil War in the light of the liberation struggles of the 1960s. A fascinating and indispensable statement of the case for 'the primacy of revolution' is to be found in a special issue of the journal *Revolutionary History* (vol. 4, nos 1/2) entitled *The Spanish Civil War: The View From the Left* (Socialist Platform, 1992) which contains both modern essays and contemporary accounts by Marxist revolutionaries. The exhilaration of the early days of working-class power and the subsequent despair after the revolution had been crushed can be sensed in two important eyewitness acounts – Franz Borkenau, *The Spanish Cockpit*, 3rd edition (*Phoenix Press, 2000), with an introduction by Hugh Thomas, and George Orwell, *Homage to Catalona* (*Gollancz, 1938). Orwell's is a sane, moving but ultimately narrow vision of the May 1937 events in Barcelona written with a pro-POUM stance, which has been taken, widely and erroneously, as an overview of the war, which it is not.

Other pro-Trotskyist perspectives may be found in the polemical essay by Felix Morrow, *Revolution and Counter-Revolution in Spain* (*New Park, 1963) and Leon Trotsky, *The Spanish Revolution (1931– 1939)* (New York: Pathfinder, 1973). The most compelling anarchist account is by Vernon Richards, *Lessons of the Spanish Revolution* (*Free-dom Press, 1972). Other important contemporary anarchist versions are to be found in Gaston Leval, *Collectives in the Spanish Revolution* (*Freedom Press, 1975); Agustín Souchy, *With the Peasants of Aragón* (*Cienfuegos/Refrac, 1982); José Peirats, *Anarchists in the Spanish Revolution* (*Toronto: Solidarity, 1979); Abel Paz, *Durruti The People Armed* (*Montreal: Black Rose, 1976) and Emma Goldman, *Vision on Fire* (*New Paltz, NY: Commonground, 1983). Most recently, there has appeared a compendious but rather sprawling account by Robert J. Alexander, *The Anarchists in the Spanish Civil War*, 2 vols (Janus Publishing, 1999).

There exists no good right-wing overview of the war in English, although readers wishing to consult one might seek out Luis Bolín's hybrid memoir-cum-survey, *Spain: The Vital Years* (Philadelphia, Pa.: Lippincott, 1967). Bolín gives his version of his own part in securing the aircraft which was to take Franco from the Canary Islands to Morocco. The politics of the Nationalist zone tend to receive coverage in biographies of Franco. The most extensive is by Paul Preston, *Franco: A Biography* (*HarperCollins, 1993). Subsequently, there has been the concise and sensible essay by Sheelagh Ellwood, *Franco* (Harlow: Longman, 1994), which comes into competition with the lively account by Juan Pablo Fusi, *Franco* (Unwin Hyman, 1987). Most recently and more substantially there is the witty psychological portrait by Gabrielle Ashford Hodges, *Franco: A Concise Biography* (Weidenfeld & Nicolson, 2000). These four critical works have some-what superseded the earlier books by J. W. D. Trythall, *Franco* (Rupert Hart-Davis, 1970) and George Hills, *Franco: The Man and his Nation* (Robert Hale, 1967). The Caudillo's admirers will enjoy Hills' book which is sympathetic without equalling the unqualified enthusiasm of Brian Crozier, *Franco: A Biographical History* (Eyre & Spottiswood, 1967). The jockeying for power of the various elements of the Nation-alist coalition are covered in detail in Blinkhorn's *Carlism*, Preston's *Franco*, Payne's *Falange* and Sheelagh Ellwood, *Spanish Fascism in the Franco Era: Falange Española de las JONS 1936–1976* (Macmillan, 1987).

The Catholic Church in the Spanish Civil War receives a finely balanced interpretation in the admirable Lannon, *Privilege, Per-secution, and Prophecy* (see above). Also of some interest is José M. Sánchez, *The Spanish Civil War as Religious Tragedy* (Notre Dame, Ind.: Notre Dame University Press, 1987), a valuable compendium of information about the national and international religious dimensions of the war. Sánchez tells a grim story of priests murdered and churches burned during the 'anti-clerical fury committed by leftists at the beginning of the war. He writes too of those Catholics murdered by the Nationalists in the name of the Prince of Peace, fourteen of them Basque priests, and also of the deafening silence which greeted such crimes in some Catholic circles. The definitive account, however, is by the Spanish Benedictine Dom Hilari Raguer, *The Catholic Church and the Spanish Civil War* (Routledge/Cañada Blanch Studies, 2006), whose meticulously researched text is an object lesson in how an ethical approach to historical issues is compatible with open-minded honesty.

For an overview of the repression in the Nationalist zone, there is Michael Richards, *A Time of Silence: Civil War and the Culture of Repression in Franco's Spain, 1936–1945* (Cambridge: Cambridge Uni-versity Press, 1998). This eloquent and moving study demonstrates how 'the violence amounted to a brutal closing down of choices and alternatives: the extermination of memory, of history'. There are also two short accounts by Paul Preston, *The Crimes of Franco* (*The 2005 Imperial War Museum/Len Crome Memorial Lecture, International Brigades Memorial Trust, 2005), and 'The Answer Lies in the Sewers: Captain Aguilera and the Mentality of the Francoist Officer Corps',

Science & Society, vol. 68, no. 3, Fall 2004. There are also several powerful accounts which give some idea of the horrors of the repression in particular areas. Ian Gibson, *The Assassination of Lorca* (W. H. Allen, 1979), is an elegantly written detective story which can still provoke a shudder of horror. Two eyewitness accounts of life in Burgos and Seville during the war are Antonio Bahamonde, *Memoirs of a Spanish Nationalist* (United Editorial, 1939), and Antonio Ruiz Vilaplana, *Burgos Justice* (Constable, 1938). They are from the pens of men who fled to the Republican zone because they were shocked by what they saw.

Spine-chilling accounts of the appalling repression of women can be found in Pilar Fidalgo, *A Young Mother in Franco's Prisons* (United Editorial, 1938), and Ramón Sender Barayón, *A Death in Zamora*, 2nd edition (*Albuquerque, N. Mex.: University of New Mexico Press, 2003), his unutterably moving account of the murder of his mother, Amparo Barayón, the wife of the left-wing novelist Ramón Sender. A target for the military rebels because of being married to Sender, Amparo Barayón fled to her native city of Zamora hoping to find safety there. In fact, she was imprisoned, tortured and eventually executed – her horrendous fate typical of what happened to many innocent women at the hands of the supporters of General Franco. Amparo Barayón's story also figures in Helen Graham, *The Spanish Civil War: The Return of Republican Memory* (*The 2003 Imperial War Museum/Len Crome Memorial Lecture, International Brigades Memorial Trust, 2003).

Some sense of the atmosphere as the Nationalists captured territory may be derived from Sir Peter Chalmers Mitchell, *My House in Málaga* (Faber & Faber, 1938). Chalmers Mitchell recounts the capture of Arthur Koestler by the deeply unpleasant Luis Bolín. The same incident is related in Koestler's own *Spanish Testament* (Left Book Club, 1937). The aftermath of the fall of Málaga is recreated in an intensely moving account by an English writer who served as an ambulance driver, T. C. Worsley, *Behind the Battle* (Robert Hale, 1939). An enormous amount may be learned about the Nationalist zone from the inexorably forensic study by Herbert R. Southworth, *Conspiracy and the Spanish Civil War: The Brainwashing of Francisco Franco* (Routledge-Cañada Blanch Studies, 2002). Even more important is Herbert R. Southworth, *Guernica! Guernica! A Study of Journalism, Diplomacy, Propaganda and History* (Berkeley, Calif.: California

University Press, 1977), an astonishing reconstruction of the propaganda effort to wipe out the atrocity at Guernica. See also Peter Monteath, 'Guernica Reconsidered: Fifty Years of Evidence', *War & Society*, vol. 5, no.1, May 1987. The compelling account by G. L. Steer, *The Tree of Gernika: A Field Study of Modern War* (Hodder & Stoughton, 1938), is one of the handful of totally indispensable books on the war. A journalist who visited Guernica in the aftermath of the bombing was Virginia Cowles who sheds much light on the Nationalist zone in her book *Looking for Trouble* (Hamish Hamilton, 1941).

On the military history of the war, there is nothing in English to match the operational histories of the war produced by Spanish army officers – in seventeen volumes on the Francoist war effort by Colonel José Manuel Martínez Bande, and in four on the Republican zone by General Ramón Salas Larrazábal. Good military accounts may be found in the books by Hugh Thomas and Anthony Beevor (see above). On Franco's strategy, see Paul Preston, 'General Franco as Military Leader', in *Transactions of the Royal Historical Society*, 6th Series, vol. 4, 1994. There is some coverage of individual campaigns in the memoirs of International Brigaders, especially of the battle for Madrid and the Ebro. The siege of Republican Madrid is best described by Robert G. Colodny, *The Struggle for Madrid* (New York: Paine-Whitman, 1958). Dan Kurzman, *Miracle of November* (New York: Putnam's, 1980) is colourful but inaccurate. A pro-Francoist account, George Hills, *The Battle for Madrid* (Vantage, 1976) is good on the military side. Geoffrey Cox, *Defence of Madrid* (Left Book Club, 1937) is a contemporary eyewitness report.

Apart from the siege of Madrid, the greatest attention has been paid to Franco's diversion to Toledo in September 1936 and the subsequent liberation of the Alcázar. This is recounted from a pro-Franco point of view in both H. R. Knickerbocker, *The Siege of the Alcázar: A War-Log of the Spanish Revolution* (Hutchinson, n.d. [1936]), and Major Geoffrey McNeill-Moss, *The Epic of the Alcázar* (Rich & Cowan, 1937). Rather more objective is Cecil Eby, *The Siege of the Alcázar* (Bodley Head, 1966). Extremely partisan accounts of the advance of the Army of Africa from Seville to Madrid may be found in Harold G. Cardozo, *The March of a Nation: My Year of Spain's Civil War* (Right Book Club, 1937); H. Edward Knoblaugh, *Correspondent in Spain* (Sheed & Ward, 1937); Cecil Gerahty, *The Road To Madrid* (Hutchinson, 1937), and William Foss and Cecil Gerahty, *The Spanish*

Arena (Right Book Club, 1937). These enthusiastic versions should be read in the light of the chilling eyewitness account by John Whitaker, 'Prelude to World War: A Witness from Spain', *Foreign Affairs*, vol. 21, no. 1, October 1942, also available in his book *We Cannot Escape History* (New York: Macmillan, 1943). There is a superb account of the difficulties facing the press corps in the anonymous pamphlet by 'A. Journalist', *Foreign Journalists under Franco's Terror* (United Editorial, 1937).

On the war in the air, the basic work is Gerald Howson, *Aircraft of the Spanish Civil War 1936–1939* (New York: Putnam, 1990). Based on prodigious research, it is full of crucial information about both sides. It has now been complemented by his book on the political and financial difficulties faced by the Republic in the procurement of arms, Gerald Howson, *Arms for Spain: The Untold Story of the Spanish Civil War* (John Murray, 1998). Ultimately, the Spanish Republic's military effort was undermined by the policy of Non-intervention which prevented it exercising its rights under international law. Howson's account superbly analyses the consequences in terms of the Republic being forced into the hands of unscrupulous arms dealers and into accepting the anything but disinterested military aid of the Soviet Union. There exist in Spanish several important memoirs by pilots from both sides. Unfortunately, in English there are only the memoirs of the Nationalist flyer Captain José Larios, *Combat over Spain* (New York: Macmillan, 1966), and those of a right-wing English pilot who went to Spain to write about the Nationalist air force, Nigel Tangye, *Red, White and Spain* (Rich & Cowan, 1937). On naval issues, it is a pity that Michael Alpert's *La guerra civil en el mar* (Madrid: Siglo XXI, 1987) is not available in English. There exist two works on British naval participation in breaking the Francoist naval blockade of the Republic – P. M. Heaton, *Welsh Blockade Runners in the Spanish Civil War* (Newport: Starling Press, 1985), and James Cable, *The Royal Navy and the Siege of Bilbao* (Cambridge: Cambridge University Press, 1979).

The International Brigades have an enormous literature of their own. The fullest general history, by Andreu Castells, has not been translated into English. A useful Soviet-produced volume is *International Solidarity with the Spanish Republic* (*Moscow: Progress Publishers, 1975), which may be contrasted with the hostile account by R. Dan Richardson, *Comintern Army: The International Brigades and* *the Spanish Civil War* (Lexington, Ky.: University Press of Kentucky, 1982). Vincent Brome, *The International Brigades* (Heinemann, 1965), is fanciful and inaccurate. There is a good scholarly survey by James K. Hopkins, *Into the Heart of the Fire: The British in the Spanish Civil War* (Stanford, Calif.: Stanford University Press, 1998). An interesting account, Robert A. Stradling, *History and Legend: Writing the International Brigades* (Cardiff: University of Wales Press, 2003), is highly critical in approach and sarcastically cynical in tone. Best of all is the comprehensively researched survey by Richard Baxell, *British Volunteers in the Spanish Civil War: The British Battalion in the International Brigades, 1936–1939* (Routledge/Cañada Blanch Studies, 2004). Baxell's work is superbly complemented by the elegant and moving study by Angela Jackson, *British Women and the Spanish Civil War* (Routledge/Cañada Blanch Studies, 2002).

The standard eyewitness accounts of the British contingent by Communist Party veterans are those by the last commander of the battalion, Bill Alexander, *British Volunteers for Liberty* (Lawrence & Wishart, 1982), and the earlier one by William Rust, *Britons in Spain* (Lawrence & Wishart, 1939, reprinted *Abersychan, Pontypool: Warren & Pell, 2004). Vivid interviews with British volunteers are collected in David Corkhill and Stuart Rawnsley, eds, *The Road To Spain* (*Dunfermline: Borderline, 1981). Tom Wintringham, *English Captain* (*Penguin, 1941); Esmond Romilly, *Boadilla* (Hamish Hamilton, 1937); Jason Gurney, *Crusade in Spain* (Faber & Faber, 1974) and Walter Gregory, *The Shallow Grave* (Gollancz, 1986) are important British accounts of the fighting on the Madrid front and elsewhere. One of the most important memoirs is that by a Labour Party volunteer, Fred Thomas, *To Tilt at Windmills: A Memoir of the Spanish Civil War* (East Lansing, Mich.: Michigan State University Press, 1996). With painful honesty and engagingly wry humour, Fred Thomas recreates both the grandeur and the misery that was the experience of the volunteers.

The American volunteers are well served by Arthur H. Landis, *The Abraham Lincoln Brigade* (New York: Citadel, 1967), the same author's *Death in the Olive Groves: American Volunteers in the Spanish Civil War* (New York: Paragón House, 1989), Alvah Bessie, *Men in Battle* (New York: Scribner, 1939); Steve Nelson, *The Volunteers* (New York: Masses & Mainstream, 1953); Sandor Voros, *American Commissar* (Philadelphia, Pa.: Chilton Company, 1961); Cecil Eby, *Between the Bullet and the Lie* (New York: Holt, Rinehart & Winston, 1969); John Tisa, *Recalling the Good Fight* (*Massachusetts, Mass.: Bergin & Garvey, 1985), Carl Geiser, *Prisoners of the Good Fight: The Spanish Civil War 1936–1939* (Westport, Conn.: Lawrence Hill & Co., 1986); Marion Merriman and Warren Lerude, *American Commander in Spain: Robert Hale Merriman and the Abraham Lincoln Brigade* (Reno, Nev.: University of Nevada Press, 1986); Milt Felsen, *The Anti Warrior. A Memoir* (Iowa City, Ia.: University of Iowa Press, 1989); Milton Wolff, *Another Hill: An Autobiographical Novel* (Urbana and Chicago, Ill.: University of Illinois Press, 1994) and most recently by Harry Fisher, *Comrades: Tales of a Brigadista in the Spanish Civil War* (Lincoln, Neb.: University of Nebraska Press, 1998). The best overview, impressively researched and beautifully written, is Peter N. Carroll, *The Odyssey of the Abraham Lincoln Brigade: Americans in the Spanish Civil War* (Stanford, Calif.: Stanford University Press, 1994). Two fascinating accounts of the experience of black American volunteers are provided by James Yates, *Mississippi to Madrid: Memoir of a Black American in the Abraham Lincoln Brigade* (Seattle, Wash.: Open Hand Publishing, 1989), and Danny Duncan Collum, ed., *African Americans in the Spanish Civil War. "This Ain't Ethiopia But It'll Do"* (New York: G. K. Hall, 1992).

The Irish experience in the International Brigades is reconstructed by Michael O'Riordan, *Connolly Column* (Dublin: New Books, 1979), and Sean Cronin, *Frank Ryan* (*Dublin: Repsol, 1979). Ireland was one of the few countries to send genuine volunteers in any numbers to fight with Franco. The apologia of the leader of the Blue Shirts, General Eoin O'Duffy, can be found in his memoirs, *Crusade in Spain* (Dublin: Brown & Nolan, 1938). A more objective view of both sides can be found in R. A. Stradling, *The Irish and the Spanish Civil War* (Manchester: Mandolin, 1999), and in Fearghal McGarry, *Irish Politics and the Spanish Civil War* (Cork: Cork University Press, 1999). Welsh involvement at home and in Spain is recounted by R. A. Stradling, *Wales and the Spanish Civil War* (Cardiff: University of Wales Press, 2004); Hywel Francis, *Miners Against Fascism: Wales and the Spanish Civil War* (*Lawrence & Wishart, 1982), George Eaton, *Neath and the Spanish Civil War* (Neath, author, 1980) and R. A. Stradling, *Cardiff and the Spanish Civil War* (Cardiff: Butetown History & Arts Project, 1996); and the Scots by Ian MacDougall, ed., *Voices from the Spanish Civil War* (*Edinburgh: Polygon, 1986). The memoirs of the

German Communist dissident Gustav Regler, *The Owl of Minerva* (Rupert Hart-Davis, 1959) are informative and, at times, moving. A unique insight into the fate of German volunteers is provided by Josie McLellan, *Antifascism and Memory in East Germany. Remembering the International Brigades 1945–1989* (Oxford: Clarendon Press, 2004).

A wide-ranging account of the solidarity of the 'Aid Spain Movement' and of the medical services of the International Brigades can be found in Jim Fyrth, *The Signal Was Spain* (*Lawrence & Wishart, 1986). A fascinating complement to Fyrth's book can be found in Angela Jackson, *Beyond the Battlefield: Testimony, Memory and Remembrance of a Cave Hospital in the Spanish Civil War* (*Abersychan, Pontypool: Warren & Pell, 2005). Also of the first importance is the moving anthology edited by Jim Fyrth and Sally Alexander, *Women's Voices from the Spanish Civil War* (Lawrence & Wishart, 1991), which should be read in conjunction with Shirley Mangini, *Memories of Resistance: Women's Voices from the Spanish Civil War* (New Haven, Conn.: Yale University Press, 1995). An account of the lives of four very different women whose lives were profoundly scarred by the Civil War can be found in Paul Preston, *Doves of War: Four Women of Spain* (HarperCollins, 2002). One of them was Nan Green, a woman whose husband fought and died in the International Brigades and who herself served in the Brigade medical services. Her memoirs have been published as Nan Green, *A Chronicle of Small Beer* (Nottingham: Trent Editions, 2004). The Spanish Republic made huge and positive difference to women's lives. A rich and fascinating account of what the Republic gave women, only for Franco to take away even more, can be found in Mary Nash, *Defying Male Civilization: Women in the Spanish Civil War* (Denver, Colo.: Arden Press, 1995).

Apart from the 'volunteers' sent to fight for Franco by Hitler, Mussolini and Salazar, there were many individual Russians, Romanians, Frenchmen and others who served in the Nationalist ranks. A major contribution to the history of the Francoist zone is constituted by Judith Keene, *Fighting for Franco: International Volunteers in Nationalist Spain during the Spanish Civil War, 1936–1939* (Leicester University Press, 2001). Two of the very few memoirs by English-speaking volunteers for Franco are the enthusiastically bloodthirsty vision of Peter Kemp, *Mine Were of Trouble* (Cassell, 1957) and the rather more sombre Frank Thomas, *Brother Against Brother: Experiences of a British Volunteer in the Spanish Civil War* (Stroud: Sutton Publishing, 1998).

A unique and fascinating account is provided by Priscilla Scott-Ellis, *The Chances of Death: A Diary of the Spanish Civil War* (Wilby, Norwich: Michael Russell, 1995). An upper-class Englishwoman who served as a volunteer nurse in the Nationalist zone, she provides a vivid picture of the contrasts between the dirt and squalor of the ordinary conscripts fighting for Franco and the high-society life of champagne, strawberries, hotels and nightclubs enjoyed by the toffs. For a biography of Pip Scott-Ellis, see Paul Preston, *Doves of War* (see above).

The response to the Spanish Civil War of the literary and artistic world has given rise to anthologies and critical studies. An interesting collection of essays is gathered in Stephen M. Hart, ed., *"¡No Pasarán!" Art, Literature and the Spanish Civil War* (Tamesis Books, 1988). Frederick R. Benson, *Writers in Arms: The Literary Impact of the Spanish Civil War* (New York: New York University Press, 1967), is a reliable survey of the better-known writers, Hemingway, Malraux, Orwell and Koestler. By far the best introduction to the subject are Valentine Cunningham's two well-selected and sensitively introduced anthologies, *The Penguin Book of Spanish Civil War Verse* (Harmondsworth: Penguin, 1980) and *Spanish Front: Writers on the Civil War* (Oxford: Oxford University Press, 1986). Also worth consulting is Murray Sperber, ed., *And I Remember Spain: A Spanish Civil War Anthology* (Rupert Hart-Davis, MacGibbon, 1974).

The international dimensions of the war have been the subject of substantial new research. Three substantial collections have been assembled by Sebastian Balfour and Paul Preston, eds, *Spain and the Great Powers* (Routledge, 1999); Christian Leitz and David J. Dunthorn, eds, *Spain in an International Context, 1936–1959* (New York: Berghahn Books, 1999) and Raanan Rein, ed., *Spain and the Mediterranean since 1898* (Frank Cass, 1999). Two older general works, by Dante A. Puzzo, *Spain and the Great Powers* (New York: Columbia University Press, 1962) and Patricia van der Esch, *Prelude to War* (The Hague: Martinus Nijhoff, 1951), are now out of date. A more modern general overview is provided by Michael Alpert, *An International History of the Spanish Civil War* (Macmillan, 1994). See also the excellent surveys by Glyn A. Stone, 'Britain, Non-Intervention and the Spanish Civil War', in *European Studies Review*, vol. IX, 1979, and 'The European Great Powers and the Spanish Civil War', in Robert Boyce and Esmonde M. Robertson, *Paths to War: New Essays on the Origins of the Second World War* (Macmillan, 1989), and Robert H. Whealey, 'Economic Influence of the Great Powers in the Spanish Civil War: From the Popular Front to the Second World War', in *The International History Review*, vol. 2, May 1983. On the Non-Intervention Committee, there is considerable information in the national studies mentioned below, especially those on Britain. A good introduction is by Glyn A. Stone, 'Britain, France and the Spanish Problem, 1936–1939', in Dick Richardson and Glyn A. Stone, eds, *Decisions and Diplomacy: Essays in Twentieth-Century International History* (Routledge, 1995). A rather dry and legalistic account can be found in William E. Watters, *An International Affair: Non-Intervention in the Spanish Civil War* (New York: Exposition Press, 1971). See also R. Veatch, 'The League of Nations and the Spanish Civil War, 1936–1939', in *European History Quarterly*, XX, 1990.

The older standard works on British attitudes are William Kleine-Ahlbrandt, *The Policy of Simmering: A Study of British Policy during the Spanish Civil War* (Geneva: Institut Universitaire des Hautes Études, 1961); K. W. Watkins, *Britain Divided* (Nelson, 1963); David Carlton, 'Eden, Blum and the origins of Non-Intervention', in *Journal of Contemporary History*, vol. VI, no. 3, 1971, and Jill Edwards, *Britain and the Spanish Civil War* (Macmillan, 1979). They all remain worth reading. However, in recent years there has been a minor revolution in the historiography of Britain's role during the Spanish Civil War. The outstanding work is by the Spanish scholar Enrique Moradiellos, *La perfidia de Albión: el Gobierno británico y la guerra civil española* (Madrid: Siglo XXI, 1996). It has not yet been translated into English but fortunately a number of Moradiellos's seminal articles have. They include 'The Origins of British Non-Intervention in the Spanish Civil War: Anglo-Spanish Relations in Early 1936', in *European History Quarterly*, vol. 21, 1991; 'Appeasement and Non-Intervention: British Policy during the Spanish Civil War', in Peter Catterall and C. J. Morris, eds, *Britain and the Threat to Stability in Europe, 1918–45* (Leicester University Press, 1993); 'British Political Strategy in the Face of the Military Rising of 1936 in Spain', in *Contemporary European History*, vol. 1, part 2, July 1992, and, most recently, 'The Gentle General: The Official British Perception of General Franco during the Spanish Civil War', in Preston and Mackenzie, *The Republic Besieged*. For a view rather more sympathetic to British policy-makers, see Tom Buchanan, ' "A Far Away Country of Which We Know

Nothing?" Perceptions of Spain and its Civil War in Britain, 1931–1939', in *Twentieth-Century British History*, vol. 4, no. 1, 1993. See also Tom Buchanan, *The Spanish Civil War and the British Labour Movement* (Cambridge: Cambridge University Press, 1991), and *Britain and the Spanish Civil War* (Cambridge: Cambridge University Press, 1997). Revealing for its unrestrained sympathies for Franco are the memoirs of the British diplomatic agent accredited to the Nationalist zone, Sir Robert Hodgson, *Spain Resurgent* (Hutchinson, 1953). Much more balanced is Sir Geoffrey Thompson, *Front Line Diplomat* (Hutchinson, 1959). The relevant volumes of the published *Documents on British Foreign Policy* contain valuable material on the Spanish Civil War: see 2nd Series, vols XVII, XVIII and XIX (HMSO, 1979).

In comparison with the lavish literature on Britain, there is relatively little on France available in English. The standard work is by John E. Dreifort, *Yvon Delbos at the Quai d'Orsay: French Foreign Policy during the Popular Front 1936–1938* (Wichita, Kan.: University Press of Kansas, 1973). The comprehensive work on French policy by David Wingeate Pike, *Les français et la guerre d'Espagne 1936–1939* (Paris: Presses Universitaires de France, 1975), has not been published in English. His earlier work, *Conjecture, Propaganda and Deceit and the Spanish Civil War* (Stanford, Calif.: California Institute of International Studies, 1968), is the best available substitute. A comprehensive American doctoral thesis, available in the better libraries, is Richard Alan Gordon, *France and the Spanish Civil War* (New York: Columbia University Press, 1971). Among the general works on French foreign policy with material on Spain are two books by Anthony Adamthwaite, *France and the Coming of the Second World War* (Frank Cass, 1977) and *Grandeur and Misery: France's Bid for Power in Europe 1914–1940* (Edward Arnold, 1995). On the domestic context of French vacillations towards the Spanish Republic, it is well worth consulting Julian Jackson, *The Popular Front in France: Defending Democracy, 1934–1938* (Cambridge: Cambridge University Press, 1988), and Jean Lacouture, *Léon Blum* (New York: Holmes & Meier, 1982)

On the role of the United States, see Richard P. Traina, *American Diplomacy and the Spanish Civil War* (Bloomington, Ind.: Indiana University Press, 1968), and Allen Guttmann, *American Neutrality and the Spanish Civil War* (Lexington, Ky.: D. C. Heath, 1963). There are a number of important studies by Douglas Little; his two articles,

'Claude Bowers and his Mission to Spain: the Diplomacy of a Jeffer-
sonian Democrat', in K. P. Jones, *US Diplomats in Europe 1919–
1946* (Santa Barbara, Calif.: ABC-Clio, 1976), and 'Red Scare 1936:
Anti-Bolshevism and the Origins of British Non-Interventionism in
the Spanish Civil War', in *Journal of Contemporary History*, vol. XXIII,
1988, and his book, *Malevolent Neutrality: The United States, Great
Britain, and the Origins of the Spanish Civil War* (Ithaca, NY: Cornell
University Press, 1985). Of crucial importance are the relevant volumes of the published US diplomatic documents, *Foreign Relations of
the United States 1936*, vol. II (Washington, DC, 1954); *Foreign
Relations of the United States 1937*, vol. I (Washington, DC, 1954);
Foreign Relations of the United States 1938, vol. I (Washington, DC,
1955) and *Foreign Relations of the United States 1939*, vol. II (Washington, DC, 1956). On the Latin American countries, see the compilation
edited by Mark Falcoff and Fredrick B.Pike, *The Spanish Civil War
1936–1939: American Hemispheric Perspectives* (Lincoln, Neb.: University of Nebraska Press, 1982).

Russian policy is covered with considerable understanding in
Claudín (see above), in E. H. Carr's sadly unfinished *The Comintern
& the Spanish Civil War* (*Macmillan, 1984) and Jonathan Haslam,
*The Soviet Union and the Struggle for Collective Security in Europe, 1933–
39* (Macmillan, 1984); Denis Smyth, ' "We Are With You": Solidarity
and Self-interest in Soviet Policy Towards Republican Spain, 1936–
1939', in Preston and Mackenzie, *The Republic Besieged*, and, most
recently Geoffrey Roberts, *The Soviet Union and the Origins of the
Second World War: Russo-German Relations and the Road to War, 1933–
1941* (Macmillan Press, 1995). Rather more the product of the Cold
War is David T. Cattell, *Soviet Diplomacy and the Spanish Civil War*
(Berkeley, Calif.: California University Press, 1957), as are the
accounts by Payne and Radosh mentioned above. The scathing
account of the Non-Intervention Committee by the Soviet Ambassador to London, Ivan Maisky, *Spanish Notebooks* (Hutchinson, 1966)
remains indispensable.

A substantial account of both Italian and German aid to Franco
can be found in Preston, *Franco*. The relevant volume of the published
German documents is an invaluable treasure store of information –
*Documents on German Foreign Policy, Series D, Volume III, Germany and
the Spanish Civil War* (HMSO, 1951). There are also some documentary
collections published at the time, of which the most useful is the

indictment of the Non-Intervention Committee, 'Hispanus', *Foreign Intervention in Spain* (United Editorial, 1937). *The Nazi Conspiracy in Spain* (Left Book Club, 1937) is an account of the activities of the Nazi Ausland-Organization in Spain. The most substantial books on Germany remain untranslated. Denis Smyth's chapter on German policy in Preston, *Revolution and War* (see above) is essential, as is the same author's 'The Moor and the Money-lender: Politics and Profits in Anglo-German Relations with Francoist Spain 1936–1940', in Marie-Luise Recker, ed., *Von der Konkurrenz zur Rivalität: Das britische-deutsche Verhältnis in den Ländern der europäischen Peripherie 1919–1939* (Stuttgart: Franz Steiner Verlag, 1986). See also two important articles by Christian Leitz: 'Nazi Germany's Intervention in the Spanish Civil War and the Foundation of HISMA/ROWAK', in Preston and Mackenzie, *The Republic Besieged*, and 'Hermann Göring and Nazi Germany's Economic Exploitation of Nationalist Spain, 1936–1939', in *German History*, vol. XIV, no.1, 1996. Even more important is Christian Leitz, *Economic Relations Between Nazi Germany and Franco's Spain 1936–1945* (Oxford: Oxford University Press, 1996). The undoubted usefulness of the study by Robert H. Whealey, *Hitler and Spain: The Nazi Role in the Spanish Civil War* (Lexington, Ky.: University Press of Kentucky, 1989), is slightly undermined by a few factual errors.

On Italy, the standard work, by John F. Coverdale, *Italian Intervention in the Spanish Civil War* (Princeton, NJ: Princeton University Press, 1977), remains immensely useful. It is beginning to be challenged on some details; see Paul Preston, 'Mussolini's Spanish Adventure: From Limited Risk to War' in Preston and Mackenzie, *The Republic Besieged*, and 'Mussolini and Franco 1936–1943', in Balfour and Preston, *Spain and the Great Powers* (see above). Although the Italian diplomatic documents for this period have still not covered the entire period of the war, a number of earlier collections in English are invaluable. The pamphlet *How Mussolini Provoked the Spanish Civil War: Documentary Evidence* (United Editorial, 1938) is an account of the March 1934 agreement made between the Duce and Spanish monarchists. The diaries and papers of Mussolini's son-in-law and Foreign Minister, Galeazzo Ciano, make compelling reading. See *Ciano's Diary 1937–1938* (Methuen, 1952) and *Ciano's Diplomatic Papers* (Odhams, 1948). Another useful volume which sheds unflattering light on the Non-Intervention Committee is *Documents on the*

Italian Intervention in Spain (no publisher, 1937). On Portuguese assistance to Franco, there is much to be gleaned from Glyn Stone, *The Oldest Ally: Britain and the Portuguese Connection, 1936–1941* (The Royal Historical Society/Woodbridge: Boydell Press, 1994). The best accounts in Portuguese are César Oliveira, *Salazar e a guerra civil de Espanha* (Lisbon: O Jornal, 1987); Iva Delgado, *Portugal e a guerra civil de Espanha* (Lisbon: Publicações Europa-América, no date) and *Portugal e a guerra civil de Espanha*, edited by Fernando Rosas, (Lisbon: Edições Colibri, 1998).

Some of the difficulties of the last days of the Republic are illuminated by Segismundo Casado's memoir, *The Last Days of Madrid* (Peter Davies, 1939). On the consequences of the Nationalist victory, the post-war repression and Franco's continuing pro-Axis sympathies, see Paul Preston, *The Politics of Revenge: Fascism and the Military in the 20th Century Spain* (*Routledge, 1990), and the richly textured study by Michael Richards, *A Time of Silence: Civil War and the Culture of Repression in Franco's Spain, 1936–1945* (see above), which traces the complex interplay between institutionalized violence, ideology, organized religion, economics and social deprivation in the humiliation and exploitation of the defeated. An important collection has been edited by Raanan Rein, *Spanish Memories: Images of a Contested Past – History & Memoir*, Special Issue, vol. 14, nos 1 & 2, (Bloomington, Ind.: Indiana University Press, 2002), with especially important chapters by Michael Richards and Angela Cenarro.

There are a number of disturbing contemporary accounts of life within Franco's Spain: Thomas J. Hamilton, *Appeasement's Child: The Franco Regime in Spain* (Gollancz, 1943); Charles Foltz Jr, *The Masquerade in Spain* (Boston, Mass.: Houghton Mifflin, 1948); Emmet John Hughes, *Report from Spain* (Latimer House, 1947); Herbert L. Matthews, *The Yoke and the Arrows: A Report on Spain* (Heinemann, 1958) and Abel Penn, *Wind in the Olive Trees: Spain from the Inside* (New York: Boni & Gaer, 1946). A horrifying account of the fate of some of those forced into exile can be found in David Wingeate Pike, *Spaniards in the Holocaust: Mauthausen, the Horror on the Danube* (Routledge/Cañada Blanch Studies, 2000). An account of the consequences of the Spanish Civil War within the post-Franco democratization process is Paloma Aguilar Fernández, *Memory and Amnesia: The Role of the Spanish Civil War in the Transition to Democracy* (New York: Berghahn Books, 2002).

Index

359